WHAT
GOVERNMENT
CAN DO

American Politics and Political Economy

A series edited by Benjamin I. Page

WHAT GOVERNMENT CAN DO

Dealing with Poverty and Inequality

Benjamin I. Page ▪ James R. Simmons

The University of Chicago Press

Chicago and London

Benjamin I. Page is Gordon Scott Fulcher Professor of Decision Making in the Department of Political Science at Northwestern University. He is author or coauthor of seven books, including *Who Gets What from Government* (1983), *The Rational Public* (1992, with Robert Y. Shapiro), and *Who Deliberates?* (1996), the latter two published by the University of Chicago Press. James R. Simmons is professor in and chair of the Department of Political Science at the University of Wisconsin, Oshkosh. He also directs the Public Administration Program there and has written extensively on public policy issues.

The University of Chicago Press, Chicago 60637
The University of Chicago Press, Ltd., London
© 2000 by The University of Chicago
All rights reserved. Published 2000
Printed in the United States of America
09 08 07 06 05 04 03 02 01 00   1 2 3 4 5
ISBN: 0-226-64481-2 (cloth)

Library of Congress Cataloging-in-Publication Data

Page, Benjamin I.
    What government can do : dealing with poverty and inequality /
Benjamin I. Page, James R. Simmons.
        p.   cm.—(American politics and political economy)
    Includes bibliographical references and index.
    ISBN 0-226-64481-2
    1. Poverty—United States.   2. Income distribution—United States.   3. United
States—Social policy.   4. Economic assistance, Domestic—United States.   I. Simmons,
James Roy, 1946–   II. Title.   III. Series.

HC110.P6P328   2000
362.5'8'0973—dc21   00-008807

⊚ The paper used in this publication meets the minimum requirements of the American
National Standard for Information Sciences—Permanence of Paper for Printed Library
Materials, ANSI Z39.48-1992.

. . . that government of the people,

by the people,

for the people,

shall not perish from the earth.

Abraham Lincoln
Gettysburg Address
November 19, 1863

CONTENTS

Preface   *xi*

1 **Introduction**   **1**
The Inequality Express   1
Inept or Impotent Government?   2
What Can Be Done   5
Plan of the Book   8

2 **Poverty and Inequality in the United States**   **11**
Economic Growth, Markets, and Americans' Incomes   11
Poverty in the United States   20
Income Inequality in America   25

3 **What Should Government Do?**   **32**
Theories of Government Functions   33
Approaches to Poverty and Inequality   46
Political and Economic Obstacles   61
Overcoming the Obstacles   74

4 **Social Insurance   76**
Old Age and Survivors Insurance (Social Security)   78
Disability Insurance   92
Unemployment Insurance   96
Medical Insurance   98
The Politics of Social Insurance   107
Improving Social Insurance   116

5 **Fair Taxes   125**
The Idea of Progressivity   127
Federal Taxes   134
State and Local Taxes   148
Taxes and Inequality   153
Tax Politics   155

6 **Investing in Education   159**
Who Should Provide Education?   161
Children and Equal Opportunity   165
Elementary and Secondary Schools   176
Training for Work   190
Higher Education   191
The Politics of Education   197
Improving Education   199

7 **Jobs and Good Wages   201**
Managing the Economy   203
Jobs and Spending on Public Goods   210
Job Training and Placement   214
Creating Jobs   219
Raising Wages   224
International Economic Policy   233
Job Politics   241
Improving Employment and Wages   245

8 **"Safety Nets" and Basic Needs   247**
Circus Imagery versus Economic Rights   247
Food   249

Contents

Housing 259

Medical Care 269

Income Maintenance 273

Politics: The War against the Poor 283

The Right to Basic Necessities 285

9 Conclusion 288

Programs That Work 290

What Remains to Be Done 293

Overcoming Political and Economic Obstacles 300

Government for the People 307

Notes 309

References 349

Index 381

PREFACE

Can governments do anything right? Many Americans seem to think the answer is "no," particularly when it comes to the problems of poverty and inequality. We have all heard stories of waste, inefficiency, and bureaucratic rigidity. We are told that antipoverty programs have failed to help the poor—they have just encouraged dependency. And some say that economic globalization has rendered governments altogether impotent. Even Social Security and Medicare, we are told, face crises and possible "bankruptcy."

This book tells a very different story. Looking at a wide range of U.S. government programs, it finds that many of them have worked quite well. Many have effectively reduced poverty and inequality without economic inefficiency, excessive red tape, or interference with individual liberties. Evidence from abroad, too, indicates that governments *can* do a great deal about poverty and inequality.

To be sure, there is plenty of room for improvement. We suggest ways to improve these programs and point out some political obstacles that will have to be overcome in order to do so.

The book is intended for general readers—anyone interested in the subject—as well as policy makers, policy experts, scholars, and students. It has several different purposes. It is an essay, taking a strong and definite stand on what can and should be done in the United States to deal with our alarmingly high levels of poverty and inequality. But it is also a sort of primer on exactly what our federal, state, and local governments *do* currently try to do about these problems. It is an exploration of "political economy," the intersection between economics and politics. And it can serve as a reference book for looking up particular programs to see how they work and what effects they have.

The book can be read in several different ways. We hope, of course, that many people will be interested in the whole thing and will read it from cover to cover. We have done our best to help you zip right through by writing as clearly and simply as we can. But some readers may find certain sections more detailed than they want. (The details have to be there for other readers.) You should always feel free to skim over such material or skip ahead. It is also perfectly fair to start at the end of the book and work back, or to go immediately to whatever chapter interests you the most.

In covering so much ground so quickly, we have undoubtedly made errors. Certainly we have left important things out, often just citing sources of more extensive evidence that readers may wish to pursue. We take some comfort from the dictum of a famous political scientist (or was it Homer Simpson?): "If it's worth doing at all, it's worth doing superficially."

The errors and omissions would be far more numerous if it were not for help from generous colleagues and friends who commented on various drafts of the manuscript. Needless to say, they bear no responsibility for defects that remain.

Lincoln Moses and Ed Greenberg slogged their way through the messy, "zeroeth draft" of the whole manuscript and came back for more. Alex Keyssar put aside his own magnum opus to give wise counsel. Jamie Galbraith and Ted Marmor delivered helpful critiques of the penultimate version.

Others made important contributions to one or several chapters. They include Betsy Aron, Ben R. Page, Tom Romberg, Mary R. Page, Mike Goldfield, Michael Wallerstein, Peter Swenson, Kathy Thelen, Fay Cook (a major morale booster), Tom Ferguson, Sandy Jencks, and Irv Garfinkel.

We also want to thank the students in Simmons's government and the economy class, and the army of antipoverty warriors, labor economists, educational researchers, social insurance experts, and others on whose work we have drawn.

We are grateful to Vilas Genke for help with the figures and especially to Scott Greer for exceptionally quick and thorough research assistance. Scott not only unearthed sources and data, but also contributed a number of ideas of his own, particularly concerning comparisons of the United States with other advanced industrial countries.

The book profited greatly from Page's 1998–99 sojourn in the supportive and distraction-free environment of the Center for Advanced Study in the Behavioral Sciences. We are grateful to the Center staff and (for generous financial help) to Northwestern University and the National Science Foundation (grant #SBR-9022192).

Most of all we are grateful to our wives, Mary and Joan, who contributed intellectually as well as dealing supportively with our absences and neglect of family life.

1

Introduction

The Inequality Express

In the mid-1990s, economist Barry Bluestone wrote of an onrushing "inequality express." The post–World War II American miracle of rising wages and rising family earnings, which for a time brought large gains even to those at the bottom of the economic heap and reduced income inequality, had come to a halt. Instead, for more than two decades beginning around 1973, the gulf between rich and poor Americans widened. The gap in earnings between well-educated and not-so-well-educated workers steadily increased, and the real standard of living of a large proportion of the workforce (particularly those with less than a college degree) may actually have declined. Bluestone, drawing on the work of Richard Freeman, Lawrence Katz, and others, traced this alarming change to a number of powerful economic and political forces, including the loss of manufacturing jobs in the United States, increased use of computers and information technology, weakened trade unions, and increasingly free international trade, capital mobility, and immigration.[1]

By the end of the twentieth century, robust economic growth had finally begun to trickle down a bit to lower-income workers. At the peak of the business cycle, with tight labor markets and high demand for workers, poorer American families at last began to regain part of the ground they had

1

lost. Still, as the twenty-first century began, inequality and poverty in the United States stood at remarkably high levels, the highest levels in the advanced industrialized world. As we will see in the next chapter, millions of poor Americans—including many full-time workers—were unable to obtain decent food, shelter, clothing, or medical care. Tens of millions of working people scrambled to make a living on wages that still, in real terms (that is, correcting for price inflation), probably fell below 1973 levels. At the same time, corporate executives and investors enjoyed enormous and rapidly growing salaries, bonuses, stock portfolios, and dividends.

In this book, we ask what, if anything, can or should be done about U.S. poverty and inequality. In particular, we want to know whether *government*—the American federal, state, and local governments—can do something about it, and if so, what. Our answer, contrary to a great deal of conventional wisdom, is an optimistic one. Although some political and economic obstacles stand in the way, we find that government can act effectively and that it can do so in ways that serve economic efficiency, contribute to economic growth, and preserve individual liberty, while at the same time reducing poverty and enhancing equality. We believe it *should* act in this way in order to benefit the vast majority of American citizens and contribute to what Lincoln called government "for the people."

Inept or Impotent Government?

In the United States, if not everywhere in the world, governments face a crisis of confidence. Advocates of free markets want governments out of the way. Politicians and pundits regularly bemoan the alleged ineptitude, inefficiency, or impotence of government. Television programs trumpet outrageous examples of wasteful government spending. True, some of this criticism amounts to firing cannons at sparrows (attacking tiny items in a federal budget that is approaching two *trillion*—two *million* million dollars), but the cumulative effect is to suggest that *all* government spending must be wasteful and inefficient, if not counterproductive.

Ordinary citizens' loss of confidence is an old story. As long ago as the late 1960s and early 1970s, with the Vietnam War, urban riots, the Watergate scandal, sharp oil price rises, and the beginnings of hard economic times for working people, many Americans began to turn away from faith in their current political leaders and government institutions. In response to opinion surveys, more and more people declared that they did not "trust the government in Washington to do what is right," that public officials do not "care much what people like me think," that people in government "waste a lot of the money we pay in taxes," and that government is pretty much run by "a few big interests" looking out for themselves. Confidence levels have never much recovered from this early drop. Toward the end of the 1990s, for example, no more than 39 percent of Americans said they trusted government "most of the time" or "just about always"; 56 percent or more agreed that public officials "don't care"; 60 percent or more said a lot of money is wasted; and as many as 74 percent said government is run by a few big interests.[2]

As we will see, however, this does not mean that Americans reject any and all government solutions to social problems. In fact, large majorities of citizens actually favor increased action on a wide range of policy fronts, from public education to protection of the environment, help with medical care, assistance with old age or disability, and help for the jobless and the needy. Large majorities regularly tell pollsters that they want to "spend more" on Social Security, medical care, and aid to education. Thus—while many Americans label themselves "conservatives," consider "liberal" a dirty word, and say they oppose big government—in important respects most Americans can be called practical liberals. Majorities have continued to be practical liberals ever since Franklin D. Roosevelt's New Deal of the 1930s.[3]

Still, there is widespread cynicism about public officials' motives, their attentiveness to ordinary people (as opposed to special interests), and their competence. There is much skepticism about what laws and policies accomplish. Some of this cynicism and skepticism is undoubtedly rooted in disappointment with what the U.S. government actually *has* done or not done, rather than what it *can* do. And some may reflect not reality, but negative rhetoric put out by antigovernment politicians and the mass media.[4]

In addition to the long-standing loss of citizen confidence, and a continued ideological onslaught by those who have always opposed the idea of active government, government today is sometimes said to face a new and more profound crisis, brought about by the increasing globalization of the economy. There is said to be a crisis of lost *capacity* to act, even of lost sovereignty. Whatever we may or may not want government to do, some observers think that governments no longer can accomplish certain tasks that were traditionally assigned to them. Especially in the areas of regulating the economy, taxing, providing safety nets, helping the needy, and dealing with extreme inequalities of income and wealth, the claim is that governments have lost their ability to act effectively. Some critics go so far as to assert that virtually all efforts at regulatory or redistributive policies are doomed to failure.

The argument is simple and frightening. With economic globalization— increasingly unfettered free trade, currency exchange, and investment, along with much faster and cheaper communication and transportation—money can fly instantly almost anywhere in the world to buy goods and services or to invest in factories. Money naturally tends to fly to places where goods and services are cheap and investment is encouraged. Nations that want to sell exports and attract investment in order to get ahead economically—or just to avoid being buried economically—must compete for investment and trade by offering cheap goods, low wages, and attractive investment climates. Among other things, this may mean low taxes, lax regulations, and avoidance of generous pensions, minimum wages, or other policies that would raise labor costs. In short, governments that want to compete in the global economy may have to "race to the bottom" by cutting back taxes, regulations, and social programs to the bone, or their goods will not sell abroad and capital will flee elsewhere. Economic globalization, the argument goes, has made governments largely impotent.

To sketch such an argument, however, is a far cry from demonstrating it to be true. As we will see in more detail as the book unfolds, there are at least three reasons why the impotence argument may be fundamentally misleading. First, like much economics-style theorizing, it posits a tendency to move toward some "equilibrium" situation—in this case, a situation in which governments can do little or nothing that might interfere with business—but it says virtually nothing about *how quickly* the theoretical equilibrium will be approached. If this alleged competitive pressure on governments is mild and proceeds only gradually, countervailing factors may arise so that the theoretical equilibrium is never reached. In any case, a process that slowly squeezed governments over the course of decades would be much less frightening than a headlong rush that occurred within a few months or years.

Second, the impotence argument is seriously incomplete. Yes, certain kinds of government policies could undoubtedly add to business costs by making labor more expensive, production more costly, or investment less attractive. But we will see that many—even most—egalitarian policies can have quite the opposite effect. They can add to the skills, motivation, and productivity of labor; the ease of transportation and communication; the attractiveness of the United States for business executives; the general efficiency of production; and the magnitude of returns on investment. Programs that upgrade the productivity and earnings of low-income workers, for example, generally help, rather than hurt, U.S. economic competitiveness. With respect to such programs, the impotence argument is dead wrong. A wide range of well-designed government policies can enhance, rather than degrade, economic competitiveness, while at the same time reducing poverty and inequality. The race among nations may be won by running not toward the bottom, but toward the top.

Third, even if there were a tendency for governments to compete by abandoning certain functions that we want performed, it would not follow that we are helpless to stop them from doing so. We might simply need to enact new kinds of public policies. If the globalized economy has negative side effects, we may need to think in terms of *globalized politics.* Global problems may require global solutions, which could be achieved through international treaties and agreements, international organizations like the United Nations, and worldwide nongovernmental organizations or social movements. If all nations are forced to meet the same obligations, competition to avoid those obligations can be controlled.

It is one aim of this book to grapple with the impotence (or "structural constraint") argument in the context of specific government programs and policy proposals. What, if anything, *can* governments do to deal with poverty and inequality in the face of competitive global pressures? We will see that some policies—especially those that build up skills and earning capacities and that get people to work—are much more promising than others. In addition, we will suggest that certain features of the U.S. *political process,* rather than global pressures, may be preventing desirable action against poverty and inequality and that it may be possible to change such features of the political process. In order to have government for the people, it may be necessary to have a more effective system of government *by* the people.

Throughout, we will analyze what the U.S. government is actually doing at present about poverty and inequality, what works and what does not, in order to address the questions of what government *can* and *should* do.

What Can Be Done

As we examine specific policies and policy proposals in many different realms—including social insurance, taxation, education, jobs, wages, and "safety nets"—we will see that different sorts of policies can have profoundly different effects on poverty and inequality. Some help to mitigate poverty and inequality, but others make them worse. Different policy alternatives differ sharply in how effective or ineffective they are, how efficient or inefficient, how they help or hurt economic growth and competitiveness, and how they expand or restrict individual freedom.

We will point out programs that are ineffective or harmful, while devoting most of our attention to those that work best. We will also offer some suggestions about what the reader can do to help enact and implement policies that work effectively against poverty and inequality. Our suggestions fall into three main types: designing effective policies, organizing to enact them, and removing political or economic barriers that work against such policies.

Designing Effective Policies

The first step toward desirable government action is to design policies that will effectively accomplish their main goals, while avoiding negative side effects. In this book, we are especially interested in policies that will effectively combat poverty and reduce inequalities of income and wealth, while at the same time maximizing such values as economic efficiency and individual liberty. In the case of policies mainly focused on other purposes—raising revenue, for example, or providing public goods—we want to identify ways of accomplishing those purposes effectively and efficiently, while at the same time reducing, or at least not increasing, poverty and inequality.

In recent years, the movement to "reinvent government" has expanded the number of effective tools available to policy makers. We have become aware of many techniques that can be used to enhance government effectiveness and efficiency, while maximizing individuals' liberty and choices. In many cases, it is possible to design programs that focus on major objectives and seek measurable results through flexible means, rather than protecting turf or bogging down in rules and red tape; programs that motivate, inspire, and empower government workers, rather than thwarting or excessively controlling them; programs that harness the force of competition to increase efficiency by setting public agencies to compete against public agencies or public agencies against private enterprise; programs that decentralize decision making to state or local governments in order to maximize diversity, flexibility, and closeness to problems or that centralize control in the federal government when necessary for uniformity or equity.[5]

Organizing to Get Policies Enacted

It is not enough to come up with good plans, however. Legislators and public officials have to be convinced to enact them and carry them out. This means that experts need to write and speak and testify to the merits of proposals. Advocates need to persuade the public that proposed policies are desirable. Citizens' groups need to organize, lobby, and mobilize the public into action.

Politics is not just a spectacle for people to watch; it is an arena of choice and action. What ordinary citizens decide to do can make an enormous difference. This book is not a "how to" manual—we will not spend much time advising the reader on exactly how to engage in political action—but those who care about public policy have many avenues for influencing what government does. The avenues include registering and voting (for state and local officials as well as presidents) and helping others to register and vote; campaigning for candidates, attending meetings, and giving money; writing to officials; protesting or demonstrating; and helping politically oriented groups that actively work for good public policies. Often broad public involvement is the key to overcoming politics-as-usual in order to get good things done.

Reforming Politics and Economics

Although politics is an arena of action and choice, the actual results of millions of citizens' actions and choices depend partly on how the arena is structured: just what the rules and processes are like. As we will see, certain features of the American political system tend to work against policies that would be in the interest of large majorities of Americans. This is especially true of barriers that restrict participation by lower-income citizens, advantages that are given to financial contributors, and disproportionate influence that is granted to organized interest groups and corporations that sometimes have interests opposed to those of the average citizen. Even in our one-person–one-vote democratic system, all too often the majority does not rule.

If political rules and processes are stacked against egalitarian policies, it is important to think about changing the rules. Effective policies against poverty and inequality would be much easier to enact if the political process were reformed, effectively enfranchising all citizens, reducing the power of money in politics, and limiting or counterbalancing corporate and interest group influence. This will not be easy; the very rules and institutions that need reforming can be expected to resist reform. But many things that are worth doing are not easy.

Certain features of the U.S. economic system may also call for reform. The political power of American business, for example (relatively small businesses as well as major corporations), together with the fact that most business firms quite naturally see profit making as their chief goal, means that they often help defeat egalitarian measures that they think would cost them money—even when those policies would be beneficial to millions of individuals and to the economy as a whole. This problem might be alleviated somewhat if such political action were made more difficult, rather than encouraged (if, for example, lobbying expenses were made not tax-deductible), or if corporations' state charters were amended to require action for certain public purposes in addition to profit making. Similarly, political action by foreign companies within the United States and by U.S. multinational corporations abroad (where their political clout is used to keep wages and regulatory costs low, producing low-cost exports, which in turn depress Americans' wages) could be discouraged by U.S. taxes and regulations and by international agreements. But we will argue that the most effective single reform would be to reduce the general role of money—any money—in politics and elections.

Several ideas about political and economic reforms will arise naturally as we deal with the politics of specific kinds of policies. We will return to explicit discussion of reform in the final chapter.

Plan of the Book

The book will proceed as follows. Chapter 2 tells the story of high and increasing levels of poverty and inequality of income and wealth in the United States, discusses some of their damaging consequences, and notes some of the causes, including the technological revolution and increased economic competition from low-wage countries.

Chapter 3 explores several theories concerning what governments should or should not do, arguing that one important government function is to reduce poverty and inequality. It outlines several different approaches to doing so, involving such ideas as equal opportunity, investment in human capital, improved wages, social insurance, and safety nets. It then points out certain economic and political obstacles to egalitarian policies and suggests how those obstacles may be overcome.

Chapter 4 analyzes social insurance programs that can (and in many cases already do) protect people against such hazards as old age, retirement, disability, illness, and injury. It considers the largest U.S. social programs, Social Security and Medicare, as well as smaller programs like Medicaid and Unemployment Insurance, analyzing their substantial but limited effects on reducing poverty and inequality. The chapter explains how the alleged "crisis" in financing Social Security and Medicare can in fact rather easily be dealt with and goes on to argue that certain proposed privatization schemes would be harmful, rather than helpful.

Chapter 5 discusses taxes. It sets forth arguments in favor of reducing income inequality through progressive taxes and indicates how that can be done without costly impairments of incentives to work, save, and invest. It shows how certain current taxes (particularly income and estate taxes) tend to reduce inequalities, but other taxes (especially sales and payroll taxes) tend to make inequalities worse, so that the current tax system, taken as a whole, has little equalizing effect.

Chapter 6 explains how a number of programs can reduce poverty and inequality by investing in the "human capital" of disadvantaged children and lower-income workers. Government can effectively help provide good nutrition and health care to children and pregnant women; provide high-quality day care, preschooling, and elementary and secondary education; and give people job training and higher education.

Chapter 7 argues that the most effective remedies for poverty and inequality involve increasing the availability of good jobs and raising the level of wages. Measures that can help do so include favorable fiscal and monetary policies, certain kinds of spending on public goods, public service employment (cheaper and better than the prison alternative), adequate minimum wages, low-wage subsidies like the Earned Income Tax Credit, encouragement of labor unions, antidiscrimination laws, and international economic policies that blunt low-wage competition from abroad.

Chapter 8 dissects the unhelpful imagery of "safety nets" and outlines new programs that could—if we wish to do so—implement guaranteed rights to minimum standards of food, housing, medical care, and perhaps income.

Finally, Chapter 9 summarizes our judgment that a wide range of existing and proposed programs can effectively help reduce poverty and inequality, while preserving individual freedom and economic efficiency. It urges that we overcome political obstacles that have prevented many such programs from being enacted.

As the book proceeds, some readers may find more detail on certain topics than they want to get into. If that happens to you at any point, we urge you to skim over the material or skip ahead to matters of greater interest. As we noted in the preface, this book can be read in many different ways. You can even jump right to the conclusion and then come back to what most interests you.

2

Poverty and Inequality in the United States

The average U.S. citizen enjoys a standard of living among the highest on the globe. Nonetheless, many millions of Americans live in poverty. Many more millions of workers struggle to make ends meet. The gap between rich and poor is much greater than in most advanced industrial countries and has grown wider in recent years.

Some amount of inequality is no doubt necessary in order to motivate people and allocate resources efficiently. But we will see that the extremely high levels of poverty and inequality in the United States are *not* required for economic efficiency, they do *not* simply reflect people's work effort and productivity, and they are *not* beyond our control. Countries as rich as our own have achieved prosperity with far less poverty and inequality. We have a choice.

This chapter begins with a brief account of the remarkable record of U.S. economic growth and the large amount of national income available for Americans to consume. It then examines the beguiling but mistaken idea that people "deserve" whatever personal income they get and goes on to describe the extent of poverty and inequality in America.

Economic Growth, Markets, and Americans' Incomes

In most respects, the U.S. economy has been a huge success. Over the course of two and a half centuries, a few small colonies of subsistence farmers and craftsmen (and plantation owners and slaves) on the eastern coast of North America have—with help from foreign capital and energetic immigrants—transformed themselves into a continentwide, affluent, industrial, and then postindustrial nation. The record of sustained economic growth has been amazing. Despite setbacks like the Great Depression of the 1930s and the stagnation of the 1970s, there has been a long-term trend of enormous increase in the value of goods and services produced by Americans. The income and standard of living of the average family have soared.

In 1800, the vast majority (94 percent) of the 5.3 million Americans lived in rural areas, in communities with populations of less than 2,500 people. Three-quarters of the labor force worked in agriculture, mostly on small subsistence farms. Water had to be carried from a spring or well; lighting was by candle and transportation by horse or foot; communication was no quicker than a person could ride or walk. By the 1870s, industrialization was well under way; more than one-quarter of Americans lived in urban areas, and barely over half worked in agriculture. But even then the annual per capita gross national product (GNP) of the United States—that is, the total value of goods and services available to be consumed by the average American—was still only $531 (this and some subsequent per capita GNP figures are given in constant 1958 dollars for purposes of comparison).[1]

By 1900, however, the per capita GNP had very nearly doubled, to $1,011. In most regions, running water and indoor plumbing were common. The recent innovation of kerosene lighting was already being replaced by gas and then electricity. Automobiles and airplanes were about to reshape transportation, telegraph lines transmitted information far and fast, and radio was on the way (but life expectancy at birth was still only 47.3 years). In just half a century more—by 1950—per capita GNP, the goods and services available to be consumed, had more than doubled once again, to $2,342 (in 1958 dollars), and life expectancy had jumped to 68.2 years. Many families could afford a car and a comfortable house with central heating, refrigerator, telephone, and various electrical appliances. Television and air conditioning were on the way. College education was becoming common.[2]

The post–World War II years, especially from 1947 to 1972 or so, were a time of particularly dramatic economic growth. For those years, we can look more closely at the cash income actually enjoyed by the average American family, converted to recent (1997) dollar values. Frank Levy calculates that in 1949 the income of the average (median) family was $18,800; it almost exactly doubled in two decades, reaching $37,800 in 1969, and continued to rise to $40,400 in 1973.[3]

The year 1973 turns out to have been an important turning point, however. As a result of sharp oil price rises and other factors, the U.S. economy then got mired in inflation, unemployment, and slow growth. General economic growth nearly stopped for a decade. Family income did even worse; it stagnated for more than two decades, hardly rising even when economic growth resumed. The $40,400 average family income figure of 1973 barely crept up to $43,600 by 1989 and remained about the same, at $43,200, in 1996[4] (as we will see, the gap between rich and poor also widened sharply during this period). Only in the late 1990s did the typical family's income once again begin to rise substantially.

Still, at the beginning of the twenty-first century, Americans were producing and consuming an enormous amount of goods and services. Looking once more at the total value produced by—and available to be consumed by—each individual American, the gross domestic product (GDP) per capita at the beginning of 2000 was over *$32,000*.[5] That is to say, if we forget for the moment about savings and investment, the American economy produced enough for each woman, man, and child in the country to consume about $32,000 worth of goods and services each year. This translated into enough for each *household* to consume more than twice that, on the order of $85,000.[6] The $85,000 figure is worth bearing in mind as we discuss the plight of working families that try to get by on only $10,000 or $15,000 per year.

Compared to U.S. production only a few decades ago, these figures are astounding. Around the world, hardly any countries match the U.S. level of per capita production. Toward the end of the 1990s, according to United Nations figures that adjust for purchasing power, the U.S. per capita GDP of $29,010 surpassed that of all other countries of the world except Luxembourg ($30,863) and Brunei ($29,773). It was somewhat greater than in any other country of Europe—several of which, however, came close. It far outclassed the level of per capita GDP nearly everywhere else, including relatively prosperous nations of Latin America (in the $8,000–$10,000 range), not to mention developing but still poor Asian countries like China ($3,130) or India ($1,670), or the most impoverished countries of Africa like Ethiopia ($510) or Sierra Leone ($410).[7]

The value of goods and services available to be consumed by the average American, in other words, was about *three times* that available to people in relatively affluent countries of Latin America, *nine times* that of China, *seventeen times* that of India, and *seventy-one times* that of Sierra Leone.

The sustained growth of the American economy has been a remarkable achievement with few if any parallels in human history. It is an achievement largely attributable to our more-or-less free-market economic system. Our system of free enterprise, market decision making, and capitalism—that is, private ownership of most of the means of production—largely created this enormous production of goods and services and these high average family incomes[8] (to be sure, government policies provided substantial assistance from the beginning and continue to do so[9]).

One important caveat, however: a rise in family incomes or GDP, as they are officially measured, does not always mean that people are better off. These statistics refer only to *monetary* transactions. Upward trends in the amount of money being earned and spent ignore offsetting costs that do not show up in dollar terms. Such costs include loss of leisure (more hours worked and more two-earner families[10]); loss of unpaid day care, cooking, housekeeping, and home maintenance, no longer provided by spouses who used to stay at home; depletion of natural resources; and degradation of the environment. Moreover, these statistics treat all increased spending as good, even if it merely represents defense against new evils like increased crime (more police, courts, and prisons) or increased disease (more medical expenses). One study that attempted to correct these defects of GDP by using a broader "Genuine Progress Indicator" (GPI) found that the average well-being of Americans only gradually increased from 1950 until the early 1970s and then gradually declined for at least twenty years after that.[11]

In any case, even if we stick to monetary transactions, per capita GDP and the income of the "average family" are statistical abstractions that can conceal much of what is happening to real people. As we have noted, it is possible for average (median) family income to decline or stagnate even when per capita GDP is rising; this happened in the 1980s. And even when *mean* family income is increasing, it is possible for most families to become worse off if a few are doing so extraordinarily well that they bring the average up. It is important to pay attention not only to how much income the economy produces in total—or on the average per person—but also to how that income is *distributed:* who gets how much income and how equal or unequal the distribution of income is. When we consider distribution along with production, the recent performance of the American economy is not such a clear success.

Just Desserts? The "Marginal Product" Theory of Wages

Most U.S. economists work with a simple theory of how the bulk of personal income is distributed: the "marginal product" (or "marginal revenue product") theory of wages. According to this theory, the "labor market" works like any other free market. Voluntary choices by individual workers and employers result in an equilibrium between the demand for labor and the supply of labor. In equilibrium, the price for a particular kind and quality of labor (that is, the level of wages paid) is set at precisely the right amount so that the last such worker to be hired gets just enough money to take the job and the employer pays just enough to equal the value that that worker will produce. (The "marginal product" is the value of the work done, the additional revenue produced, by that last or "marginal" worker).[12]

According to this theory, everyone who does work of the same value—for any employer anywhere (adjusting for transportation costs and the like)—ought to get this same marginal product wage. Wage levels ought to adjust themselves upward or downward—smoothly and frequently—with any shift in supply or demand. If more labor of a particular type is needed, the wage tends to go up; if more people want to do that sort of work while demand stays constant, the wage goes down. The theory implies that employers get the labor they need at a reasonable price and workers get whatever income their skills and efforts can produce.

The marginal product theory has profound implications. For one thing, if wages are set in this fashion, then wage levels seem to be "natural," and we are tempted to conclude that governments or anybody else ought to be wary before mucking about with them. Economists, bringing their mathematical armory to bear on this matter, can easily prove—under certain assumptions—that any interference with free labor markets (setting minimum wage levels by law, for example) is inefficient, wasteful of economic resources, and therefore presumably harmful.

Moreover, the marginal product theory seems to imply that the market automatically sets wage levels so that they are *fair*. If everyone is paid just what her or his labor is worth, why complain? What distribution of income could be more just than a distribution based on merit and effort?

Since the time of Alfred Marshall, the marginal product theory of wages has been taken as axiomatically true by most U.S. and British economists. It has become a cornerstone of modern economic theory.[13] But there does not exist much empirical evidence about how well or how badly this theory describes what actually happens between real workers and real employers. As we will see in the next section, wages are set in a variety of ways that very likely deviate from compensation for marginal product. First, however (and perhaps even more important), we need to explain why—to the extent that the marginal product theory is correct—it does *not* follow that wages set as that theory describes are necessarily fair or just. Nor does it follow that *total income,* which includes not only wages, but also such things as capital gains on inherited stock, is necessarily fair or just.

One obvious problem is that, according to the theory, a worker's pay depends not on what she or he actually produces, or even on what the average worker of her or his type produces, but on what is produced by the *marginal* worker—the last one hired to do a particular kind of job. All other workers of the same kind are paid according to what that last, marginal worker produces. And the theory itself assumes that there are declining returns to labor—that every previous worker produced more revenue than the last one.[14] Those previous workers therefore get paid *less* (often much less) than the value they themselves produce. The resulting "producer's surplus" generally constitutes *profit* (or, as most economists prefer to put it, "return on capital"), which ordinarily goes to owners or stockholders. This may or may not be fair, but no conclusion about its fairness follows from the marginal product theory of wages. Economic orthodoxy tells us that there must be some profits in order to get people to save and invest, but it says little about whether or not a bigger share of the value they produce ought to go to workers rather than the owners of capital.[15]

Furthermore, the notion that workers are paid for what "they" produce (at the margin) is deeply ambiguous. Virtually all production is joint: it depends on cooperative interaction among a number of people, as well as the use of tools and machines that embody past labor and inventions, and a whole social infrastructure. Employers undoubtedly try to assess roughly how much new workers add to the value of production, taking all this background for granted. But to separate any individual worker's true contribution from the contributions of others may be impossible, and if it could be calculated, it would have little or nothing to do with the concept of marginal product.[16]

Even supposing that we could determine exactly how much value an individual produces, would that production invariably reflect "merit" that should be rewarded? Some people may be born smart and strong, while others are physically impaired or not very bright.[17] Some people are brought up by supportive parents who nurture and educate them and give them every advantage, while others are damaged, abused, or held back by poverty and deprivation. Some enjoy perfect health, while others are struck down by illness or injury. Some inherit their parents' family business or stock portfolio; others get nothing. These differences are largely a matter of good or bad luck. Would it be fair for unhappy accidents of genes, childhood upbringing, injury, or disease to condemn some people to meager incomes forever afterward, while their more fortunate fellows prosper?

To be sure, there are practical and ethical reasons for letting individuals' levels of effort have some effect on their incomes. Most of us feel that those who try hard should get some material reward. This feeling is consistent with the idea of using material incentives to encourage work effort and to enhance the efficient allocation of people to jobs. But it certainly does not follow that everyone should be blessed or condemned exactly according to the "verdict of the marketplace." As Robert Kuttner asks, Do we want *everything* to be for sale? [18]

To allow market forces of supply and demand totally to determine wages would not be fair or just because this would mean that workers' incomes would be subject to many influences beyond their control, including events that are altogether arbitrary and capricious. Suppose, for example, that a worker who has labored hard for years and has developed outstanding skills is suddenly replaced by a machine or that the factory suddenly closes and moves operations to Mexico. Suppose, that is, that demand for a particular worker's labor suddenly vanishes. Or suppose that the supply of competing workers suddenly grows, due to large-scale immigration or to a recession that throws millions of people out of work. Do we really want to call the resulting job loss or drop in wages fair and just? Do we want to insist that nothing be done about it?

Even to the extent that the marginal product theory is correct, therefore, it would be foolish to passively accept its results as producing a fair distribution of income. In addition, there are reasons to believe that the theory is incomplete and deficient in ways that further undermine the claimed sanctity of market-determined wages.

Who Actually Gets Ahead?

Not all income comes from wages. Substantial amounts of income, in the form of dividends, interest, rent, or capital gains, derive from the ownership of capital: stock, bonds, real estate, or other valuable assets. Some people acquire large amounts of capital through inheritance or gift, not through any effort of their own.[19] Despite mythology about "people's capitalism," most income from capital goes to a rather small number of people and contributes significantly to the overall inequality of incomes. As James Galbraith points out, for example, the highest-income 1 percent of families in the early 1990s got less than half of that income from wages or salaries; most of the rest came from capital gains and interest on stocks and bonds.[20] In *Top Heavy,* his careful study of wealth inequality, Edward Wolff showed that the richest 1 percent of American households held about half (48 percent) of all the financial wealth in the United States.[21] In chapter 5, we will suggest that it would make sense to tax income from capital at the same rates as workers' wages—not at lower rates, as is done at present.

Wages, salaries, and self-employment income earned from work constitute the largest part of personal income (as much as 80 percent of Census-reported money income).[22] The wages received by any particular worker are influenced by a variety of factors, some encompassed in the marginal product theory, and some not; some under the worker's control, and many not. These factors include characteristics and behaviors of workers themselves (skills, effort, and productivity, but also personality, friendship networks, gender, and race) and such external factors as the levels of employment and unemployment in the economy as a whole, the structure of the particular industry where the worker is employed, and the size and composition of the potential workforce.

When business is booming—for example, when there is full or nearly full employment and very few people are unemployed—both the level of wages and the equality of the wage distribution tend to rise. Most workers' pay goes up, and the low-paid tend to catch up somewhat with their higher-paid fellows. When the economy falls into recession or depression, on the other hand, workers' wages tend to decline, and many people—especially those on the low end of the income scale—lose their jobs. These economic fluctuations are obviously beyond the control of the individual worker. But (as we will see in chapter 7) they can be influenced—and inevitably *are* influenced—by government "macroeconomic" policy, including manipulation of the money supply and interest rates. We need to consider whether and how macroeconomic policies might be deliberately used to affect peoples' wages and the extent of inequality.

Similarly beyond the individual worker's control are a host of other external factors: a baby boom or large-scale immigration that increases the number of competing workers, increased imports of competing goods, the rise or decline of particular economic sectors, the gain or loss of a monopoly position by the worker's employer, and "downsizing," automation, or the relocation of factories abroad. Such external factors can strongly affect a worker's wages (and her or his measured "marginal product"), but they have little or nothing to do with any change in the individual's level of skills or effort. Again, however, a variety of government policies—including taxes, spending, and regulation—can and in many cases inevitably *do* affect these factors. Again, we will want to consider whether and how government policies might be deliberately used to help people who are hurt by events beyond their control.[23]

When it comes to the characteristics of individual workers, of course a variety of factors that affect a worker's productivity—intelligence, skills, education and training, work habits, experience, ability to work with people, aspirations and motivation—also affect that worker's wage or salary. A person's level of formal education, in particular, is increasingly important to whether or not she or he gets ahead. A college degree or postgraduate work can make a lot of difference. To the extent that we are concerned about poverty and inequality, we will want to consider what government might do to help everyone obtain good education and training and in other ways maximize their productivity.

Here, however, we emphasize two other points. First, even when all measurable characteristics of individuals are taken into account, a great deal of variation in wages remains unexplained. Some people do much better or worse than others for reasons that apparently have nothing to do with education, skills, or other productivity-related characteristics. Much of this variation seems to result from what can simply be called luck. It makes a difference where in the country people happen to grow up, for example, or which particular employers they happen to hook up with. (Wages are often higher, for example, where there are strong labor unions or where firms have monopoly profits to share; wages frequently diverge from labor-market outcomes for the roughly one-fifth of workers with jobs dependent on government.) Family problems can make a difference, as can personal charm (or lack of it) and the personal networks one has access to. Prep school classmates are likely to be more useful than friends from a ghetto high school.[24]

19

Second, people's incomes are strongly affected by their family backgrounds, especially the occupations, educational attainment, and income (the "SES," or socioeconomic status) of their parents. According to one calculation, for example, the sons of the most privileged one-fifth of American families earned about 75 percent more than the sons of the least privileged one-fifth. Families exert their influence through a variety of mechanisms, including providing a genetic inheritance of intelligence (a relatively small factor) and other personal traits; enabling children to get more education (a big factor); getting children admitted to higher-prestige colleges; providing useful social networks; and passing on money and other assets through inheritance.[25]

To be sure, family background is not an ironclad determinant of who gets ahead. Shiftless heirs sometimes squander inherited millions, and a messenger boy does occasionally become CEO. But family background accounts for a rather large proportion of the variation in incomes—perhaps 40 percent of it.[26] Social mobility in America is far from unlimited. Sons from the most privileged fifth of families, for example, have had something like a 36 or 38 percent chance of ending up in the top fifth themselves and face hardly any danger of falling down to the bottom fifth[27] (if family background made no difference, their chances of ending up in the top fifth would be 20 percent—exactly equal to their chance of ending up in the bottom fifth). Thus the happenstance of what family one is born into has a substantial effect on how high or low one's income will be in later life. Families tend to perpetuate inequality. This, too, makes it difficult to argue that people's incomes represent their just desserts.

Poverty in the United States

Despite the very high incomes of most Americans, many millions of others live in poverty. At the end of the twentieth century, after more than two hundred years of sustained and very successful economic growth, some 34 million people, 12.7 percent of the entire U.S. population, lived in families that received annual cash incomes below the official poverty line, which averaged just $16,660 per year for a family of four (only $13,003 for a family of three).[28] And $17,000 a year does not go very far for four people. Nor does it compare very favorably with the average of about $85,000 in GDP available for each American household.

The level of poverty had declined sharply during the 1960s (from about 22 percent in 1959 to 12 percent in 1969) as a result of government anti-poverty policies and economic growth, but it edged up again in the late 1970s and then stayed in the 13 to 15 percent range.[29]

As Rebecca Blank has pointed out, most of America's poor are quite different from media-encouraged stereotypes of predominately black, inner-city-ghetto-dwelling, nonworking, never-married welfare mothers or dangerous drug-addicted young men who have been mired in poverty for many years. When TV producers want pictures of "typical" poor people, they naturally turn to easily located urban ghettoes. But the resulting pictures are not typical; they are *stereotypical*. They contribute to a misleading portrait of the poor as "Other," alien, quite different from the rest of us—less likely to win sympathy from the middle-class white majority.

In truth, as of the mid-1990s, only about *12 percent*—one in eight—of poor Americans lived in urban ghettoes. Fewer than 20 percent—one in five—lived in families headed by never-married mothers. African Americans and Hispanics were indeed more than twice as likely as non-Hispanic whites to be poor (so were Native Americans), but only 27.7 percent of the poor were black, and an additional 20.1 percent were Latino, while 48.1 percent were white. In more than half of poor families, at least one member worked for at least part of the year. In contrast to the image of unbreakable long-term dependency, among all Americans who were poor at some time over a thirteen-year period about *half* were poor for only one to three of the thirteen years. Indeed this random sample indicated that fully *one-third* of all Americans were poor at some time during the thirteen-year period, usually just for a short but painful spell.[30]

It is still true, as Michael Harrington pointed out long ago,[31] that poor people are largely invisible to the middle-class majority. Most of us consciously or unconsciously form images of poverty based on misleading TV images. For this reason, it may be worth repeating: many more poor people are white than black. Very few live in urban ghettoes. Few live in families with never-married mothers. Most have a worker in the family.

As must be obvious from the fact that one-third of all Americans experience poverty at some time, the poor are a very diverse and heterogeneous lot. Thanks to Social Security and Medicare, however, relatively few of the elderly (fewer than 10 percent at any one time) are now poor. Poverty in the United States is now heavily concentrated among *children,* who have not been helped by government as much as the elderly have. In Blank's data, 40.8 percent of all the poor were younger than 18. In fact, nearly *one-fifth* of all American children now live in poverty, a frightening statistic that is higher than in any other industrialized country.

This is related to the rise of families headed by single mothers, who by 1993 headed 60 percent of poor families with children. To put it another way, about 43 percent of all poor people now live in families headed by a single parent, almost all of them women. But in order to counter stereotypes, it is important to note that the increase in women-headed families does not represent some unique pathology of the poor; it mirrors a societywide trend that encompasses middle-class people as well. Moreover, as we have noted, few poor single mothers resemble the never-married, sexually profligate teenagers that pundits and politicians (mostly male) love to fulminate against. Many of these women have escaped bad relationships or have been divorced or abandoned by the men in their lives, and they do not have unusually large families. The reasons for poverty among single women and their children are not hard to discern: they have only one potential wage earner in the family, most of the women have limited skills and education, many are tied down by child-care responsibilities, and women are typically paid less than comparable men.[32]

In any case, as we discuss government programs that might or might not help the poor, it will be important to keep in mind the heterogeneity of the poor population. Significant numbers of poor people are old (9.4 percent), single men (8.8 percent), single women living alone (13.4 percent), members of married-couple families (34.9 percent), white (48.1 percent), working (most), and poor only for short spells (most), while a small but important minority suffers from the pervasive ghetto-based problems of the usual stereotype. No one "solution" to poverty can possibly fit all these diverse people. Poverty is a complex, multifaceted problem that requires complex and varied solutions.[33]

The data that we have been discussing are based on the official U.S. government definition of poverty, which has some quirks and oddities that we need to mention, since they affect debates about how many poor Americans there are and what the trends have been.

The official poverty measure was originally devised in the 1960s using Agriculture Department estimates of how much money a family of a given size needed in order to buy adequately nutritious food. For families of three or more people, the appropriate "economy food budget" was simply *multiplied by three* (since the average family in 1955 had spent about one-third of its money on food), in order to yield the poverty line for that size of family. Each year the poverty lines are increased by the same percentage as the Consumer Price Index (CPI) has risen, in order to keep up with inflation. But the purely family-based nature of the measure is a bit strange; unrelated people living together are not counted as a "family." And uniform poverty lines for the whole country probably lead to an overstatement of felt poverty in rural areas and small towns (where housing costs are low) relative to big cities (where they are high). Moreover, there is a peculiar, neither-fish-nor-fowl treatment of government benefits. Cash transfers to the poor are included as income (we would prefer that they not be, so that we could easily examine the extent of poverty before any government action is taken), while in-kind benefits are excluded and taxes paid are not subtracted. The exclusion of in-kind benefits like Food Stamps probably led to excessively pessimistic estimates of postgovernment poverty trends during the 1970s, when such benefits were rapidly expanding. Various improvements in the poverty measure have been proposed.[34]

Still, the existing, widely used poverty measure generally gives a correct impression of how many Americans are extremely poor and who those people are. For our purposes, the main point is that the official poverty measure sets a very low income threshold indeed and does not count as poor those people who are raised above the line by government cash-transfer programs. It definitely does not overstate the extent of the "pregovernment" poverty problem that we might or might not want government to address. Many more people would be poor if government did nothing to help.

The consequences of poverty are real and pervasive. Poor people get less nutritious food to eat. They have much worse health and shorter life expectancies. They live in cramped and often dilapidated dwellings, without the appliances and amenities that most of us take for granted (as we will discuss in chapter 8, some are homeless). They have great difficulty providing their children with proper food, health care, or schooling, let alone college or good prospects for a middle-class job.

Even though the United States has tremendous wealth and has per-capita economic production near the top among the world's countries, we are also exceptional among advanced countries in our level of poverty. One careful comparison of poverty rates for various countries in the mid-1980s, for example, found that the 13 percent rate in the United States was two to three times as high as in other countries with similar average standards of living.

The rate was about 7 percent in Canada and Australia, 5 percent in France and the United Kingdom, and 4 percent or less in Sweden, Germany, and the Netherlands.[35] More recently the United Nations Human Development report calculated that by European Union standards the United States in the early 1990s had 19 percent of its population below the poverty line, which put us much higher than any Western European country (the only other countries with poverty rates above 12 percent were the United Kingdom, at 13.5 percent, and Australia, at 12.9 percent). An interesting comparison is with Switzerland, which resembles the United States in having a very high GDP, very high levels of inequality, and many super-rich people, but provides much better for the poor.[36]

Living on the Edge: The Working Poor

Many millions of Americans with full-time working family members are poor or live on the edge of poverty. Cold statistics about dollar incomes and percentages do not tell the human story of what it is like to live as a low-income worker in the United States. Nor is it easy for middle-class desk-sitters like the present authors (or many of our readers) to imagine what it is like.

It is eye-opening, for example, to read Barbara Ehrenreich's wry account of her brief foray into life as a food server and room cleaner in Key West's "hospitality industry." The number of hours of hard work required to pay bare living expenses is numbing. The slop and stink in the bowels of the chain restaurant that Ehrenreich calls Jerry's, the nasty and capricious foremen at the Hearthside, the rules against bathroom breaks or talking to fellow employees—such working conditions are totally foreign to those of us who spend hours under our own control in a clean room, tapping on a keyboard and staring at a computer screen. Yet such conditions do not show up as negative "income" in the statistics.[37]

Equally foreign to most of us is the idea that low-wage workers may not have access to a cheap supermarket, or a freezer for economical food storage, or even enough savings for a deposit plus the first month's rent on an inexpensive apartment (which may be too far from the job anyhow). Instead, they often have to pay a premium for convenience-store groceries or fast food. Some must pay a hotel by the day or week for shelter or even sleep in a car. Such extra costs of living, too, do not show up in the usual statistics.

If we are blessed with good health insurance and a pension plan, it may not occur to us that many working people cannot afford the drugs and medical care they need to prevent minor afflictions from turning into major handicaps. For millions of working Americans, an employer pension or an IRA is only a dream.

Full-time work in America simply does not guarantee escape from poverty. In the mid-1990s, some 5.6 million children (more than 38 percent of all poor children) lived in poverty despite having at least one parent who worked fifty or more weeks that year. These working-poor families received little public assistance. Most were white, about half were married couples, and almost half lived in the South. They were almost equally distributed among cities, suburbs, and rural areas. Most (62 percent) had graduated from high school, though few (only 27 percent) had gone beyond that level of schooling; declining job opportunities and declining wages for adults who had not been to college held their incomes below the poverty line.[38]

In the spirit of the work requirements of new welfare laws, we may want to use a somewhat more demanding definition of full-time work by families. If we do so, insisting that two parents together work at least an average of thirty-five hours a week for all fifty-two weeks of the year (but counting single parents with a child under six who worked at least twenty hours), in 1996 there were 5.0 million children—about one-fifth of all poor children—living in working families with incomes below the official poverty line.[39]

Simple arithmetic makes clear how it is possible that the families of full-time workers can live in poverty. At the end of the 1990s, when the federal minimum wage was $5.15 per hour, a minimum wage worker who worked for forty hours a week, fifty weeks a year, earned only $10,300 per year—far below the $16,660 poverty threshold for a family of four (not to mention the roughly $85,000 available to every American household if our GDP were distributed equally to all families). In real value—adjusting for inflation—the minimum wage dropped sharply during the 1970s and 1980s. In terms of 1997 dollars, it fell from a peak of $6.19 in 1967 to a low point of just $4.34 in 1989 and recovered only part way, to $5.15, toward the end of the 1990s.[40]

Income Inequality in America

Poverty, of course, is partly in the eyes of the beholder and the sufferer. We may have a sense of certain absolute levels of deprivation that outrage our consciences: lack of what we think of as minimal food, shelter, or health care. But a bit of reflection makes clear that any conception of poverty—even one based on such "absolutes"—is actually *relative*. It depends on how other people live in the same society at the same time.

An American family of four, for example, with an income just below the poverty line—say, an income of $16,000 per year—looks positively rich when compared with the average person in Ethiopia or Tanzania, where the economy produces only some $500 or $600 per person. Poor Americans are poor *relative to other Americans.* But this does not mean that they are "not really" poor. Human beings are social creatures who live in interaction and in comparison with others. A person deprived of things that everyone around him has is likely to suffer a sense of inadequacy, a loss of dignity and self-respect. Thus poverty is partly a state of mind, based on one's relative standing in one's own society and community.[41]

Moreover, a person with a given level of income may actually be worse off in objective terms if she or he happens to live in an affluent society. In an America where nearly everyone has a car, where public transportation has atrophied, the need for a car in order to get to work or the store or an appointment becomes much greater. People without an automobile are seriously deprived. Much the same is true of telephones, TV sets, computers, and other items that most of the world deems luxuries. As Amartya Sen puts it, relative deprivation in terms of incomes can yield absolute deprivation in terms of *capacities.* Being relatively poor in a rich country, one may need more income to achieve the same *social functioning,* including taking part in the life of the community. Merely to appear in public without shame may require more expensive clothing in a rich country than in a poor one.[42]

There is evidence that most Americans explicitly recognize the relative basis of poverty. When asked by survey researchers how much money it takes to "get along" in their community, most respondents give a figure somewhere near one-half of the *median* income of Americans: that is, half as much as the average American gets, where the average is taken as the amount exactly between that received by the higher half and that received by the lower half of the population. Americans, of low and high income alike, accept the idea that one who falls far below the median income is deprived and should be considered poor.[43]

The importance of relative incomes means that we need to consider the general extent of *inequality* in the distribution of income: the magnitude of gaps between the incomes of rich and poor, between high- and low-income people. In the United States, such gaps are very wide and have increased markedly since the early 1970s.

Perhaps the simplest way to explore the extent of income inequality in the United States is look at Census figures on the amount of money income earned by different "quintiles," or fifths, of households. In 1998, the lowest-income fifth of American households got an average of only $9,223, and the second lowest fifth averaged only $23,288. Half of all American households earned less than $38,885. By contrast, the top fifth of households averaged $127,529 in annual income.[44]

A handy way to assess the extent of inequality is to compare the proportion of total aggregate income received by all the people in the bottom one-fifth of the population with the proportion received by the top one-fifth. In 1998, the 20 percent of U.S. households with the highest incomes got fully *49.2 percent* of all the cash income reported to the Census Bureau's Current Population Survey. That is, the best-off fifth of American families received about *half* of all the income in the country. The bottom fifth, by contrast, got only *3.6 percent.* On the average, then, those on top enjoyed incomes about *fourteen times* as high as those on the bottom. The extent of inequality appears even more extreme if we look separately at the families at the very top of the income distribution. The top 5 percent of families alone received 21.4 percent of all the income in the country, meaning that on the average they enjoyed incomes about *twenty-four times* as great as families in the bottom fifth.[45]

Extreme as this inequality appears, Frank Levy and others have pointed out that the Census figures actually tend to *understate* it because they do not include capital gains—a major source of income for the very rich—and they round off the very highest incomes (some amounting to many millions of dollars) to just $1 million.[46] Still, the figures are useful. Over time, they make clear a trend of substantially increasing inequality. In 1974, the bottom fifth of households got 4.4 percent of the income, which slowly declined over the rest of the century to 3.6 percent. Meanwhile the share of the top fifth grew from 43.1 to 49.2 percent, and the income share of the top 5 percent rose even more sharply, from 15.9 to 21.4 percent[47] (see figure 2.1).

A variety of other kinds of data and measures tell much the same story. Sheldon Danziger and Peter Gottschalk, for example, recalculated Census data on *family* (as opposed to household) incomes over time in a sophisticated fashion that takes account of variations in family size (this is particularly important since families have grown smaller, presumably needing less income), includes unrelated individuals, and weights larger families more heavily in the statistics. According to these data, the real incomes of both

Figure 2.1   Percentage of Aggregate Income Received by Each Fifth of
Households, 1967–98

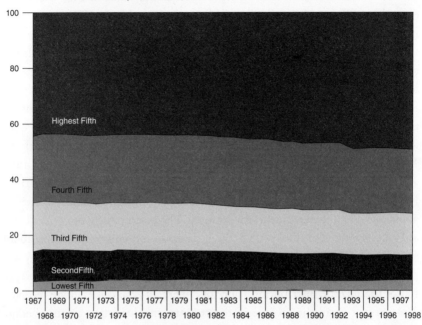

Source: 1998 U.S. Census, CPSO Money Income in the U.S., B-6, table B3.

high-income and low-income families grew markedly between 1949 and
1969; in fact, those on the bottom gained the most. Between 1973 and 1991,
however, families in the bottom tenth lost a lot of ground; their mean incomes dropped by 19.1 percent. Those in the lower middle part of the distribution pretty much stagnated. But those with higher incomes gained, and
the top tenth enjoyed an increase of fully 21.5 percent. Thus inequality
among families greatly increased.[48]

The causes of this increased inequality do not lie chiefly with the changes
in family structure that are sometimes blamed for it.[49] Instead, the causes
are largely rooted in the decline or stagnation of wages (particularly the
wages of less-skilled men) that we have already mentioned. The so-called
"skills premium" for education has greatly increased, not only because of the
increased importance of computers and information technology, but also
because competition from low-wage countries—operating through cheap
imported goods, the movement of factories and capital abroad, and immigration of low-wage workers—has drastically undercut the low end of
U.S. wages.[50]

But the increased income inequality in the United States also reflects, at the same time that millions of people's incomes were declining or stagnating, a huge upsurge of incomes among the very *top* income earners. The entrepreneurs of the 1980s and 1990s cashed in big. Executives' compensation, in salaries, fringe benefits, and especially stock options, soared. American CEOs enjoy compensation many times as high as the CEOs of comparable firms abroad, and the link with their economic performance is tenuous at best.[51] Fortunate people who got stock options—or bought or inherited common stock—early in the last two decades of the twentieth century (in the summer of 1982, for example, when the Dow Jones Industrial Average [DJIA] fell below 800) enjoyed an enormous bonanza as the DJIA climbed to a level of 11,000 in 1999.[52] That was a *1,275 percent gain.* To put it another way, the average value of blue chip stocks—mostly owned by very wealthy people—was multiplied by nearly *fourteen times.*

Andrew Hacker, using a wide variety of sources, has painted a compelling picture of who these very high-income people are. They include the 9 percent of Americans enjoying the "$100,000 life," the fortunate 70,000 or so households earning $1 million or more a year, and those at the very top, the handful of Americans (137 in 1996) that *Forbes* magazine identified as having personal wealth of more than $1 billion (George Soros, for example, actually earned $1.5 billion in 1995 alone).[53] With the American dream in mind, we may well cheer the chance to get rich. But *this* rich? When millions of hard-working people are barely getting by?

A compact way to summarize the extent of inequality with a single number is to calculate a "Gini coefficient," which varies from zero (if everyone in the population gets exactly equal incomes) and grows toward one when income is more and more concentrated—nearing the limit of 1.0 when every bit of income is received by a single person or family in a large population. Gini coefficients calculated over time for Census data on family incomes show the familiar trend toward increasing inequality. A Gini of 0.388 in 1968 rose to 0.456 in 1998.[54]

Among advanced Organization for Economic Cooperation and Development (OECD) countries, the United States has an exceptionally high degree of income inequality, standing in what Denny Braun calls "a class by itself" at the top of the inequality pyramid. In the 1980s and 1990s, among ten countries with comparable data, the United States had by a substantial margin the highest Gini coefficient for disposable household income: about 0.34, compared with 0.30 or less for the other most unequal countries (the United

Kingdom, France, Australia, and Canada), while Finland, Sweden, Norway, and Belgium had much lower Gini coefficients in the 0.22 to 0.24 range. And U.S. inequality had recently increased more than in any other country but Britain.[55]

By other measures, too, the United States leads the inequality pack. The United States has had the highest percentage of low-income persons among fifteen advanced OECD countries. Looking at the "ninety-ten" or "rich-to-poor" ratio (the total income of the top 10 percent divided by the total income of the bottom 10 percent), the U.S. ratio of 5.94 was about one-and-a-half times as high as that of any of the next most unequal countries, Canada, Australia, and the United Kingdom.[56] The United States stands closer than other advanced countries do to the very high levels of inequality found in many less-developed countries of Latin America, Africa, and Asia.[57]

According to the 1999 United Nations *Human Development Report,* the United States had the worst "human poverty" score (based on survival rates, literacy rates, long-term unemployment, and the proportion of people below half the median income) of all seventeen advanced countries measured.[58]

Ideally, as we set the stage for examining what (if anything) government can or should do about poverty and inequality, we would like to know how much poverty and inequality there *would* be in the United States *without* any government action at all. In order to assess how big a problem there is for government to address, we would like to figure out the hypothetical, purely *"no government"* or *"pregovernment"* distribution of income, based on how much income people would have received without getting any income transfers, paying any taxes, or being affected by any other government spending programs, regulations, or other actions. Despite some heroic early efforts by Richard Musgrave, Morgan Reynolds, Eugene Smolensky, and other scholars, however, any effort to estimate "pregovernment" incomes is bound to be elusive. Government is so inextricably involved with the economy in so many ways that it is impossible to identify them all and subtract them out. Indeed it is impossible to conceive of a modern economy existing without a substantial government role.[59]

Still, the Census Bureau has calculated the distribution of income among American households in a variety of ways (some eighteen different ways), including one—definition #4—that comes fairly close to the concept of total "pregovernment" income (it includes realized capital gains and health insurance fringe benefits, but does not subtract any taxes or add in any direct government benefits).[60] This measure shows income to be even more un-equally distributed than the usual money-income statistics do. In 1998, for example, 11.7 percent of households got more than $100,000, while more than 25.6 percent got less than $15,000 (the Gini coefficient was a startling 0.509). On the other hand, according to a fairly thorough "postgovernment" measure that adds all cash and noncash transfers and subtracts taxes (defi-nition #14), only 6.5 percent of households got more than $100,000, and only 14.3 percent got less than $15,000. This distribution was considerably less unequal (with a Gini coefficient of 0.405), indicating that government action significantly reduced income inequality.[61]

When looking at income statistics, including those given earlier in this chapter, it is important to remember that they usually reflect a variety of government actions. Always they include the effects of macroeconomic and other regulatory policies, as well as spending on public goods. Often, as in the earlier Census figures we cited, they include government cash transfer payments as income. Sometimes (as in the OECD disposable income figures above) they also subtract taxes paid. When taxes and transfers are taken into account, U.S. incomes generally look somewhat less unequal than when they are not, but more unequal relative to other countries—most of which have more egalitarian government policies. The figures that are most relevant for our present purposes are those that come closest to reflecting no government action at all.

Clearly the high level of income inequality in the United States does not follow inevitably and automatically from market forces that fairly reward individuals' skills and efforts. The extent of inequality is largely beyond the control of individual workers. But the evidence from other wealthy countries indicates that such extreme poverty and inequality are not inevitable. Collec-tively, it would seem, we have a choice. Now it is time to turn directly to the question of exactly what, if anything, government can or should deliberately do about poverty and inequality.

3

What Should Government Do?

What should government do about the extensive poverty and the extreme and growing inequality of income and wealth in the United States?

One possible answer to this question is "nothing." Perhaps we can trust market forces to fairly reward merit and punish sloth; let the chips fall where they may. (Of course, this would ignore one of the main points of the last chapter.) Don't government programs inevitably violate individual freedoms, waste resources, and get bogged down in bureaucratic inefficiency? Are we sure that anything *can* be done about poverty and inequality without causing dependency and making the problems worse? Perhaps everyone should just concentrate on getting ahead and forget about those who fall behind.

We will argue that there are persuasive answers to each of these concerns. But issues of freedom, efficiency, and government capacity and effectiveness must be taken very seriously. This chapter begins by discussing the general pros and cons of action by government or by private markets; it outlines several possible government "functions" within a primarily free-market economy. It then explains why we believe that one important function of government should be to deal with poverty and inequality. Next comes the question of just *how* that might be done. Several different approaches are discussed, noting the strengths and weaknesses of each: using progressive taxes and income transfers, providing equal opportunity, investing in human

capital, assuring the availability of jobs at good wages, providing social insurance, and guaranteeing access to basic necessities (these approaches will come
up again in later chapters of the book). Finally, we consider certain economic
and political obstacles to carrying out egalitarian policies—especially obstacles involving economic globalization and unequal political power—but
argue that the obstacles can be overcome.

At certain points in this chapter, we introduce elements of economics-style
reasoning in order to illuminate arguments for and against government action. Some important technical terms are italicized and defined (often par-
enthetically) in language that is as simple and clear as we can make it. We
recognize, however, that some readers may find some of these concepts difficult or may be put off by terms that sound odd and unfamiliar. If that
should happen, we urge you to *forge ahead*. Skim through any troublesome
passages—or skip them altogether—and get on with the rest of the book.
You can always come back to this chapter later.

Theories of Government Functions

A number of influential ideas about what governments should do can be
traced back to the emergence of modern social and political institutions in
England, where conflicts between individual rights and government power
provoked a great deal of thought. Thomas Hobbes, for example, writing at
a time of chaos and civil war, formulated a vision of government that remains
compelling for many Americans. Hobbes argued that individual human beings ("men," in the parlance of the day) give up their autonomy to a sovereign
government for the sake of mutual defense and the establishment of law and
order. That is, the chief function of government should be to establish order.[1]

As the economy, society, and government of England evolved, the theory
of government functions evolved as well. The early emergence of barons'
checks on monarchical power, exemplified by the Magna Carta, was accompanied by theories of individuals' natural rights (later, constitutional rights),
upon which government—even a sovereign king—must not infringe. The
rise of Parliament, including a House of Commons that increasingly represented an emerging middle class, was accompanied by theories of government by the consent of the governed. John Locke, a leading advocate of
government by consent, also located the functions of government firmly
within the framework of an emerging free-market economy. To Locke, the

principal functions of government included keeping order in the sense of preventing people from killing or stealing from each other, but he saw this as essentially bound up with protecting private *property,* the main foundation of a market economy. Locke declared that "[t]he greatest and chief end, therefore, of men's uniting into commonwealths and putting themselves under government is the preservation of their property."[2]

In England and the United States, prevailing theories of the proper functions of government came to be embedded in—indeed derived from—theories of the functioning of a free-market economy. Adam Smith, the great political economist who glorified the "invisible hand" of competition among private entrepreneurs—competition that, he claimed, usually promotes the general good—fought against government interference with the private economy through tariffs, quotas, price regulation, or spending on pomp and splendor. Smith thought that government should provide the foundations for a private economy: keep order, protect property and enforce contracts, and provide a supply of money, but not do a lot more.[3]

Establishing Foundations for a Market Economy

This function of government—the most fundamental of all, in the eyes of many modern economists and businesspeople—now seems so self-evident that it often goes without saying. Practically everyone in the industrialized West—and, increasingly, people around the world—believes that government should keep public order, define and protect property rights, enforce contracts, and create and manage the money supply.

In order for markets to work well, it is clearly essential to *define and protect property rights.* Legal provisions are needed to determine exactly how ownership of various kinds of property is established, what rights owners have, how those rights are enforced, and how ownership can be altered. Only when property rights are clear and enforceable is it possible for people to buy and sell goods, hire employees, accumulate capital, and build up businesses. Only with well-defined and transferable property rights can goods be produced, traded, and consumed in an efficient fashion. And only government has the authority and legitimacy to create and enforce property rights.

The basic idea is simple enough. One of the most ancient functions of governments has been to establish who owns which land and personal property and to protect them against theft or destruction. Police forces and courts are needed to punish or deter violations of property rights. The law must make clear just what people can and cannot do with their property and how they can sell or lease it to others or pass it on to heirs by inheritance. Constitutional or other provisions may also be needed to limit the ways in which government itself can interfere with private property.

In a complex modern economy, however, the definition and protection of property become very complicated. New forms of ownership must be invented and implemented. Limited-liability corporations, for example, which are so crucial to the high-volume production and distribution of goods and services, exist only because governments recognize them as legal "persons"— entitled to own, to contract, to sue and be sued—while shielding their owners (stockholders) and managers from most forms of personal liability. The corporation is a creature of government. For a modern economy to work properly, government laws and regulations must deal with many abstract forms of property, including corporate stocks and bonds and rights to ideas ("intellectual property"). They must define the nature and powers of partnerships, trusts, and a host of other institutions. They must spell out the meaning of, and enforce, a welter of different provisions in commercial contracts. And they must make clear when and how private property rights have to give way to other public and private purposes, through liability laws, zoning, taxes, condemnation, and the like.[4]

Governments permit corporations to be organized and to act as legal persons, for example, not because there is some sort of natural "right" to do so, but because corporations are thought capable of bringing benefits to society as a whole. In return for the valuable legal privileges given to them, therefore, it might not be unreasonable for government to require that corporations meet specific social obligations. Such obligations could be enforced through such measures as revising state-granted corporate charters, imposing serious criminal penalties for illegal behavior, depriving them of tax breaks or subsidies in cases of serious infractions of civil law, and perhaps even withdrawing political rights (to lobby and the like) upon criminal conviction, just as people convicted of felonies lose the right to vote.[5]

In addition to defining and protecting private property, governments need to *create and manage a supply of money,* that is, of a medium of exchange that people can use conveniently to buy and sell things with. Only governments have the power and the legitimacy to declare what is and what is not "legal tender," to print paper money or moneylike obligations including Treasury bonds and notes, to guarantee that money will maintain its value, and to regulate the size of the money supply so that it is neither too small nor too large.

One reason we need to mention these obvious functions of government is to make clear that it is artificial to distinguish sharply between "public" and "private" in a modern economy. The idea of a free market without government—an idea that some libertarians seem to embrace—is an illusion. Governments create and enforce the property rights and other legal arrangements that make modern markets possible. And governments not only create markets, but also inevitably alter and modify markets by making choices among a host of alternative legal arrangements, many of which may have important implications for poverty and inequality. It would be rather peculiar to attack the legitimacy of any and all government "interference" with the private economy when government action makes such an economy possible. The real question is what sorts of government action are *desirable* and what sorts are not.

Some modern descendants of Adam Smith, enjoying the nearly worldwide triumph of free-market ideology, offer us a particularly narrow, constricted theory of what governments should do. They emphasize the importance of individual freedom, especially economic freedom, and decry government activity of almost any sort. Beyond the bare functions of providing law and order, enforcing contracts and property rights, and managing the money supply, they say that the main duty of government is to leave us alone. Milton Friedman's powerful tract, *Capitalism and Freedom*, details a long list of things the U.S. government has done, but that governments should *not* do.[6] As another writer puts it, "The central idea of libertarianism is that people should be permitted to run their own lives as they wish"; they should not be forcibly protected from themselves, and they do not have an enforceable claim on others.[7]

Yet Western economic theory also holds within it the seeds of quite different theories of government. Adam Smith himself, while suspicious of much of the activity of his contemporary British government, had no illusions about the universal efficacy of markets. Indeed, he wrote compellingly of persistent efforts by businessmen to collude, to fix prices, to evade the pressures of market competition. Implicit in Smith's work is an analysis of market failures, including monopoly and oligopoly pricing, which may require government action. Moreover, Smith offered an extensive account of "public works" that government should provide—not only defense and justice, but also works to facilitate commerce (roads, bridges, canals, harbors; forts and ambassadors abroad) and measures to educate the youth and to promote religion.[8]

Others, further developing classical and neoclassical economic theory, have elaborated on the idea of market failures. Arthur Pigou, for example, explored what he called "neighbourhood effects" (now usually called *externalities*), in which people not party to (external to) economic transactions may nonetheless be affected by them. People in the neighborhood of a steel factory that belches smoke or a chemical plant that pours toxins into a river or lake may suffer grievously. Yet—absent some sort of special legal rights or government regulation—the polluters may have no incentive to compensate for this harm or prevent it. Quite aside from questions of fairness, such a situation is economically inefficient. It leads to a misallocation of resources: more production of steel, chemicals, and pollution than a perfect system of all-inclusive property rights (including rights to clean air and water) and voluntary economic transactions would produce.[9]

Providing Public Goods

Building on Pigou's insights about neighborhood effects, economists have developed theories of *public goods,* or *social* or *collective goods*, invoking such examples (imperfect examples) as clean water, clean air, national defense, and public order. Markets alone generally fail to provide public goods in an optimal fashion. Sometimes they fail to provide them at all. In order to promote economic efficiency, therefore, governments may have to act.[10]

This is most obvious in the case of an ideal, theoretically "pure" public good. A pure public good is one with completely *nonrival* and *nonexcludible consumption.* Nonrivalness means that there is no rivalry among consumers: no matter how many people consume such a good (perhaps the view of a beautiful mountain, for example), the cost of producing it does not increase. Nonexcludibility means that once the good (say, clean air) is produced, no one can be excluded from consuming it or be forced to pay for doing so. If a good has the characteristic of nonexcludibility, private markets will fail to produce it no matter how many people want it. When consumption is nonrival, the price (which is economically most efficient if it is set equal to marginal cost) should ideally be zero because it costs nothing for an additional person to consume the good. But what sort of businessperson would produce a good and then sell it for nothing? With nonexcludibility, there is no way to require consumers to pay any price at all, so, again, who would produce it? Economic theorists have shown that the result is highly inefficient.[11]

Take the traditional (though rather archaic) example of a lighthouse, which has some of the features of a public good. Consumption is more or less nonrival: it costs no more to let fifty ships—or five hundred ships—use a light than it costs to let a single vessel use it. Also, once the light is shining, it is hard to exclude any ship from seeing it or to force a ship to pay for doing so. Left to themselves, therefore, private entrepreneurs have little or no incentive to build lighthouses. If we want to prevent ships from breaking up on the rocks, governments may have to act.[12]

Of course, real-world situations are not quite so neat as the theory suggests; no purely public goods actually exist. Consumption is seldom, if ever, completely nonrival, except perhaps for the case of information; in most cases, congestion or other factors introduce a degree of rivalness (too many ships in a channel trying to use a lighthouse might make it dangerous for other ships to use it). Much more common than pure nonrivalness is *increasing returns to scale* over some range of production, so that the cost of serving each additional consumer goes down, but does not reach zero. Similarly, exclusion is rarely impossible; more often it is just *costly* (if pressed, for example, one might devise a lighthouselike navigational aid that broadcasts a scrambled and apparently directionless electronic signal, decodable only with a device that shipowners could be required to rent or purchase).[13] Moreover, the nature and importance of public goods are contingent on technological developments; lighthouses come and go (space satellites and global positioning devices pose similar but not identical problems). Further, nonrivalness and nonexcludibility are not invariably found together; it is possible to have one without the other.

Thus there are many messy situations in which private markets may fail in whole or part and government may need to step in. Short of purely nonrival consumption, for example, increasing returns to scale may (if exclusion is possible so that prices can be exacted for consumption) create a *natural monopoly*. In a natural monopoly situation, a single firm has incentives to take over the whole market (could this be true of "network externalities" and certain types of computer software?) and produce very cheaply at high volume, but to charge prices that are well above the ideal, marginal-cost level. This provides one important rationale for antitrust policy, for price or rate regulation, or for direct public provision of goods and services—with government either taking over entirely or else providing competition with a private monopolist.

Short of complete nonexcludibility, the difficulty or costliness of excluding people from consuming goods (or preventing them from producing bads) often results in positive or negative *externalities:* good or bad impacts on people not involved in ("external" to) market transactions (as we noted, externalities are the same thing as Pigou's more mellifluously labeled "neighbourhood effects"). In unregulated private markets, externalities lead to inefficient overproduction of bads like pollution and to underproduction of goods like the preservation of natural wildlife and scenery. The existence of externalities therefore is often invoked to argue for government action in realms that do not involve pure public goods. These include national defense (if a private entrepreneur were to create a nuclear deterrent force, it would be difficult to exclude from protection individual citizens who refused to pay), police and courts, environmental protection, product safety, education (businesses and society as a whole may gain from well-educated workers and citizens), research and development, public health, promotion of morals, support of the arts, and a host of other things. As we will see, many of these policies affect poverty and inequality in one way or another. Moreover, poverty and inequality themselves may create negative externalities, providing a rationale for government action on those grounds.

Market failure can also result from systematic *asymmetries of information,* where some people know crucial things that others cannot easily find out. An example is the *adverse selection* problem in health insurance and pension schemes. Unusually illness-prone people may flock to buy private health coverage, or unusually long-lived people may rush to buy private pension annuities, since fees cannot be adjusted to the customers' privately held information about their own characteristics. This may drive premium rates above what healthier or shorter-lived people can afford. Universal, government-run programs like Medicare or Social Security may be needed to overcome this defect of the market.[14]

To be sure, as critics have insisted—especially in the antigovernment climate of recent years in the United States—market failure alone does not necessarily justify turning to government. The costs of "government failure," in the form of political waste, bureaucratic inefficiency, or loss of personal liberties, may exceed the benefits of any improvement that government could make on imperfect market solutions.[15] Few would actually assert that monopoly prices and unrestricted pollution are always more bearable than government efforts to regulate them.[16] Short of that extreme position, though, it is still clear that the mere existence of externalities or increasing returns does not by itself mean that government should act. We must consider the whole range of possible costs and benefits. This often entails difficult measurement problems. (How, for example, does one put a dollar value on the preservation of an old-growth forest or on the saving of a human life?)

Once it is suggested that government should act to deal with a market failure, we may face many choices about exactly what sort of policy tools to use. If private enterprise fails to provide a public good, should the government go into business and produce it itself? Or should it contract out the job? Or provide tax incentives, financial subsidies, or regulations to persuade private businesses to do what they would not otherwise do? And what level of government—national, state, local—can best do what needs doing? Through what type of institution—executive, regulatory, legislative, or judicial? Clearly (as we noted in chapter 1) it is desirable to choose policy tools that maximize such values as effectiveness, economic efficiency, equality, and individual freedom.

We will see that efforts to provide public goods or to deal with externalities, increasing returns, information asymmetries, and so forth inevitably have implications for the matter of main concern to us, poverty and inequality. No public good is equally valuable to everyone; some chiefly benefit the poor, while others mainly benefit the rich. Moreover, the particular means of providing public goods (contracting out, for example, as opposed to hiring public employees) often has implications for the distribution of income. In deciding exactly *how* government should act, it may make sense to pay attention to the impact on poverty and inequality, along with issues of effectiveness, efficiency, and liberty.

Ensuring Economic Growth and Stability

A third function of government advocated by many economists and others is that of promoting economic growth and stability—ensuring that the entire economy grows at a desirable rate, does not suffer from excessively high levels of unemployment or inflation, and does not fall into damaging recessions or depressions.[17]

Economic theory does not offer very firm prescriptions about these matters. There is no agreed formula stating how much current consumption should be foregone for the sake of economic growth. Indeed, the relative importance of various causes of economic growth—aggregate demand, investment in plant and equipment, technological innovation, workforce education, public works infrastructure—is subject to debate, so it is difficult to assess exactly what should be done about them. There is even sharper disagreement about inflation and unemployment. In the short run, at least, there may exist a trade-off between the two: when unemployment declines, inflation tends to increase. Macroeconomic theorists disagree about which is the greater evil, what level of unemployment—if any—is "natural" (below which inflation is likely to accelerate), and what, if anything, government can and should do. Similar arguments concern whether and how government should try to smooth out economic fluctuations, counteracting the business cycle.[18]

In the 1980s, a chorus of conservative economists and policy advocates argued that government cannot and should not do much about any of these things except to fight inflation; efforts at short-run stimulation of the economy are futile because people see through their temporary nature and adapt in ways that defeat the policy efforts. Government, they said, should simply keep the money supply steady, stand aside, and let the great engine of free enterprise chug down the tracks, producing whatever growth and employment it can.[19] The appeal of this sort of laissez-faire doctrine tends to fade, however, when things go badly wrong—as they did in the 1990–91 recession, one of the most severe economic contractions since World War II. High rates of inflation or unemployment, deep recessions, and slow economic growth invariably lead to calls for government action. Most Americans believe that the government has some degree of responsibility to make the overall economy work properly. For that matter, government probably has no choice but to try: it is so deeply involved in the economy that it is bound to have profound effects, and it may as well try to make those effects positive rather than negative.

One set of tools for macroeconomic policy making involves *fiscal* policy: the overall levels of taxes and spending, and the balance or imbalance between them. Budget deficits, representing an excess of spending over tax revenues, tend to stimulate aggregate demand, which in turn (under certain conditions, at least) produces higher levels of employment, counteracts recessions, and promotes higher levels of economic growth. The thought of

John Maynard Keynes, though much contested, retains considerable vigor: many economists and others still argue that the government ought deliberately to run substantial deficits in times of recession in order to stimulate economic recovery. Other economists, especially in the period after the Reagan-era surge in annual U.S. budget deficits, have maintained that reducing the deficit and then paying off part of the accumulated national debt should be the highest priority in American politics. Deficits were in fact reduced and then eliminated during the 1990s—an important achievement that probably contributed to economic growth, but came at the cost of years of constricted social spending.

Arguments about deficits are complicated by confusion over measurement. The U.S. government's budgeting ignores the standard accounting distinction between spending for investment and spending for current consumption; instead, it treats all investments as if they represented expenses in the year of outlay. Thus official tallies of "current accounts" deficits have probably overstated the extent to which current expenses actually exceeded revenues.[20]

A second tool of macroeconomic policy involves management of the money supply and interest rates. By printing paper money or by issuing bonds, notes, and other moneylike obligations, the government can have major effects on interest rates, inflation, unemployment, and economic growth. "Tight money," when money is made hard to borrow by means of slow growth in the money supply and/or direct raising of interest rates by the Federal Reserve Board, tends to reduce inflation, but also to slow growth and to increase unemployment. An expanding money supply and low interest rates have the opposite effects. The question of precisely what monetary policy should be pursued (increase the money supply exactly as much as productivity grows? faster? slower?) is very much a matter of contention, and alternative macroeconomic policies are likely to affect different groups in society differently.

Without question, however, governments do actually make such decisions; they cannot escape doing so. And the choice of macroeconomic policies can have profound effects on poverty and inequality, as we will further discuss in chapter 7. Historically, economic growth has eventually trickled down to help the poor; a rising tide has tended to lift all boats—though, as we saw in the last chapter, it did not do so in the 1970s and 1980s. Choices between unemployment and inflation can affect the rich and the poor quite differently. Wealthy creditors who loan their money out at fixed interest rates—the holders of bonds, for example—hate unanticipated inflation, which erodes the value of their assets, whereas ordinary working people are much more devastated by unemployment.

Dealing with Poverty and Inequality

A fourth possible function of government, the one of most interest to us in this book, derives from the fact that market outcomes may produce a highly unequal distribution of income and wealth. We may want government to do something to help the poor or to reduce inequality. Even Milton Friedman has taken this point. *Capitalism and Freedom* at one point hedged on the issue, maintaining that it is "difficult to justify" either accepting or rejecting an ethic of market-driven incomes equal to people's marginal product. But it also expressed openness to an extensive income-redistribution program in the form of a "negative income tax," which, Friedman argued, would minimally upset market allocations.[21] Others have taken it to be a major function of government, if not *the* major function, to provide a safety net for the neediest and to reduce excessive inequalities in wealth and income.[22]

One important argument for government action of this sort flows from the philosophy of utilitarianism, which underpins much of Western (especially Anglo-American) thinking about politics and society. Utilitarianism posits that the chief criterion for judging the performance of governments or economies should be whether or not they maximize the total satisfaction or happiness—the aggregate sum of "utilities"—of the entire population of individuals.[23] This utilitarian principle suggests a rather broad view of the functions of government. So, at least according to one interpretation, does the preamble to the U.S. Constitution: government should "promote the general welfare." Or, as Abraham Lincoln put it, government should be "for the people."

It turns out that the utilitarian principle, combined with certain empirical assumptions, leads to the conclusion that the general satisfaction is increased when inequality of income is reduced. The basic argument proceeds as follows. People tend to have declining marginal utility for money: that is, an additional dollar of income means more to a person when he is poor than when he is rich. If we assume that this is the case and that everyone has identical utility functions for money—that is, the same total amount of money would make different people equally happy (this is not likely to be exactly true, but perhaps it is close enough to draw reasonable conclusions)—

and if we also assume that there exists a fixed amount of money to be distributed (not very plausible, but again perhaps close enough), then each dollar taken from the rich and given to the poor will increase the happiness of the latter more than it detracts from the happiness of the former, thus increasing the total sum of satisfaction in society.

If the above assumptions are perfectly met, then redistribution should proceed to a state of complete equality, which will maximize total happiness. Even if the assumptions are not fully correct—if there exist epicures, for example, who would gain more than others at the same income level from an additional dollar or if too much equality would reduce incentives to work or invest and thereby diminish the amount of income available to redistribute—utilitarian logic provides a powerful argument for some degree of government action to reduce market-produced inequalities of income and wealth.[24]

This sort of individualistic, utilitarian reasoning does not appeal to everyone. But several other lines of thinking, based on a number of different ethical or religious values, likewise suggest that poverty and inequality should be a concern of government.

The communitarian ideal of good public order and a peaceful, law-abiding society, for example, is likely to be threatened by extreme inequalities. As even Thomas Hobbes noted, when material inequality is extreme, the poor may become desperate and riot, steal what they need, or revolt in civil war.[25] Angry have-nots are a threat to the haves. Further, a sense of community and harmonious, friendly social interactions are likely to decline if some people are so deprived as to be consumed with envy and hatred of the well-off. As R. H. Tawney put it, "[G]reat disparities . . . poison relationships and communications between individuals and groups."[26]

To be sure, neither raw self-interest nor a narrow sort of communitarianism necessarily points toward a very egalitarian society. Worry about public order may not, in itself, dictate very strong government moves to equalize incomes because people on the bottom of the heap can sometimes be made remarkably tolerant of their lot. The current situation in the United States has not produced constant riots (though it has probably contributed to crime and disorder). Also—to some powerful people—segregation, high walls, prisons, and even repression may seem cheaper than large-scale income redistribution. Some well-off people may care only about their own small, homogeneous, perhaps gated, communities.

Still, a broader communitarianism that encompasses *all* citizens does point in the direction of government action to reduce severe inequalities. As Charles Fourier noted, extreme inequality divides people, hinders genuine social interaction, and undermines community. Love, friendship, familiarity, and other interpersonal relations are distorted by social inequality and poverty. Privation produces multiple kinds of dissatisfaction, including illness, pain, shame, envy, frustration, fear, and loathing. It promotes class division and hardens and vulgarizes the wealthy—encouraging idleness, arrogance, dissolution, and ostentation. It necessitates an unproductive workforce devoted to serving and protecting the affluent.[27]

Taking a particular social contractarian approach, John Rawls's theory of justice asks us to make income-distributional decisions from the perspective of an "original position," ignoring whatever privileges we may now enjoy and contemplating the possibility that we might have ended up in the place of the least fortunate. If we are highly risk averse, Rawls argues, we should adopt a "maximin" criterion: we should arrange things so as to maximally improve the lot of the least-well-off member of society.[28] This, of course, would call for a substantial degree of equalization. Rawls's approach is designed to induce sympathy for others from a starting point of rational self-interest.

Few of us, of course, actually perform utilitarian calculations or Rawlsian thought-experiments. Our ethical and religious ideas and feelings take many different forms and come from many different sources. But most of us care about other human beings, consider every individual valuable, and want to see everyone treated well. We may put this in terms of the Golden Rule, or Jean-Jacques Rousseau's exhortation to feel compassion for those in need because we can imagine our own needs in a similar situation, or Henry Sidgwick's "extended sympathy," or some other formulation.[29] If we have even a rudimentary sense of common humanity, a number of considerations point us toward taking action against poverty and inequality.

If we love individual freedom and want all people to enjoy it, for example, we must recognize that there is not much freedom for the destitute. Disability, illness, hunger, and exposure to the elements are not conducive to a wide range of choices or to full self-development. Nor is bondage to a dead-end, low-paying job. Similarly, if we cherish the value of equal opportunity, the idea that everyone should have an equal chance at the "starting line" of life's competition, we must realize—at least when pressed—that accidents of birth and environment greatly advantage some and severely handicap others. Without compensatory action by government or some other agency, formally equal opportunity is likely to be an illusion. If we believe in fair treatment for all human beings, we are bound to see that much deprivation results from factors beyond people's control and requires collective help.

None of these values—not social order, sense of community, individual freedom, self-development, equal opportunity, or fair treatment—points toward total and complete equality. Each of them calls up a somewhat different vision of exactly what government should do. Nor, as we noted, does the utilitarian criterion of maximizing aggregate happiness prescribe perfect equality. The danger of losing some productive investment and work indicates that we should stop short of complete leveling. Just how far we should go depends both on how strong our egalitarian values are and on empirical questions about the precise terms of what Arthur Okun called the "big tradeoff" between efficiency and equity. As Okun put it, a bucket that carries (redistributes) income from one person to another may be leaky.[30]

In this book, we will be much concerned with the question of just how leaky—or how watertight—the "Okun bucket" actually is in the case of various specific policies. As we will see, the empirical evidence does not in fact establish the existence of such rigid barriers against redistribution as are often assumed in popular rhetoric. In a number of cases, equity and efficiency can go harmoniously together. The efficiency and practicality of measures to deal with poverty and inequality depend partly on just what our aims are and how well we design policy tools to accomplish them—subjects we turn to now.

Approaches to Poverty and Inequality

To accept the idea that government should play some role in dealing with poverty and inequality does not settle exactly what that role should be. We will consider several different possible approaches that embody a variety of possible goals and a variety of methods to accomplish them. These include guaranteed incomes, progressive taxes and income redistribution, equal opportunity, investment in education and human capital, guaranteed jobs at good wages, social insurance, and safety nets.[31] Several of these approaches will be prominent in later chapters of the book.

Guaranteed Incomes

The simplest and boldest approach to inequality is to directly redistribute income, taking cash from the rich and giving it to the poor, guaranteeing everyone a certain minimal level of income. With sufficient redistribution of this sort, presumably poverty would be much reduced or eliminated, and every person would enjoy a decent standard of living. At the limit (which is seldom if ever advocated), a very high guaranteed income would ensure nearly complete equality of incomes in the whole population.

The idea of this sort of redistribution of income enjoyed some currency in the United States during the 1960s and 1970s. Proposals for a "guaranteed income," "demogrants," a "negative income tax," or "family allowances" were embraced by many politicians and policy experts on both the Left and the Right, including Milton Friedman. Advantages of such plans were said to include the simplicity of the policy tools involved (just taxing the rich and giving the proceeds to poor and low-income people), the freedom of choice allowed to recipients (they can spend the money any way they want), and the efficiency of the operation (low administrative costs and minimization of economic distortions).[32]

The debates surrounding presidential candidate George McGovern's proposed "demogrants" and the Nixon administration's defeated Family Assistance Plan, however, made clear not only that most of the rich do not want to be taxed heavily to fund such programs, but also that sympathy with the poor and a desire to help them do not necessarily translate into widespread public support for large cash transfers or guaranteed incomes. What about work? Would it be fair to compensate those who do not work at all with incomes just as high as those of people who work desperately hard? Wouldn't such a policy create perverse incentives? Wouldn't it discourage people from working and encourage dependency on handouts? [33]

In actuality, considerable evidence indicates that most poor people are willing and eager to work, so long as they can find jobs that pay reasonable wages and so long as they can deal with transportation, child care, and the like. Several large-scale social experiments in the 1960s and 1970s found that guaranteed incomes, even fairly substantial incomes, had only small effects of decreasing hours of work and did so only among certain population subgroups. (The finding of significantly higher divorce rates among those with guaranteed incomes, which some took to show that income support undermines "family values," could equally well be seen as showing that relief from economic fears and pressures frees people to escape from bad marriages.)[34] Moreover, the total loss to society from decreased work due to a modest level of guaranteed incomes would be limited because most of the people affected have relatively low skills and productivity; the work foregone by them would probably not be very valuable.

But the actual cost of lost work is not the only issue. Fairness to those who work hard, the goal of clearly rewarding and approving of work, and the desirability of giving even the most humble among us a sense that they are contributing to society all push toward dealing with poverty and inequality in some way other than simply guaranteeing large cash payments to everyone. The widespread opposition to even small and narrowly targeted "welfare" payments under the old Aid to Families with Dependent Children (AFDC) program, together with the widespread insistence that all able-bodied aid recipients should work (even if the cost of training, transportation, and day care exceeds the value of what they can produce), indicates that in the United States any major effort to deal with poverty and inequality probably must include provisions for work by all who can plausibly be considered able to work. Just who and how many are in fact able, of course, is very much subject to dispute.

Still, we will revisit the idea of guaranteed incomes in chapter 8 after we have reviewed a variety of other kinds of programs.

Progressive Taxes and Income Redistribution

Guaranteed cash incomes are only one particular manifestation of a broader and more widely accepted strategy: that of using *progressive taxes* (taxes that take higher percentages of income at higher income levels), together with a variety of spending programs, to redistribute income from relatively affluent to relatively poor or low-income citizens.

Progressive taxes, which we will discuss further in chapter 5, have been advocated by a long and distinguished series of tax philosophers and policy thinkers, from nineteenth-century British economists to the long-reigning chief expert on U.S. taxes, Joseph Pechman.[35] Indeed, progressive taxes are integral to almost any government effort to combat poverty and increase equality, because tax money spent on low-income people obviously does most to equalize incomes if it comes from the rich, not if it is extracted from the poor or middle classes.

But it does not follow that spending must take the form of universal cash grants that amount to a guaranteed income. Income redistribution can be accomplished in a wide variety of ways, including narrowly targeted and means-tested cash transfers, in-kind transfers, education and training programs, wage subsidies, public employment programs, and even spending on public goods that happen to benefit mainly low-income citizens. We will discuss the advantages and disadvantages of specific kinds of spending programs in various later chapters. From the point of view of the general strategy of income redistribution, the main questions are just *how equal* people's posttax, postbenefit incomes can or should be made, and to what extent the inequality of private incomes is moderated by the whole range of government programs.[36]

Equal Opportunity

A different approach to poverty and inequality involves letting private markets determine incomes—or at least accepting whatever inequality results from differences in efforts, skills, and productivity—but having government remove unfair barriers to getting ahead and make sure that everyone has an equal chance at the "starting line" before competition begins. This idea of an equal start, followed by a fair competitive race, is deeply ingrained in our culture.

Most thinking about equal opportunity focuses on two general areas. One involves eliminating artificial and irrational barriers to success, such as discrimination based on race or gender. The other involves helping children from impoverished backgrounds to avoid or overcome various handicaps: providing prenatal health care and nutrition in order to prevent low birth weights or other biological damage to newborns, preschooling to teach social and intellectual skills not fostered at home, hot school meals and medical care to maintain physical health and well-being, high-quality public schooling, and, when necessary, compensatory education to provide skills needed in the workplace. Irwin Garfinkel, Jennifer Hochschild, and Sarah McLanahan, for example, emphasize that equal opportunity requires helping children.[37]

Without question, it is a good idea to eliminate irrational discrimination. Policy measures for children, too, can make a great difference in reducing poverty and inequality. They can prevent or overcome many severe physical and mental deficiencies that would otherwise doom people to failure in the unforgiving competition of the marketplace. Moreover, such policies are often quite cheap and cost-effective. We need not believe the rosiest estimates—for example, that prenatal medical care programs may save as much as *ten times* their cost by preventing subsequent medical expenses and income losses and that preschooling programs may produce benefits worth about *five times* their costs [38]—in order to be convinced that such programs are very much worthwhile.

At the same time, we will argue that conventional conceptions of equal opportunity are often too limited. There are real difficulties with the notion of letting a competitive race run, unhindered, after some definite "starting line." At what point, exactly, are we to supposed to cease helping people because the race has already begun? Not with the first grade of school, surely; disadvantages from subsequent years of weak elementary schooling—or, for that matter, from malnutrition or untreated disease—may haunt people for the rest of their lives. But should we say hands off after, say, sixth grade? Being stuck in an inferior high school (where even the valedictorian may be unable to get into a good college) [39] can ruin a teenager's future job prospects, not to mention the dangers to health and life itself that can result from living in a deprived and perhaps violent neighborhood. Contrary to the footrace imagery, there can be no single, natural childhood or postchildhood starting point to the competitive struggle for economic success. The race begins before birth and continues every day of one's life. A serious approach to equality of opportunity, therefore, logically should acknowledge the need to help people at any stage of their lives when they are disadvantaged by circumstances largely beyond their control.

Moreover, any serious approach to equality of opportunity has to grapple with exactly which factors we propose to make equal. Obviously people cannot have completely equal opportunities unless the net results of *all* economically relevant factors beyond their control are equalized. Such factors are legion. They include not only the nutrition, medical care, and schooling that children get, but also the quality of social and intellectual stimulation they receive at home and from their peers, all of which depend heavily on their parents' resources and choices. Parents, not children, mostly determine whether the children live in good or bad neighborhoods, with good or bad schools and helpful or hurtful peers; whether or not there are books and computers at home; whether or not social adjustment, cognitive skills, and ambition are nourished and encouraged. True, children make choices, too, and should be encouraged to make good ones. But parents largely determine whether or not there will be money for a computer, for travel, for college. Indeed, parents—through genetic inheritance, as well as their teaching, their examples, their resources, and their life choices—in many respects affect what sort of person a child will become.

It is for these reasons that people's family background has been found to account for about half the variation in their occupational status, and perhaps 40 percent of the variation in earnings.[40]

Because of the important role of parents, neighborhoods, and peers in affecting economic success—together with the high degree of inequality among parents—even the most vigorous government efforts to compensate with medical, nutrition, and schooling programs are likely to fall short of providing truly equal opportunities for today's children. So long as we leave parents largely responsible for their children (and challenges to that arrangement are rare), a serious effort to ensure true equality of opportunity for children would have to reduce severe inequalities among parents. Or it would have to compensate for those inequalities in other ways, or limit the variety of possible incomes that the children may attain. Either way, true equality of opportunity would require a considerable measure of equality of results. The familiar, well-worn dichotomy between opportunity and results is misleading. We will discuss equal opportunity further in chapters 6 and 7.

Education and Human Capital

Closely akin to the idea of equal opportunity is the idea that government should make special efforts to invest in *"human capital"* (a bloodless phrase referring to the productive power of individuals), in order to improve people's chances to do valuable work and earn high market incomes. Conceptually the idea of human capital is a broad one, including everything that makes people productive, such as physical and mental health, physical skills and strength, achievement motivation, cognitive ability, work habits, interpersonal skills, general knowledge, and technical expertise. It encompasses the inner confidence, the self-respect, and the active engagement in life tasks that Anthony Giddens champions.[41] Like a thoroughgoing effort at equal opportunity, therefore, a serious attempt to endow everyone with a high level of human capital would entail a broad range of programs involving nutrition, medical care, parenting and child care, work experience, and lifelong education.

In practice, most proposals offered under the rubric of investment in human capital focus on education and training, particularly formal schooling and job-retraining programs. Investment in education has many strong advocates—from Gary Becker to Robert Reich—and powerful arguments on its side. It does not "interfere" with markets in the way that some government programs do; instead, it subsidizes the creation of a strong labor force, something that businesspeople as well as workers can appreciate. Education is widely seen as a public good, bringing broad social benefits, but likely to be underproduced by private markets (firms that invest in training their workers, for example, may find that the workers quit and take their new skills to higher-paying jobs elsewhere). And, to the extent that increased income inequality results from an increased "skill premium" (perhaps brought about by the increased importance of computers and information technology along with low-wage competition from abroad), to raise American workers' skill levels seems a highly appropriate response. Before he became secretary of labor in the first Clinton administration, for example, Robert Reich wrote an eloquent plea for training a new generation of "symbolic analysts" who would emerge as winners in global economic competition.[42]

It is hard to disagree with this logic (though a few die-hard opponents of government manage to do so), especially since the human capital approach promises to promote equality together with—rather than in conflict with—economic growth and competitiveness. In chapter 6, we will see that properly designed educational programs can indeed help accomplish both sets of goals and can do so in an efficient and freedom-enhancing manner.

At the same time, however, it is important to recognize that if "human capital" is construed too narrowly, if only formal schooling and training programs are supported, the effects on income inequality may be rather modest. Millions of people may still be left behind due to untouched deficiencies of health, motivation, social skills, and the like, which hamper their ability to do productive work. Moreover, to the extent that income differences reflect factors other than differences in skill or productivity—inherited wealth, for example, or the good luck of employment in a prosperous sector of the economy versus the bad luck of a no-growth sector[43]—then even a complete equalizing of skill levels would have little effect on income inequality. Likewise if there remain relatively menial, low-productivity jobs that still have to be done by someone. Income levels might remain highly unequal; small differences in educational credentials might serve only as handy cues for picking lucky winners.

Available Jobs at Good Wages

Since labor markets do not perfectly determine incomes according to skills and productivity, since low-productivity tasks persist, *and* since it is highly unlikely that everyone's human capital can be thoroughly equalized, programs aimed at promoting equal opportunity or investing in human capital are not likely, by themselves, to achieve a very high degree of income equality. They may simply result in slotting somewhat different people (perhaps arbitrarily) into still-highly-unequal economic positions. Neither poverty nor inequality may be greatly affected.

Under realistic circumstances, it is at least equally important—maybe more important—to make sure that jobs actually exist for everyone and that all jobs, even the most humble ones, pay reasonable wages. William Julius Wilson has emphasized the crucial importance of jobs and wages, as have most contemporary experts on the economics of poverty and inequality, including Rebecca Blank, Sheldon Danziger, and Peter Gottschalk.[44] Many different kinds of government programs can affect the availability of jobs and the level of wages.

One key component in this approach—urged by James K. Galbraith, among others—involves macroeconomic policy.[45] As we mentioned, fiscal policy (levels of spending relative to taxes, deficits versus balanced budgets, and the like) and monetary policy (the amount of money put into circulation, and tight or loose interest rates) have enormous effects on economic performance and on the level and distribution of wages. When interest rates are low and government spending is high, the economy tends to grow rapidly, unemployment drops, workers are more in demand, and wages—especially at the bottom end of the scale—tend to rise markedly. Inequality is reduced. Tight money and restricted government spending, on the other hand, tend to slow the economy, reduce the demand for workers, leave many people unemployed, and cause wages to drop, especially among those with already low incomes.

Government *must* make choices about fiscal and monetary policy; it cannot help doing so in the normal course of its functions of providing a money supply and taxing and spending for public goods and other purposes. It makes sense, therefore, to make macroeconomic policy choices with a clear eye on how they affect poverty and inequality.

Moreover, government is a major consumer in the economy. Government policies involving procurement of goods or services affect levels of employment and wages. Defense policies that utilize large, well-paid volunteer armed forces, for example, can provide employment and good wages to many relatively low-skill individuals, while also upgrading their skills. Military policies that rely heavily on expensive, capital-intensive, high-tech weapons systems, on the other hand, mostly benefit high-income engineers and technology firms. Many choices about which policies to pursue and how to pursue them will affect the availability of jobs, the level of wages, and the extent of income inequality.

It may also be possible to use direct government employment as a method of helping low-income people by subsidizing their wages (that is, paying higher than the market rate), while at the same time accomplishing important public purposes like building infrastructure or cleaning up the environment. In the 1930s, for example, the Works Progress Administration (WPA) built roads and bridges, and the Civilian Conservation Corps (CCC) blazed trails and planted trees on national lands, employing people that the Great Depression had thrown out of work.[46] Similarly, in the late 1970s and early 1980s, the Comprehensive Employment and Training Act (CETA) helped counteract a deep recession by placing jobless people in state and local government offices and elsewhere. Public service employment is sometimes criticized as wasteful and inefficient for paying higher-than-market wages, but wage subsidies are part of the point: such programs may get useful work done by less-skilled individuals and help them receive decent wages even when the private market would not do so.

Providing public service jobs, whether involving infrastructure, the environment, or other projects of public concern, may not only help the people who get those jobs, but also, by offering good wages in competition with private enterprise (that is, by increasing the demand for labor), drive up wages generally so that other workers are not stuck with subpar earnings. Public employment can reduce income inequality in the society as a whole.

A natural extension of the idea of public service employment is that government might *guarantee jobs* at decent wages to everyone, as an employer of last resort. The idea of guaranteed jobs has been quite popular with the American public, though not generally with business firms that would have to pay higher wages or with the politicians who listen to those firms.

The chief objections to some of these policies concern issues of efficiency and economic growth. Public employment, in particular, is often assumed to involve wasteful, unproductive "make-work," or, at best, to be inefficient because it is not subject to the discipline of market competition. Yet it is not clear that such defects are unavoidable. Competition could be introduced, for example, either among public agencies or between them and private firms bidding for government contracts. Vigorous public management might ensure that effective work is done for important social purposes. Again, however, the very goal of equalizing incomes suggests that getting the work done for the cheapest possible pay should not necessarily be the chief consideration in such programs. It may well be worthwhile to pay more than the minimum in order to redistribute income by paying for work, producing social approval and enhancing self-respect in the way that only work, rather than welfare or other transfer payments, can.

A clever way to raise *after-tax* wages for low-income people, without relying on direct government employment, is to subsidize private wages by means of something like an Earned Income Tax Credit (EITC), which provides a tax refund to low-income workers. In this way, effective wages are raised, but private markets continue to determine what sorts of work get done.

Minimum wage laws might also help raise the incomes of those at the bottom of the scale. Generations of economists have taught that minimum wages are inefficient because they forbid employment at low wages that would clear the market, producing unnecessary unemployment (if a person cannot produce enough to be worth the minimum wage, presumably no one hires him). Yet we will see in chapter 7 that recent research has cast doubt on this apparently obvious proposition. In real-world situations, increases in minimum wages apparently have not measurably increased unemployment. Moreover, even if this finding were mistaken and some small amount of unemployment resulted, we might well feel that the gains of ensuring that more people get acceptable wages would be worth the costs of leaving some very-low-wage work undone plus providing relief for the unemployed. Better yet, guaranteed public service employment at the minimum wage level might eliminate any specter of unemployment.

As in the case of guaranteed incomes, the most fundamental objections to job- and wage-related programs would apply if wages were equalized (through high wages for those on the bottom and confiscatory income taxes at the top, for example) so extensively as to seriously, and on a large scale, undermine incentives to work or to save. True enough—if the bulk of high incomes were taken away in taxes, then some people probably would not work as hard to get those high incomes. (To a surprising extent, on the other hand, many high achievers appear to work for reasons of power, prestige, self-fulfillment, and inner drive, rather than for enjoyment of material rewards; they would continue to strive even if the effort brought them little money.[47]) Similarly, if people were not permitted to earn high incomes, savings rates—generally higher among the wealthy—would likely decline, reducing investment and economic growth.

Just how big these costs from a given amount of income equalization would be, however, must be established by empirical research, and just how much cost we are willing to bear in any necessary "big trade-off" must be determined by our values and choices. Merely to assert a tendency toward some loss of economic production is not sufficient to establish that such policies are not desirable.

We will address these issues further in chapter 7, where we discuss specific kinds of job and wage policies. Again, much rhetoric about negative economic effects of redistributional programs appears to be greatly exaggerated. Some programs designed to increase equality can actually improve economic productivity as well. West Germany's experience with an active labor market policy, for example (which made it very difficult to fire employees), apparently increased productivity by encouraging firms to train workers intensively and to engage in what Wolfgang Streeck calls "diversified quality production."[48]

Social Insurance

Whatever we may or may not do about ensuring the equal opportunity for children to get ahead, equalizing human capital, or guaranteeing the existence of jobs at good wages, it will still always be true that people's life circumstances can be badly damaged by events beyond their control. Such events can create pressing new needs or make it impossible for people to earn an adequate amount of money.

Many devastating events are not only beyond people's control, but also quite sudden and unpredictable. A debilitating and expensive-to-treat disease, a crippling injury, or the death of a crucial family wage earner may occur at any time to almost anyone, producing a particularly capricious sort of inequality that is almost universally deplored. Why should someone be plunged into destitution simply because a drunk driver sent her or him to the hospital, because a hurricane smashed the house, or because a stroke killed the family's chief wage earner?

The obvious remedy for such disasters is insurance. Insurance can help the unfortunate deal with medical expenses and lost income, spreading the costs over a large, affluent, and mostly luckier population (or over the mostly happier lifetime of victims).

At first glance, this may seem a matter for private insurance that people will buy for themselves. Can't the market deal with it? As we have noted, however, the private market for many kinds of insurance is flawed because of the problem of *adverse selection* of individual purchasers (employers, less subject to this problem, help insure only a fortunate fraction of the population). Since those most prone to risk of loss—whether because of genetic predispositions, bad life circumstances, or other reasons—need (and tend to seek) insurance most, and since insurers cannot obtain complete information about individuals, the insurers must charge everyone high premiums and thus discourage lower-risk people from buying insurance at all. Moreover, even if insurers knew everything about individuals' risks, we might well resist the idea that those burdened with hereditary or other uncontrollable risk factors should have to pay extra premiums for their misfortunes. This sort of inequality certainly does not reflect lack of "merit." And in a purely voluntary insurance market, there may also be a tendency for some people to *"free ride,"* refusing to insure themselves and counting on society to pick up the tab, perhaps belatedly and at extra expense, through hospital emergency rooms, public aid, and the like.

For these reasons, there is a compelling argument in favor of compulsory *social insurance* against unforeseen and uncontrollable disasters—insurance that covers everyone (thus eliminating problems of adverse selection or free riding) and that covers everyone at an equal or nearly equal price, thus mitigating the unfairness of uncontrollable factors that increase some people's risks. Social insurance against disease (including mental illness), disability, loss of parents or spouses, and the like is a feature of virtually all advanced industrial countries, for good reason. Theodore Marmor, among others, argues that social insurance is and should be absolutely central to the U.S. version of the welfare state.[49]

There are also good reasons to provide social insurance against certain events that are not unforeseen, but are nonetheless uncontrollable: retirement, for example, when old age arrives and the ability to work diminishes or disappears. Retirement insurance is designed to prevent the travesty of casting aside old people—who in preindustrial societies generally enjoy respect and even reverence—and condemning them to an impoverished existence if they have not, on their own, managed to accumulate substantial savings or a large private pension.

But why, you may ask, should retirement insurance be compulsory? Given the inevitability and foreseeability of the need, can't we count on people to provide for themselves? Don't government pension systems cause people to reduce their private savings (thereby perhaps slowing economic growth) and to stop working too early?

The answers to these questions depend partly on empirical issues: for example, to what extent private savings actually are reduced (as we will see in chapter 4, evidence of reduced work or substantial decreases in savings rates is not in fact very compelling[50]). Answers also depend on one's general views about government activity and about whether or not we want to help people who make serious mistakes.

Suppose that required contributions to social insurance do somewhat reduce private savings and that the proceeds (surpluses credited to the Social Security Trust Fund, for example) are invested in other government programs—perhaps programs to improve public education or to protect the environment. Should we conclude that there is a loss to society because this money is not going into private investment? Not necessarily. Even if the fruits of public investment do not immediately show up as dollars of gross domestic product, they may be every bit as valuable as, or more so than, the returns on private capital. (Even if private investment proved to be more fruitful, of course, we need not give up compulsory public social insurance; proceeds from the required contributions could simply be invested in private rather than public securities.)

Suppose further that, in the absence of social insurance against old age, a number of people would not make adequate provision for retirement—because putting aside money would pinch their low incomes too tightly or simply because they are not good at planning ahead. Do we want to put them on the dole when they get old, further undermining the incentives of others to save? (The free-rider problem again.) Or should we heartlessly say tough luck, no relief, and let the burden fall on any children they may have? Isn't it better to avoid this dilemma by requiring all workers to contribute throughout their lifetimes to compulsory social insurance for retirement?

Finally, if we wish to make collective decisions about the distribution of income across generations or among individuals (perhaps by charging proportionally less and paying out proportionally more in benefits to those with very low lifetime incomes), the existence of a comprehensive social insurance system provides a means for doing so through adjustment of tax and benefit levels. That is, a social insurance system provides the opportunity not only to help equalize incomes over an individual's life cycle and in the face of uncontrollable catastrophes, but also to increase equality among different individuals. To "privatize" such a system and to insist that individuals take care of themselves might be profitable for some affluent people who could invest their savings lucratively, but it would deprive society of a chance to make incomes more equal.

As our discussion of retirement insurance suggests, issues of social insurance become more complicated when they involve controllable behavior that can affect the likelihood or the consequences of negative events. Any insurance system in which risks are affected by controllable behavior is subject to the quaintly named problem of *"moral hazard"*—the problem that people who are insured may no longer have such strong incentives to avoid bad or risky behavior and may therefore engage in more such behavior than they would without the insurance (fire insurance companies, for example, worry that people they cover may become more prone to smoke cigarettes in bed). If we want to discourage a particular kind of behavior, we may hesitate to insure people against its consequences. Some critics of social insurance make this the centerpiece of their opposition; they are so determined to provide incentives for good behavior, and to root out any sort of laziness, error, or immorality, that they would abandon virtually any effort to assist the unfortunate on the grounds that a few weak souls might take unfair advantage of the help.[51]

Yet human life is full of behavior that is partly controllable and partly not—alcoholism, for example, or drug addiction, or disorganized work habits that may be partly rooted in genetic predispositions or mental illness. In such cases, should we help those who fall or simply let them crash? Are we willing to pay no price at all, in terms of excessive generosity to a few advantage-takers, for the sake of helping those who desperately need help? Or can we devise ways to help, while minimizing perverse incentives? We will address such questions in chapters 4 and 8.

Safety Nets and Basic Necessities

The metaphor of a "safety net" suggests that the competitive struggle of life is not a race, but a high-wire act. It implies that we want to encourage everyone to do aerial acrobatics, gyrating as energetically and skillfully as possible, but if they fall, we want to save them—at the last minute, in a minimal and perhaps embarrassing fashion—from the deadly consequences of a plunge to earth. We will make fun of this safety-net metaphor in chapter 8; we prefer the idea of providing people with a solid floor, rather than a swaying wire and a last-minute net. Still, safety-net imagery does hint at the idea of social insurance (protecting people from the consequences of largely uncontrollable disasters). Additionally, it implies that people should be saved from *any* precipitous fall, even if it is partly their own fault.

What if we do everything feasible to ensure true equality of opportunity and to prevent disasters, what if we provide comprehensive social insurance against uncontrollable troubles, and yet some people—perhaps through a messy mixture of unwise behavior and bad luck—still end up in terrible shape? What should we do? Simply let them suffer? Let drug addicts destroy their bodies and minds? Tell the homeless to go ahead and sleep on sidewalk grates?

Many Americans would say no. Surely an affluent society can afford a measure of forgiveness. Surely we can afford to catch those who fall—even those who fall because of carelessness or willfulness—and limit their suffering. Even if we reject the idea of a guaranteed income, we may want to ensure that everyone has at least a minimal level of certain specific goods and services: enough food to live on, medical care, decent shelter. To withhold such help would be to fulfill, unnecessarily and in a particularly painful fashion, the prophecy that the poor *will* be always with us. To give the help would not be very expensive. It would not greatly reduce overall income inequality, but would at least relieve the plight of some of the most deprived Americans.

It is here, however, that the wrath of moralists and incentives-enthusiasts becomes most fierce. What, coddle people who engage in stupid, lazy, or immoral behavior? Give up on deterring them from doing so? Tempt others to take the evil path? To some critics, the slightest chance of bad side effects of this sort is enough to warrant abandoning altogether anyone who is not "truly needy" and "deserving" of help.

To most of us, on the other hand, the issues are more subtle. Just how great will these costs be? Just how much undesirable behavior will be tolerated or caused? How much in such costs are we willing to pay for the sake of human decency? Finally, can we design programs that will avoid perverse incentives and minimize these costs? As we turn to specific safety-net-type programs in chapter 8, we will argue that such costs can be quite low and easily affordable if programs are designed sensibly and well.

The approaches of guaranteeing incomes, imposing progressive taxes, providing equal opportunity, investing in education and human capital, ensuring the availability of jobs at good wages, and providing social insurance and safety nets embody somewhat different goals and methods. We believe that each approach can help, and that the different approaches complement each other. In order to deal with the complex and variegated problems of poverty and inequality, it is necessary to do several different things at the same time. This will become apparent in later chapters as we analyze specific kinds of existing and proposed government policies.

First, however, we must consider certain possible political and economic obstacles to reducing poverty and inequality.

Political and Economic Obstacles

Suppose we are convinced that the government should deal seriously with poverty and inequality by taking one or more of the above approaches. If the arguments for doing so are sound and appealing, one might assume that a majority of our fellow citizens would be convinced and that, in a democracy, the majority's will would then be carried out. Alas, things are not so simple. Even if the values and interests of a large majority of citizens were to dictate that their government should act against poverty and inequality, certain economic or political obstacles may stand in the way. Two general types of obstacles may be particularly important, stemming from economic globalization and competition among nations, and from political inequality within the United States.

Economic Globalization and Competition among Nations

In discussing what government should do about poverty and inequality, we have pointed out the need to take into account a wide range of economic considerations having to do with efficiency, productivity, and economic growth. If a proposed redistributive program were to cause severe decreases in work efforts or sharply reduced savings rates, leading to substantially less economic production and lower-than-possible average incomes, we might well decide that it was not worth the cost—not, on balance, a good idea. But we have suggested—and will try to demonstrate further as the book proceeds—that this, from the point of view of the United States alone, need not be a major problem. In some cases, such costs are nonexistent; some egalitarian programs can help rather than hurt economic productivity and growth, especially if they are well designed. In other cases, there may be some costs, but they can be kept low enough that we may well consider them affordable.

In the context of economic globalization and a world market, however, these concerns come into the picture in a different and profoundly disturbing way. Even if we are quite sure, when thinking of ourselves as an independent national unit—a self-determining sovereign state—that a majority of our fellow citizens would benefit from egalitarian and antipoverty policies, when we shift our viewpoint and begin to take into account our position in the global political economy, these same policies may suddenly look undesirable or impossible to carry out. In this sense, our independence and sovereignty may be threatened; our government may be unable to do things that we want it to do and that we have always taken for granted it has the power to do.[52]

In chapter 1, we outlined the reasoning behind this alarming possibility. Substantial redistribution of income presumably requires high, progressive taxes that take a sharp bite out of the incomes of the wealthiest and most successful citizens, along with other measures that raise the costs of doing business, raise the price of goods we produce, and lower the rate of return on capital, while benefit programs attract low-income people from abroad to enjoy them.

If our economy were isolated from the rest of the world, with impermeable barriers that blocked any economic transactions or migration from occurring across our borders, we might well find the economic costs of redistribution endurable; we might well, as Okun, Rawls, and many others have suggested, be willing to give up some of our total or average consumption in order to improve the lot of the worst off. But economic globalization, with increasingly free, high-volume trade, immigration, and mobility of capital, may fundamentally change the picture. At the very same time that globalization increases the need for redistributive programs by lowering low-income wage levels and increasing inequality, globalization may also make redistributive programs more costly and difficult to pursue.

Free trade means that we can buy cheap goods from abroad. But in order to buy them, we have to sell something—either our own goods, which some redistributive programs may make more expensive and harder to sell, or our assets—and it is disquieting to contemplate selling our valuables in order to consume cheap imports. Freer immigration could mean that millions of low-income people from other countries would come to the United States to benefit not only from our affluent private economy, but also from any generous redistributive policies we pursue, thus costing taxpayers more and putting a strain on the system. (On the other hand, immigration may be an economic plus;[53] it also has other benefits, as we will note in chapter 7.) And some high-income people could move out of the country to the Bahamas or elsewhere (at least for tax purposes), reducing the revenues available to fund programs. Most important of all, free mobility of capital means that if multinational corporations and investment bankers decide that doing business in the United States is too expensive, that returns on capital are too low, they can move elsewhere to low-wage, low-tax, nonregulating countries—getting a better deal for themselves, but leaving us with less production, less economic growth, and smaller tax revenues to fund government programs.

In short, one might imagine that economic globalization could make redistributive programs more costly and even self-defeating. It might increase the demand for and the expense of social programs (by driving down U.S. wages and attracting needy immigrants), while reducing the tax money available to pay for such programs. And by enabling wealthy individuals and corporate capital to flee redistributive programs altogether (not just reduce work or savings efforts), globalization might add greatly to otherwise endurable productivity losses. All the worse if nations consciously compete to tax, spend, and regulate as little as possible in order to attract capital, to maximize production and exports, and to avoid encouraging low-income immigration. Such competition could result in an international "race to the bottom," in which countries vie for the dishonor of doing the least about social concerns like the environment, poverty, and inequality.[54]

How seriously should we take such a prospect? How hard does economic globalization actually squeeze the modern state? Have we altogether lost sovereignty, lost the capacity to make policy for ourselves? These questions must be answered in a comparative context, considering, for example, what has been happening in the Social Democratic welfare states of Europe. There, welfare states have been pressured, but endure.[55]

Without question, the forces of economic globalization are powerful. Without question, they do put some new pressures and constraints on governments, making certain kinds of redistributive programs more difficult to carry out. Fortunately, however, we will see that in many cases the magnitudes of these effects are not overwhelming. A mere *tendency* to increase the costs of redistribution need not be very troubling if that tendency is small or moderate. Again, many important kinds of redistributive programs—particularly those involving equal opportunity, prevention of easily avoidable harms, and investments in health, education, and other aspects of human capital—actually help rather than hurt economic competitiveness; they are not threatened by the forces of globalization. Indeed, recent evidence suggests that existing egalitarian programs in various countries around the world may, on balance, *help* rather than hurt economic growth. The economies in countries with highly unequal incomes (the United States, Australia, and Switzerland, for example) have tended to grow more slowly than those with much more equality (Japan, Belgium, Finland, and Germany).[56] Finally, we will argue that certain kinds of redistribution that are put at hazard can be handled at the global level, by international treaties and agreements. We can respond to economic globalization with political globalization. Announcements of the demise of the welfare state are premature.

In analyzing the impact of a globalized economy, it is important to distinguish clearly among different kinds of programs, as we will do in the remainder of the book. But we will also want to consider the possibility that a further way—perhaps the chief way—in which globalization obstructs redistributive programs may be *political*. Economic globalization may alter the political bargaining power of such actors as multinational corporations and trade unions, with important effects on what sorts of policies are chosen.

Political Inequality

A distinct, though related, set of possible obstacles to dealing with poverty and inequality is rooted in the way politics works, particularly in certain features of the American political system that may produce an unusually high degree of *political inequality*. If all citizens do not in fact have equal voices in policy making, if some people and groups (particularly high-income groups) have much more power than others, then redistributive policies—even policies that would fit the interests and values of large majorities of citizens—may not be enacted.

Political inequality in the United States may arise from at least three major sources: (1) highly unequal political participation (low-income people and minorities less often register, vote, work in campaigns, or give money than high-income people do), (2) the political power of corporations and other organized interest groups that tend to represent the well-to-do, and (3) a two-party political system that may better represent major investors and certain groups of party activists than ordinary working people or the poor.[57]

Lower-income Americans, according to survey evidence, tend to be more supportive than higher-income people of such programs as Food Stamps, welfare, and assistance for African Americans.[58] But they may have less political influence, less voice in shaping public policy, than higher-income citizens, who tend to resist such programs.

Unequal Participation. A large body of research has demonstrated that in the United States low-income people participate much less in politics than do high-income people. This is true of the most basic act of political participation, voting in elections: the higher the income, the higher the rate of voting turnout. In a major study of participation, Sidney Verba, Kay Schlozman, and Henry Brady found that only 52 percent of survey respondents with family incomes under $15,000 reported that they had voted in the last presidential election, but 86 percent of those with incomes over $75,000 said they had voted. Shortly after the 1996 presidential election, 74 percent of people with incomes over $75,000 told the Census that they had voted, but only 33 percent of those with incomes under $10,000 did so.[59] Low-income people often have even less clout in "off-year," nonpresidential elections.

This is nothing new: ever since survey-based voting studies were first conducted in the 1940s, scholars have invariably found that low-income people vote less than high-income people. Yet it is not inevitable or uncontrollable; in fact, the United States is unusual in this respect. In most European countries, high proportions of citizens turn out to vote—often 80 or 90 percent of them, in contrast to the U.S. rates of just 50 percent or so of citizens voting in presidential elections and a miserable 35 percent or so in off-year congressional elections (even fewer in many local elections). Moreover, in most European countries, there is little or no class bias in participation: low-income people are not much more or less likely to vote than are high-income people.[60]

One reason for this unusually great degree of political inequality in the United States is that we have a two-party system, which is thoroughly institutionalized by various constitutional and legal provisions, including single-member legislative districts, a one-person elected presidency, and legal obstacles against third parties getting on the ballot.[61] In a two-party system, both parties tend to make rather vague and centrist appeals, not creating stark electoral contrasts and not greatly stirring up citizens. If citizens are not given sharply defined choices between candidates or the option of voting for a distinctive package of policies they want, they have less reason to care about the result and less reason to vote. What Anthony Downs called the "expected party differential" is small, and a rational citizen has little reason to turn out.[62] Countries with multiparty systems, in which there are more parties with more distinctive stands, tend to have higher rates of voting turnout—about 9 percentage points higher.[63]

Moreover, the United States lacks a particular kind of political party that has played a crucial part in the politics of many European countries: a Social Democratic party, explicitly run by and for working people and organized labor, which mobilizes working people and the poor and gets them to the polls.[64]

Steven Rosenstone and Mark Hansen have demonstrated the key role of political mobilization in stimulating political participation, and the general failure of party mobilization to reach low-income Americans. Our Democratic Party, though it embraced many low-income people during the New Deal years of the 1930s, was never a purely working-class party and appears to have drifted further from that role in recent years. During the last two or three decades, neither the Democrats nor the Republicans have worked very hard to get low-income people involved in politics. Indeed, there are reasons to suspect that both U.S. parties are content to let poor people stay at home and not upset the parties' ability to appeal to middle- and upper-middle-class voters.[65] As we will see, this may result from the particular configuration of activists and money-givers who back the Republican and Democratic parties.

The class bias in voting turnout also reflects a number of legal rules and arrangements—many of them traceable to "good government" (and anti-ethnic-immigrant, anti-working-class) impulses of the Progressive period between 1896 and World War I—that reversed a century-long pattern of high participation and made it harder for everyone, but especially for low-income people, to vote. (Recently Alexander Keyssar has extended Walter Dean Burnham's classic analysis by documenting efforts to disenfranchise working-class Americans during much of the nineteenth century.)[66] Unlike most advanced countries, we do not hold our elections on a Sunday or a special holiday; instead, we insist that voters somehow get off from work or steal a little time from their families. We do not, as some countries do, *require* people to vote; we leave it up to individual initiative. We do not take public responsibility for putting together a comprehensive list of people eligible to vote; instead, we require that citizens personally register, in times, places, and manners that are not always easy and are sometimes quite obscure or difficult. Even the act of voting itself is not always made quick and simple; polling places are sometimes located in out-of-the-way spots or burdened with long lines of frustrated would-be voters.

The federal "Motor Voter" law and various state laws allowing postcard registration, easy absentee voting, and the like have somewhat improved this situation. Still, the U.S. electoral system remains basically designed to ensure a low turnout by its citizens, especially low-income citizens. Legal and administrative barriers to registration and voting make a real difference.[67]

Those who do not vote, of course, cannot expect to affect the outcome of elections and cannot expect election-oriented politicians to pay much attention to them. The 1994 congressional elections, in which far-right Republicans led by Newt Gingrich swept into control of the House of Representatives, is an interesting example; surveys showed that the average American was not enthusiastic about this "revolution," but too few working-class and low-income people voted to overcome the impact of party activists and higher-income voters.[68] Again and again, the outcome of elections hinges importantly on who turns out and who does not.

Some scholars have questioned the importance of low turnout by suggesting that those who do not vote express views and policy preferences very similar to those of people who do vote. This is sometimes true, especially in presidential elections, but it ignores an important point. Several of the same factors that discourage low-income people from voting—especially the absence of a working-people's party that would mobilize workers and stand for policies friendly to them—also reduce the clarity of political discourse and choices. This leaves people confused about which candidates and policies would help them. A lack of distinctive *expressed preferences* by low-income nonvoters does not refute the proposition that if those people were activated, mobilized, and engaged in politics, their choices—and the results of elections—would be quite different. The European experience supports this conclusion.

In any case, the unequal political participation that disadvantages low-income people goes well beyond the act of voting. Election outcomes are affected not only by who turns out to vote, but also by who provides other resources that can be transformed into votes—especially by what sorts of people try to persuade their friends about politics, work to elect candidates, run for office, and give money to campaigns. In each of these respects, and also in activities outside the electoral context that affect policy making (writing letters to officials, working in political groups, and the like), low-income people tend to participate at much lower rates than high-income people. The class bias in participation tends to be similar across many of these activities, but it is much sharper with respect to the critical factors of affiliating with political organizations and giving money to political campaigns.

Verba, Schlozman, and Brady, for example, found that the 34-percentage-point gap in voting rates between high- and low-income people (86 percent versus 52 percent voting) was nearly matched by a 24-percentage-point gap in informal community activity and a 25-percentage-point gap in contacting officials (50 percent of higher-income people, but only 25 percent of lower-income people, said they contacted officials). But the voting gap was exceeded by a 44-point gap (73 percent versus 29 percent) in affiliation with political organizations and by a huge 53-point gap (56 percent versus 3 percent) in giving campaign contributions. Americans with more resources give much more time and money to political activity.[69] People's family backgrounds and their levels of income and formal education work through a number of intervening variables to have a profound impact on the extent to which they take part in politics.[70]

Unequal participation, then, is a major factor in American politics that may affect the kinds of policies that governments enact. If the political system tends to heed the voices of a high-participating, high-income, and generally less egalitarian minority of citizens, and to ignore some of the views and interests of a lower-income majority, then any long-term effort to get government to address problems of poverty and inequality may have to consider efforts at political reform as well.

The Power of Interest Groups and Corporations.   A second aspect of political inequality that may get in the way of egalitarian policies is the political power of corporations and organized interest groups that are hostile to redistributive programs.

Interest group power is a complicated issue. It is very difficult to detect how much influence groups actually have. If politicians pay more attention to organized groups than to ordinary voters, they are not eager to admit doing so. Any blatant trading of votes for money, which is illegal, is carefully kept secret and only occasionally comes to light.[71] It is very difficult to pin down the effects of other possible mechanisms of influence: groups' use of money and activists to elect friendly politicians, their provision of information and their use of special "access" to officials, and their fabrication of "grassroots" campaigns to shift public opinion or impress officials.

A number of political scientists have essentially given up on this issue. They have accepted politicians' "Who, me?" disclaimers at face value and concluded that groups have no power at all, or they have looked in the wrong places and found nothing, or they have despaired of conclusive results and professed agnosticism. Even scholars who have noticed a suspicious correspondence between groups' money giving and politicians' votes sometimes insist that extortion (politicians coercing groups into contributions by threatening negative action) is more common than bribery, or they just point out causal ambiguity in the evidence and settle on inconclusiveness.[72]

Nonetheless, there are strong reasons to believe that interest groups have a substantial impact on policy making—an impact that tends to go against the interests of ordinary citizens, especially on major redistributive issues. Extensive group activity and money giving are certainly well documented; corporations and business associations make enormous campaign contributions, run large Washington offices, and send hordes of lobbyists to Capitol Hill. Increasingly they also try to shape public debate through the media.[73] Clearly interest groups and corporations believe that their political money is well spent.

It is also clear that the main thrust of interest group activity tends to be hostile to redistributive policies. "Pluralist" political scientists once argued that the interest group system is benign because all interests tend to be represented (at least by "latent" groups) and they all tend to balance each other out. But theoretical analyses of the free-rider problem, which makes it especially difficult for large and diffuse groups (e.g., low-income citizens) to organize, have established reasons to expect a bias toward producers' groups— representatives of corporations and professional people, rather than ordinary citizens.[74] Empirical evidence supports this expectation. As E. E. Schattschneider put it, the flaw in the pluralist heaven is that the heavenly chorus sings with a strong upper-class accent. Business and the professions are well organized and active. By contrast, organized labor in the United States, unlike many other countries, is extremely weak; unions cover less than 15 percent of the U.S. workforce and have a political budget far smaller than that of business. In the 1995–96 electoral cycle, for example, business gave some $147 million to political action committees or PACs (70 percent of which went to Republicans), while labor gave only about one-third as much: $49 million (92 percent of it to Democrats).[75]

Quantitative studies have helped establish the existence of certain links in processes of interest group influence. It is clear, for example, that money makes a difference to electoral outcomes. The better-funded candidate does not always win, but candidates without money do not have much of a chance.[76] It is reasonable to infer, therefore, that the enormous amount of money spent by interest groups helps elect officials friendly to their interests. Further, the evidence indicates that campaign contributions lead to active support of group-backed legislation in key legislative hearings.[77] Some formal theoretical work highlights the likelihood that interest groups gain influence through their control of information.[78]

In the end, however, the most persuasive evidence of interest group influence is of a more historical or journalistic sort. A number of such studies reveal a combination of clear group goals, extensive group activity, demonstrated contacts with politicians, and the enactment, after such contacts, of policies that fit the groups' goals. Classic works detailing this sort of evidence include those of E. E. Schattschneider on businesses' scramble for tariffs and Grant McConnell on private interests' domination of land and water policy. Another striking example is David Gibbs's archival work on how American diamond merchants in the 1960s obtained favorable U.S. policies toward the Congo.[79]

Especially important for our purposes is the wealth of evidence of an extensive "right turn" by business interests since the late 1970s. Since that time, much of American business has poured money into conservative think tanks, books, articles, and TV; funded Ronald Reagan in 1980 and many right-wing candidates since; and worked actively to cut taxes on the wealthy and to demolish or defeat social welfare programs.[80] In subsequent chapters, we will consider interest group activity concerning specific programs, including the recent attacks on Social Security and Medicare. The antiegalitarian features of public policy in the United States may be best understood in terms of political influence exerted by business and other organized interest groups.

Of course, not *all* "pressure groups" represent business or the professions. Washington also houses organizations representing workers, the elderly, women, and other large population groups. And there is a dynamic collection of progressive "public interest" groups and think tanks, ranging from the small Indian Law Resource Center (12 employees, a $1.5 million budget), the Economic Policy Institute, the Center for Budget and Policy

Priorities, and the Environmental Working Group, up to the high-visibility, large-membership Common Cause.[81] A well-aimed study, press release, or lawsuit can sometimes win against big-bucks opposition. It is partly for that reason that we are not altogether pessimistic about the prospects for political change.

Money, Activists, and Political Parties. A third source of political inequality in the United States is the particular nature of our political parties. Both of our major parties may be strongly influenced by wealthy investors and ideological activists who are less egalitarian than the average citizen.

A common but misleading way of looking at political parties is simply as aggregations of like-minded citizens. If that were true and if roughly half of Americans called themselves Republicans, while the other half lined up as Democrats, parties would not have a very profound role in policy making. They might differ somewhat from each other, so that policy would zigzag a bit from Left to Right as one party replaced the other in power, but in the long run, public policy would reflect some sort of compromise between the two, rather closely reflecting the wishes of the average citizen.[82]

But the picture of parties as collections of citizens is seriously incomplete because parties are also *organizations* or coalitions that depend on a variety of resources in addition to ordinary citizens' votes. Parties must rely heavily on the person-power of *political activists* to do the work of organizing and campaigning to elect their candidates, and they must rely on money from campaign contributors or *financial investors* to pay the enormous expenses of politics—media buys, staff salaries, campaign materials, and the like. Activists and investors, in turn, can exact a price for what they give: they can insist that their party not always please the average American voter or the average party identifier, but rather sometimes take particular (and perhaps extreme) stands on issues of special interest to the activists and investors.[83] Thus the policy preferences of the particular set of activists and investors belonging to a party coalition may have important effects on the policies that the party advocates and enacts.

Without question, there are important differences between the Republican and Democratic parties' coalitions. Since the New Deal, for example, the Democrats have generally been more friendly than the Republicans toward programs to address problems of poverty and inequality. This difference regularly shows up in surveys of the views of activists and money-givers, as well as party identifiers. It manifests itself in congressional voting patterns, executive branch policies and proposals, macroeconomic policy, and the general ebb and flow of legislation.[84] This is the familiar stuff of American politics. Republicans generally fight Democrats over redistributive policies, and policy often changes when the control of government switches from one party to the other. It is evident, for example, that most of the major egalitarian social programs in the United States, including Social Security, Medicare, Medicaid, and large-scale federal aid to education, originated under Democratic administrations.

A much less familiar but very important point, however, is that certain elements of *both* parties—especially their financial contributors—may deflect *both* parties away from advocating certain progressive policies that most ordinary Americans favor. This is particularly important in the case of the Democrats, who are thought of as being the working-people's party—or as close to such a party as exists in the United States.

Alexander Heard, a pioneer of research on money in elections, long ago showed that both parties rely on money from big contributors. Their financial constituencies have differed somewhat from each other, with Republicans getting the bulk of contributions from the biggest firms, especially manufacturers, bankers, and brokers, whereas the Democrats have got more money from merchandising, hard and soft drinks, construction and building materials, publishing, advertising, and entertainment, as well as the professions, public officeholders, and labor unions.[85] Clearly these financial constituencies want somewhat different things. Republican-oriented manufacturers hope for low taxes, low labor costs, and little (if any) social welfare spending, while Democratic-oriented contractors want big highways and public buildings, and Democratic broadcasters and trial lawyers want friendly regulatory and legal provisions. Especially important for us, however, is the fact that the Democratic Party, as well as the Republican, depends on money from business and the professions. Most big Democratic contributors (with the exception of labor unions, whose importance has sharply declined) are affluent people whose enthusiasm for taking from the rich and giving to the poor is distinctly limited.

Thomas Ferguson's archival research on money and politics in the 1930s has indicated that standard accounts of Franklin Roosevelt's New Deal coalition as a popular assemblage of working-class people and ethnic and religious minorities miss a critical piece of the story. The New Deal coalition also included major financial investors, among whom a key part was apparently played by certain internationally oriented, capital-intensive firms. These firms went along with—and sometimes actively participated in shaping—such measures as the pro-union National Labor Relations Act and the Social Security Act (which did not cost these capital-intensive firms much money) in return for concessions including a strong free-trade policy that facilitated their international business.[86] As Michael Webber and William Domhoff's research indicates, many firms that contributed to the Democrats in 1936 may have had different (or additional) motives; many were based in the traditionally Democratic South, were headed by Jews, and/or espoused "corporate liberal" values.[87] But even the most liberal firms did not share all the aims of the average American worker.

Although by far most of the cash from business and finance in the 1930s went to the Republicans (just as it does today), a few key firms and affluent individuals provided funds that were essential to make the Democratic Party viable in our money-driven electoral system. They also tended to tilt the party in a somewhat less egalitarian direction (of course, the progressivism of the Democratic Party was also limited by the importance of the then-solidly-Democratic South, whose legacy of slavery, racism, and a quasi-feudal economy has had a profound continuing effect on American politics[88]).

Ferguson, together with Joel Rogers, has traced the later fate of the investor side of the New Deal coalition and found changes that today much more seriously affect the political feasibility of egalitarian policies. For many years after the 1930s, a similar capital-intensive and internationally oriented group of investors backed the Democrats and played important parts in Democratic policy making. A roll call of investment bankers, financiers, and associated lawyers prominent in Democratic administrations (especially as secretaries of state, defense, and treasury) would include the names of Averell Harriman, John J. McCloy, Robert Lovett, James Forrestal, Dean Acheson, Douglas Dillon, Cyrus Vance, Robert Altman, and Robert Rubin.[89] Beginning in the middle and late 1970s, however, many investors deserted the Democrats. Foreign economic competition (along with the Organization of Petroleum Exporting Countries [OPEC] price shocks and stagflation) was pinching too hard. Formerly Democratic firms turned against taxes, against concessions to labor, against government regulation, and against social welfare programs. These firms, along with the vast bulk of American business, poured money into the 1980 and 1984 Reagan campaigns. The Reagan administration then did its best to cut back egalitarian and redistributive programs. This "right turn" in American politics did not reflect a change in what ordinary citizens wanted, but rather a change in the preferences of major investors and money-givers.[90]

The partial revival of the Democratic Party since the Reagan years, according to this analysis, has come at a high price. The Democrats put back together a financial constituency including some of the same old capital-intensive, internationally oriented investment banking and other firms, along with important contributors from the fields of entertainment, telecommunications, trial law practice, computers, and medical technology, but only by adopting "new Democrat" economic policies of the sort advocated by the conservative Democratic Leadership Council.[91] Some ordinary citizens who voted for Bill Clinton in 1992 were surprised to find that his administration, strongly influenced by Treasury Secretary and former Goldman Sachs investment banker Robert Rubin, quickly dropped its advocacy of an economic stimulus program. Instead, it turned its emphasis to deficit cutting and the promotion of free trade—both of which tend to increase rather than decrease income inequality. Clinton, apparently to his own surprise, found himself hostage to the bond market.[92]

The financial constituencies of both political parties, then, may constitute significant barriers to the enactment of egalitarian policies. This has probably become all the more true in recent years as the political power of business (particularly as opposed to that of labor) has grown and as the vast majority of business firms have come to oppose social spending programs. We will have more to say about political obstacles as we discuss specific programs.

Overcoming the Obstacles

The point of our analysis is definitely *not* that economic globalization and political inequality make it impossible in the United States for government to do anything about poverty or inequality. Quite the contrary. We believe that many things can and should be done.

Instead, our point is that we need to be alert to these issues in designing, selecting, and working to enact progressive programs. Just as we need to design policies that maximize economic efficiency and individual liberty along with equality, we need to craft policies that will minimize the inclination—and/or the ability—of capital to flee the country.

Similarly, it is not sufficient simply to come up with attractive policy ideas and to assume that they will prevail on their merits. We need to analyze the political forces that will work for or against them—including but not limited to the expressed preferences of the average voter. And we need to *act,* not just think about it. We need to mobilize the public and to counteract the moneyed political opposition in all feasible ways.

In some cases, the manner in which programs are designed and promoted may significantly affect the lineup of political forces, so that careful program design can help win necessary support from political activists and interest groups. In other cases, biases or imperfections in the political system may be so important that egalitarians should give high priority not just to working for substantive policies, but also to carrying out reforms of the political process. In all cases, an understanding of political dynamics is likely to help inform the strategy and tactics by which concerned people can succeed in organizing, working politically, and getting their programs enacted.

4

Social Insurance

As we saw in the previous chapter, there are compelling arguments in favor of government-run social insurance programs to protect people against the risk of losing income due to old age and retirement, death of a wage earner, disability, unavoidable unemployment, or medical expenses. In most social insurance programs, people make regular contributions (pay taxes) while they are working, in return for the assurance that they will get help if and when one of these misfortunes befalls them. For reasons of efficiency as well as equity, private markets cannot generally provide satisfactory insurance of this sort. Only a system of compulsory coverage and central regulation works well.[1]

Social insurance programs are intended to benefit large parts of the population. Ideally, in order to pool risks widely and to prevent anyone from falling into destitution for reasons beyond her or his control, they should cover the *entire* population. This means that most of the beneficiaries are people who have had substantial incomes during their working lives and are (or were) members of the middle class. At the same time, however, social insurance programs have major effects in alleviating certain kinds of poverty and inequality, because a great deal of poverty and inequality would otherwise be caused by the misfortunes that these programs address.

Taken together, social insurance programs constitute by far the largest spending programs of the U.S. federal government. Most of them are authorized under the Social Security Act of 1935 or under amendments that have been added over the years. Old age, survivors, and disability insurance are often lumped together under the rubric of "Social Security," or OASDI, while the program of public medical insurance for the aged is known as Medicare. Medicare, the universalistic social insurance program for the aged, must be distinguished from Medicaid, a smaller, means-tested program intended chiefly for the poor—which, however, has been evolving into a more general social insurance program and will be so treated in this chapter. (A third important program, not involving direct government spending, consists of large tax subsidies for employer-provided health insurance—worth about $78 billion of foregone revenue in 2000.[2])

These are very large programs. The total U.S. federal government budget for fiscal year 2000 was about $1.8 *trillion:* 1,766 *billion* dollars. Social Security (OASDI) alone, paying benefits to some forty-five million beneficiaries, spent about $409 billion—more than 23 percent of the entire budget. Medicare spent about $217 billion, an additional 12.3 percent. And Medicaid added about $115 billion, 6.5 percent of the total. These three programs together, then, added up to about $740 billion (roughly $2,700 for each American), approximately 42 percent of the whole federal budget.[3]

When we combine Social Security, Medicare, and Medicaid with all the rest of the smaller federal social insurance programs—including retirement, medical, and disability insurance for federal military and civilian employees, veterans, railroad workers, and others, as well as income stabilization for farmers and unemployment insurance—they amounted in 2000 to a grand total of about $957 billion in outlays. That is more than half (54.2 percent) of the entire federal budget (see table 4.1).

In this chapter, we will discuss the main social insurance programs, beginning with Social Security retirement pensions and moving on to disability insurance (including Workers' Compensation and Supplementary Security Income), unemployment insurance, and medical insurance (including Medicare and Medicaid). We will note the very important yet limited effects they have on poverty and inequality. Toward the end of the chapter, we will discuss political factors that have led to this particular configuration of programs and will propose changes that could make them more effective.

Table 4.1   Social Insurance in the Federal Budget

	$ Billions	% of Outlays
Old Age and Survivors Insurance	($439.9)	(24.9%)
OASI (Social Security)	352.5	20.0
Federal employee retirement		
(military and civilian)	78.9	4.5
Railroad, veterans, and D.C.	8.4	0.4
Medical insurance and medical care	(369.4)	(20.9)
Medicare	216.6	12.3
Medicaid	114.8	6.5
Veterans	18.6	1.0
Federal employees, Indians,		
coal miners, children, others	19.5	1.1
Disability insurance	(107.7)	(6.1)
DI (Social Security)	56.1	3.2
Supplementary Security Income	31.4	1.8
Veterans	18.9	1.1
Coal miners, workers' comp, federal		
employees	1.3	0.1
Unemployment insurance	28.1	1.6
Farm income stabilization	12.0	0.7
Total social insurance	957.2	54.2

Source: Estimated Fiscal Year 2000 dollar figures from U.S. Office of Management and Budget, *Budget of the United States Government, Fiscal Year 2000* (Washington, D.C.: U.S. Government Office, 1999). Percentages calculated by the authors; figures have been rounded.

Old Age and Survivors Insurance (Social Security)

The bulk of Social Security payments goes in monthly checks to about twenty-eight million retired workers who previously paid payroll taxes for the program. Benefits are roughly proportional to how much a worker paid in. The average retiree receives Social Security benefits equal to about 44 percent of his or her preretirement income earnings: in 2000, about $804 per month, or $9,600 per year. That is certainly no gravy train, but it provides crucial help for most retired people. Some three and a half million spouses and children of these retired workers get benefits averaging about half as large. In addition, Social Security pays substantial benefits to over seven million survivors (spouses and children) of deceased workers.[4]

Clearly Social Security benefits are not sufficient by themselves to pay for very comfortable, let alone luxurious, retirement. Old Age and Survivors Insurance (OASI) provides only a basic minimum; it is generally assumed that most people supplement it through employer pension plans and/or their own savings. To encourage this, substantial tax subsidies are given to employer retirement plans (about $84 billion worth in 2000) and to individual retirement accounts and Keogh plans (about $15 billion).[5]

Still, many old people rely very heavily on Social Security. About two-thirds of Americans over age sixty-five get at least half their income from Social Security payments, which account for about 40 percent of all income that goes to the elderly population. For the lower-income two-fifths of the elderly, Social Security provides fully *80 percent* of their income. Women, who tend to live longer than men and to have lower lifetime earnings and lower private pensions and savings, depend especially heavily on the program. Women make up about 60 percent of all beneficiaries, and Social Security provides about 51 percent of all the income received by elderly unmarried women, including widows.[6]

The Social Security program as a whole is very efficient. As mainly a tax-collecting and check-mailing enterprise, with the advantage of huge economies of scale, it is quite cheap to administer. Administration costs only about $3.5 billion per year, less than 1 percent of the program's total budget. This compares very favorably with the 10–15 percent in administrative costs typically incurred by private insurance companies.[7]

Effects on Poverty

Social Security makes an enormous contribution to preventing and alleviating poverty among elderly people. According to the 1999 federal budget document, without Social Security fully 61 percent of unmarried elderly beneficiaries and 41 percent of the married ones would have fallen into poverty. But counting Social Security benefits, only 16 percent of the unmarried beneficiaries and only 3 percent of the married ones fell below the poverty line.[8] Looking at the entire U.S. population of people aged sixty-five and older, if Social Security payments had been removed from their incomes (and everything else stayed the same), their poverty rate in the 1990s would have been an alarming 52 percent, rather than the actual 14 percent. OASDI contributed 32 percent of the incomes of nonpoor aged families and fully 71 percent of the incomes of poor aged families.[9]

Savings and Work Incentives

These figures probably somewhat overstate the program's impact on poverty, however, by ignoring the likelihood that without Social Security some people would have kept working or saved more on their own for retirement. For example, despite improved life expectancies and better health, only some 16–17 percent of men older than sixty-five are now in the workforce, compared with 54 percent in 1930 before the program existed.[10] Econometric efforts to estimate the precise magnitude of Social Security's effect in reducing work by the elderly have generated considerable scholarly controversy and political heat; the truth is elusive. To some degree, Social Security payroll taxes may also have replaced private savings, though probably not to the extent that Martin Feldstein and some others once thought. Estimates differ widely; most fall in the range of zero to fifty cents for each dollar of expected "Social Security wealth."[11]

The 1980s and 1990s saw fierce political attacks on Social Security, emphasizing the alleged "bankruptcy" of the program (a matter to which we will return) and trumpeting allegedly massive negative impacts on work and savings. These were supposed to be major problems that reduced American productivity, competitiveness, and economic growth. Now, however, we can view these matters from a more calm perspective. Both the magnitude of the effects and their harmfulness were grossly exaggerated. The decisions in recent decades of more elderly people to retire by age sixty-five, for example, have resulted from many factors, including the rise in employer-based and other private pensions, not just the establishment and expansion of Social Security. Most of all, they have resulted from the enormous overall rise in productivity and standards of living since the 1930s. Most Americans—both individually, in their own savings and retirement decisions, and collectively, as citizens and voters supporting Social Security—have decided that one excellent use of our increased wealth is to allow old people to retire from work.[12]

Likewise, private savings (most of which come from retained corporate earnings, not from individuals) are affected by many factors, of which Social

Security is only one—and a rather small one, at that.[13] Moreover, it is not clear that the displacement of private savings is necessarily a bad thing. Most payroll taxes go directly into benefit payments, on a pay-as-you-go basis, so that they go to consumption, rather than savings. But for more than a decade, the Social Security program has contributed on the order of $100 billion per year in surpluses of payroll tax revenues over benefits paid out (in 1999, the Social Security surplus, including interest on trust fund assets as well as payroll tax revenues, was at least $125 billion).[14] Some of that revenue has been used to pay off the national debt, amounting to *public* savings. Much of it has been used to pay for other government programs. To the extent that those payments represent long-term investments in such things as education, military equipment and preparedness, environmental protection, roads and other infrastructure, and so forth, they may be just as productive as the investment that flows from private savings, even if the returns do not always show up in gross domestic product (GDP) figures as dollars of national income.

In any case, there can be little doubt that Social Security greatly reduces poverty and enhances incomes among the elderly. It is striking that in 1959, before Social Security benefits were expanded, 35 percent of all Americans over age sixty-five had incomes below the official poverty line; by 1995, only 10.5 percent were poor. Poverty is now more than twice as prevalent among children as among the elderly. The role of Social Security is particularly evident in the sharp 9-percentage-point drop in poverty among the aged during the early 1970s, when Social Security benefits were substantially increased and when, for the first time, average benefits exceeded the official poverty threshold.[15]

Without Social Security, then, the number of poor people in the United States—which toward the end of the twentieth century stood at 35.6 million, or 13.3 percent of the population[16]—would undoubtedly be much larger. Social Security probably has more impact on reducing poverty than any other government program. Rebecca Blank, in her landmark book on poverty policy, called the expansions of Social Security "crucial" in reducing poverty among the elderly.[17]

Limited Redistributive Effects

At the same time, we need to recognize that the antipoverty effect of Social Security is incidental to the main purposes of the program. It deals only with certain kinds of poverty, and its effects even on them are limited.

Social insurance programs are designed to cover all or nearly all of the population, most of which is middle class. In the case of retirement insurance, virtually all working people (about 96 percent of them) are covered, from the lowest-paid worker to the highest. What people get out of the system is roughly proportional to what they put in. That is, a person who was never able to work gets no benefits; a person who for many years earned enough to pay the maximum in payroll taxes gets maximum benefits. Thus Social Security retirement insurance serves primarily as a *forced savings* program that compels people to contribute payroll taxes while they work, in return for guaranteed benefits when they retire. (The program also requires smaller payments from all workers to insure against the risk of disability or the loss to dependents of a wage-earning spouse or parent.) Thus Social Security prevents destitution due to catastrophic disability, and it saves from poverty those who could not or would not otherwise provide for their own retirement, but it does so chiefly by subtracting the costs of those protections from workers' own earnings. Hence there is considerable justification to the feeling that Social Security benefits are an "entitlement."

To put it another way, Social Security old age insurance mostly helps smooth out a person's lifetime earnings. It reduces *income inequality over an individual's life cycle,* but it does not much reduce *inequality among the lifetime incomes of different individuals.*

Social Security deviates from being a pure forced savings or compulsory insurance program, however, in two main ways. First, its benefit levels are guaranteed; they are set by law, not by a varying market return on investments. Benefits for new retirees rise as wages rise, and benefits for the already retired are increased to keep up with inflation through cost-of-living allowances (COLAs). In the early years of the program, benefit levels were substantially higher than they would have been if contributions had been privately invested. (This sort of intergenerational transfer was easy, within the pay-as-you-go financing of the system, when the number of new workers was growing rapidly and their payroll taxes could be shared among a small number of retirees. It gets harder to accomplish as a large demographic bulge of baby-boom workers retires and a smaller base of working people is left to pay the payroll taxes.)

Second, Social Security has never made payments to individuals exactly in proportion to their contributions. The lowest-income workers get benefits somewhat higher than their payroll tax contributions would justify. For example, the ratio of retirement benefits to preretirement earnings for very low-income workers has averaged around 57 percent, whereas average-income workers get about 42 percent and high-income workers get only about 24 percent of their preretirement earnings (but they also pay a lower proportion in taxes).[18] This does tend somewhat toward equalizing different individuals' lifetime incomes. But the effect is a moderate one because the low incomes that are augmented are so very low to start with and are augmented only modestly in dollar terms.[19]

It would be possible—indeed, it would be technically and administratively easy—to change the Social Security program so that it would have more impact in counteracting both poverty and inequality. One step would be to reduce the benefits to retirees who get high incomes from other sources by making all benefits subject to the income tax (most recipients would owe no tax anyhow because their total incomes are so low). Opinion polls indicate that most Americans favor this measure,[20] but the policy-making trend has gone in the opposite direction. The amount of total income below which Social Security benefits are not taxed has gradually been raised, reaching $17,000 in 2000 for sixty-five- to sixty-nine-year-olds. This resulted in a "tax expenditure" (foregone revenues) of about $22 billion in 2000.[21]

Another way to make Social Security more progressive would be to increase the benefits of those at the bottom of the economic scale—in other words, to ensure a subsistence income for the elderly even if they were never able to earn much when they worked. It should be possible to guarantee that *no* old American is poor.[22] Yet another step would be to use general tax revenues to pay for part of the program, using the progressive income tax, rather than relying on the current Federal Insurance Contributions Act (FICA) payroll taxes, which are regressive—that is, they take proportionally more money from low-income than high-income people—because they impose a flat-rate tax on all income up to a certain point and then no tax at all (we will discuss the tax side of Social Security further in chapter 5). A similar effect would be achieved through the payroll tax itself by raising or eliminating the "cap" that exempts all annual earnings above a certain point ($76,200 in 2000) from Social Security payroll taxes.

Bankruptcy?

But what about the impending "bankruptcy" of Social Security? Is the whole program about to disintegrate? Is it a pipe dream to consider any sort of redistribution or expansion of benefits? Dire predictions of "bankruptcy," "insolvency," "collapse," and the like have, since the 1980s, become a regular feature of the American scene.[23] What is the truth of the matter?

The truth is quite different. Yes, sometime around the middle of the twenty-first century—unless the program is altered or present guesses about immigration, fertility, or economic growth turn out to be wrong—a large number of baby-boom retirees relative to current workers will probably put a strain on the Social Security system.[24] This may require one or more policy changes: some combination of getting higher returns on the revenue saved for this purpose, raising payroll taxes, using general tax revenues, reducing benefit levels, extending the retirement age, adding state and local government workers to the system, promoting faster economic growth, and/or taking similar measures. But the magnitude of the problem is often exaggerated; it can be managed rather easily, in a variety of different ways.[25] Predictions of crisis, "trillions of dollars of shortfalls," and the like are based on the very peculiar assumption that we will make no adjustments in the program, even though we have repeatedly adjusted it in the past and will have decades in which to do so again.

It is possible that there will be no problem at all. According to more optimistic economic projections, economic growth will be sufficient to pay benefits at the planned levels for at least seventy-five years into the future. And with each year of robust economic growth in the late 1990s, reasons for optimism increased.[26]

In any case, even if the more pessimistic projections are correct, the notion of "bankruptcy" in this context is grossly misleading. The U.S. government is not an individual or a business. It cannot legally declare bankruptcy. It need never do so because it can meet its obligations in a variety of flexible ways through taxing or borrowing. The idea of Social Security "insolvency" rests on an accounting fiction that is useful up to a point, but that can become a serious impediment to understanding and can provoke unwarranted panic.

In harmony with the insurance or forced savings analogy, Social Security is formally set up in terms of an "OASDI Trust Fund," into which payroll tax receipts are paid and then—to the extent that they exceed the amount of benefits paid out—are "invested" (historically they have been put into U.S. Treasury bonds). Amidst the cries of crisis, it has often been ignored that for many years Social Security has been running surpluses of revenue received over benefits paid out. It is expected to continue running surpluses, on the order of *$100 billion per year,* well into the future. Only around 2020 or later do the system's "actuary" (chief accountant) and most experts expect the annual surpluses to stop.[27]

Some people—including the administrators of the program, who are required by law to do so—talk as if these enormous surpluses are put into a sort of piggy bank, where they accumulate (and earn interest) until they are needed to meet the future needs of a larger retiring population. Then, the story goes, we will take these pennies out of the piggy bank and add them to ongoing payroll tax revenues to pay Social Security benefits until all the pennies are gone and current taxes are insufficient to cover benefit obligations. At that point, recently estimated to come in 2029, or 2032, or perhaps 2040—fortunately the day of supposed doom keeps receding—the system will become "insolvent"; its assets will be "exhausted." (It is worth remembering that such dates depend on economic projections that are highly uncertain; under more optimistic assumptions, the supposed day of reckoning will not arrive until 2070—or may never come at all. Even if it does arrive, incoming tax revenue will still be sufficient to pay two-thirds to three-quarters of planned benefits.)[28]

But there is no piggy bank. Just as President Roosevelt's original idea of a "fully funded" pension scheme (with each worker's payroll taxes saved for his or her own retirement) never came off, even current surpluses have not really been saved.[29] What has usually happened when Social Security surpluses have been paid into the so-called Trust Fund is that they have been "borrowed" by the government—that is what Treasury bonds are for—to be used for other programs. The money is no longer there. It is gone; what exists is a government *promise,* an IOU, to pay it back.

It is actually rather difficult for the federal government to "save" or "put aside" surplus tax revenues. One way is to invest them in private securities. Another, which was embraced toward the end of the 1990s by both President Clinton and congressional Republicans, is to use such revenues to pay off part of the national debt. Then—assuming that the reduction in disposable incomes does not have a depressing effect on the economy—it is hoped that increased private investment will increase economic growth so that more goods and services will be available later for Social Security (or other programs) to use. To keep payroll taxes high and other spending programs low in this way may also help prepare everyone politically and psychologically for future increases in Social Security spending and (presumably) for higher taxes.

In any case, however, most of the payroll tax revenue has always been used, as it comes in, to pay benefits. In its financing, Social Security has mostly been a pay-as-you-go program, in which benefits to current retirees are paid for by the payroll taxes of current workers, and partly a borrow-the-surpluses-for-other-purposes program. The trust fund concept is helpful for assuring workers that the money they contribute in payroll taxes will be returned to them upon retirement. But in fact, this assurance really rests on the faith and credit of the government's promise to do so (very substantial faith and credit), not on the physical accumulation of contributions in a piggy bank.

The non–Social Security use of huge Social Security surpluses, which largely escaped notice for many years, has had some important consequences. In 1983, for example, when Social Security was allegedly saved from financial collapse by cutting benefits and increasing payroll taxes, what actually happened was that taxes and benefits were set at stringent levels that would be needed at some rather distant time in the future. In the meantime, enormous surpluses were generated to be used for other purposes: most notably the Reagan military buildup or (to look at it another way) income tax cuts. Supporters of Social Security were snookered. In effect, regressive payroll taxes were used instead of progressive income taxes to pay for part of the military buildup and other government activities. Oddly, during the 1980s and 1990s, many "deficit hawks," determined to cut the large Reagan-era budget deficits at all costs, talked as if the Social Security program were somehow responsible for those deficits. In fact, however, Social Security revenues from the payroll tax substantially exceeded Social Security benefit payouts, and the surpluses were regularly used to offset deficits in other programs that were supposed to be funded by general tax revenues.[30]

The trust fund and piggy bank fictions are probably useful for reinforcing the social insurance and compulsory savings concepts. They also help remind us that it is proper to pay back to the Social Security program the many hundreds of billions of dollars that were "borrowed" from it, repaying with funds from general revenues, that is, from the more egalitarian personal income tax.

But once we acknowledge that the piggy bank does not exist, we can stop worrying quite so much about the magical date on which it is supposed to be emptied. We can instead focus on what may be a real problem: how, in the long run, to make sure that tax revenues for Social Security are sufficient to pay for the benefits that are paid out. Instead of fretting about a mythical "bankruptcy" in 2040 or 2070, we should focus on the possibility that within the next couple of decades (perhaps as soon as 2020), under currently scheduled tax and benefit levels, the outgo may begin to exceed the income. If so, we need to plan how to bring them into reasonable balance over the long term.

Fortunately, despite much apocalyptic rhetoric, this turns out to be surprisingly easy. For clarity, it helps to avoid scare talk about "trillions of dollars of shortfalls" over several decades and instead to put revenue shortfalls into the context of the many more trillions of dollars of wages that workers will be earning. According to the trustees of the Social Security system (based on the usual—rather pessimistic—"intermediate" economic forecasts), over the next seventy-five years or so the total difference between projected income and costs for OASDI is only about *2 percent* of the total (currently FICA-taxable) payroll earnings during that period.[31]

In other words, if payroll tax receipts were raised now by just 2 percent of payrolls and kept at that level or if income taxes were raised an equivalent amount, benefit levels could be left untouched, and the program would be in financial balance over a period covering the reasonably foreseeable future. There is room for such a change; U.S. tax rates are low compared with those in most other advanced countries. The chief actuary of Social Security calculated in 1998 that merely eliminating the "cap" and imposing payroll taxes on high incomes that were then exempt—while paying those people full benefits under the existing schedule—would eliminate a bit more than two-thirds of the projected shortfall in revenues over a seventy-five-year period.[32] Many Americans would probably be surprised to learn that the Social Security "crisis" would mostly vanish if people with incomes over $70,000 or so were simply required to contribute to the system.

In the currently tax-averse climate of Washington, few have endorsed this particular solution. But many leading experts on Social Security, including Robert Ball, Henry Aaron, and Robert Reischauer, have pointed out that a variety of rather moderate cuts in benefits or other policy changes could likewise bring revenues and expenditures into balance for seventy-five years or more. Various official commissions have agreed. Possible cuts include reducing the COLAs that increase benefits to compensate for inflation (arguably the currently used Consumer Price Index may overindex inflation, though the opposite may be true of the special expenses of the elderly), postponing the retirement age further than the already scheduled gradual move from age sixty-five to sixty-seven, counting more (lower-income) years of past earnings in the benefit-calculation formula, or subjecting all Social Security benefits to the income tax. Broadening coverage of the system to include all state and local government workers would help. The investment of some Trust Fund assets in common stocks is another possible option.[33]

It is good to know that these relatively mild measures would solve the projected problem, but we urge great caution about benefit cuts. Benefits are rather modest now. Social Security cuts of almost any sort are highly unpopular with majorities of the American public, and even technical-sounding cuts are not likely to escape public scrutiny.[34] We see no good reason to thwart the citizens' will on this very important issue.

The superficially attractive idea of "extending the retirement age," in particular, would actually mean imposing a rather harsh cut on seniors in the sixty-five-to-seventy age range, many of whom cannot work (and would simply go without the benefits) or should not be forced into working. True, a number of elderly people could contribute a lot to society and gain personal fulfillment by working in fields like education and day care. They should be encouraged to do so, both for their own sake and for the sake of others. But we recommend using the carrot, not the stick. Generous income supplements along the lines of the Earned Income Tax Credit could be given to old people who work for low wages, thus raising their incomes, while also reducing Social Security payouts and/or increasing payroll tax revenues. Age discrimination by employers could be more vigorously combated, public service positions could be created for the elderly, and the like. But forced delay of retirement would go against most older people's strongly felt desires and against historical trends that are more than a century old. Those of us who love our work should remember that many other people are stuck with unrewarding toil.

If the shortfall problem turns out to be real, our own preferred solution is to initiate moderate tax increases, raising or removing the payroll tax cap and/or drawing from general tax revenues. That way the wealthiest Americans—who profited so lavishly from the skewed economic booms of the 1980s and 1990s—will pay a bigger share of the Social Security bill. Certainly the remaining uncovered state and local employees should be included in the system. The idea of some investment of Trust Fund money in common stocks is also worth exploring so long as investment decisions are carefully insulated from politics.

But the main point is that there are many options. Whatever particular package of policy changes is chosen, it will not be difficult to maintain the long-term financial viability of the Social Security system. We are confident that the American people and their elected representatives are up to this job. Other countries with impending demographic bulges of retirees (Germany, for example) face much more difficult problems because their tax and benefit levels are higher to start with and they will have even fewer workers than we will to support future retires.[35]

Privatization?

In 1964, Republican presidential candidate Barry Goldwater suggested that Social Security should become "voluntary": that those who wanted out of the system should be able to make their own arrangements for retirement. Opponents charged that this would wreck the Social Security system, and voters expressed little enthusiasm for the suggestion. Some thirty-five or forty years later, however, considerable respectability was achieved for a similar—but much more skillfully promoted—idea: that Social Security should be partly or wholly "privatized," making people responsible for investing part or all of their savings as they wish.

Why not? Couldn't many people make more money that way? Wouldn't such a system increase individual freedom?

Private saving for retirement is definitely a good idea. The U.S. system assumes that most working people will save through employer plans or on their own; Social Security is intended only as a supplement or a guaranteed floor. It makes sense for government to encourage private saving, either through favorable tax treatment (like the existing tax breaks worth about $100 billion a year—an amount that dwarfs most antipoverty programs) or by direct subsidy of matching funds for investment, which would be much more helpful to low-income people. But to dismantle the guaranteed minimum benefits of Social Security would be quite another matter.

The general arguments in favor of publicly run, compulsory social insurance that we discussed in chapter 3 clearly apply to this case. If saving for retirement were made entirely voluntary, we would have to anticipate that many people would be improvident or unlucky. If they reached old age destitute, unable to care for themselves or their families, either their children (if any) would be stuck with the bill or society would very likely—and quite properly—feel obliged to help them, at the taxpayers' expense. But these people would be "free riders," taking advantage of public benevolence without having made their own contributions. Only a system of compulsory savings during everyone's working years can avoid this free-rider problem. Moreover, people need insurance against the risk of an unusually long life in retirement that would deplete their private savings. But such insurance, involving fixed benefits and open-ended duration of payments, is likely (if voluntary) to suffer from a severe "adverse selection" problem. People whose health experiences or family histories make them expect to live an unusually long time will rush to sign up. Premiums will have to be set very high to pay for these costly customers (this is why private annuities are so outrageously expensive). Others, who do not expect to live so long, will either have to overpay or be deprived of coverage. The adverse selection problem, the free-rider problem, and considerations of fairness to children all provide strong arguments for a universal, compulsory system, in which everyone is forced to save for retirement.[36]

So why not require saving, but leave people free to choose how to invest their money? Couldn't they get better returns by careful investment in the stock market, rather than accepting Social Security's fixed benefits? Yes, some probably could, especially certain savvy and affluent young people — who (perhaps forgetting what their parents did for them) may not like the idea of supporting a large bulge of baby-boomer retirees with their payroll taxes, while doubting just what their own future Social Security benefits will amount to. (Of course, they have much less reason to fear loss of Social Security benefits — and those benefits are a better deal — than many media reports have indicated; and they are free to save on their own, with tax subsidies, in any case.) But any such gain would come at the cost of undermining several important features of the Social Security system: its insurance of survivors and long-lived retirees, its intergenerational transfers, and especially its redistribution across income groups. Unless special provisions were made, privatization would allow the affluent young to stop contributing to the old and poor. They could keep all their money for themselves. The result would be very damaging to many old people, including low-income people who do not have much money of their own to invest in the stock market and could no longer rely on Social Security's fixed benefits.[37]

If privatization were carried out at the same time that the promised Social Security benefits were guaranteed to current and/or future retirees, there would be an enormous *transition problem*. In effect, each working person would have to be taxed or contribute *twice:* once to fund his or her own retirement and once to take care of retirees under the current pay-as-you-go system. Otherwise privatization, sometimes touted as a solution to the projected Social Security deficit problem, would actually make the problem *worse.* But if current benefits were taken away from people who have been paying payroll taxes regularly, a major promise by the federal government would be broken.

Private accounts would be subject to large fluctuations in value as the stock market goes up and down, so that retirees would be at the mercy of what their accounts were worth at the particular time they retired. Moreover, as Peter Diamond has pointed out, many assumptions about the future returns from private investments have been wildly overoptimistic, neglecting the likelihood that the booming stock market of the 1990s will eventually drop—or at least slow its growth.[38]

Private control of investment would also make the free-rider problem reappear in a new guise. Some people would be tempted to engage in high-risk speculating, hoping for big gains, but expecting to be bailed out if they failed. Such bailouts would encourage free riders and undermine any counsel of prudent investing. But absent bailouts, people who invested carefully, but got unlucky—and bad luck for some is inevitable—would be left without the income security that is the central purpose of retirement insurance. Especially disastrous, of course, would be bad luck that hit several years' worth of retirees all at the same time, such as a stock market crash that shrunk the value of their savings just as they were about to retire.

Some privatization plans address these problems by proposing private investment of only a portion of each individual's payroll taxes. But partial privatization, involving many small investment accounts, entails very high administrative costs—especially if people are given wide investment choices (and without choices, why bother?). According to one assessment of the evidence, about 28 percent of the total value of such accounts could be swallowed up by administrative expenses. Other estimates go as high as 45 percent.[39] Politically, partial privatization could damage the residual Social Security program by setting in motion an unraveling process. The minority of people (mostly young and high-income) who would tend to do especially well with private accounts, and who have substantial political clout, could be expected to agitate to privatize a larger and larger share of contributions. The more they succeeded, the heavier the burden on the remaining public program would be if it tried to accomplish any income redistribution at all, and the stronger the impulse of the affluent to get out of it. The end result could very well be the destruction of the public old age insurance system.

To us, it seems wisest to encourage private retirement savings outside the Social Security system, but to leave that system intact.[40]

Disability Insurance

Much smaller than Social Security's OASI retirement and survivors program, but still substantial, is its program of Disability Insurance (DI). Disability Insurance helps about five million disabled workers and nearly two million of their family members every year, at a cost of roughly $56 billion.[41] Disabled workers receive, on the average, benefits that are a bit lower than those of retirees; spouses and children of the disabled get much less.[42]

The rationale for this program is clear. It is a rather pure form of social insurance against the risks of disabling injuries or diseases that deprive people of the ability to work and earn incomes. This kind of devastating harm can hit anyone suddenly and arbitrarily, through no fault of his or her own. Moral hazard is not much of a problem—hardly anyone argues that people consciously or carelessly become disabled in order to claim insurance benefits, so the risks are fundamentally insurable. But reliance on private markets would be unwise for reasons of free riding (society probably should and would help people regardless of their failure to insure themselves), adverse selection (high-risk people would tend to buy the insurance and drive up rates beyond what others should or could pay), and equity (even if private insurers could effectively risk-grade premiums, why should the terribly unlucky have to pay more? And what about people who are disabled at birth or in childhood and could not hope to buy private insurance?) In short, these are just the sorts of risks that social insurance is supposed to cover.[43]

At the same time, disability insurance is not without controversy or difficulty. There is sometimes room for honest disagreement—or misrepresentation—concerning whether a particular individual is or is not too disabled to work, and for ideological battles over how many people are in fact disabled. In the early 1980s, Congress and the Reagan administration, fearing that this program might cause "dependency" and convinced that hundreds of thousands of recipients were fraudulently claiming benefits or failing to report that they had recovered and could work again, changed the rules, challenged many people's eligibility, and stopped paying benefits. (In 1982, only 29 percent of applicants for DI benefits were accepted, down from 45 percent in the 1970s.) Many thousands of former recipients appealed, and about two-thirds of them were eventually reinstated—after months of hassle and expense during which some disabled people became destitute or died. A General Accounting Office (GAO) study of denials and terminations found that only 15 percent of those terminated had actually been able to return to work, and even they were mostly limited in the amount and kind of work they could do. Moreover, the GAO did not find the health and functional limitations of those denied benefits to be appreciably different from those who had been allowed benefits.[44]

After this Reagan-era debacle, and under pressure from the courts, restrictions on eligibility for DI benefits have become less draconian, and the number of recipients has gown once again from its 1984 low point of 3.8 million back to the earlier (1978) peak of 4.9 million and beyond. But federal administrators worry about this growth and continue to scrutinize eligibility. For fiscal year 1999, for example, the Clinton administration reported that the Social Security Administration planned to process 1,637,000 reviews of eligibility of the recipients of DI and SSI (Supplementary Security Income) disability benefits, up from 690,000 disability reviews in 1997. This is the main reason why the administrative costs of DI, at around 3.3 percent of the program's budget, are high compared with those of OASI (about 0.6 percent) (although they are still quite low compared with private insurance).[45]

Increasingly efforts are being made to help and encourage disabled people to return to work by preventing employer discrimination, by helping with rehabilitation and employment services, and by improving physical access to work, transportation, and public facilities. The Americans with Disabilities Act and court decisions based on it represent important steps in this direction.

Social Security Disability Insurance (DI) is not the only government program designed to help the disabled; in fact, it provides only about one-third of the benefits that disabled people receive.[46] Most of the rest comes from programs that are restricted to certain sets of people or certain circumstances in which disabilities are incurred, such as Workers' Compensation (state-run programs with small federal contributions), SSI (about $31 billion in annual federal outlays, chiefly for the very poor), veterans' programs (about $19 billion), and programs for coal miners and government employees (about $1 billion) (look back at table 4.1). We will discuss these programs now.

Workers' Compensation

Workers' Compensation is similar to Social Security DI in that it is based on contributions taken out of the earnings of working people (through a tax on employers' payrolls) and pays higher benefits to those who have been earning more. Its "merit rating" of employers provides financial incentives to prevent accidents. But Workers' Compensation covers only injuries received at work (occupational illnesses would be hard to trace to a particular employer), and it pays rather modest benefits—much less, for example, than would ordinarily be recovered in tort lawsuits for dangerous or negligent practices by employers that cause workplace accidents. Historically, in fact, Workers' Compensation seems to have been instituted in the early 1900s precisely in order to substitute for lawsuits and to shield employers from liability.[47]

Workers' Compensation consists of highly variable (and poorly documented, hence little understood) state-financed and state-run programs that generally undertake to pay some two-thirds of an injured worker's previous wage—subject, however, to a rather low maximum figure, generally below $500 per month. The maximum varies widely from state to state: in the mid-1990s, it was $760 in Illinois, but only $264 in Mississippi. Workers' Compensation also pays lump sums for major injuries like loss of an arm (again, the sums vary widely, from $228,000 in Illinois down to $25,000 in Massachusetts), as well as some medical expenses, very limited rehabilitation services, and compensation to survivors in the event of fatal injuries. About 87 percent of all wage and salary workers are covered, but Workers' Compensation excludes many of the nation's most poorly paid workers, such as farm workers, domestics, and casual laborers. Women appear to be particularly disadvantaged.[48]

No one knows how many people actually receive Workers' Compensation payments or how much the average beneficiary gets. But total cash compensation has been substantial, already rising above $25 billion by the early 1990s.[49] Despite the narrow targeting on work-inflicted injuries, the exclusion of many of the poorest workers, and the skimpy benefits, this program clearly makes a contribution to preventing poverty among the particular set of disabled people who have suffered work-related injuries.

Federal Government Employees

Employees of the federal government, both military and civilian, have historically enjoyed a system of retirement and disability insurance analogous to Social Security's OASDI, but with the addition of a defined-contribution (private investment) Thrift Savings Plan for retirement. Taken together, the retirement and disability programs for civilians cost about $47 billion per year. There is also a small federal employee workers' compensation program. (Military retirement pensions cost about $33 billion; disabled members of the armed forces are handled under veterans' programs.)[50] Since 1983, new employees have been covered by Social Security.

Veterans

Another program restricted to a particular set of people is that designed for military veterans. Veterans with disabilities resulting from—or coincident with—military service can receive monthly compensation payments based on the degree of their disability. These payments do not depend on income and can be received together with other benefits like Social Security. In addition, the family survivors of veterans who die from service-connected injuries receive payments in the form of dependency and indemnity compensation. They are, like Social Security benefits, automatically "indexed" to increase as the cost of living increases.[51]

The number of disabled veterans and survivors of deceased veterans receiving benefits totals more than 2.7 million. In 2000, they got nearly $20 billion in benefits,[52] enough to make a significant reduction in the number of people who otherwise would have been poor.

Supplementary Security Income

Supplementary Security Income (SSI) is administered under the Social Security system. It is not exactly the same sort of social insurance program as those we have been discussing because it is not restricted to workers or former workers, it is not dependent on their contributions, and it does not pay benefits in proportion to what individuals put into the program. Instead, it is means-tested and is restricted to very low-income individuals.

At the same time, SSI—like several other programs that we will discuss here as well as in chapter 8 under the rubric of "safety nets"—can reasonably be seen as providing social insurance in a broader sense. SSI helps family members of the disabled who otherwise might bear the whole burden. It insures people against the risks of certain kinds of harm that may be incurred long before their working lives can begin. These include harms that occur in early childhood or even at birth that may impair the ability to work or may altogether prevent a person from ever working. The usual social insurance model, in which everyone is expected to work and to pay premiums on social insurance, obviously does not apply to such work-preventing or work-impairing risks. Yet a broader and more humane concept of social insurance—in which family members and others make the tax contributions—clearly does apply.

SSI is one of the few U.S. government programs that help people who suffer major physical or mental disabilities (total blindness, for example) before they have a chance to become ordinary workers, military veterans, or government employees. SSI, in effect, offers a small guaranteed income to those who are certified as disabled, with maximum benefits in 2000 of $512 per month to a single individual living alone with no other income or $769 to a couple with no other income.[53] Benefits are gradually reduced as other income rises, so that payments in the mid-1990s averaged only about $376 per month to individuals and $612 to couples. Recipients must exhaust most of their financial assets before getting anything. Supplementary Security Income covers more than five million disabled people, who constitute about three-quarters of the entire SSI caseload.[54]

The general American aversion to guaranteed incomes seems not to hold in this case of worthy or "truly needy" individuals who cannot work and whose inability to work is clearly beyond their control.

Unemployment Insurance

Unemployment Insurance (UI) under the Social Security Act (together with smaller, parallel programs for veterans, railroad workers, and federal employees) is designed to offer temporary help to full-time working people who lose their jobs due to layoffs, plant closings, or other factors beyond their control. At the turn of the twenty-first century, UI was budgeted at about $25 billion. It paid some eight million claimants benefits that averaged about $200 per weekly check, or a little over $800 per month, for a maximum of twenty-six weeks. This gives substantial help—though not a princely sum—to the fraction of unemployed people (roughly 35 percent in the mid-1990s) who get benefits.[55]

UI, like Workers' Compensation, is largely state-run. It is subject to only a few federal regulations about industries and workers that must be covered.

This leads to highly variable and—in some cases—rather skimpy coverage. UI is funded by a payroll tax on employers (which, however, is largely or entirely passed through to workers in the form of reduced wages) of around 6 percent. But this applies only to the first $7,000 of an employee's annual earnings, so that the tax amounts to only about 2.5 percent of employers' total payrolls and is rather regressive—low-income workers pay the highest proportion of their earnings. Employers who have a history of high unemployment pay more than those with a low history, thus reducing the subsidy to cyclical industries and curtailing the problem of moral hazard (otherwise, employers with regular ups and downs in business might arrange periodic layoffs to save themselves labor costs, while their employees were supported at others' expense). Thus the program has a regulatory function of encouraging employers to keep stable levels of employment. It also provides some automatic economic stabilization by increasing outlays during recessions.[56]

Unemployment benefits should be subject to relatively little stigma because they are based on past earnings and they are taxable. They should be particularly helpful because they may be supplemented with other income or other government benefits. As presently constituted, however, UI has several disadvantages. It is not in fact free of hassle (long waits in line) or stigma. It is also severely limited in scope of coverage, in duration, and in level of payments; in each of these respects, UI has eroded in effectiveness since its peak year of 1971.[57]

UI has always been aimed at temporary rather than long-term unemployment. It generally limits benefits to twenty-six weeks, so that those who are unemployed for a long time eventually run out of payments. This is true even when national economic conditions are bleak. A 1970 provision automatically extending benefits by a modest thirteen additional weeks in case of national recession was repealed in the budget-slashing year 1981, and states are now only permitted (not required) to offer such an extension when their own unemployment rates are high.[58]

The program excludes many workers, especially those who are self-employed or work in small businesses, who work part-time, or who are employed in agriculture or as domestic workers. Many of the lowest-income American workers, and especially many women (for whom flexible, part-time employment is often the only option), are therefore not covered at all.[59] Taken together, the restrictions on coverage and duration of benefits mean that only a small fraction of unemployed people now receive unemployment compensation. Whereas fully 81 percent of the unemployed did so in April 1975, in 1995 the figure was just 36 percent (it actually hit a low point of only 26 percent in 1987). In 1997, too, the "insured unemployed" represented only about 35 percent of the estimated number of unemployed.[60]

Furthermore, those who *are* covered by UI do not get much. Benefit levels vary widely by state; the maximum payment in some states is more than three times as great as in others. The average benefit, which had climbed steadily to a peak of $159 per week in 1971, subsequently dropped by 12 percent to $136 per week in 1995 (both figures refer to constant 1988 dollars). States have historically paid benefits of between 50 and 70 percent of an individual's previous earnings—only, however, up to a rather low maximum benefit level. As a result, the national average weekly benefit is only a small fraction of the average covered weekly wage: only 37 percent in the early 1990s. One reason for the decline in benefits is that the federally imposed minimum amount of earnings that must be covered has stayed constant in dollar terms (at $7,000), but has eroded dramatically in terms of the proportion of total wages covered, from more than 90 percent in 1940 to less than 29 percent in 1992.[61]

UI is of critical importance in staving off abject poverty—for a while— for a certain small fraction of Americans who are covered and become unemployed through no fault of their own. But the limited coverage and scanty benefits mean that UI has a limited effect on poverty and hardly any effect at all on the overall inequality of incomes. UI could be made much more effective by raising the level of wages covered far above the current $7,000 (thereby permitting a substantial increase in benefits and making the taxes much less regressive), by greatly expanding the types of jobs covered (particularly now that flexible and part-time jobs are increasingly common), and by extending the duration of benefits, especially in times of national recession. Arbitrary variations from state to state in coverage and benefits could be reduced by tighter federal regulation.

Medical Insurance

The most conspicuous gap in the American system of social insurance concerns medical care. The dangers of ill health and injury represent just the sorts of risks that social insurance is supposed to cover. Injury and disease are generally beyond the individual's control. They can strike anyone suddenly and unexpectedly. They can temporarily or permanently destroy the ability to earn income, and they can eat up enormous amounts of money in hospitals', nursing homes', and doctors' fees. Private medical insurance does not work very well. Private insurers, fearing adverse selection (that the sickest people will flock to them), set premiums high. They strive to ferret out health information on individuals so they can raise premiums for high-risk, high-cost people (with "preexisting conditions," for example) or turn them away altogether. In order to maximize profits, they try to "cream" the population, insuring only the healthiest people. Those who most need medical insurance, therefore, are least likely to find a willing private insurer. If they do find one, they are likely to face very high rates, which they may not be able to pay.

Barring a system of direct public provision of medical care with doctors employed by government—which seems to be very popular in Britain, but has few backers in the United States—only a universal, compulsory system of social insurance can pool the health risks for the entire population and ensure that everyone will have access to doctors and hospitals.

Yet the United States does not guarantee medical insurance to everyone. This is quite unusual in the advanced industrial world. Virtually every other advanced country offers its citizens universal coverage. Germany started a health system for workers in the nineteenth century, and most European countries instituted universal coverage not long afterward. Our Canadian neighbors finally turned to a universal system in 1971. Even the Australians, whose cowboy-style individualism rivals that of Americans, got on the bandwagon in 1975, leaving the United States standing alone.[62] At the turn of the twenty-first century, about 45 million Americans—more than 16 percent of the U.S. population, including 47 percent of the working poor—lacked medical insurance.[63]

Not only do other countries' universal systems produce health results as good as or better than ours, but also they do so at *much less cost* than our system does. The United States spends about 14 percent of its gross national product (GNP) on medical care. Canada, France, and Germany provide universal coverage to their populations at a cost of just 8 to 9 percent of GNP. The United Kingdom, Japan, and Australia do it even more cheaply, for between 6 and 7 percent of GNP. Particularly striking is the comparison between the United States and Canada before and after the Canadians moved to a universal system in 1971. Medical costs in both countries had been rising at similarly rapid rates, but after 1971, costs leveled off significantly in Canada, while they raced ahead in the United States, leading to a large and increasing gap between the two countries.[64]

Instead of universal, comprehensive public medical insurance, our system is confined to the elderly and the poor.

Medicare

After repeatedly rejecting of the idea of national health insurance (in 1935, 1948, and the early 1960s, for example),[65] the U.S. Congress enacted Medicare for the aged in 1965. Many advocates of universal medical insurance saw this as a natural first step, since the elderly are particularly vulnerable: their medical needs tend to be greatest, their incomes tend to be very low, and they generally lack access to employer-based or other group-based private insurance coverage. In 1963, in fact, nearly half of all Americans aged sixty-five or older lacked hospital insurance altogether. Serious illness among the aged put great financial strain on their children and in many cases stripped elderly people of all their assets and threw them into poverty.[66]

Medicare has dramatically improved this situation. By the late 1980s, for example, when more than a third of young Americans lacked medical coverage for all or part of a two-year period, 99.3 percent of the elderly were covered by medical insurance during that same period.[67]

Medicare is far bigger than the small disability and unemployment programs we have just been discussing; it stands second only to Social Security (OASDI) as our largest social insurance program. Toward the end of the twentieth century, Medicare covered about thirty-eight million people (thirty-three million aged and five million disabled), nearly one-quarter of whom received payroll-tax-supported Hospital Insurance (HI, or "Part A") payments that averaged $3,600 each. Most of these people—thirty-six million of them—also paid modest monthly premiums of about $44 to join the optional Supplemental Medical Insurance (SMI, or "Part B") branch of Medicare. (The premiums paid only about one-quarter of the cost of SMI. The rest was subsidized from general tax revenues.) About 87 percent of SMI enrollees received some Medicare payments for physicians' fees or other covered expenses during the year. For 2000, Medicare's HI was budgeted to spend about $144 billion, and SMI was budgeted at about $92 billion. Taken together (after subtracting credits for premiums and collections), the two Medicare programs were budgeted to spend about $217 billion, or more than 12 percent of all federal outlays (recall table 4.1).[68]

Medicare is a substantially redistributive program. HI taxes are imposed at a uniform rate of 2.9 percent of earnings (*all* earnings, unlike OASDI taxes), so that higher-income people pay more, but the benefits are the same for everyone.[69] Although SMI charges a flat dollar premium, the bulk of SMI funding comes from the federal income tax, which is substantially progressive: that is, higher-income people pay more in dollar terms and as a proportion of their incomes. Thus higher-income working people pay for a larger proportion of Medicare health insurance than low-income people do. Not only are capricious, health-related poverty and inequality among the elderly reduced, but also overall lifetime equality among all citizens is somewhat increased.

Medicare Hospital Insurance (HI) covers inpatient hospital expenses for up to ninety days per benefit period, with a lifetime reserve of an additional sixty days. Payment includes room and board in a semiprivate room, pharmaceuticals, and nursing and other services (but not doctors); it also covers hospice services and limited skilled nursing care.[70] SMI covers a wide range of physician and outpatient services, including diagnostics, surgery, and radiology. It also covers ambulance services, medical supplies, clinical services, anesthesia, and blood transfusions.[71]

This does not, however, mean that all of the medical expenses of the elderly are comfortably covered by Medicare. Far from it. Increasingly, old people have had to pay co-payments and deductibles. HI requires a one-time payment, before Medicare coverage kicks in, equal to the average cost of one day in the hospital (about $800 at the end of the 1990s). Then, if hospitalization lasts longer than sixty days, there is a deductible equal to one-quarter of a hospital day (about $200) for each day until regular benefits run out at day 90. If patients use their one-time reserve of sixty days' coverage, the deductible goes up to half a hospital day. SMI covers only 80 percent of physician charges as set by a fee schedule, so that patients have to pay at least 20 percent of the bill—and more than that if the doctor turns down "full assignment" and charges more than the scheduled rate.[72] (Increasingly nursing homes and other providers will not accept Medicare patients.)

Even more important than co-payments are the limits on Medicare's coverage. The program has not (except during hospital stays) covered drugs, which can be very expensive. It does not (since the repeal of the short-lived amendments of 1988) cover catastrophic illnesses for which hospital stays exceed the specific limits. And it has extremely limited long-term care coverage. Private "Medigap" insurance—regulated in 1990 so that ten standardized packages are offered—fills some of the gaps in Medicare coverage, but is very expensive, so that some 20–30 percent of the elderly (including some with the lowest incomes and greatest needs) cannot afford and do not purchase it.[73]

As a result of Medicare's limits on coverage and requirements of co-payments, together with the high cost of Medigap insurance, the elderly have had to spend a higher and higher proportion of their own income on medical expenses. In 1965, before Medicare, about 13 percent of elderly people's incomes went to out-of-pocket health care costs. In 1977, with Medicare's help, that figure had fallen to 7 percent. But by 1995, it had crept back up to 11 percent.[74]

"Bankruptcy" Again?

Despite the limited coverage of Medicare, however, the program faces serious financial problems. Even more quickly than Social Security, Medicare is coming under pressure. This is largely due to rising medical costs, including the huge investment (by what Lawrence Jacobs calls the "supply state") in high-cost, low-benefit technology.[75] It will be exacerbated by a decline in the ratio of working people (who pay Medicare payroll taxes) to elderly people covered by the program. The ratio of 4 to 1 at the turn of the century is expected to drop to 2.2 to 1 by 2030, when longevity has increased further and many baby boomers will be older than sixty-five. The SMI supplemental medical branch of the program is less directly vulnerable, since only about a quarter of its financing comes from payroll taxes; the rest is drawn from general tax revenues. But, of course, there will be fewer general taxpayers as well. The HI Trust Fund was at one time predicted to become "insolvent" (in the peculiar bookkeeping sense that we discussed above) in 2001, which was only extended to 2010 by the Balanced Budget Act of 1997. More important, already in 1995, HI expenditures began to exceed the program's annual income, even before the start of baby-boomer retirements around 2010.[76]

Does this mean that the program will soon "go bankrupt" and collapse unless it is drastically curtailed? No. As we noted before, the concept of bankruptcy does not apply to federal government programs. As with Social Security, various options are available for keeping the program financially sound. The chief differences are that for Medicare the time pressure is greater and that the rising costs of medical care constitute an additional factor that must be taken into account.

Even if Medicare were not changed at all, the revenue shortfalls could—if we wished—be made up by increasing payroll taxes (by about 1 percent of payrolls) and/or using general tax revenues. But U.S. medical costs are already out of line compared to those in other advanced countries. Practically everyone agrees that it is important to restrain the growth of medical costs.

Cost Containment

Total medical costs in the United States soared from less than 6 percent of the U.S. GDP in 1960 to 11 percent in 1987 and about 14 percent in 1997. Government spending on Medicare has increased even more rapidly, from $7.3 billion in 1970 (about 10 percent of total U.S. health expenditures) to 36.4 billion in 1980 and almost $123 billion in 1991, when it represented fully 37 percent of total U.S. health expenditures. The twenty-one million Medicare enrollees in 1972 increased to nearly thirty-five million by 1991. As a proportion of the whole federal budget, Medicare expenditures more than doubled from about 4 percent in 1970 to almost 8.9 percent in 1990.[77]

The growth in Medicare expenditures has resulted from a hard-to-disentangle combination of increased numbers of elderly people and longer life spans, together with factors that affect the entire health care system: improved quantity and quality of care, including dramatic improvements in medical technology (but also wasteful technology), and rapid inflation in medical costs (medical inflation was 484 percent between 1965 and 1985, compared to a 350 percent increase in the general Consumer Price Index). Medical inflation has been partly driven by the availability of large amounts of public money to pay for fee-for-service medical care—with the fees mostly set by doctors and hospitals.[78] This has created a moral hazard problem for both doctors and patients, who have often lacked financial incentives to avoid overusing medical care.[79]

Medicare has in fact been relatively successful at containing costs, however—more successful than private insurance companies. The cumulative growth rates in per-capita health care spending since 1970 show private health insurance costs soaring ahead of Medicare during the 1980s and 1990s.[80]

In the U.S. health care system as a whole, efforts at cost control have involved major changes in the incentives and reimbursement arrangements of care providers. Health maintenance organizations (HMOs) were strongly promoted by legislation in 1973; they have incentives to cut costs because they receive fixed annual premiums from each enrollee and keep whatever profits remain after expenditures are made. HMOs have definitely helped reduce medical inflation, but vigorous efforts at cost containment can drive patients elsewhere and therefore become self-limiting. HMOs may have largely lost control of costs now that they cannot easily engage in cost shifting. To the extent that they do contain costs, HMOs run the risk of decreasing the quality of care, especially for the least aggressive patients (often those of low income and education).[81]

For Medicare, a particularly successful cost-containment strategy has been the shift to HI hospital reimbursement by "diagnosis related groups" of ailments, or DRGs. In 1983, a Prospective Payment System (PPS) was set up, in which hospitals are no longer reimbursed on a fee-for-service basis for whatever treatment is given to each patient, but instead receive fixed payments for each patient, depending only on which of 468 DRGs their health problem falls into. That is, the hospital gets a fixed fee for a given type of illness and thus has incentives to cut costs in treatment. The result appears to have been some slowdown in the growth rate of hospital costs, which averaged only 3.2 percent annually for the first three years of PPS, compared to 7.8 percent for the three years before. At the same time, however, some hospitals may have evaded the DRG scheme by shifting costs elsewhere or by cutting care in ways harmful to patients. Moreover, the impact of this kind of program appears to be limited; if reimbursement rates are squeezed too hard, some hospitals or health care plans may opt out of the Medicare system and refuse to accept Medicare patients. At the end of 1998, HMOs announced that they were eliminating coverage of about 414,000 Medicare patients in twenty-nine states.[82]

Similarly, limits on physicians' fees through a fee schedule determined by a "resource-based relative value scale" (RBRVS), adopted in 1989, cut fees for surgery and other services. The cuts were delayed somewhat under doctor pressure, and studies of their impact vary, but they appear to have helped contain costs.[83] Again, however, if Medicare squeezes doctors' fees too hard, some may opt out of the system and get their money from private, fee-for-service patients.

Judging by the comparative evidence on other countries' systems, by far the most effective cost-containment measure would be to change to a system of universal health insurance with a single payer (the federal government), which would set coverage standards and negotiate the fees with all providers. Theodore Marmor and others have argued that the Canadian model, in particular, could work quite well in the United States. Changing to such a system would not only cut costs, but also reduce paperwork, administrative expenses, and anxiety and broaden Americans' access to health care. David Himmelstein and Steffie Woolhandler present a striking set of U.S.-Canada contrasts: Canadians are more likely to get necessary care and are much more satisfied with their system. Canadians receive more attention from physicians and get longer hospital stays; they get safer surgery, plenty of transplants, and faster breast cancer treatment. And all this comes at much lower cost because Canadians pay much less for administrative overhead, advertising, drugs, and high-tech gadgets.[84]

Long-Term Care and Medicaid for the Middle Class

Unlike Medicare, Medicaid (also enacted in 1965) is a means-tested program intended for the poor. We consider it a social insurance program, however, both because it represents a fragmentary beginning to general medical insurance and because it has in fact evolved, in certain respects, to become part of the general social insurance package that covers most Americans. That is, Medicaid has partly shifted from an antipoverty program to a middle-class entitlement program.

This has happened because Medicare for the elderly does not generally cover long-term care, whether at home, in the community, or in nursing homes. In the early 1990s, for example, Medicare paid only about 3.7 percent of nursing home bills. Private Medigap policies that do cover long-term care are extremely expensive (the mother of one of our colleagues pays over $7,000 a year for such a policy). Many people cannot afford them. Yet millions of the elderly need long-term care; over 7 million did so in the mid-1990s, about 1.5 million of them in nursing homes. Because life expectancies and the number of retirees are growing so rapidly, the nursing home population is expected to more than double by 2018. Expenditures on nursing homes have skyrocketed much faster than medical expenses generally; they grew from

$4.9 billion in 1970 to $69.6 billion in 1993, an increase of an amazing 1,320 percent. Many families have been shocked to discover just how expensive nursing homes are. Already in the middle 1990s, they charged an average of about $37,000 to care for one patient for a year. That is enough to wipe out the lifetime savings of most old people, and their children, very quickly.[85]

To some extent, Medicaid has dealt with this problem. Medicaid covers not only those who are initially poor, but also the "medically indigent," who become poor as a result of medical expenses. Many nursing home residents who start out paying their own bills use up all their income and assets. Then Medicaid takes over. Thus Medicaid has ended up paying for a much larger portion of long-term care than Medicare does—already three times as much in the early 1990s. The elderly do not make up a large portion of all Medicaid beneficiaries (only 11.5 percent in the mid-1990s, down significantly over the previous two decades), but their care is so expensive that they accounted for 31 percent of all Medicaid spending—a proportion that has been rising rapidly.[86]

Increasingly, many older Americans have come to see Medicaid as a middle-class entitlement, giving them social insurance against the most catastrophic long-term medical expenses for the elderly. This is not an unreasonable idea. One would certainly expect that social insurance ought to cover long-term medical care. But the use of Medicaid for this purpose has some odd effects. Its means-tested structure unfairly stigmatizes some who use it and unfairly deprives others who do not or cannot. Further, the requirement of spending down all one's assets creates perverse incentives to avoid saving or to illegally conceal or transfer assets. And Medicaid's focus on nursing homes entails considerable unnecessary expense. Care in the home or community can often be equal in quality, cheaper (less than one-third the cost), and more pleasant for the elderly. The state of Oregon, operating under a special federal waiver, has had considerable success at using Medicaid and other funding to support home health care, while restricting aid to those who truly need it. The result was an actual reduction (by 8 percent) in the number of nursing home beds at the same time that the elderly population was growing by 40 percent. Oregon managed to hold down nursing home expenditures to just 38.5 percent of long-term care expenditures, the lowest proportion in the country; only one other state's proportion fell below 50 percent.[87]

We will have more to say about Medicaid's benefits for the non-elderly poor in chapter 8 on "safety nets" and basic needs.

The Politics of Social Insurance

The politics of social insurance in the United States has often involved high visibility, broad conflict, and active participation by general public opinion and the political parties. What is sometimes less fully appreciated, however, is that organized interest groups and corporations have also played critical parts.

Political Parties

One crucial aspect of the role of political parties is obvious to all observers of American politics: in the establishment of social insurance programs, the Democratic Party has almost invariably taken the lead, and the Republican Party has resisted. The centerpiece of the U.S. system of social insurance, for example—the Social Security Act of 1935—was proposed by the administration of Democratic President Franklin D. Roosevelt, with input from progressive Democratic officials and experts around the country (especially from Wisconsin). It was enacted in Congress by nearly straight party-line votes, with the overwhelming bulk of the support coming from Democrats, whose numbers had been greatly increased by voters' reactions to the Great Depression (in the House of Representatives, every Republican but one voted to recommit the bill).[88]

Much the same thing is true of the Social Security amendments of 1939 (adding survivors insurance) and 1956 (adding disability insurance); the proposers and supporters were predominantly Democrats. It is true also of the important 1972 Social Security amendments, which expanded benefits and added coverage of the disabled to SSI. (President Nixon seemed content to let the congressional Democrats run most of domestic policy, so long as he had a free hand in international affairs.) Right up to the present day, congressional Republicans have tended to favor cutting benefits and considering privatization, while most Democrats have advocated preserving or extending benefits and retaining the general system of public social insurance.

Similarly, Medicare and Medicaid legislation was enacted in 1965—breaking the decades-long barrier against serious federal involvement in health care—only because Democrat Lyndon Johnson was president and large majorities of Democrats had been elected to Congress in the Goldwater electoral debacle of 1964. The House voted along party lines; in the Senate, only eighteen Republicans and eight Southern Democrats opposed the program on a crucial amendment vote.[89]

The same pattern holds for virtually all the social insurance programs we have considered—and indeed for a wider range of social programs. The main factor organizing political conflict in the United States is substantial disagreement between the Republican and Democratic parties. There are significant differences between ordinary voters who identify with one or the other of the parties, but party differences in policy preferences are much sharper among party activists, including delegates to the national presidential nominating conventions, and among public officials—including presidents and members of Congress. Year after year, the best predictor—and an increasingly sharp predictor—of how members of Congress will vote is their party affiliation, which is closely linked to a liberal-conservative dimension on domestic policy.[90]

Public Opinion

Ever since the 1930s, overwhelming majorities of Americans have enthusiastically supported the enactment and expansion of Social Security and other major social insurance programs. In December 1935, for example, 89 percent of the public told Gallup interviewers that they favored "government old age pensions for needy persons," and surveys over the next few years found 90 to 94 percent support. Year after year, substantial majorities say we are "spending too little" or should "do more" on Social Security. Even in the face of alarmist talk about budget deficits and "bankruptcy," majorities of the public have resisted almost any sort of cut in benefits, from reducing basic benefit rates to slowing down cost-of-living adjustments or extending the retirement age. The idea of partial or wholesale "privatization" of Social Security through mandatory individual retirement accounts—a great favorite among economists, conservative politicians, and (not incidentally) stockbrokers—has met with considerable public skepticism, especially when costs and risk factors are mentioned in survey questions.[91]

The enthusiasm for Social Security has been especially strong among parts of the population who have been affiliated with the Democratic Party—lower-income, working-class people (especially members of labor unions) and ethnic, religious, and racial minorities. But popular support has extended across virtually the entire population.

Similarly, large majorities of Americans have consistently supported Medicare and Medicaid. Well before 1965 (when those programs were enacted), large majorities of 75 to 85 percent said that government ought to "help people to get doctors and hospital care at low cost." Since 1965, equally large majorities (78 to 87 percent) have seen medical care as a "right" to which all citizens are entitled. Substantial majorities have also said that government should "do more" or "spend more" on health and have favored a "national health insurance" system that would cover everyone. To be sure, there has been some resistance to *federal* government involvement in this area, but in response to a late-1990s Pew survey that gave people many choices concerning who should be "primarily responsible" for ensuring access to affordable health care, a majority picked the federal government. Proposals to limit or cut back Medicare or Medicaid invariably arouse heavy public opposition. When the Canadian national health plan was described in a survey, a large majority of Americans supported it, while hardly any Canadians (just 3 percent) said they would prefer the U.S. system.[92]

Given the fact that the American public overwhelmingly supports our social insurance programs and wants to expand them, why has there been so much political resistance to enacting them—and why have there been such vigorous efforts to curtail or dismantle them? More broadly, why does the United States have such a limited and incomplete system of social insurance, far less comprehensive or generous than in most other advanced countries? In a democratic country, where the citizenry is supposed to rule, how can this be? Part of the answer to this question may involve the role of corporations and organized interest groups, which is different here than in many other countries.

Corporations and Organized Interest Groups

As we pointed out in chapter 3, it is very difficult for scholars to pin down the precise effects that organized interest groups and corporations have in American policy making, but there is reason to believe that their impact is considerable. They provide much of the money and many of the activists that are essential for winning elections, thus tending to elect public officials who are friendly to groups' interests and happy to give them access. Corporations and other organized groups profoundly influence the course of public debate and public opinion about policy by sponsoring and funding studies, books and articles, press releases, op-ed pieces, TV commentary, and advertisements.[93] They have direct inputs into the policy-making process, not only by giving favors to policy makers, but also by testifying in legislative hearings, providing information, and even drafting politicians' speeches and legislation. Groups cannot always get what they want, but they often have blocking power to stop policies they oppose.[94]

Once we recognize the importance of organized interests in policy making, we can begin to understand some patterns of public policy in the United States by examining what kinds of policies various interest groups have sought and how powerful those groups are.

The most important fact about the politics of social insurance is probably the same fact that profoundly shapes American politics generally and that distinguishes our political system from those of most other advanced countries: we have tremendously strong, politically well organized corporations, trade associations, and professional groups, but a very weak labor movement. Organized labor in the United States is far weaker than in most other advanced countries. In most advanced countries, about half or more of the workforce belongs to unions; only in the United States and France is the percentage down in the teens. We completely lack the centralized institutions for wage bargaining that are crucial to labor's strength.[95] Largely as a result of the weakness of organized labor, we also lack a Social Democratic party to represent workers. Our Democratic Party, despite its achievements in enacting some social insurance programs, is a pale substitute for a European-style Social Democratic party, just as our system of social insurance is a pale reflection of European systems.[96]

In the United States, the political strength of business firms (most of which have opposed social insurance programs) and the weakness of labor (which has supported them), together with the absence of a labor-dominated political party, have regularly tilted the outcome of political struggles away from social insurance. Regardless of what most citizens may need or want, the outcomes tend to fall short of full, people-friendly programs.

Even the great 1935 triumph of Social Security is illuminating in this regard. For many decades longer than most European countries, the United States resisted any comprehensive system of old age pensions. Only "soldiers and mothers" got some piecemeal social welfare coverage.[97] The Social Security Act was passed only under the most extreme conditions—in the midst of the Great Depression, which had weakened and demoralized business while raising trade unions and popular social movements to a peak of political power.[98]

Moreover, the specific process of drafting and enacting the Social Security

Act (and its New Deal sibling, the Wagner Labor Relations Act, which facilitated the organization of workers into unions) illustrates the critical role of business in American politics and the limits that role imposes on the social insurance system. Crucial to the Democratic Party of the New Deal period was the support of not only workers, labor unions, immigrants, ethnic and religious minorities, and the like, but also certain key business leaders.

As Thomas Ferguson has argued, many pro–New Deal businesspeople came from capital-intensive, multinationally oriented firms that were apparently willing to trade their acquiescence to certain progressive social policies for free-trade measures that would help their international business. In addition, as Peter Swenson points out, certain firms that themselves offered fringe benefits to their workers supported public social insurance in order to eliminate lower-cost competition from businesses that refused to do so (others sought stimulation of mass-market consumption). Top officials from these relatively progressive firms, including Gerald Swope of General Electric, Walter Teagle of Standard Oil, and Marion Folsom of Kodak, played important parts in shaping proposals that became the Social Security Act of 1935. Further, as Swenson argues, officials' *anticipation* of broader business acquiescence was probably even more important than this direct participation.[99] But this reliance on business support very likely ensured that U.S. programs would be more limited than those initiated by union-backed Social Democratic parties in Europe.

Policy making in the United States, of course, should not be viewed as a simple struggle between business and labor, whose interests do not wholly conflict, and neither one of which may be unified in a particular case. Jill Quadagno has argued, for example, that the delayed and limited nature of Social Security resulted partly from the late unionization of U.S. mass-production workers and the key role of autonomy-seeking craft unions.[100] Moreover, the plantation-based agricultural interests dominating the South (which exercised considerable power in Washington because of its one-party Democratic rule and the seniority system that gave them control of congressional committees) wanted to lock labor on the land through a poor-law approach to welfare. After hindering social welfare proposals for many years, the Southerners successfully insisted on excluding from initial Social Security coverage virtually all agricultural workers, thus leaving unprotected many poor whites and nearly all black people.[101] Further, the program's blatant biases against women (dependents' benefits were paid to the husbands, not to the wives, for example, and benefits were denied to former spouses divorced before retirement age) had little to do with class conflict and much to do with sexism and assumptions about traditional family structure.[102] Still, conflict between employers' desires for profits (low wages, low taxes) and employees' desires for high wages and benefits has shaped many political clashes over social insurance in the United States. The employers have won more often than in other advanced countries.

Medical insurance illustrates this point. Most labor-intensive businesses, which are usually affiliated with the Republican Party, have strongly opposed any payroll tax–based medical insurance program, which raises their labor costs—just as Social Security, Unemployment Insurance, and other social insurance programs do.[103]

Medical insurance, however, also engages a different aspect of interest group politics. Medical specialists in the United States are much more affluent than their fellows in other countries (in Canada, for example [104]); many of them are organized into the potent, politically active American Medical Association (AMA). Indeed, doctors used to be virtually *required* to join the AMA, at the cost of hospital and other privileges if they did not (now more belong to specialist organizations). For many years, the AMA spoke for "medicine" as a whole. It dominated policy making in the health area and was widely regarded as one of the most powerful interest groups in American politics. It fiercely opposed any interference with the "doctor-patient relationship" or any sort of "socialized medicine"—notably including national health insurance, which the AMA was instrumental in defeating at each critical historical juncture.[105]

For years up through the 1960s, the AMA resisted the programs that became Medicare and Medicaid tooth and nail. It spent some $1.2 million (a lot of money at that time) on advertising and lobbying; it besieged Washington, ran scary ads, and put up folksy posters in doctors' offices.[106] Contrary to the usual pattern, the AMA lost that battle. But it is important to see that in many respects it won the war. Medical insurance was narrowly restricted to the elderly and the poor. Moreover, the practice of medicine was kept private, on a fee-for-service basis, with physicians mostly free to charge whatever the market would bear (they made sure that official fee-review panels were dominated by doctors). With government providing lots of new money, the market would bear more and more. The result—that the programs that doctors had opposed vastly enriched doctors—may seem ironic, but in fact it was a natural and predictable outcome of a process in which the AMA played a critical and very powerful part, especially in shaping the agenda of what was considered possible.

One key to understanding the hard sailing that U.S. social insurance programs encountered in the 1980s and 1990s is to see that important business investors in the Democratic Party, who had supported the original Social Security Act in 1935 and who had backed Medicare and Medicaid and other programs during subsequent decades, in the late 1970s tended to turn against progressive social policies and abandon the Democrats. As we noted in chapter 3, there were sound business reasons for doing this. Economic competition from abroad, especially from Germany and Japan, began to put a squeeze on profits. So did the "stagflation" (simultaneous economic stagnation and inflation) that had resulted from Vietnam-era deficits and the quadrupling of energy prices by the Organization of Petroleum Exporting Countries. Some internationally oriented businesses, eager to protect third-world markets against perceived Soviet meddling, came to prefer heightened military rather than domestic spending. Other firms (chemicals and paper, for example) felt pinched by the costs of new environmental and workplace regulations. For all these reasons, government regulations, taxes, wage-raising measures, and social spending no longer seemed affordable. Virtually all of American business started campaigning to cut taxes, eliminate regulations, and reduce social spending—the bulk of which goes to social insurance. In the 1980 election, most of the Democrats' money dried up or defected to Ronald Reagan and the Republicans.[107]

The outpouring of business money for Republican candidates, beginning with the Reagan landslide of 1980, and the much-increased funding of conservative think tanks, studies, and publicity—rather than any shift in the opinions of ordinary citizens—fueled the subsequent policy "right turn" against social insurance. That outpouring of political money continued, in various forms, for more than a decade after 1980. It helped energize budget-cutting frenzies after the Reagan-era tax cuts had created huge deficits. Business money contributed to the efforts to "put entitlements on the table" for budget cuts; it helped publicize the "crises" in Social Security and Medicare and helped tout privatization plans.[108]

The debacle of the Clinton health reform plan in 1993–94 represents a painful variation on this story. The plan itself—as opposed to the inspiring rhetoric with which it was launched—was cobbled together not so as to give the public what it wanted and needed (universal insurance along the lines of the Canadian single-payer system), but to gain crucial business support.[109] Several Silicon Valley electronics firms, plus the Ford Motor Company and others worried about the mushrooming cost of their medical fringe benefits, initially backed the idea of universality in return for cost cutting. Various health care providers were brought along by keeping their pieces of the pie intact. But the firms motivated by cost cutting lost enthusiasm as HMOs (temporarily) began to cut costs anyhow, drug companies and others began to fear a squeeze on their prices and profits, and, most notably, a segment of the insurance industry, fearing loss of markets, launched a devastating media blitz against the plan that included the famous "Harry and Louise" ads. The Clinton plan sank without a vote. Few mourned the demise of this particular bureaucratic monstrosity, but an opportunity for serious reform was lost—again largely because of business resistance to comprehensive social insurance.[110]

Only in the late 1990s, with renewed economic growth and increased prosperity, did some businesses' opposition to social insurance begin to moderate somewhat. Together with the modest revival of organized labor and the growth of progressive social movements, this (once the impeachment nastiness of 1998–99 was over) improved the tone of American politics significantly and may have created openings for policy improvements.

Doctors, insurance companies, and other business firms may have most of the money, but they are not the only relevant players. The American Association of Retired Persons (AARP), for example, with some thirty-five million members, is also a formidable presence in Washington. AARP—sometimes tarred as just another "special interest," but surely more representative of millions of Americans than, say, the American Petroleum Institute—is skillful at mobilizing its constituency to enact, improve, and defend social insurance programs for the elderly.[111]

Economic Competition and Structural Constraints

But what about "structural" constraints on the capacity of governments to provide social insurance? Are not social insurance entitlements, which take up a very large share of the federal budget, precisely the government programs that most increase U.S. labor costs and most threaten our international competitiveness? How can we expect to sell goods abroad or to compete at home with cheap, low-wage imports if our labor costs are inflated by substantial payroll taxes? Does not this consideration require us to participate in a race to the bottom, cutting social insurance programs as sharply as possible in order to compete? Or to put it another way, does not international economic competition impose a structural constraint on government action, making it impossible (unless we wish to commit economic suicide) to offer generous or expanded coverage?

Yes and no. It is crucial to make distinctions among different kinds of programs. Certainly some of the very generous social insurance provisions in European countries—which are generally much more expensive than those in the United States—have come under competitive pressure. This is particularly true of programs that benefit members of the workforce without encouraging them to work, like Germany's long paid vacations and very generous unemployment insurance.[112] Excessive expansion of our own UI would probably entail some competitive costs. But no such constraint prevents the United States from adopting a national health insurance plan, which would actually be *cheaper* than the present system and would improve our economic standing, as well as providing better care for more citizens. Business firms that lobby against such plans are not somehow embodying structural logic; they are generally pursuing narrow self-interests or are misled by ideology.[113]

Old age pensions are a particularly tempting target for budget cutters because they are very expensive and seem to involve unproductive "consumption." At some point, no doubt, overly generous payments to retired people could seriously raise the costs of U.S. products and create a competitive disadvantage. But we are far from that point. The income floor that Social Security and SSI presently provide to elderly people is minimal indeed. Unless we as a society decide to engage in wholesale euthanasia of older people (a prospect that does not appeal to the present authors), there is no effective way to extract much money from their support. Cuts in Social Security would mostly have to be made up for by retirees' children or by public aid of one sort or another, so that the net costs to society would stay much the same (though not the relative costs to capital and labor or the costs to particular income groups). Similar considerations apply to disability payments. Considerations of humanity aside—and we hope they are not set aside for long—the temptation to save money by starving "unproductive" members of society is largely based on an illusion.

The chief practical use of these competitive and structural arguments is to direct our attention toward exactly *which* kinds of programs might be harder to sustain than others, which kinds may be ripe for expansion, and which sorts of program improvements might increase efficiency and economic productivity along with equity.

Improving Social Insurance

The social insurance programs we have described—especially the biggest ones, Social Security and Medicare—have helped millions of Americans to avoid disastrous financial consequences from events beyond their control: disability, expensive injury or illness, old age, unemployment. By doing so, they have greatly reduced certain kinds of poverty, particularly among the elderly. According to U.S. budget documents, in the mid-1990s about one-quarter (26 percent) of all social insurance benefits—that is, $90 billion worth—helped reduce the poverty gap. Those $90 billion amounted to twice as much money as the poor got from all means-tested programs (including Medicaid, which was not included in the social insurance sum). In other words, U.S. social insurance programs are our largest antipoverty programs.[114]

By requiring contributions from people while they are working and paying benefits to them when they are ill, old, or otherwise removed from the workforce, social insurance programs smooth out people's lifetime streams of income, significantly reducing certain kinds of inequality: inequality due to ups and downs in a given individual's life or due to certain misfortunes that happen to hit some people rather than others. Moreover, by offering protection against the risks of such catastrophes as severe illness or disability, social insurance programs reduce uncertainty and anxiety for many more millions of people—the bulk of the population—who will never actually suffer the misfortunes that they are insured against.

At the same time, social insurance that is funded by compulsory contributions and offers benefits roughly proportional to contributions obviously cannot have a very powerful effect on overall income inequality among individuals. To the extent that social insurance programs simply force people to buy insurance that is worth about what they pay for it, those programs do not have any impact at all on the enormous differences in lifetime income between one person and another. Most of the statistics on U.S. poverty and income inequality that we presented in chapter 2 were computed *after* taking into account cash transfers from social insurance and other government programs. Even when all payments from Social Security, Unemployment Insurance, Workers' Compensation, and the like are added to people's incomes, it is still true that the top one-fifth of Americans get many times (about four-teen times) as much annual income as the bottom one-fifth. The poor people we discussed were poor *after* taking into account cash payments from social insurance programs.

In our view, U.S. social insurance programs could be improved by increasing their redistributive features—by increasing the extent to which they help unfortunate people who do not fare well in the labor market and are not able to pay much in contributions or taxes. This could be done by increasing minimum benefits (that is, by paying adequate benefits regardless of contributions) and by asking higher-income people to pay more of the programs' costs—for example, by raising the "cap" on the amount of income that is subject to Social Security payroll taxes.

Moreover, we have seen that U.S. social insurance programs have a number of gaps and imperfections even from the pure middle-class-insurance point of view.

Medical Care

By far the highest priority for improving social insurance in the United States, we believe, should be to reshape our system of medical insurance in such a way as to ensure much better access to care for everyone, along with broader coverage of drugs and long-term care, while controlling the escalation of costs.

One might assume that these goals would sharply conflict with each other, that broader and more universal medical care is bound to cost more. Surprisingly, however, that is not the case. At present, we fall so far short on each of these goals—with some forty-five million people uninsured and millions of others underinsured, but with medical costs far greater than in any other country—that it would actually be possible to improve coverage and reduce costs at the same time. As Theodore Marmor, Jerry Mashaw, and Philip Harvey put it, we are currently getting the worst of both worlds: private medicine, but little freedom of choice for patients or providers, combined with high public expenditures, but continuing anxiety about access to care.[115] The problem is that we have been spending many billions of dollars of public money on a complicated, private, still mostly fee-for-service medical system that is largely free to seek profits by maximizing the use of expensive treatments, while we have not imposed public requirements of universal access to care or sufficient controls on costs.

The emerging HMO/managed care system has its own special problems, including perverse incentives of medical care providers (seeking to hold costs down at the cost of lower quality), their general freedom from legal liability, and the difficulty consumers have obtaining information about providers' strengths and weaknesses. This has generated a substantial public backlash.

The obvious solution is the one that has been adopted by virtually all advanced countries except the United States: to move to a "single payer," national health insurance system. The advantages of universal coverage for equality of citizens and for peace of mind of the population are apparent. The advantages for cost control are less obvious, especially if one fixates on a simple economic model of supply and demand: when demand is increased by extending coverage, won't prices and costs go up? As medical economist Victor Fuchs and others have pointed out, however, national health insurance actually *reduces* medical costs in the countries that have it by reducing administrative costs, by restraining excessive investment in high-cost technologies and unneeded hospital capacity, and by using centralized government buying power to drive down prices. It also reduces costs by paying prospectively (for example, setting hospital budgets at the beginning of the year), rather than retrospectively (reimbursing fees-for-service)—thus giving providers strong incentives to control costs, while forbidding them to deny patients care. True, this entails some rationing of care in order to ensure that only necessary care is given. But rationing always occurs in one way or another. Current U.S. rationing is based mainly on the wealth of the patient, a questionable criterion that gives better treatment to rich foreign visitors than to our own citizens. Patients are likely to accept rationing by doctors more readily than rationing by accountants. The evidence indicates that health outcomes under national health insurance are as good as or better than they have been under the expensive, hybrid U.S. system.[116]

A particularly promising model for the United States is the medical system of Canada, a country with many similarities to our own, including a federal system. In Canada, the federal government prepays each province a substantial proportion (roughly 40 percent) of the costs of all necessary medical care. This federal grant requires that each province set up a program that is *universal* (covering all citizens), *comprehensive* (covering all necessary hospital and medical care), *accessible* (no special limits or charges), *portable* (each province recognizes others' coverage), and *publicly administered* (under control of a public, nonprofit organization). All ten provinces maintain medical insurance plans satisfying these criteria. Hospitals' budgets and physicians' fees are set annually in vigorous negotiations between provincial governments and the providers of care. Patients choose their own doctors; doctors bill the provinces; hospitals are paid through global budgets, not itemized billings. As in the United States, most hospitals are public or nonprofit, and physicians practice in diverse individual or group settings. Large majorities of Canadians express great satisfaction with their system.[117]

The U.S. federal and state governments are perfectly capable of running a national health insurance system similar to that of Canada. Indeed, various versions of national health insurance (NHI) for the United States—recently including the McDermott-Wellstone single-payer plan—have been thoroughly worked out and extensively discussed. All that is needed is the political will to enact such a system. To be sure, because of the Byzantine complexity of the current U.S. medical care system, the transition to NHI has to be designed with particular care, and time must be allowed for adjustment. The maze of private medical insurance companies, for example—whose chief contributions sometimes seem to be paperwork, anxiety, and confusion—must be given time to seek profits in other fields.[118] But the technical feasibility of egalitarian, effective, and efficient national health insurance has been demonstrated around the world.

While we are improving medical insurance, we should also remember that medical care is by no means identical with health. In fact, people's overall health, including life expectancies, infant mortality, and vulnerability to various injuries and diseases, appears to be affected much less by medical care than by general standards of living. Key factors include the quality of food people eat, the kind of shelter they live in, the cleanliness of the water they drink and the air they breathe, the quality of sanitation systems, and a host of other aspects of environments and lifestyles. There are enormous differences in these respects between poor and rich countries, but even rich countries vary widely. The United States, for example, has had much higher infant mortality than the Netherlands, Scandinavia, Australia, New Zealand, Japan, or France.[119] And infant mortality, life expectancy, and general health are worse among poor than affluent Americans.

If we wish to improve Americans' health, therefore, we need to consider a wide range of measures in addition to medical insurance. Efforts at healthier eating, more exercise, safer sex, and generally increased health consciousness can be helpful. Improved nutrition and living conditions for the poor could also make a big difference. Government programs that affect the quality of the environment—especially the quality of air and water—and workplace health and safety are important as well, as are product safety and the taxation and regulation of dangerous goods like guns, tobacco, and alcohol. Oddly, while the United States is a prodigal spender on medical care, we have historically neglected public health and the prevention of injury and disease.

Improved medical insurance, then, should be supplemented by improved public health programs. The political obstacles against doing so are significant, however. In just one year, for example, the tobacco industry spent $40 million on a nationwide advertising blitz against proposed increases in cigarette taxes and regulations. Tobacco companies also spent more than $43 million on an intensive lobbying campaign that besieged the Capitol with 192 lobbyists, including the former top Senate leaders of both parties: Howard Baker (Republican) and George Mitchell (Democrat).[120] The tenacity of the National Rifle Association in resisting gun control is well known. Still, experience has shown that mobilized citizens and public opinion can overcome such obstacles.

Social Security

Some proposals to "save" Social Security through privatization and the like are reminiscent of the Vietnam War notion that we could save villages by destroying them. Whether intentionally or not, such proposals—and the accompanying rhetoric about "crisis" and "bankruptcy"—tend to erode Americans' faith in a socially guaranteed basic retirement income, thus pushing us toward the inegalitarian, inhumane alternative of forcing every person to fend for himself or herself.

As we have indicated, we are confident that the demographic pressures on the Social Security system can be dealt with through relatively small policy changes. Moderately increasing payroll tax revenues by raising the cap on income subject to tax, perhaps together with the use of some general revenues, would solve most of the problem. Experience suggests, however, that payroll taxes should not be raised too quickly or the money may be used for other purposes. Since there is no federal piggy bank to put surplus Social Security revenue into until it is needed, the best that can be done is probably to pay down national debt or (with careful safeguards) to invest some Trust Fund money in private equities. To encourage—but not force—some elderly people to retire later and keep doing productive work would also be helpful.

It may be useful to think of the baby-boom population bulge as a temporary piece of bad luck that works against a certain group of workers and retirees. From this point of view, the bulge constitutes another noncontrollable risk against which we should socially insure people. This is one reason that it may make sense to borrow the money to pay for part of the benefits for this group, repaying the debt through general tax revenues, much as we have done for wars and other national emergencies. This should be a temporary measure; we could return Social Security to a payroll tax–based, pay-as-you-go basis after the population bulge passes through the system.[121] Fortunately, we have plenty of time and plenty of options for handling this problem. No short-term decision is likely to be final.

We believe that even in the context of financial pressure it should be possible to make the Social Security system somewhat more progressive. Raising the cap on payroll taxes would be one step in this direction; another would be to increase benefits among the lowest-income recipients.

Unemployment Insurance

The capricious state variations, narrow coverage, low benefit levels, and restricted duration of unemployment insurance all cry out for reform. Tightening federal regulation, extending benefit periods (especially during recessions), broadening coverage (particularly for women working part-time), and raising the level of wages covered would all be steps forward.

A common objection to unemployment insurance has been that *moral hazard* is a particularly acute problem: if UI is made too attractive, people may be encouraged to become unemployed or (more likely) to make less than a wholehearted effort to regain employment, and employers may be encouraged to lay people off.[122] Hence, the argument goes, UI benefits must be kept meager and clearly inferior to the fruits of working. True, moral hazard is potentially a serious problem, much more serious with unemployment insurance than with most other kinds of social insurance. Still, it is clear that the vast majority of UI claimants are unemployed for reasons beyond their control. It is also clear that private provision of unemployment insurance is simply not feasible.

The solution is to offer reasonably adequate unemployment insurance benefits (better than are now offered), but only within a context in which work is widely available and people are required, as well as helped, to pursue it. As the Beveridge Report in the United Kingdom put it, "[The] only satisfactory test of [genuine] unemployment is an offer of work."[123] Moreover, the best *cure* for unemployment is a job. The best way to insure against unemployment due to plant closings, industry shifts, recessions, global competition, and the like is to make sure that everyone has a chance to work when able to do so and that people are compensated when—but only when—they cannot. There is no point and no equity in trying to deter or punish unemployment when no decent jobs are available.

The kinds of policies necessary to ensure that everyone has a chance to work and get good wages are discussed in chapter 7; they involve macroeconomic policies, government procurement policies, public service employment, and a variety of regulations—even international treaties and agreements. To attain the objectives of unemployment insurance—in other words, to protect people from the hazard of involuntary unemployment—requires a broader conception of social insurance that goes well beyond existing programs.

Toward a Broader Conception of Social Insurance

The basic idea of social insurance is a sound one: to protect everyone from risks they cannot control, while requiring that they work when possible and contribute to the cost of insurance while they are working. But as this idea has been worked out in U.S. public policy, social insurance covers only a rather circumscribed set of risks for limited groups of people. A clear understanding of the many other types of risks that can afflict people, and of the limited sense in which individuals can control such risks, leads to a considerably broader conception of what social insurance should do.

Our growing scientific understanding of genetic and environmental influences on human behavior helps us to see that in many cases behavior that we once saw as the result of conscious choices—sometimes morally condemned choices—is actually under little, if any, conscious control. Often people really can't help it. This is apparent, for example, in the health area. Health-threatening obesity turns out often to be more a matter of genetics than of greed or deficient self-control. Mental illness often has a genetic component. Alcoholism and drug addiction are frequently linked to family histories. In a completely different realm, it is apparent that unemployment often results from systemic factors: a nationwide recession, or pressures of global economic competition, or shifts between industrial sectors—rather than any error or deficiency on the part of an individual—may suddenly wipe out a long-held and well-performed job.

More broadly, a host of personal factors that affect people's incomes and life chances, from intelligence and creativity to levels of ambition, motivation, and physical or mental health—to say nothing of money and other assets that parents may provide—are themselves profoundly affected by genetic endowment, family upbringing, and the peers and neighborhoods by which people are surrounded. Over these matters the individual has only very limited control. To be born or brought up with limited intelligence, ambition, or skills, or with poor health, is to face a high likelihood of living a deprived and limited life. It may also mean never being able to earn enough to make the financial contributions to social insurance programs that will ensure satisfactory benefits.

A broader view of social insurance would consider people's chances of being stuck with deficient genetic endowments or a deficient upbringing—or landing in a hostile environment—as being risks against which society should at least partly insure its members. John Rawls's conception of the "original position" is helpful in this regard. If we exercise our empathy and imagination, if we temporarily disregard our own good luck and contemplate what social arrangements we would seek if faced with the possibility of being cursed rather than blessed by heredity and environment, we are likely to choose a broad conception of social insurance in which everyone is substantially protected against these fundamental sorts of ill fortune.[124]

The problem, of course, is that individuals do have *some* control over what they do or do not achieve. Any effort *fully* to insure everyone against the unhappy consequences of heredity and environment would create a serious problem of moral hazard. Parents would have less incentive to invest in their children's futures; individuals would have less reason to better themselves or to strive to overcome the odds. This is simply another way of saying that any effort to ensure complete equality of incomes would be very costly. To the extent that material incentives are important (and surely they count for something), entirely to eliminate differential rewards for individual achievements would mean failing to encourage behavior that we want to encourage and tolerating behavior that we want to discourage.

Merely to point out the existence of a moral hazard problem and to reject the feasibility of total equality, however, is not to rule out the desirability of *some* level of social insurance against fundamentally bad luck in genes or environment. Just what level of insurance is desirable should depend on how much control human beings actually have over a particular kind of behavior, how much impact material incentives have on that behavior, and how much we care about it. The trend of evidence increasingly suggests that many people who do poorly in labor markets do so for reasons largely beyond their control. Moreover, nonmaterial incentives—such as desires for self-fulfillment and social approval, as well as love for others—can often provide plenty of motivation for people to work hard and to better themselves even if there are not great economic rewards for doing so.

As we go on in this book to discuss education, jobs, and safety nets, it will be useful to keep in mind that an expanded conception of social insurance may provide new arguments in favor of government programs in those areas. Why, for example, should society not try to insure children against the misfortunes of inadequate food at home, lack of medical care, or poor schooling? Children, who fall outside the work-and-contribute logic of traditional social insurance programs, would be sorely neglected if we limited ourselves to those programs. Similarly, why should we not ensure adults against disappearing jobs or declining wages that result from recessions, plant closures, industry restructuring, or global competition? Broad social insurance could help such people develop the abilities to work, give them opportunities to do so, and support those who could not.

Before we turn to these topics, however, we must look at the taxes that fund government spending programs, inquiring into what effects taxes have on poverty and inequality and how they can be made more equitable.

5

Fair Taxes

Taxes play a critical part in what government does or does not do about inequality of income and wealth. If taxes are *progressive*—that is, if high-income people pay higher percentages of their income in taxes than low-income people do—then incomes tend to be less unequal after taxes than before. The tax system reduces income inequality. But if taxes are *regressive*—that is, if high-income people pay *lower* percentages—then the tax system increases inequality. If taxes are *proportional,* with everyone paying about the same percentage of his or her income, there is no net effect on income inequality.

The idea of progressive taxation has a long history in the United States. Personal and corporate income taxes, in particular, have long been seen as means to finance the federal government according to people's ability to pay and to reduce extreme differences in incomes. As we will see, however, over the years this redistributional effect has been reduced by a succession of loopholes and rate reductions in income taxes and by increased reliance on other taxes that are proportional or regressive, especially payroll taxes.

Which taxes bite deepest? Figure 5.1 shows what share of federal government revenue has been produced by different types of taxes since just before World War II. Since the middle of the war, individual income taxes have regularly produced the most revenue, providing some 40 to 45 percent of all federal government receipts most years (about 48 percent in 2000). Corporate

Figure 5.1   Percentage of Federal Government Revenue, 1940–2005

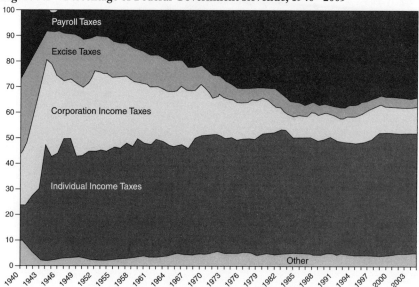

Source: U.S. Office of Management and Budget, *Budget of the United States Government, Fiscal Year 2000,* historical table 2.2.

income taxes, on the other hand, which provided about one-third of all federal government revenues during World War II and about one-quarter for several years after the war, then declined to a low point of just 6 percent in 1983, rebounding only to 10 percent in 2000. The slack has been taken up by social insurance payroll taxes, which accounted for only 11 percent of federal revenues in 1950, but grew to 16 percent in 1960, 23 percent in 1970, 31 percent in 1980, and fully 37 percent of federal revenues in 1990 (34 percent in 2000). "Excise" taxes—that is, federal sales taxes on alcohol, tobacco, gasoline, and other specific goods—long ago, in the form of tariffs on imports, constituted the major source of all federal revenue. But excise taxes have sharply declined in importance so that they now account for less than 5 percent of federal revenue (3.7 percent in 2000). Estate and gift taxes provide even smaller shares.[1]

State and local tax revenues, on the other hand, come about one-third from property taxes, one-quarter from general sales taxes, and just one-fifth from income taxes.[2] We will see that the progressive ideology that once animated federal tax policy has never fully extended to state and local taxes, many of which—especially sales taxes—are regressive. At present, therefore, the net effect of all federal, state, and local taxes taken together is not very redistributive. The gap between rich and poor remains just about as wide after taxes as before.

In this chapter, we discuss the arguments for progressive taxation and the objections to it, especially those related to savings and work incentives. We then look at different kinds of taxes one at a time, beginning with the federal personal income, corporate income, payroll, excise, and estate and gift taxes, and moving on to state and local property, sales, and income taxes. We note how each tax works, what effects it has on the rich and the poor, and how it might be made more equitable. Finally, we examine evidence that the tax system as a whole does not now do much to reduce income inequality. We consider political factors—including organized interest groups—that have undermined the fairness of our tax system, and argue that an aroused public could much improve the situation.

Taxes are complicated. Some important aspects of tax policy are rather technical and just cannot be made to sound very exciting. If at any point in this chapter you run into material that you find boring or too detailed, we urge you to skim or skip over it entirely. But be sure to look at the section on "Tax Politics," which concludes the chapter.

The Idea of Progressivity

Benefits Theory

One theory of fair taxation is largely independent of progressivity: it holds that tax burdens should be set equal to the *benefits* that different individuals derive from government. If we ignore the social, cooperative aspects of production and the many ways in which people's incomes diverge from their "marginal product" or the value of what they produce (recall the discussion of this issue in chapter 2), then we might accept the idea that people are *entitled* to whatever they earn—an idea that John Locke saw as rooted in natural law or the "natural order."[3] From this concept of entitlement, it seems to follow that government should not take away anyone's income or wealth without providing equivalent benefits. As formulated by Erik Lindahl and others, benefit theory holds that an individual's taxes should be set so as to approximate as closely as possible the price that individual would be willing to pay voluntarily in order to get whatever government benefits accrue to her or him. Such a system would mimic the virtues of competitive markets in private goods. It should lead to efficient provision of public goods, calibrating the quality and quantity of such goods in accordance with citizens' desires, and it would ensure justice or fairness in the sense of not interfering at all with private property.[4]

Benefit theory might happen to lead to somewhat progressive taxation if it were true—as appears likely—that rich people get more benefits than poor people from such government programs as national defense and law enforcement (they have more property to protect). But that misses the main point. Government cannot possibly do much to increase equality if it gives everyone benefits exactly proportional to the taxes they pay. Only a combination of taxes and benefits that takes more from the rich and gives more to the poor can increase after-government equality. That fact (even more than the nightmare that would result from trying to assess the subjective value of different people's benefits) constitutes the chief flaw of relying exclusively on the benefit theory of taxation. To do so would rule out using the tax system deliberately to redistribute income from rich to poor. That is, it would rule out using taxes to perform the government function with which this book is most concerned.[5]

Redistribution and Ability to Pay

As we noted in chapter 3, there are strong arguments in favor of income redistribution as one function of government. If we begin with a fundamental ethical premise of impartiality, then we should care about what happens to other people just as we care about ourselves. Impartiality among different people is at the heart of many religious and philosophical precepts, from the Golden Rule to Kant's "categorical imperative" and Sidgwick's "rational benevolence." It animates Rawls's injunction that we should put on a "veil of ignorance" when contemplating questions of justice, setting aside our own position in society.[6] If we adopt this kind of impartiality or empathy, and if we go along with the widely accepted view that people are risk-averse or have declining marginal utility for money (that is, a given amount of additional income is worth less to people who already have a lot), then it follows that some degree of income equalization is desirable. One natural way to accomplish it would be to tax high-income people proportionally more than people of low income.

This argument for tax progressivity is closely related to the phrase "ability to pay." The point is not merely the obvious one that people with high incomes are able to pay more taxes because they have more money, but also that they can pay *proportionally* more—a higher percentage of their incomes—because an extra dollar does not mean as much to them as it does to someone with less money.

John Stuart Mill, for example—though not himself an advocate of progressive taxation—saw the distribution of wealth as a "matter of human institutions" subject to collective decision, and he was not happy with the inequalities that he observed in Britain in his time. Mill emphasized the importance of ability to pay, which he equated to *equality of sacrifice*.[7] This key idea, when modified to mean *minimum total sacrifice*—that is, designing taxes so that their subjective burden on the whole population is reduced to a minimum—and combined with the idea of comparable, declining marginal utility for money among all individuals, led F. Y. Edgeworth to formulate a theory prescribing highly progressive taxation.[8] Arthur Pigou brought the idea to full fruition. He noted that we need not really believe that everyone has identical utility functions, but lacking other information, it is simply best to suppose that people are temperamentally alike. It follows that taxes should be progressive so long as they do not interfere too much with savings and economic growth.[9]

Thus the most influential theory supporting the idea of progressive taxation is much the same as the utilitarian theory of income redistribution that we sketched in chapter 3. It relies on the same principal assumptions: that people have declining marginal utility for money (again, that an extra dollar means less to you if you already have a lot of money), that we can at least roughly compare different people's utilities, that we should act as if utility functions for money are about the same from one person to another (a given level of income will have about the same effect on different people's happiness), and that—at least within a reasonable range of tax rates—pretax incomes will stay about the same as tax rates change. To the extent that these things are true, the total sum of human happiness will be increased when income is taxed away from the rich and spent for the poor.

Objections

Objections to progressive taxation generally focus on one or more of these assumptions.[10] Some economists, for example, resolutely deny the possibility of comparing the happiness or utility of different people. Many critics object that different people's utility functions are certainly *not* identical, and some (especially non-economists) dislike the idea of taking account of utility differences in any case—do we really want someone to be taxed less because he enjoys money more? Virtually all critics worry about the possibility that high progressive tax rates may reduce the amount of income available to be taxed—and may reduce overall welfare—by reducing savings, work effort, and economic growth.

We do not believe that the objections concerning interpersonal comparisons and the shape of utility functions have much merit. Some people who want to reject the possibility of interpersonal comparisons may be confused about the meaning of the ordinalist revolution in economics, which has permitted most of economic theory to be formulated in terms that do *not require* cardinal measurement or interpersonal comparisons of utility.[11] But this does not in any way forbid us from thinking about such matters when they *are needed,* as they are in the case of any serious discussion of welfare or justice. We simply cannot say much about whether or not a tax is fair without considering whether the harm it does to one person is greater or lesser than the good it does for another person. Economists as economists may choose to declare themselves mute on such matters (in practice, few do[12]), but we as citizens and social thinkers cannot afford to ignore questions of justice, equity, and fairness.

No one said that such judgments are easy. Still, we must make them, and we do make them all the time. They are actually easier to deal with in the case of taxation than in many other issues that one encounters. For one thing, in a given society at a given historical period, it does not seem very far-fetched to judge that most individuals have roughly comparable evaluations of material circumstances—that is, that their utility functions for money tend to be rather similar. Once we accept that rough similarity, Pigou's observation has special force: if we are going to talk about justice at all, we must assume something, and we are likely to do better by assuming identical utilities than anything else. Moreover, such an assumption defuses one of the most telling criticisms of utilitarianism, that it privileges epicures. By acting as if everyone has identical utility functions, we take into account the main factors that contribute to overall happiness, but we do *not* in fact give any advantage to people who claim to have especially refined capacities for enjoyment.[13] Finally, the assumption of identical utility functions also means that we need not worry much about exactly what shape those functions have. So long as the utility of an extra dollar declines as a person's income increases—a proposition that Edgeworth declared to be "universally admitted"—it makes little difference how quickly it does so; substantial tax progressivity is still called for.[14]

The more important objections to progressive taxation involve the practical concern that negative effects of taxes on savings and work might reduce the size of the economic pie and make society as a whole worse rather than better off. This issue requires serious discussion.

Effects on Savings and Work

Recent arguments against tax progressivity have mostly focused on the issues of savings and work effort. In the mid-1980s, for example, an article on "The Trade-off between Equality and Efficiency" by Edgar Browning and William Johnson claimed to find that increased equality would lead to extremely high losses of economic production. Their estimates made redistribution look enormously costly. But those estimates depended on using weak data, mischaracterizing the status quo, and then contrasting the presumed status quo with a particularly clumsy and inefficient redistributive scheme.[15]

In the heated ideological climate of the 1980s, even the most careful scholars sometimes got carried away. Jerry Hausman, for example, introduced his analysis of how taxes affect work—based on highly sophisticated methods and good data from the Panel Study of Income Dynamics—with the dramatic claim that his study "contradict[ed]" the "comforting view" that income and payroll taxes cause little reduction in labor supply and do little harm to economic efficiency. As commentator Gary Burtless pointed out, however, Hausman actually found that *most* individuals are not very responsive to taxation. His estimates of high average responsiveness and high welfare losses depended crucially on the finding that a few people on the extreme tail of the work/leisure preference distribution responded very strongly. But estimates for extreme individuals are necessarily less reliable, and Hausman's were highly sensitive to particular assumptions he made.[16]

Some scholars—including Joseph Pechman, the dean of U.S. tax experts—never accepted these gloomy assessments. Pechman noted that there is not in fact any theoretical, a priori reason to expect negative effects from high or progressive taxes on either work or savings. In both cases, it is possible that "income effects" (people's efforts to get more income when taxes take some away) may overcome "substitution effects" (the tendency to substitute leisure for work when the rewards for greater work effort are reduced). Empirical studies, Pechman said, indicated only a small effect of taxes on families' primary wage earners, though higher taxes do apparently tend to discourage secondary earners (spouses) from working as many hours as they otherwise would. Historical trends "do not . . . support the view that taxes have had a significant effect on aggregate labor supply." The effect of taxes on savings, Pechman declared, is "even more ambiguous." The prevailing view, he said, is that saving does respond to the after-tax rate of return, but the magnitude of response is uncertain.[17]

More recent work has tended to confirm Pechman's view. In his overview of a series of empirical studies on progressive taxation, Joel Slemrod judged that the "1980s brand of elasticity pessimism" (the assertion of large negative effects on work and savings) was "overstated." The experience of the 1980s indicates that taxes can exert a powerful influence on the timing of economic activity (a rush to cash in capital gains in 1986, for example, just before the capital gains tax rate was raised) and on the financial and legal structuring of economic activities (e.g., the nature and extent of tax shelters). But the 1980s experience also has lowered the best estimates of the tax responsiveness of labor supply and saving. Thus the Reagan era's "supply side" tax cuts and special incentives to save did not in fact increase personal savings rates, which continued to decline.[18]

Studies using experimental data from the elaborate Negative Income Tax experiments yielded particularly low estimates of tax effects on labor supply, clustering tightly around zero,[19] but the results of other recent studies have not been very different. Even the old idea that women are more deterred by taxes has come into question,[20] perhaps because more are now primary wage earners.

It is important to note, however, that taxes *can* have significant effects. The specific structure of rates makes a difference. For many years, the effective tax rates on poor people (including loss of welfare benefits) were 100 percent or more of their earnings: that is, they actually *lost* money by working. No matter how strong people's work ethics are, perverse tax incentives of that sort can discourage some from working. On the other hand, measures like the Earned Income Tax Credit (EITC), carefully designed to encourage work by subsidizing wages and removing the subsidy only slowly with increased income, can be made bigger and more progressive with little or no negative effect on economic efficiency. Equality can be increased more efficiently by the EITC approach than, for example, by flat cash transfers or increased tax exemptions.[21] Analysis of the Negative Income Tax experiments indicated that, for the low-income segment of the population, some reforms that would yield greater after-tax equality would indeed cause large losses in work effort and large distortions in the labor market, but that other reforms involve less economic loss or actually *reduce* distortions among the low-wage population by reducing the high tax rates imposed on poor wage earners.[22]

Surely it is true that if taxes were made so highly progressive as to be confiscatory at the high-income end of the scale, bad things would happen. This is especially so with increased capital mobility around the globe: capital, and perhaps high-income people as well, would flee the country to low-tax havens. But the econometric studies indicate that the United States is very far from that point. Indications are, in fact, that tax progressivity could be substantially increased without harming the economy, if it were implemented in sensible ways.

From a comparative point of view, it is important to remember that the total U.S. tax burden is considerably lower than in nearly all other rich advanced countries. In 2000, total U.S. tax receipts amounted to about 34 percent of the gross domestic product (GDP). The figure was a shade lower in Australia and Japan, but significantly higher in the United Kingdom and Canada (41 percent and 43 percent, respectively); substantially higher in Germany, the Netherlands, Italy, Austria, Belgium, and Finland (all at 45 percent or more of GDP); and much higher in Norway, France, Denmark, Switzerland, and Sweden (all above 50 percent).[23] This suggests that there would be substantial room for U.S. taxes to increase without putting us at a competitive disadvantage with Canada or the main economic powers of Europe, who are our chief trading partners and competitors.

To be sure, some of those countries—especially the ones with the highest tax burdens and most extensive welfare states—have felt pressured by globalization and have been cutting back. But this is a relative matter; what is seen as austerity in Sweden or Denmark still involves far higher levels of taxes, services, and income redistribution than in the United States.[24]

The evidence is also ambiguous on exactly what pressures globalization creates and how strong they are. Corporate taxation has declined nearly everywhere, and corporation income taxes would seem especially vulnerable to the threat of global capital mobility—not only can capital move away from high-tax countries, but also, with even less bother, multinational corporations can use creative accounting to shift apparent profits from high- to low-tax locales. (To evade high personal income taxes, on the other hand, would usually require leaving one's home country—a costly step for most Americans.) Yet Dennis Quinn found that, across countries, increased financial liberalization and enhanced capital mobility were actually associated with *higher* levels of corporate taxation. A broader trend toward less redistributive taxation by most nations may result from the sorts of competitive economic pressures that Duane Swank has documented, but the evidence suggests that those pressures are rather small.[25] The main impediments to progressive taxation are probably political, rather than economic.

Federal Taxes

The Individual Income Tax

The federal income tax on individuals—which, as we have seen, is the largest single source of federal government revenue—is supposed to be the jewel in the crown of tax progressivity. From the 1890s—when the modern income tax was first seriously proposed—until 1913, when the income tax was enacted after passage of a constitutional amendment, the redistributive rhetoric was ferocious. Advocates spoke of attacking the great concentration of wealth, and opponents feared "communism." [26]

During World War I, income tax rates were in fact made highly progressive, with large exemptions and high marginal rates that applied only to the very wealthiest Americans—for example, a 77 percent tax on incomes over $1 million (a huge sum at that time) in 1918. After a dip in the 1920s, very high *nominal* income tax rates—that is, official statutory rates as published in the tax schedules—applied throughout the 1930s and the two subsequent decades. From 1950 to 1963, the official tax rates on the highest incomes stood at 91 or 92 percent—higher than most of us would favor imposing, and enough, if those rates were actually effective, to bring about an extraordinary redistribution of income and wealth.[27]

No major redistribution of income ever occurred, however, for three reasons. First, by the time of World War II, when the peak marginal rate on the highest incomes reached 94 percent, substantial taxes had been imposed on the middle and working classes as well, making the income tax mass-based and somewhat reducing its overall progressivity.[28] Second, from the beginning—and increasingly over time—a series of exclusions, deductions, and tax shelters undermined progressivity by allowing much or most of wealthy people's incomes to escape taxation. Third—and partly in recognition of the fact that effective tax rates were far lower than the published rates—policy makers eventually made sharp cuts even in the nominal, published rates for high-income taxpayers.

It is important to see that much of what economists consider income is *excluded*—is not taxed at all—or is only partially taxed under the federal income tax. Most notably capital gains—increases in value of stocks, bonds, real estate, artwork, and other assets—are not generally taxed at all unless and until they are "realized," that is, until they are turned into cash. There is a practical argument in favor of this exclusion: namely, that it is difficult to keep track of changing values of assets except when they are sold and a market value is established. In some cases, too, it would be a hardship to force liquidation of assets in order to pay taxes. But capital gains, which accrue mostly to the wealthiest individuals, constitute a very high proportion of the income of those people. To exclude unrealized gains from taxation is to leave much of the income of the very wealthy tax-deferred or even tax-free, especially since many gains are *never* realized. The increased value is passed along without taxation to heirs or trust funds or (if given away as charitable contributions) actually produces tax deductions. The recipients get a stepped-up "basis" and are not taxed on these gains either. Moreover, even *realized* capital gains have generally (since 1921) been given special treatment. The law has taxed them at lower rates than wages and salaries by excluding half or more of realized gains from taxation and/or by applying a special low rate to them.[29]

The result has been to make the *effective* tax rates on high-income people—that is, the amount of taxes they actually pay as a percentage of their total, broadly defined income—much lower than the nominal rates published in the rate schedules. There were noisy complaints about apparently outrageous tax rates of 92 percent and the like, but in practice no one paid taxes at anything close to that rate (no one, that is, except perhaps the occasional confused millionaire or lottery winner who lacked a good tax accountant).

In the years in which nominal rates on high-income taxpayers looked high, the preferential treatment of realized capital gains made a particularly dramatic difference. In 1976, for example, the nominal tax rate of 69 percent on income over \$1 million was turned into an effective rate nearly 20 per-centage points lower, merely by the exclusion of some capital gains.[30] If *un-realized* gains were included in income figures, the drop would be revealed as much greater, and the effective tax rates of high-income people would be seen to be even lower. Little wonder that lawyers and accountants scrambled to invent tax shelters—like cattle and oil partnerships for New York dentists—that turned ordinary income into capital gains or offset income with bogus capital "losses."

A similar bonus for the well-off results from the exclusion or nontaxation of what economists call the "imputed rent" of owner-occupied dwellings. The value that people enjoy from living in homes that they own is consider-able. Although we do not ordinarily view it this way, it makes sense to think of the value enjoyed as income, as a return on investment, just like dividends from stocks or bonds. It would not be difficult to include a fixed percentage of the market value of every owner's home as income. But the income tax ignores it. This exclusion is worth far more to the owner of a multimillion-dollar house than to the owner of a modest apartment, and it is worth noth-ing at all to a renter. It means that a significant part of the total income of high-income people—namely, the enjoyment of living in expensive homes—is not taxed at all.

Again, when the nominal tax schedule is progressive, a given dollar amount of tax *deductions*—which are subtracted from income before the tax rate applies—is worth much more to high-income than to low-income people. And generally high-income people have bigger dollar deductions, as well. This is true even of the popular deduction for interest on home mort-gages, which has been misleadingly sold as a break for the middle class. Thus in the period of apparently very progressive tax rates, extensive deductions for home mortgage interest, state and local taxes, charitable contributions, and the like greatly reduced the effective tax rates on high-income people. In 1976, for example, deductions reduced the nominal tax rate on income of \$1 million and over by 18 percentage points. Together, deductions plus the preferential treatment of capital gains cut the nominal 69 percent rate nearly in half. Other factors brought the actual effective rate down to just 28 percent.[31]

As a result of all the exclusions, deductions, and tax loopholes—plus underreporting of income, which is especially prevalent among independent business and professional people—even in the years with very high nominal tax rates on high incomes, hardly anyone actually paid those rates. The pathbreaking study by Joseph Pechman and Benjamin Okner, which merged data from several sources, found that in 1966—a year in which the published tax schedule looked very progressive and the top nominal rate was 70 percent—the effective rates were quite low and not progressive at all over the upper-income ranges. Computed as percentages of broadly defined "adjusted family income," the income taxes paid by families with incomes of $1 million and over were not 70 percent, but only somewhere between 12 and 17 percent of income! Moreover, families with incomes in the $100,000 to $1 million range actually paid taxes at slightly *higher* effective rates than the very top income earners did.[32]

In subsequent years, the income tax law has changed significantly. But the situation of low and only mildly progressive effective tax rates has not much altered; instead, the lack of progressivity has just been more openly acknowledged. The chief change has been to flatten out the nominal tax rates by cutting the top rate markedly and then eliminating the series of brackets that used to tax increasingly higher incomes at increasingly higher rates—moving to a mostly two-rate system. At the same time, changes in the law have eliminated some—but by no means all—of the deductions, loopholes, and tax shelters that had made the nominal rates close to meaningless and had distorted people's economic decisions. The 70 percent top marginal rate of the 1970s, for example, was cut to 50 percent beginning in 1982, as part of a Reagan-era Christmas tree of benefits for the well-to-do. The top rate was then cut even more sharply to 28 percent in 1988, by the 1986 legislation that abandoned graduated rates almost completely (leaving only two tax brackets, of 15 percent and 28 percent) and also broadened the tax base and closed many loopholes, attempting to rationalize the tax code without affecting its level of (non)progressivity.[33] Small changes in 1990 and 1993 (moving to four brackets, taxed at 15, 28, 33, and 39.5 percent) only moderately increased the top rates and the progressivity of the income tax.

In a follow-up to his study with Okner, Pechman found that the effective rates of the income tax became slightly less progressive between 1966 and 1970 and again between 1970 and 1975. They became a bit *more* progressive in 1980, but then markedly less so in 1985, after the initial Reagan tax cuts. Even in 1980, before those cuts, the effective average tax rate on incomes of $1 million and over was only 11.7 percent.[34] Rather far from "confiscatory" taxation. More recently Richard Kasten and others found that, despite the ups and downs, there was not much net change in the progressivity of federal income tax rates between 1980 and 1993. A drop in the effective taxes of the highest-income individuals may have been concealed, however, because this study omitted the much-increased unrealized capital gains of the wealthy, as well as imputed rent and other untaxed income.[35]

What is clear is that during the 1980s and 1990s, a period in which income inequality greatly increased—as the wages of working people remained stagnant, while the salaries, dividends, and capital gains of upper-income people grew enormously—the effective rates of the individual income tax remained low and only mildly progressive. Any serious effort to reduce income inequality in the United States would have to consider substantial increases in income tax progressivity, with particular attention to capital gains.

The Corporate Income Tax

Like the personal income tax, the federal income tax on corporations has long been thought of as a major tool for redistributing wealth. It began modestly, at a rate of 1 percent, in 1909. During World War I, the rate was increased to 12 percent, approximately the level at which it stayed for two decades. (In addition, an "excess profits tax" was instituted to reduce war profiteering; it actually provided most of the tax revenue raised during the war.[36]) During World War II, the rates of the corporate tax once again increased markedly (again supplemented with an excess profits tax) to as much as 53 percent on income just over $25,000. Once more the ratcheted-up rates stayed about the same for many peacetime years, stabilizing at 52 percent on income over $25,000 in the 1950s and 48 percent during the 1970s.[37]

Gradually, however, the effective rates of the corporate income tax were eroded by more and more generous treatment of depreciation, which allowed corporations quickly to subtract from taxable income much larger fractions of the value of their capital assets than were actually disappearing due to exhaustion or wear and tear. This "accelerated depreciation" was liberalized in 1954, 1962, and most notably in 1981, when the "accelerated cost recovery system" allowed businesses to pretend that assets lost their value long before their useful lives were really over. In addition, an "investment tax credit" in force most years between 1962 and 1985 further reduced taxes when new equipment was purchased. The Tax Reform Act of 1986 eliminated the investment credit and tightened up depreciation allowances somewhat, but at the same time, it lowered the general corporation tax rate from 46 to 34 percent.[38]

Largely as a result of growing loopholes, the corporation income tax came to produce relatively less and less revenue. As we noted earlier, it accounted for about one-third of all federal government revenue during the World War II years and roughly one-quarter in the 1950s, but only about one-fifth in the 1960s and only about 15 percent in the 1970s, 9 percent in the 1980s, and a very slightly increased 10 or 11 percent in the 1990s and 2000s (refer back to figure 5.1).

Very likely this trend has also reduced the progressivity of federal taxes as a whole. We cannot be absolutely sure because corporate taxes may not be entirely borne by the owners of corporations; it is possible that they are partly *shifted* forward to consumers in the form of higher prices or backward to workers as lower wages. To the extent that such shifting occurs, of course, the tax is much less progressive than if it falls wholly on the mostly high-income and very wealthy owners of corporations or of capital generally. We must therefore discuss this complex and controversial issue, at least briefly. Readers who prefer to be spared the technical details should skim quickly over the next two or three pages.

Now the hard part. If firms try to maximize profits in the manner generally assumed by economic theory, they cannot shift the tax in the *short run* because all their decisions about prices and quantities remain the same. Only if they pursue some sort of "cost plus margin" or "targeted after-tax rate of return" strategy—which seems implausible outside special situations like regulated public utilities or collusion among small numbers of oligopolistic firms—can they possibly shift the tax to workers or consumers. Any effort to do so would ordinarily allow competing firms to outsell their products or hire away their workers.[39]

In the *long run,* however, an unshifted corporate income tax clearly affects investment by reducing the rate of return on corporate equity. There is less incentive to invest in corporations, and such investment presumably declines until after-tax rates of return are equalized with the noncorporate sector. If the supply of capital is fixed, this means that investments are made in less productive noncorporate firms, reducing the marginal rate of return so that the tax is borne by capital in general.[40] But if total investment declines, then the productivity of labor decreases, and at least part of the tax may be borne by workers. Just to complicate matters further, if investment is financed by borrowing—a more and more common procedure—then the deductibility of business interest eliminates these investment effects, and the tax is wholly borne by the owners of the corporation.[41]

And to complicate things still more, all the above reasoning assumes that corporations are operating within a closed national economy. But in a more open economy, with capital now much more mobile across international borders, the logic is somewhat different. If one country imposes a higher corporate income tax than another, capital may be able to flee to the lower-tax country. By this process, capital may relocate until the real after-tax rate of return is equalized worldwide. If so, the tax will be borne by other factors of production—the most important being labor, affected in the form of lower real wages.[42] This sort of "supply side" reasoning, plus somewhat specious complaints about "double taxation," was used to justify Reagan-era corporate tax cuts.[43]

All this theoretical confusion and controversy has not been resolved by empirical evidence, which appears to be inconclusive. Over time, there has not been a growth in unincorporated business at the expense of corporations (the corporate form simply has too many advantages); quite the contrary. Nor have after-tax rates of return gone down since substantial corporate taxes were imposed—in fact, they are much higher. But exactly what this means in terms of what *would have happened* without the tax is unclear, as is the long-run effect of the tax.[44]

Uncertainty about the impact of globalization affects not only the *incidence* of corporate taxation (that is, whom the tax falls on, who actually pays it), but also the question of whether international economic competition now imposes constraints on the feasibility of the tax. The logic of globalization may pinch more tightly here than with other taxes. Corporate profits are so directly involved that it seems plausible that some capital flight, some shifting of the tax to other factors of production, and hence some competition among nations to lower corporate taxes, may well occur.

As we have noted, the ease with which accounting tricks can shift a multinational firm's apparent profits from one country to another may reduce the feasibility of imposing corporate income taxes, even without any profound investment-flight effects. But the importance of such effects has almost certainly been overstated. For one thing, corporate taxes do not represent only costs; they bring corresponding benefits through government programs that increase returns on capital by raising labor productivity, providing infrastructure, and making life more attractive to workers and executives. For another, capital that seeks low taxes without the political risks and special costs of developing countries (e.g., corruption and political instability) may not have many places to flee to. An estimate of the effective marginal tax rates on corporate-source income in nine advanced industrial countries, using identical ("King-Fullerton") methodologies, puts the United States close to average. Moreover, trends between 1980 and 1990 show no race to the bottom at all: three countries (Australia, France, and Germany) cut their effective tax rates, but six countries (Canada, Italy, Japan, Sweden, the United Kingdom, and the United States) actually *increased* the overall effective tax rates on corporate-source income.[45] There is no evidence to warrant overheated rhetoric against corporate taxes. Nation states—especially when they control a huge market like that of the United States—are not impotent even in the realm of corporate taxation.

Because of theoretical and empirical uncertainties about the corporate tax, scholars interested in the effects of taxes on income inequality generally offer alternative estimates based on different incidence assumptions. Pechman and Okner, for example, found that in 1966 the corporate income tax may have been either highly progressive or just about proportional, depending on which set of assumptions was used.[46] Pechman found essentially the same thing for 1970, 1975, 1980, and 1985.[47] In any case, however, the sharply declining level of effective tax rates has meant that the corporate income tax has brought in less and less money—and has therefore had less and less potential impact on the income distribution. The same point is made by Don Fullerton and Diane Rogers's lifetime income–based study, which used a sophisticated general equilibrium model to conclude that the corporate income tax took about the same proportion of people's income across the whole income range. The distribution of effective rates was fairly flat or somewhat "U-shaped"—actually highest on the *lowest* income category—mainly because the tax was largely offset by tax credits, accelerated depreciation, and interest deductions on debt, so that there was little net "source-side" impact to fall on owners of capital.[48] We would add that this finding for 1984— right at the Reagan-era nadir of corporate taxation—should not be taken to mean that the corporation income tax could not be *made* progressive by closing some or all of the many loopholes.

A fair tax system would integrate personal and corporate income taxes in a way that ensured a high degree of progressivity, while minimizing the problem of capital flight or accounting trickery. There is an argument for maintaining some level of corporate taxation to pay for the many legal advantages granted by the corporate form and to make sure that corporate profits are not entirely accumulated and kept free of taxation. But heavier reliance on the personal income tax has two major advantages: the personal tax can easily and indisputably be made highly progressive, and—with the appropriate provisions—it could capture the gains of individuals who choose to live in the United States even if they send their capital (or paper profits) elsewhere. The best solution would probably be to tax corporate profits—whether or not distributed as dividends—directly to their corporate stockholders, either by making unrealized as well as all realized capital gains subject to the individual income tax or by treating corporations like partnerships and allocating all their net profits and losses among the individual stockholders. Either way, the income of the highest-income individuals could be taxed at much higher rates than at present, and there would be much less opportunity to exploit the existence of low-tax countries.[49]

Payroll Taxes

While corporate income taxes have been producing a smaller and smaller proportion of federal revenue, a larger and larger share has been coming from the payroll taxes associated with Social Security, Medicare, and Unemployment Insurance (remember figure 5.1). Already by the mid-1990s, in fact, more than three-quarters of all Social Security–covered workers paid more in payroll taxes than in any other tax, even the income tax. There is not much dispute about who bears the payroll tax burden: workers do. Not only do they pay the roughly 7.5 percent of covered wages that is called the "employee's" share, but also most economists agree that workers also pay the roughly 7.5 percent "employers'" share (which is not mentioned on pay slips) because employers treat it as simply another cost of labor and subtract it from wages.[50]

Among advanced industrial countries, U.S. payroll taxes are not in fact all that high. At about $4 for each hour worked by manufacturing workers, our payroll tax rate in the mid-1990s somewhat exceeded those of Britain, Canada, and Japan, but was less than the rates in most of Scandinavia, the Low Countries, or Germany (the top payroll taxer, at $6.26 per manufacturing hour).[51] That suggests there is room to raise these taxes, if necessary, to bolster Social Security and Medicare.

But there is no substantial doubt about whether payroll taxes are progressive or regressive. They may be somewhat progressive at the very lowest income levels (since people without any earned income do not pay[52]), but over the upper part of the income range, they are *quite regressive*. This is because payroll taxes are imposed at a flat percentage rate, but the covered income is "capped" at a fixed dollar level beyond which there is no tax at all. The Old Age, Survivors, and Disability Insurance (OASDI) cap, which is automatically adjusted annually for rises in average wages, was set at $76,200 in 2000. Thus a person who earned $80,000 or so in covered wages or salary paid the maximum Social Security payroll tax: an "employee's share" of $4,724, exactly the same dollar amount as paid by a person who earned $800,000 per year, or $8 million, or $800 million.[53] As a percentage of people's income, therefore, the fixed amount of tax is far lower for the wealthy than for the working poor or the middle class. A payroll tax amounting to 15 percent of income for someone who earns under $80,000, for example, will take only 7.5 percent of income from a $160,000 earner, less than 1 percent (0.75 percent) from someone earning $1.6 million, and a barely detectable percentage from the fortunate person taking in $16 million a year.

Thus estimates of the incidence of payroll taxes generally show them to be somewhat progressive in low income ranges, proportional for quite a while, and then very regressive.[54] (Fullerton and Rogers, analyzing incidence on a *lifetime-income* basis and taking into account presumed general-equilibrium shifting to consumers, found that payroll taxes in 1984 were quite regressive over all the income groups studied.[55])

To be sure, one should not exaggerate the regressivity. Payroll taxes are probably roughly proportional, rather than regressive, over a range that includes most Americans' incomes. Further, effective progressivity at the very bottom of the scale has been increased by the EITC refundable tax credit for part of the first few thousand dollars earned (though this applies mainly to persons with children and does not help those without any earnings). And regressivity at the top end has been reduced somewhat by regular increases in the level of the "cap" on income subject to tax (though automatic adjustments have no appreciable effect on progressivity in terms of *relative* wages, as calculated among the proportions of the population at the higher and lower ends of the scale[56]). Still, the relatively small numbers of people at the top end of the scale, where payroll taxes are regressive, earn enormous amounts of income free of the tax. This is why—as we noted in chapter 4— altogether removing the cap and imposing Social Security payroll taxes on *all* wage and salary income, while also paying full benefits on that income according to current benefit formulas, would provide enough new revenue to make up fully *two-thirds* of the trillions of dollars of Social Security revenue shortfalls that pessimists project will occur over the next seventy-five years.[57] It would also make the payroll tax proportional, rather than regressive.

One apparently plausible reason to question whether payroll taxes are really regressive comes from the contention that they should not be viewed as taxes at all, but rather as *contributions* to the Social Security, Medicare, and Unemployment Insurance programs that they fund. Such a view is consistent with the social insurance logic of those programs. It leads to the conclusion that the programs, with taxes and benefits taken together, are somewhat progressive—but significantly less so than when benefits alone are considered. Similarly, to remove payroll taxes from consideration with other taxes would make the whole tax system look more progressive. But one good reason for treating them at least partly as taxes is that, during recent decades, many hundreds of billions of dollars in surplus payroll taxes have been used (in effect) for general government programs; it makes sense to treat their source as a tax that produces general revenue.[58] Moreover, as we face the prospect of baby-boom retirements with possible payroll tax shortfalls for funding social insurance programs, one option is to use general revenues to meet the temporary emergency. It makes sense to compare the distributive justice or injustice of increasing payroll taxes with that of using the more progressive individual income tax.

In the end, either view is justifiable so long as the analyst picks one and sticks with it. We can say that the Social Security contribution-and-benefit system is less progressive than the benefits seem by themselves because the contributions are regressive. Or we can note that payroll taxes are regressive. We should not double count by asserting both things at once, but we should certainly not undercount by omitting payroll contributions/taxes from discussion of *both* social insurance and taxation. The latter trick has been used more than once to make the U.S. combination of social insurance and taxes look more progressive than it actually is.

Federal Excise Taxes

Federal excise taxes are essentially sales taxes imposed at the federal level on gasoline, alcohol, tobacco, firearms, and a few other goods. Excise taxes, along with tariff duties on imported goods, were once the main sources of federal revenue, but they have shrunk to a very small fraction: they provided only about 3.7 percent of all revenues in 2000 and a bit less in subsequent years.[59]

The chief arguments in favor of excise taxes are, first, that they are easy to administer and, second, that they can be used to discourage harmful behavior like drinking, smoking, and shooting people. Taxes on cigarettes, in particular, have been raised in recent years in some states (though increases have been fiercely and successfully resisted at the federal level), partly in order to raise money to defray the public health costs of smoking and to help save people from the deadly consequences of getting the addictive habit (studies indicate that by raising cigarette prices, substantial taxes do in fact somewhat cut purchases). The logic of taxing alcohol is much the same. Similarly, a high tax on gasoline would help pay for the public costs of driving (wear and tear on roads, congestion, air pollution) and would reduce unnecessary driving.

Most European countries have followed this strategy, and many have used the revenue for mass transit and health programs that have an egalitarian impact. Curiously, however—perhaps because of the enormous political power in the United States of the oil and gas, automobile, concrete, and road construction industries—our gasoline taxes are very low and have been continually eroded by inflation. Virtually every advanced country but the United States and New Zealand has gasoline taxes that constitute more than half the price of gas at the pump. Their taxes are much higher than ours (usually four to eight times as high) and seriously discourage gas guzzling.[60] Also of very minor importance (perhaps for similar political reasons) are U.S. taxes on firearms, which have been imposed only on machine guns and certain short-barreled weapons. Discouragement of firearms through high taxes would seem to be a singularly appropriate social use for tax policy.

The chief argument against U.S. excise taxes, now that "luxury taxes" (on furs, yachts, and the like) have mostly been abolished (why?), is that the remaining excises are very sharply regressive throughout the whole income scale. On the average, millionaires do not drive a lot more miles, smoke a lot more cigarettes, or drink a lot more booze than ordinary workers do; in fact, they actually tend to consume less alcohol and tobacco—so they do not generally pay many more dollars of taxes on those goods. But a given dollar amount constitutes a much smaller fraction of total income for high-income people than for low. The arithmetic here is much like that of a payroll tax with a very low cap on taxable income. Excise taxes are even more regressive, though, because they hit people who have little or no earned income at all. The burden of, say, $600 worth of excise taxes is quite substantial—10 percent—on someone who makes only $6,000 per year, but it is only 1 percent on someone who makes $60,000. The burden just about vanishes from sight (at 0.1 percent of income) for someone making $600,000.

There are not many disputes about the incidence of excise taxes: consumers of the taxed goods do pay. Over the range of actual tax rates, demand for goods like gasoline and cigarettes is generally rather *inelastic* (that is, not enough people quit buying the taxed goods to cut much into manufacturers' and distributors' profits), and supply is generally *elastic*. That means that the taxes raise prices to consumers without much reducing the quantity they buy.

Since consumers pay, practically all estimates of excise tax incidence show sharp regressivity. In 1985, for example (according to Pechman), the lowest twentieth of income earners paid about 5.4 percent of their income in federal excise taxes, while the top twentieth paid only 0.4 percent.[61] High regressivity is also (for similar reasons) characteristic of the much bigger general sales taxes and many versions of "value added" taxes that are sometimes proposed as substitutes for the federal income tax. Such a change would dramatically undercut the already tepid progressivity of the federal tax system.

To be sure, efforts to calculate tax incidence on the basis of smoothed-out, *lifetime* income tend to make excise and sales taxes look somewhat less regressive. Such analyses figure that people who are poor for just a few years should be seen as paying taxes in those years at the lower percentage rate corresponding to their (higher) long-term income, rather than at a high percentage of those years' actual (lower) income. But the "permanent income hypothesis" on which lifetime calculations are premised does not perfectly describe reality, the data are incomplete, and the rate calculations are questionable. Even if they were correct, we should not ignore the real burden that high taxes in low-income years impose. Higher expected earnings in the future are not much help in dealing with such burdens. People cannot generally borrow against them, for example.[62]

Estate and Gift Taxes

Federal estate and gift taxes are potentially quite different from excise taxes because they are (or could be) very progressive. They could easily be designed to apply heavily to the gifts and bequests of very wealthy people and little or not at all to others. Since wealth is acquired through cooperative social effort and since government helps property owners in many ways, most people consider moderate estate or inheritance taxes to be quite appropriate.

If we really believe in equal opportunity, and if we want to break up dynasties of economic and political power, much higher estate and gift taxes may be in order. Indeed, it may be difficult to justify allowing the inheritance of wealth at all. Why should a rich person's heir, who did nothing to earn the wealth, get an enormous head start that may deaden his or her own efforts? The most plausible justification for allowing inheritance of intangible property would seem to be the practical but limited aim of providing additional incentives (the pleasure of making future bequests) for those who do produce and accumulate wealth. But this justification is not very compelling; there are already strong incentives to enjoy the power, respect, and personal consumption that wealth brings.[63]

Existing U.S. estate and gift taxes do have a significantly progressive structure. Estate and gift tax rates are made the same ("unified") in the hope of hindering people from avoiding taxes by choosing whether to give or not give away property before death. The nominal rates are somewhat graduated (though much less so than in the past), rising from 33 percent on estates just above the exemption level to 39 percent on taxable estates larger than $21 million. More important, because the tax applies only above a high exemption level, the tax affects only the wealthiest Americans. Only the top 1.4 percent of estates, 32,000 of them, paid any estate taxes at all in 1995.[64]

But the tax is not nearly so heavy or so progressive as it looks. The high exemption level—$665,000 in 1998, scheduled to rise to $1 million ($2 million for couples) by 2006—that restricts the tax to the very wealthiest Americans means that many large estates escape taxation altogether. Actual effective tax rates are rather low because of the exemption, as well as various deductions and credits (mainly for charitable contributions and state taxes paid), and because the portion of estates that goes to spouses is exempt. Official Internal Revenue Service figures show that in the mid-1990s, estates under $1 million paid only 3 percent, those under $2.5 million paid 12.5 percent, and the rate rose to 31 percent before dropping to only 22 percent for estates of $20 million or more, which have big deductible contributions to charity. But those percentages apply to *net* estates, after subtracting expenses and amounts retained by spouses.[65] Taking a broader view, for one year that Pechman studied, on the $34.1 billion reported in taxable estates, just 14.7 percent was actually paid in taxes. Even gross estates in the $5 million to $10 million range paid only an average of 14.9 percent, and those over $10 million paid a bit less.[66]

Pechman's figures, too, actually *overstate* the proportions of wealth that are paid in taxes because the figures refer to estates as they existed and were reported at the time of death. But this is only a fraction of the wealth that actually passes from one generation to the next. High-income taxpayers can afford the services of skillful tax lawyers and accountants, who help them avoid many taxes, particularly by transferring their wealth before death so that it never shows up in taxable estates. Careful planning can avoid gift taxes as well.

One simple technique is to repeatedly give carefully calibrated, medium-sized gifts to one's heirs for a number of years before death. A husband and wife can each give up to $10,000 every year to as many different people (including children and grandchildren) as they want, entirely free of gift tax. Over a period of twenty years, a gift each year of $20,000 to each of six children and grandchildren would add up to the tidy sum of $2.4 million (plus accrued interest)—entirely free of taxes. This is one reason that gift tax revenues have been minuscule.

More sophisticated devices for the transfer of truly large fortunes include various kinds of "generation-skipping" trusts and charitable foundations. Such techniques have the disadvantage of restricting control by grantors and heirs; some old-time robber barons who set up foundations years ago would probably be appalled at how their money is being spent. Still, smart lawyers can generally find ways out of most estate and gift taxes for the very wealthy, while preserving substantial control from beyond the grave.[67]

The extent to which great wealth escapes taxation in the United States is surprising, especially at a time when inequalities in wealth have increased dramatically. The fairness of the tax system would be increased by more serious taxation of large estates and gifts.

State and Local Taxes

Historically the largest single source of revenue for state and local governments, taken together, has been the property tax. Property taxes—imposed mainly on houses and commercial real estate and mostly devoted to funding the public schools—account for more than three-quarters of local taxes and about one-third of combined state and local taxes. They amounted to about $226 billion in 1998.[68] The second largest, but rapidly growing, source is general sales taxes imposed on retail purchases. In third place—but also increasingly important—are state income taxes, which differ from the federal version in that most make less effort at progressivity; some set a flat tax rate on all income above a rather low threshold level. We will discuss them in order of size.

The Property Tax

Property taxes, like the corporate income tax, have bedeviled and divided students of tax incidence. The traditional view was that property taxes are a combination of a tax on land and a tax on structures, with the tax on land borne by landowners and the tax on structures shifted in whole or part (in the form of higher rents) to tenants, who tend to have much lower incomes. But the "new view"—no longer so new—is that the tax is a combination of a uniform national tax on capital and an excise on local capital. If so, indications are that the tax is in large part borne by the owners of capital, who tend to be wealthy and to have high incomes.[69] The more plausible assumption for purposes of comparing the incidence of one tax with that of another (that is, dealing with widespread use or nonuse, increase or decrease, of the property tax) is that this tax falls mainly on the owners of capital in general.

Empirical studies that accept this view of incidence generally conclude that the tax is somewhat progressive, at least at the high end of the income scale. Pechman and Okner, for example, with their broad measure of income, found that in 1966 the property tax was more or less proportional— at around 2.5 percent—in the low- and middle-income ranges; it then rose fairly sharply in the high-income range, reaching 9.6 percent on incomes over $500,000 and 10.1 percent on incomes over $1 million.[70] In his updated studies on tax incidence over the next two decades, Pechman found that the effective rates were mildly progressive every year. But the level of average rates declined across the board, so that the tax came to have less total redistributive effect. In 1970, for example, effective rates ran from 2 or 3 percent in the low- and middle-income ranges up to 8.9 percent for the top 1 percent of income earners, but in 1985, the effective rates ran from just 0.7 percent at the bottom to only 4.4 percent at the top.[71]

Fullerton and Rogers's analysis of tax incidence based on *lifetime* rather than annual incomes supports this finding of substantial progressivity at the top of the income range, but they also found high rates at the very bottom. This possible "U-shaped" incidence results from a combination of three patterns: (1) the tendency of high-income people to have more capital (relative to their incomes), which is hit by the tax; (2) a tendency of middle-income people's incomes to peak late in life, causing them to save less and to be taxed relatively less on capital than lower- or higher-income people; and (3) a tendency of low-income people to spend a bigger share of their income on housing, the cost of which is raised—in this model—by the property tax.[72] But this alleged "uses-side" effect on low-income people's housing costs is controversial and depends on assumptions that do not make the whole burden of the tax fall on capital in general. Moreover, lifetime incidence studies treat everyone as a rational life-cycle planner who saves up, spends down, and uses perfect capital markets to smooth out lifetime incomes. They ignore the very real burdens on people who are hit by capricious fluctuations of income, which cannot be remedied simply by borrowing, since predicted future earning are uncertain and are not fully accepted as security for loans. Tax burdens on people high and low in *annual* income are relevant.

In any case, the "property tax revolt" of the 1970s and 1980s, using populist rhetoric, but propelled largely by wealthy property owners,[73] led to a decline in property taxes and increased reliance on other taxes, which almost certainly increased the regressivity of state and local taxes.

All empirical studies face the problem of calculating how much people actually pay in property taxes—in the simple sense of what their tax bills are, before any shifting—since self-reports are not always accurate. Statistical attributions based on housing quality and the like miss many variations in assessed valuations and in actual taxes paid. Assessment practices vary widely (a multimillion-dollar mansion in Bel Air may pay less than half as much in taxes per square foot as a modest home in middle-class Baldwin Hills). Expensive homes may often be valued far below their market worth, and businesses—particularly those that get states competing against each other for their presence—often win lucrative tax concessions. These vagaries of administration probably lead to lower taxes on high-income people, and less progressivity, than standard studies tend to reveal.[74]

Property taxes could be made more progressive and more fair by better standardizing assessment practices so that owners of equal-value property are treated equally and so that the wealthiest property owners do not escape full taxation.

State and Local Sales Taxes

Sales and excise taxes of various sorts are the biggest single source of revenue for *states,* bringing them about $216 billion in 1997,[75] and they play a significant part for many local governments as well.

There is not much doubt about who bears the burden of general sales taxes: consumers do. (The tax rates and the elasticity of demand are not generally high enough to appreciably reduce demand and shift part of the burden to producers.) Since low-income people spend a larger share of their income on consumption, a general sales tax that covers nearly all consumption goods falls most heavily on those with low incomes. Sales taxes are clearly regressive.

Virtually all empirical studies confirm this. Pechman and Okner found that in 1966 sales and excise taxes taken together were quite regressive, with effective rates declining steadily from about 9 percent on the lowest-income group to barely 1 percent on incomes of $500,000 and over.[76] Pechman's studies over the next two decades found similar effective rates and a similarly high degree of regressivity in every year studied.[77] The Fullerton and Rogers lifetime incidence study probably understated sales tax regressivity, ignoring heavy tax burdens on the temporarily poor and exaggerating burdens on the rich (by omitting unrealized capital gains from their income base). But even that study found sales and excise taxes, taken together, to be substantially regressive over 90 percent of the population.[78]

To be sure, states have made some efforts to limit the regressivity of sales taxes—for example, by exempting from tax essentials like food, utilities, and prescription drugs, which are particularly important to low-income people.[79] Metcalf's lifetime-income incidence study actually claimed that these exemptions, together with the elimination of federal tax deductibility (which used to favor high-income people), have made sales taxes *progressive* on the average.[80] But not only does this study tend to understate sales tax regressivity for the same reasons that we have noted most lifetime analyses do, but also other flaws like the use of annual consumption as a very rough proxy for lifetime incomes make the results particularly questionable.[81]

Again, the increased reliance by states on sales rather than property taxes has almost certainly increased the regressivity of the state and local tax system. A study by Citizens for Tax Justice identified the "terrible ten" states that most highly tax the poor and middle class, sparing the rich. The terrible ten were Washington (where the poorest fifth of families paid 17.1 percent of their income in taxes, while the top 1 percent of families paid only 3.9 percent), Florida, Texas, South Dakota, Tennessee, Louisiana, Pennsylvania, Illinois, Alabama, and Michigan. Most of these states rely heavily for their revenue on sales and excise taxes.[82]

State Income Taxes

A relatively small but rising portion of state and local tax revenue comes from state-level income taxes, which produced 28.9 percent of state tax collections in 1980 and 33.7 percent in 1990 (about 22 percent of combined state and local taxes in 1990).[83] But these taxes are not nearly so progressive as the federal version. They often apply a flat tax rate across most or all of the range of taxable income, which makes it a proportional tax. Some states have excluded capital gains or taken other measures that tend to produce regressivity.

Recently, however, some states have broadened their income bases, increased standard deductions, and eliminated various tax shelters, making their income tax systems more progressive. There is a great deal of variation from state to state. A few states have strongly progressive rate structures. California's marginal rates, for example, rise steadily with income, from just 1 percent on the first $10,000 to 9.3 percent on everything over $67,000. Iowa, Montana, New Jersey, and Ohio also have quite progressive income taxes, as do states like Vermont and Rhode Island that piggyback on the federal tax by simply charging a percentage of one's federal liability. But other states have straight proportional systems: Illinois, Indiana, Michigan, and Pennsylvania, for example, impose a flat 3 or 4 percent tax on all income. And several of the "terrible ten" regressive states have no income taxes at all.[84]

It is very difficult to do empirical analyses of the overall incidence of state income taxes, with their bewildering variety of rates and structures. Few scholars have tried to do so separately from the larger federal income tax. One effort, by Metcalf, indicates that—whether income is computed on an annual or a lifetime basis—state and local income taxes were substantially progressive (though not very high) in both 1984 and 1989. There was some drop in top-income effective rates—and hence a drop in progressivity—between the two years, despite state reforms and despite the decreased value of federal deductibility after 1986.[85] But these findings must be taken with caution because of weak income data, as well as the problems with its lifetime estimates noted above.

Even if state income taxes have become somewhat progressive on the average, there is reason to doubt that they can ever become a major instrument of income distribution. Really high effective rates on high-income people would be too easy to evade by transferring income—or, if necessary, physically moving—to lower-tax states. It is hard for any subnational government unit in our federal system to enact strongly redistributive policies, as Paul Peterson's seminal book *City Limits* made clear.[86] States are somewhat better off than localities in this regard, but only the federal government, dealing with the whole American population, can hope to engage in substantial redistribution of income or wealth. Yes, the United States as a whole also faces competition from other countries, but the U.S. economy is large and can be treated as at least partly closed. For people who want to avoid progressive taxes, it is a lot harder to move from the United States to Mexico than from Vermont to New Hampshire.

Still, it is far better—in terms of effects on poverty and inequality—for states to rely on income or property taxes, rather than sales taxes, for their revenue. Even the weakest state income taxes at least have the advantage of producing substantial revenue in a fashion that is proportional or somewhat progressive, in contrast to regressive sales taxes. And if state income taxes are made seriously progressive, like those of California or the federal-piggybacking states, they can have a significant egalitarian effect.[87]

Taxes and Inequality

When all federal, state, and local taxes are taken together, they apparently do not have much net effect on income inequality in the United States. The progressivity of federal (and, to some degree, state) income taxes, together with the milder progressivity of the small and declining property and corporate income taxes, is largely offset by the regressivity of payroll, sales, and excise taxes.

Pechman and Okner's classic study, which considered eight different sets of incidence assumptions about the various taxes, found that in 1966, even under the most progressive ("1c") assumptions, the total effective rates of all taxes were nearly proportional over most of the income range. Rates rose from 22.6 percent on $5,000–10,000 incomes to just 26.4 percent on incomes in the $30,000 to $50,000 range (remember that, in 1966, $50,000 was a lot of money). The effective rates then climbed substantially at the top, reaching 49.3 percent on incomes over $1 million. Under the least progressive ("3b") assumptions, there was virtually no progressivity at all—effective rates went from 28.1 percent on the very lowest incomes to 29.0 percent on the very highest, with a bit of a dip in the rates for middle-income people.[88] If—as our pluralistic instincts suggest—the truth lies somewhere between these extremes, the total tax system, taken as a whole, was very mildly progressive.

Pechman's updates of these estimates over the next two decades showed little change except right at the end of the period he studied, in 1985. In that year, at the peak of Reaganism, any progressivity in U.S. taxes had almost completely vanished. Even under the most optimistic incidence assumptions, effective rates rose from 21.9 percent on the first income decile to just 25.5 percent on the top 1 percent of incomes. Under the least progressive assumptions, the tax system had become significantly regressive.[89]

Presumably some of the earlier modest progressivity of the system has been restored by post-1985 changes in federal tax law. On the other hand, the increasing reliance on payroll and sales taxes, and the shift from federal toward state and local spending and taxing, does not bode well for tax progressivity. A number of states during the 1990s appear to have made their taxes more regressive, often by raising sales taxes during years of economic stringency and then cutting income—rather than sales—taxes during better times.[90]

Fullerton and Rogers's lifetime-income findings are quite similar to those of the original Pechman and Okner annual-income study. They found that overall U.S. taxes are roughly proportional across middle-income groups, though progressive at the very bottom and at the very top of the income distribution. Total effective rates (measured as lifetime "equivalent variation" from a proportional tax on labor endowment) were about 6 percentage points and 11 percentage points higher in the next-to-top and top income categories than in the lowest lifetime-income category.[91] Such rate differences, of course, come nowhere near the sharp progressivity that we associate with the old published rates of the federal income tax.

What should we make of all this? The bottom line is that the system of U.S. taxes, taken as a whole, does *not* substantially contribute to the redistribution of incomes. Taxes do not take nearly enough from the rich to bring lower-income people up to a minimal middle-class living standard or to provide them and their children with equal economic opportunities, let alone achieve equality with the very wealthy.

In the mid-1990s, in fact, Congressional Budget Office data showed that the top 1 percent of highest-income American families received fully *11.4 percent* of all the *after-tax* income in the country, just as much as was received by the entire bottom 35 percent of the population put together. After-tax income shares had become far more unequal since the late 1970s. While the top 1 percent of families enjoyed an average gain of 72 percent in their after-tax income between 1977 and 1994, the bottom *two-fifths* of all American families actually suffered a *decline* in after-tax income.[92] Clearly the U.S. tax system had not reversed, or even much slowed, the inequality express.

If we want more equality, we should work for a more progressive tax system. Efforts for greater tax progressivity, however, are bound to run up against obstacles from the same political forces that produced the current tax system. We need to consider just what those political factors are in order to see how they might be overcome.

Tax Politics

Tax policy in the United States has emerged through a long historical process in which changing revenue needs have interacted with several political factors. The preferences of the general public have been important, especially in times of crisis or highly visible conflict, and especially when the public has been mobilized by a popularly based political party. But in more normal times, the wishes of well-organized interest groups—especially powerful business corporations—tend to prevail.

For the first hundred years or so of U.S. history, the very limited revenue needs of the small federal government were met by low, easy-to-collect (but generally regressive) import duties and excises. Tax politics largely concerned which economic interests and geographical regions would bear the burdens. Grain farmers, for example, did not like excise taxes on distilled spirits (it took troops to put down the 1794 "Whiskey Rebellion").[93] During much of the nineteenth century, Southern agriculturalists affiliated with various incarnations of the Democratic Party—who wanted low tariffs and free trade in order to export their produce abroad and to buy cheap imports—repeatedly conflicted (even to the point of trying to "nullify" federal legislation) with Northern manufacturers who sought high protective tariffs and who worked through the Federalist and later the Republican Party.[94]

The increasing industrialization of America meant that more revenue was needed to fund a growing federal government. Enormous amounts of tax revenue were also needed to respond to national emergencies like the Civil War, World War I, the Great Depression, and World War II. Each of those crises contributed to an enduring transformation of the tax system. In each case, political leaders won popular consent to great financial sacrifice by emphasizing the *fairness* of new taxes and by linking them to moves toward democracy and equality in American society.[95]

Thus the United States first experimented with a progressive income tax during the Civil War. The move from the 1890s through 1913 to reinstate such a tax was largely energized by Populist, Progressive, and Socialist movements outside the two-party system.[96] But the 1913 tax legislation enacted (with bipartisan support) by Woodrow Wilson and the Democrats was only mildly progressive. A truly progressive personal income tax, along with a corporate tax and an excess profits tax, resulted only from the sudden need for new revenue and for broad public support in World War I.

The new tax regime was just trimmed, not replaced, during the business- and Republican-dominated 1920s. Much more progressive taxation was enacted—again because of needs for both revenue and public support—under Democratic leadership responding to the Great Depression. (Franklin Roosevelt's New Deal helped establish the modern pattern of Republican-Democratic disagreement over distributive justice in tax and other policies.) In World War II, once more for the sake of revenue and public support, the income tax was kept progressive, while it was also broadened to impose heavy taxes on working people and the middle class.[97]

In the times of crisis that have determined the main outlines of our modern tax system, then, the wishes of the general public—highly aware of tax issues and crucially needed to support policy changes—have played an important part. In more normal times, however, tax politics tends to revert to arcane, low-visibility struggles in which special interests often get their way. Over several decades after World War II, tax progressivity was eroded as business groups won increasingly generous depreciation allowances, tax credits, and other special provisions. Many small loopholes were initiated in low-visibility settings (the proverbial midnight end-of-session meetings of the House Ways and Means Committee, for example), where business lobbyists could prevail with no one the wiser.[98]

A sometimes-more-benign variant of low-visibility tax politics has involved the quiet enactment of special *tax expenditures* for social purposes. We consider some aspects of this "hidden welfare state" (the Earned Income Tax

Credit, for example, and subsidies of pensions and retirement accounts) to be quite positive. As Christopher Howard points out, however, the reliance on support from moderate-to-conservative lawmakers and from organized groups of employers and providers has sometimes deflected these measures away from their ostensible social aims and subsidized special interests instead. Social policies embedded in the tax code also tend to escape accountability and control, and tend to crowd out more direct programs.[99]

Some regressive tax changes have occurred when Democratic presidents including Kennedy and Johnson, losing interest in redistributive tax measures—and indeed embracing supply-side, economic-growth logic of the sort voiced in the 1920s by Andrew Mellon—actively worked for the investment tax credit and other breaks for business.[100]

More recently, too, major changes in tax policy have lacked the high level of public involvement and the appeals to equity and progressivity found in the early struggles over the enactment and expansion of the income tax. In 1981, for example, the extraordinary tax cuts targeted mainly for business and the well-to-do (which produced more than a decade of large budget deficits) resulted from a remarkable outpouring of corporate campaign contributions, public relations campaigns, and lobbying, with help and orchestration from the Reagan administration.[101] The Tax Reform Act of 1986 managed, against all conventional wisdom, to overcome the short-term interests and the frantic efforts of many business lobbyists.[102] But it did so (in a bipartisan, technocratic fashion) mainly in order to make efficiency gains—not to increase equity or progressivity, except at the very bottom of the income scale. Its flatter rate structure ratified the move away from a progressive income tax. Its broader income base had only the *potential*—not yet much realized—to permit a new system of progressive rates with fewer loopholes.

There have been some limited signs of renewed Democratic Party interest in progressive taxation, including the important Clinton administration–initiated expansion of the EITC (which had the advantage of pleasing many Republicans with its work incentives, at the same time that it has greatly helped low-income working people and moderately increased the battered progressivity of the income tax). In the Clinton years, the two-bracket structure of the income tax was also stretched out to a more progressive four or five brackets of effective rates, peaking at about 40 percent. These modest measures certainly did not transform the unequal distribution of Americans' incomes, but they did demonstrate that there was room to make U.S. taxes more progressive without harming the economy. Taxes were raised a bit and made more progressive (helping to balance the budget). What followed, contrary to alarmist predictions, was not an economic crash, but rather a sustained economic boom.

The experience of the last century suggests that major increases in tax progressivity occur only when the public is central to the process—when, as E. E. Schattschneider put it, the "scope of conflict" is broad—and when policy makers are forced to pay close attention to what citizens want.[103] There is survey evidence that most Americans favor fair and moderately redistributive taxation; most oppose loopholes and want taxes to reflect people's ability to pay. (Most are also willing to pay *more* taxes to fund programs they favor.)[104] But the public's views carry little weight in normal, low-visibility tax politics. Mobilization of the citizenry is essential. So is education of citizens about little-known features of the taxes that are imposed on them.

Popular mobilization is easiest to achieve in the compelling context of a national emergency and with strong leadership from a popularly based political party. But it may be possible for vigorous grassroots movements—and public interest groups like Citizens for Tax Justice—to stimulate political leadership in more normal times.

With popular mobilization, it might be possible to achieve the sorts of tax reforms that Donald Barlett and James Steel, among others, have urged: to apply the income tax to all income ("from whatever source derived," as the Sixteenth Amendment puts it), to end regressive itemized deductions like the mortgage interest credit, to restore higher rates (perhaps the 70 percent marginal rate) at the top of the income scale, to abolish the special treatment of capital gains (but we would allow income averaging and inflation indexing in order to avoid taxing illusory gains or applying excessive rates), and to tax all unrealized capital gains at death.[105] Similarly, at the state level, an aroused public might be able to push state governments to stop relying so heavily on regressive sales taxes and to move toward progressive income taxes.

6

Investing in Education

In dealing with poverty and inequality, it makes sense to put a high priority on training and education. So long as people's incomes are largely determined by the outcome of labor markets, the "human capital" that they carry within themselves—their skills, talents, work habits, and even their energy and aspirations—is crucial to the wages and salaries that they will earn. Human capital strongly affects the quality and quantity of work that people can do, which in turn strongly affects their incomes. And human capital is largely a result of education and training.

If we want people to rise out of *poverty,* therefore, a very natural strategy is to make sure that they get good education and job training so they can do valuable work that will earn them substantial incomes. It would be unrealistic to imagine that *all* poverty could be eradicated in this way (training cannot always overcome severe physical or mental disabilities, for example), but a great deal could be accomplished.

By the same token, education is absolutely critical to the idea of *equal opportunity.* If people are to have an "equal chance" to achieve economic well-being, they need to start the competitive race with equal skills and talents. In the information age, physical strength and stamina may no longer be so necessary, but cognitive and verbal skills are essential. To the extent that people are born significantly unequal or fall behind in infancy due to bad luck in their choice of parents and home environment, therefore, substantial *compensatory* education may be necessary in order to provide them with any semblance of an equal start. It is also important to work directly to prevent disadvantages of birth, nutrition, and health from taking their toll before formal schooling begins.[1]

Education is also important to any effort at achieving generally less *unequal incomes*. This has been particularly obvious since the sharp widening of income inequality associated with a so-called skills gap. During a twenty-year period that lasted into the 1990s, as the incomes of the most highly educated Americans leapt forward, the real wages of poorly educated, less-skilled workers stagnated or actually declined (recall the discussion in chapter 2). One obvious remedy—advocated by Robert Reich and many others—is to improve the skills of those at the bottom of the economic heap.[2]

There may be limits to how much can be accomplished through formal schooling. To some degree, for example, it is possible that educational credentials merely serve to sort people out (regardless of their actual productivity) among a relatively fixed set of jobs that provide highly unequal rewards. To the extent that this is true, and formal education is more concerned with credentials or "screening" than with productivity, increases in people's levels of education may merely reshuffle who gets lucky at job placement—perhaps just sharpening the impact of small distinctions in credentials—without actually reducing income inequality.[3] Indeed, it is not clear that most present or future U.S. jobs actually require a high level of formal education. Still, to the extent that the marginal product theory of wages is correct, to raise the skill levels of those with the lowest incomes should definitely raise their earnings and reduce income inequality.

This is a long chapter because it deals with much more than just formal schooling. First we analyze why education (broadly construed) is a matter for government, rather than solely private action. Then we reexamine the idea of equal opportunity, arguing for a broad understanding of what is required in order to give children equal chances in life. This takes us to the sensitive subject of family planning and how to discourage irresponsible childbearing, which can put children into near-hopeless situations. We move on to the importance of enforcing child support from disappearing fathers, the key role of adequate nutrition and health care for pregnant women and infants, the importance of school lunches and breakfasts, and the crucial part that can be played by preschooling, including Head Start and day care.

The chapter then turns to formal elementary and secondary schooling. We discuss the fact that American children face sharply unequal school opportunities, the evidence that money and other resources matter, and the crippling effect of residential segregation. Education research indicates that it is possible to improve the education of poor and working-class children if we are willing to make the effort. We also inquire into the effects of instituting charter schools, voucher programs, or other forms of school "choice," some of which may reduce inequality, while others exacerbate it. Next we go on to higher education, its effects, and problems of racial and other sorts of discrimination. Finally, we look at the decentralized politics of education and sum up our recommendations for improving schooling and children's opportunities generally.

As usual, if you get bogged down at any point, please skip ahead.

Who Should Provide Education?

Practically everyone agrees that education is important for combating poverty, providing equal opportunity, and reducing income inequality—and for other purposes as well, such as promoting economic growth and improving the civic competence of citizens in a democracy. The question becomes exactly how education should be produced and distributed. Precisely *who* should invest in precisely *what sorts* of efforts to improve human capital? Workers themselves? Employers? Parents? Philanthropies? Government? If government, at what level—national, state, or local? And by what means—by directly providing schooling, contracting out, or subsidizing private institutions?

Among some libertarians, the automatic answer is "Let the market handle it." Let people invest in their own human capital and that of their children. Let private entrepreneurs respond by competing to provide the kinds of education and training that people are willing to pay for. Give consumers a choice, and markets will ensure that successful educational institutions thrive and failures die out.

There is some evidence that market competition and consumer choice can in fact produce excellence in education. Exhibit "A" is the U.S. system of higher education. Our privately funded, tuition-charging colleges and universities—along with a number of outstanding public institutions—have become the envy of the world; they attract tuition-paying students from around the globe. At the elementary and secondary level, a relatively small but vigorous set of private schools has sometimes led the way in school quality. At the time of writing this book, there is considerable momentum behind the idea of extending competition and choice to more schools, through vouchers or charter schools—a topic that we will discuss later in this chapter.

At the same time, advocates of privatization in education must grapple with several uncomfortable facts. The vast preponderance of elementary and secondary education in the United States is in fact provided by government, mainly state and local government (later we will discuss the profound implications of state and local financing). At the end of the twentieth century, about 89 percent of all the 53 million U.S. elementary and secondary students were enrolled in public rather than private schools.[4] Also, private schools generally take in far too little tuition to meet their costs; they stay afloat only through subsidies from affluent alumni, from the government, and from churches—especially from the Roman Catholic Church, which runs about 79 percent of the private elementary and secondary schools in the United States and enrolls about 85 percent of the 6 million private students.[5] Even higher education in the United States is mostly provided by public institutions, which enroll 78 percent of the roughly 15 million college and university students.[6]

In light of this predominant government role, one might ask why a primarily public system of education emerged in the first place and why it has persisted for decades in the United States, as well as in every other advanced country around the world. Could there be good reasons for it?

Several theoretical considerations do indeed point toward good reasons for a strong government role in education. Take job training. Employers presumably know best what skills their workers need and have easy access to those workers; employers would seem to have incentives to build up their own workers' skills and productivity, and to do so in the most efficient possible fashion. Some do. But a serious problem of positive *externalities* prevents employers from investing in human capital to the extent that would be optimal. Workers, unlike machinery or buildings, can decide to take the company's investment and go somewhere else, thus benefiting the worker and the new employer, but not the company that made the investment. Involuntary servitude is unconstitutional, and even the most clever and ingenious measures short of slavery fail to guarantee that the employer-investor will capture the full value of investments in human capital. Not surprisingly most employers severely limit such investments.[7]

Historically, U.S. public schools first emerged in New England in the 1830s, just as industry was beginning to replace family farming and this externality problem was beginning to arise among nonfamily employers.[8]

So why don't workers invest in themselves? To some extent, they do. Many Americans make extraordinary efforts to learn useful skills, studying on their own, working up the skill ladder on the job, and paying their own way through college or trade school. Again, however, there are strong reasons to doubt that workers can make the level of investment in their own human capital that would be optimal for society. For one thing, many people simply do not have the money and cannot get it. Absent a government program (like the G.I. Bill or guaranteed loans), they cannot generally borrow what they need for investments of this sort, even if such investments would be very profitable, because *information asymmetries* and monitoring problems make private financial markets imperfect. The average person cannot borrow—at a reasonable rate of interest—enough to fund the training she or he needs because private lenders have no way to be sure that that person will be able to pay back the loan and no way to force him or her to do so. *Moral hazard* can be a problem as well; one who goes too deeply into debt for schooling may decide not to strive hard in order to pay it back. Default rates tend to be high.

Even government provision or guarantee of loans would not do the whole job because the benefits of job training go beyond their economic value to the individual who is trained. Positive externalities include economic growth and the future taxes that more productive workers will pay. Moreover, if we are concerned about poverty, inequality, and equality of opportunity, we should not force everyone to fund her or his own training. It makes sense to help people who have limited resources, without imposing enormous debt burdens that will keep them lagging far behind their more fortunate fellow citizens.

Compelling reasoning of this sort applies not only to specifically job-related training, but also to higher education generally. When it comes to college or postgraduate education, employers are mostly out of the picture. They can seldom take the risk of investing many tens of thousands of dollars in the education of a single individual. (They only occasionally do so, to add highly specialized skills to the toolkit of a few employees with well-demonstrated company loyalty.) By the same token, it is even harder for an individual to borrow tens of thousands of dollars for higher education than it is to borrow a few thousand for job training. And such a loan, if somehow finagled, would often impose an insurmountable repayment burden on the poor and people of modest resources. Parents sometimes help, but their ability and willingness to do so are highly variable.

The problems for elementary and secondary education are even more daunting. Employers are of very little help, except for occasional fringe benefits that they may give to employees' children. Children themselves are generally too young to get private loans even if such were available, and many are too immature and ill-informed to make sensible decisions about the role of education in their futures. Surely we do not want to charge six-year-olds with the duty to pick and pay for their first grade classes. For devotees of private markets, parents are the best hope; most parents love their children and are willing to make great sacrifices for them. But many parents lack the resources to pay for good schooling. (In the mid-1990s, full tuition at the average nonreligious, private elementary school was $4,693 per year, and the comparable secondary school tuition averaged $9,525: heavy burdens indeed for middle-class families with several children. Tuition at Catholic and other religious schools was considerably lower, but still burdensome.[9]) Besides lacking financial resources, many parents lack the necessary information, judgment, or willingness to squeeze their own consumption in order to invest in their children's education at a level that would be optimal for those children and for society as a whole.

In the case of elementary and secondary education especially, these considerations are joined by the need to provide several wholly or partly *public goods*. These include the common language, history, and culture that help create a coherent society; universal literacy and the basic knowledge to make democracy work; and the minimal levels of skill and orderly work habits to make people employable, not wholly dependent on private charity or public support. For these reasons (some of them, of course, sharply disputed), the arguments for government involvement in elementary and secondary education are especially compelling, and a major government role has been undertaken in all advanced societies as they have industrialized. In the United States, free and often compulsory public elementary schooling was widely established by the last quarter of the nineteenth century.[10]

It is sometimes assumed that there is less need for government involvement in preschooling. When two-parent families were the rule and at least one parent—usually the mother—generally stayed at home with the kids, parents could be counted on to do most of the work of caring for small children during the day and preparing them for formal schooling (at least this was the middle-class ideal; large numbers of farm, working-class, and minority women have always had to work). As single-parent families have become much more common, however, and as most mothers have begun to work outside the home, preschool care and education at home cannot be taken for granted.

In terms of dealing with poverty and inequality, there are important questions about the preschool years. Do parents read to kids? Are there books, educational toys, computers at home? Lack of computer access or technical literacy may create a gulf between the affluent and the rest. Are there lively and intelligent peers in the neighborhood to serve as role models? All too often, no. Where do children go during the day if no one is home? Are parents able to find, judge, and afford good day care? Often they are not. Anyone who cares about poverty, inequality, or equal opportunity, therefore, is likely to favor a government role in preschooling, as well as other levels of education. Arguably, preschooling may be the most critical schooling of all.

In our view, then, there are persuasive arguments in favor of government involvement in every level of education—especially, but not exclusively, in preschooling and the earliest years of schooling. The chief questions concern exactly *what sort* of government (national or local, for example) and exactly *how* government should intervene. The answers may vary with the type of education we consider.

Children and Equal Opportunity

Equal opportunity is a slippery concept with several possible meanings. In one narrow version, it accepts that individuals have (are born with or acquire early in life) very different "abilities," which are relatively fixed—or are simply taken as given—and will lead to very different life chances, very different prospects for success in the competitive race. In this sense, "equal opportunity" merely means that people with *similar abilities* and tastes at any given point in their lives should receive the *same treatment*—for example, the same educational opportunities or curriculum.[11] That is, people should face no artificial barriers, such as discrimination on the basis of race, ethnicity, or gender, and they should have *equal access* to education regardless of such factors as their income or wealth.

Advocates of a broader concept of equal opportunity acknowledge that people may be born unequal in various respects, but insist that most "abilities"—whether involving physical strength, mental acuity, specific work skills, energy, ambition, or creativity—are by no means fixed. Abilities can change as a result of people's own efforts and with the help of parents, peers, schooling, and work experiences. Abilities are especially plastic early in life, when small differences in experience (good nutrition and mental stimulation, for example) may make lifelong differences. But people's abilities continue to change throughout their lives. Broader views of equal opportunity generally focus on efforts to *equalize abilities,* either in advance of some competitive "starting line" or throughout people's lifetimes.

Divergent views of this "starting line" issue define further differences among theories of equal opportunity. For those who focus on the metaphor of a competitive running race, the point of equal opportunity is apparently to make sure that the runners all line up along a line with the same distance to run, have no special hurdles to jump or distractions to face, and—presumably—start out in good physical health and have access to similar track shoes, running clothes, nutrition, and training regimes. Many aspects of such a race are equalized, then, but others are not: the effort that athletes put into training and running, for example, and the quality of their muscles and co-ordination (which may be influenced by genetic inheritance). Once the starting gun fires, there is no more equalizing—the runners take off, and the fastest wins.

Those who speak of equal opportunity at the "starting line of life" seem to have in mind that the competitive race starts at some definite moment: not at birth, and presumably not with entry into first grade; perhaps with graduation from elementary school into the big, bustling world of middle school? To provide equal opportunity in this sense means to do everything possible (well, perhaps not quite everything, but a lot), up to that point, to *equalize the expected value* of each person's *lifetime income*—or at least the expected value of income for all who make the same amount of effort.[12]

"Effort" as a factor affecting success is particularly tricky for this line of thought. Advocates of equal opportunity want to encourage maximum effort by rewarding success, but must acknowledge that the extent of effort itself partly reflects motivational "abilities" that people may acquire early in life (for example, intrinsic motivations to learn and achieve[13]). Who will actually win and who will lose cannot be predicted (it will depend partly on chance); to ensure this sort of equal opportunity is to ensure that, *before* the race starts, runners have an equal chance to win.

This is no trivial matter. Actually to achieve equal opportunity in this sense—so that, say, every thirteen-year-old in America would have an equal probability of attaining future fame and fortune—would require extraordinary efforts. Every child would have to be assured of good nutrition, healthy surroundings, intellectual stimulation, physical and social training, good role models, and, not least, excellent preschooling and schooling. Moreover, any residual biological inequalities would have to be dealt with by overcoming them or providing compensating assets. For a world in which grossly unequal childhood environments are legion, this would be a tall order.

Yet we have suggested that even this rather sweeping program rests on an artificially limited concept of equal opportunity because the notion of a definite startling line is untenable. The competitive race starts anew every day of our lives. Our abilities change throughout our lives, often in ways that we cannot control: as the result of a crippling illness, for example. The core logic of equal opportunity—the idea that everyone should have an *equal chance* to do well—really implies that everyone should be helped to have the *same expected future income at every point in life*. This, of course, is virtually the same thing as prescribing equal incomes for everyone, since any chance fluctuations that affect future expectations would immediately be corrected and only fleeting variations among individuals would remain. That is, as we said in chapter 3, the logic of equal opportunity, when fully worked out, tends to lead to equality of result.[14]

Many advocates of equal opportunity pull up well short of this conclusion. They limit the concept one way or another: by imposing some arbitrary but definite starting point after which no effort is made to equalize "abilities," for example, or by excluding certain human variations (e.g., in genetic endowment) from any efforts to compensate or equalize. Often motivation and effort are treated as unrelated to initial endowments and as subject to no societal influence other than a system of material incentives in which differential incomes are held out as rewards for work. Or various "liberties" that restrict equal opportunity are taken as inviolable.[15]

Some narrow versions of equal opportunity have a severe, "devil take the hindmost" quality. Once a few blatantly unfair barriers to success are removed, they offer no sympathy to people with other sorts of disadvantages or bad luck. A peculiarly restricted treatment of effort often ignores the many ways other than material incentives by which society can help people develop the motivation, ambition, and good work habits that are essential to more truly equal opportunity. Much can be done in infancy, in early childhood development, and in schools. Chinese and Japanese schools, for example, apparently achieve a great deal by assuming that students' "abilities" are very nearly equal—everyone is capable of doing the work—and that the school's job is precisely to encourage everyone to make the effort to realize that capacity.[16]

For the purposes of this chapter, it is striking that in *all* concepts of equal opportunity, even the narrowest, education plays a major role. There are differences in emphasis. Those who focus on equal treatment of people with equal abilities emphasize nondiscrimination and *equal access* to all levels of schooling. Those who want to equalize abilities before some late-childhood "starting line" emphasize *early childhood* preschooling and schooling, including compensatory education. And those who want to equalize abilities and life chances throughout lifetimes favor *lifelong* efforts (including compensatory efforts) to build up equal human capital for everyone.

We ourselves lean toward broader rather than narrower conceptions of equal opportunity. Even readers who disagree, however, should see that *any* plausible version of equal opportunity calls for major educational efforts and supports an important role for government action.

Before Birth

First things first. An unwanted child, a child born to a deprived and desperate single parent (perhaps a teenager), or a physically or mentally disabled child born to a malnourished or drug-abusing mother, is not likely to enjoy equal opportunity. One very important way to reduce poverty and inequality therefore is to prevent it in as many cases as possible by reducing the likelihood of children being born damaged or cast into hopeless situations as infants.

About one in four births in the United States (three of every five black births, though this proportion is falling) is now out of wedlock. Many of those children are born into single-parent families, many into low-income situations, and nearly a third to mothers under twenty years of age. True, it is easy to create a needlessly alarmist picture from such sound bites: "out of wedlock" does not mean no stable relationship. "Single" parent does not mean never-married (in the early 1990s, for example, fully *92 percent* of all children living with single mothers had divorced or separated, rather than never-married, mothers). And even some young, low-income, never-married mothers are capable of good parenting. Still, there is a problem.

Families headed by young mothers are seven times as likely as other families to be poor and are extremely likely to end up needing public assistance.[17]

People who cannot properly care for children should be persuaded and helped not to bear them. This is not a promising area for legal regulation; most Americans would reject any government attempt to decide who can have children when. But education and moral persuasion are another matter. Those who deplore poverty and inequality would do well to think through how to educate teenagers and poor people concerning the perils of childbearing under inauspicious circumstances. It not only harms the mother's educational and job prospects, but also disadvantages, if it does not doom, the child.

Moral crusades to encourage chastity and sexual abstinence among teenagers are fine with us, therefore, if someone can figure out a way to make them work. But "just say no" to sex seems to be a very hard sell, particularly among older teens. In practice, such campaigns may tend to distract from (or deliberately substitute for) the important practical step of encouraging birth control. It should be easy to prevent most *unwanted* births into bad situations; the technology is available. The evidence indicates that low-income women—those most at risk of launching their own children into an impoverished existence—are more than twice as likely as higher-income women to have an unwanted birth. Merely providing universal access to birth control information, devices, and services therefore might well play a significant part in preventing poverty.[18]

The federal government—along with private organizations like Planned Parenthood—has in fact actively promoted family planning services. Starting in 1967, states were required to make family planning services available to Aid to Families with Dependent Children (AFDC or "welfare") recipients. A 1970 law established a population affairs office and authorized federal funding for family planning services, training, information, and educational programs through Title X of the Public Health Service Act. Title X helps fund about 4,200 family planning clinics (concentrated in low-income areas, with free care for the poor) and serves some 4.2 million women each year. By the mid-1990s, federal and state governments spent about $725 million per year on family planning, about 87 percent of it from the federal government—most now through Medicaid (46 percent), but a critical component (21 percent) still through Title X, and some through the social services block grant and the maternal and child health block grant. The 1996 welfare law offered additional incentives to the states to reduce out-of-wedlock births, but it is not yet clear that this will increase family planning efforts.[19]

The federal effort has greatly increased access to family planning: the number of women served by federally funded programs rose from nearly one million in 1968 to four million two decades later. Roughly five of six clients had low incomes—incomes below 1.5 times the meager poverty line. But the fact that more than eight million poor and near-poor women of childbearing age need organized family planning services and that few can afford private physicians means that there is considerable room for improvement. Funding for family planning has actually declined since its peak in the late 1970s, and there are periodic efforts to end it altogether.[20]

The problem, of course, is political conflict over contraception and abortion. Curiously, some who claim to cherish "life" favor banning any form of artificial contraception, condemning many unwanted babies to misery. Abortion, once a furtive and illegal refuge of the desperate, is now seen by increasing majorities of Americans as a birth control technique of last resort—or at least as an option that women should be allowed to have, free of government interference. The *Roe v. Wade* Supreme Court decision of 1973 established a constitutional right to abortions and struck down restrictive state laws (particularly in the first three months of pregnancy). But the 1989 *Webster* and 1992 *Casey* decisions permitted mandatory waiting periods, distribution of tendentious antiabortion "information," parental consent requirements, and other measures to discourage abortion, which many states have been quick to enact. In addition, conservative legislators cut back funding for family planning beginning in the 1980s, and the Hyde amendments drastically curtailed Medicaid funding for abortions—so that the number of federally funded abortions declined from 295,000 in 1977 to merely 165 in 1990.[21]

Since teenagers, minorities, and the poor are more likely than others to want abortions—poor women are three times more likely to have them than nonpoor women—and since well-off women can afford to fly to permissive states or foreign countries to get abortions, abortion restrictions and funding cuts disproportionately hit the poor and tend to increase the reproduction of poverty. The same is true of the campaigns of harassment, intimidation, and even killing of abortion providers, which (despite protective federal legislation) have resulted in severe shrinkage of abortion services. Some 86 percent of U.S. counties, most of them rural, but some including large cities, now have not a single abortion provider. Like it or not, conflicts about abortion are also conflicts about U.S. poverty and inequality.

Child Support

A related issue is that of fly-by-night fathers who fail to provide child support. As Sar Levitan and others have commented, defaulting on a consumer loan often draws tougher treatment than does failure to support one's children. Only about one out of three divorced, separated, never-married, or unmarried mothers receives child payments at all, and the payments that are made tend to be skimpy, averaging little more than $3,000 a year—hardly enough to provide children with good food, clothing, and housing, let alone a stimulating social and intellectual life. Even among the one-half of parents awarded child support payments along with custody as part of legal judgments, only about 37 percent have actually received payments, and only about one-quarter have got full payments. Single mothers left without child support have a rough time trying to provide their children with equal opportunities. Impunity for irresponsible fatherhood also encourages the careless procreation of more poor children by people who should not have them.[22]

Increasingly the federal and state governments have pursued these disappearing fathers. Federal laws in 1975, 1984, and 1988 mandated guidelines for appropriate amounts of child support, required states to enforce support, and helped them with funding. The federal Family Support Act (1988) and other legislation mandated genetic tests in contested paternity cases and authorized liens on property, garnishment of wages, withholding of income tax refunds, and alerting of credit agencies about deadbeat dads. The same law also established a federal parent locator service so that fleeing fathers could not just vanish across state lines. In 1992, it was made a federal crime to willfully fail to pay past-due child support while living in another state. A few years later the federal government was spending $2.1 billion annually on child support enforcement and was collecting almost $6 for every $1 spent. But not all states have taken full advantage of their new authority, and the number of single mothers needing child support has grown faster than help in getting it.[23]

Enforcement of child support is no panacea because many disappearing fathers are marginal characters with low incomes and little ability to pay. Still, as deadbeat dads increasingly get entangled in wage withholding, property liens, and even community service requirements and loss of their driver's licenses, there is hope of significantly helping their children and, as the word spreads, of discouraging irresponsible paternity. Child support collections rose by some 80 percent during the 1990s.[24]

Chapter Six

Health and Nutrition

Another critical factor for ensuring equal opportunity at the very start of life is adequate *prenatal* and infant nutrition and health care. Poor nutrition by pregnant women tends to lead to high infant mortality, low birth weights, and poor health—sometimes major disabilities—in children. Food Stamps, which enable most poor citizens to obtain subsidized food, can help; the evidence indicates that most families do in fact buy more food in total as a result of receiving Food Stamps, though improved nutrition is a more complicated matter. Perhaps even more important in this connection is the Supplemental Food Program for Women, Infants, and Children, known as "WIC," which has been shown to be quite effective in raising birth weights and improving the health of both mothers and infants. This program is also highly cost-effective even in the narrowest sense: a study commissioned by the Department of Agriculture in the late 1980s found that every WIC dollar spent on prenatal care for mothers saved from $1.77 to $3.13 in Medicaid costs for mothers and newborns.[25]

The obvious benefits of WIC have made it a popular program. In 2000, some $4.1 billion was spent on WIC, and it reached about 7.5 million women, infants, and children with nutrition assistance, nutrition education and counseling, and health care, including prenatal care. During the 1990s, participation grew by about 30 percent, and by the end of the decade, the program was helping half of all America's infants.[26]

Starting in 1984, federal legislation required the states' Medicaid programs to give health coverage to all pregnant women and young children who meet state income-assistance guidelines, whether or not they receive financial aid. In the mid-1990s, Medicaid served 18.7 million children: one out of every five children in the United States, including one of every three babies born in the United States. Again, the evidence indicates that this has big positive effects. Between 1979 and 1990, as the fraction of women eligible for Medicaid if they became pregnant expanded from 14 to 34 percent, there were associated reductions in both infant mortality and low birth weights. Still, many pregnant women are not reached because loose federal guidelines result in wide disparities among states' eligibility criteria. At one point, benefits were given to people with incomes up to 75 percent of the poverty threshold in Alaska, but denied to anyone above 13 percent of the poverty line—excluding everyone but the truly dirt poor—in Mississippi.[27]

The federal government has also helped create and fund community health centers in low-income areas. In the 1990s, it spent about $700 million per year on a block grant assisting 550 health centers that provided primary health care to some five million patients, about 60 percent of whom identified themselves as poor. Another block grant to the states, amounting to $674 million in the mid-1990s, supports maternal and child health in low-income families. But both these block grants (created in 1981 by the Reagan administration to consolidate and squeeze down various categorical programs) have come under continued financial pressure, so that many uninsured near-poor women and children still have nowhere to go for primary health care.[28]

School Breakfasts and Lunches

Nearly all Americans embrace a concept of equal opportunity that goes at least this far: children who are born so unlucky as to have a weak or fragmented family, few resources, and an unhelpful neighborhood should be "given a chance" through acceptable levels of nutrition, medical care, and preschool training. One important element of equal opportunity is adequate nutrition while children are at school or preschool.

The federal government spends over $6 billion a year to help provide breakfast, lunch, and milk to more than thirty million children in public and private schools and day care centers. Most of this goes to subsidize school lunches for more than 25 million children (more than half of all U.S. elementary and secondary school students), including about 11.8 million children from poor homes who receive free lunches and 1.7 million children from near-poor homes who get reduced-price lunches (affluent children get smaller subsidies). The impact of school lunches is unclear, however; subsidized low-income children are more likely than others to participate in the program, and participation is associated with consuming more food energy during the day, but this may be partly because bigger eaters sign up in the first place. There are also questions about the fat content and the nutritional value of the meals. Moreover, millions of poor children do not receive these lunches because of complicated eligibility procedures and off-putting stigmas (separate lines or tables or distinctive tokens) that discourage them from applying.[29]

Of particularly direct relevance to equal opportunity is the much smaller school breakfast program, focused on low-income areas, which spent about $817 million per year in federal funds in the mid-1990s to give free or reduced-price breakfasts to some 4.7 million children—many of whom would otherwise start the day with an inadequate meal or none at all. Children who eat breakfast are clearly able to perform better in school, and school breakfast participants get more nutrients than nonparticipants, though it is hard to be certain that the program actually increases breakfast eating in schools that offer it and it is hard to link program participation specifically to school performance. There is also a small federal program that provides milk to about 60,000 children in institutions that do not participate in other child nutrition programs, and there are larger programs that provide "summer food" to about 1.9 million children in various institutions and to about 1.2 million children in child care centers. Curiously, given the crucial importance of child nutrition to equal opportunity, the child and adult food care program—which mainly supports meals in child care centers and family day care homes—was cut sharply, by about $2.5 billion, in the 1996 welfare revisions.[30]

Head Start and Day Care

One of the most popular and successful programs to come out of the Great Society antipoverty efforts of the 1960s is Head Start. Head Start now has an annual budget of about $5 billion and serves some 877,000 children from poor families, including a relatively small number (about 45,000) under age three in "Early Head Start." Head Start has focused on basic social and intellectual skills, featuring low student-teacher ratios and active parental involvement, including employment at Head Start centers of a number of mothers of program participants—an effective way to train parents in good child-rearing practices, while also caring for children.[31]

Early research on compensatory education was discouraging because it seemed to indicate that there was no long-term gain on standardized IQ or achievement tests by children who attended enriched preschools. But subsequent research, including a nationwide study of siblings, has generally found that Head Start and other such programs have led to substantial gains in test scores and school attainment, as well as lower frequencies of being held back in school or ending up in special education classes. There appear to be real, long-term improvements in IQ and other cognitive test scores. The intensively studied Perry Preschool Program in Ypsilanti, Michigan, with particularly strong enrichment and highly trained teachers, has shown especially large and enduring effects that include higher high school graduation rates and higher employment rates and earnings among adults. So (based on an experimental research design) has the Abecedarian Project in Chapel Hill, North Carolina.[32]

If the less robust Head Start programs were brought closer to Perry School standards—locating them more often in schools, for example, with better trained teachers—and were extended to the millions of poor children not now served, they could, over the long term, significantly reduce poverty and inequality in the United States. This would be particularly true if Head Start were expanded from the current part-day schedule to full-day, full-year day care operations so that mothers could work full-time, and if they were opened generally to three-year-olds and younger infants. By enabling mothers to work, day care has a strong impact on poverty among small children. In France, an extensive day care program has helped bring the child poverty rate down to about 6 percent, whereas the rate in our own, wealthier, country is 21 percent.[33]

The popularity of Head Start has brought the program bipartisan support and spared it from the most vicious budget cuts of the 1980s and 1990s. Almost incredibly, however—given the program's popularity and success and its central role in providing equal opportunity—funding has been sufficient to enroll only about *one in five* impoverished children. Within a federal budget in the $2 *trillion* range (that is, 2,000 billion dollars), the extra $10 billion or so needed to triple the size of Head Start would hardly be noticed.[34] For any serious advocate of reducing U.S. poverty and inequality, the full funding of Head Start and related pregnancy and early childhood programs like WIC and Medicaid should receive very high priority.

This is particularly true since government is increasingly helping with preschool child care in ways targeted largely at the middle class. One such federal program—costing about $2.4 billion in 2000—is the child and dependent care tax credit. This is a moderately progressive measure, worth the most money to families with adjusted gross incomes below $30,000 or so, that gives taxpaying families credit for a proportion (up to 30 percent) of actual child care expenditures below certain limits. We consider this a useful and sensible program that contributes to gender-based fairness, as well as productivity, by enabling more women to work outside the home—as about half the mothers of infants now do. But it is of very limited benefit to very low-income people because the credit is not refundable, and hence is worthless to those with incomes too low to incur income taxes. And delayed payment of a refund does not immediately help with up-front, out-of-pocket payments for child care. Also significant (costing about $1.4 billion in 2000), but of even less use to the poor, is the exclusion from income taxation of employer-provided day care benefits. Such benefits go mostly to high-income workers, and each dollar's worth of tax exclusion (as opposed to a tax credit) is worth most to those in the highest tax brackets.[35]

On the other hand, rapidly growing grants to the states through the Child Care and Development Fund—budgeted at $4.5 billion in 2000—have increasingly helped provide child care services for children from low-income working families and families with parents moving from welfare to work. Those services reached some 1.75 million children in 2000. Combined with funds from the welfare law revision specifically designed to help make it possible for former welfare recipients to work, they are projected to reach about 2.4 million children in 2004. In the past, many poor mothers and children have been excluded from help because of age restrictions, limited state matching funds, and state use of "exemption" options, so that there have been long lines of people awaiting assistance and others have been excluded entirely; the Clinton administration appears to have made considerable headway on this front.[36]

Several European countries have done better than the United States by providing free or highly subsidized day care to everyone. In the United States, with already established private day care centers and a marked bias against direct government provision of services, a reasonable way to move toward such a system might be through the grants to states mentioned above. Better, however, would be a program of universal vouchers for purchasing day care, with the value of the voucher highest (or the cost lowest) for low-income people and a smaller subsidy for the affluent.[37]

Elementary and Secondary Schools

Financing and operating elementary and secondary schools is the largest single function of state and local governments in the United States. Much of the action occurs in some 15,000 local school districts, funded by local property taxes and—increasingly—by general state revenues. The states now provide nearly half of the roughly $300 billion per year spent on schools and impose a variety of standards on curricula, textbooks, administrative procedures, and the like. The federal government plays a much smaller part, providing only some 7 percent of total expenditures, nearly all of that filtered through the states.[38] But federal legislation and court decisions have been particularly important in the areas of civil rights and discrimination based on race or gender, bilingual education, help for persons with disabilities, and assistance to low-income students or areas.

The provision of free, universal elementary and secondary school education has long been seen as a great triumph of American democracy. In this instance, in contrast to most aspects of the welfare state, the United States has actually led the way. The U.S. system of public elementary schools was mostly in place by the last quarter of the nineteenth century, whereas England and other European countries continued bifurcated, largely private school systems into the twentieth century. The quicker U.S. start may have had to do with our need to build many new schools as western lands were settled, as well as the relative weakness of class divisions and the strength of a certain limited ideology of equality. In any case, urbanization, industrialization, immigration, and changes in the family (especially the development of a working class employed for wages outside the home), along with democratic politics and reformist institutions, led in most U.S. cities to full-fledged systems of public elementary schools that were age-graded, free, often compulsory, hierarchically organized, and taught and administered by professionals. High schools largely took their present form during the Great Depression of the 1930s, when job scarcity made it sensible for teenagers to stay in school.[39]

For most of the last century, U.S. public schools have been widely praised for accomplishing many things: training an industrial workforce, helping "Americanize" immigrants from many foreign cultures, training Americans in democratic citizenship. Public schools have also been seen as providing a major ingredient of equal opportunity, educating the poor and those of modest means free of charge and doing so in *common schools* along with the well-off and people of diverse cultural backgrounds, all sharing a common curriculum.[40]

Unequal Schooling

Recent historical research has cast doubt on just how golden the "golden age" of U.S. public education was, however. There were, for example, many class-related battles over local autonomy for working-class communities *versus* centralized control by upper-middle-class administrators and officials, and the latter generally won. And equality has always been achieved only within local areas, not among them. But more important, even local equality in public schooling soon began to break down. The common curriculum, for example, eroded in high schools after a 1918 National Education Association report advocated designing curricula to meet the needs of the new majority of students, most of whom were not going on to college. The subsequent fragmentation of courses, and eventually tracking, undoubtedly helped prepare students for the kinds of lives and work they were most likely to encounter, but it also limited schools' effects on social mobility and equality.[41]

Over many decades, the ideal of the common school for diverse students—implemented by including everyone from a given residential area—also increasingly was thwarted by residential segregation along lines of ethnicity and social class. After World War II especially, affluent and middle-class whites, with help from government Federal Housing Administration loans and new federal highways, moved out of the cities into homogeneous suburbs with homogeneous and relatively affluent schools.[42] They left working-class people, the poor, and minorities behind in inner cities, attending increasingly segregated and impoverished public schools. Today, for example, cities like Detroit, Cleveland, Gary, Milwaukee, and Chicago, with 25–40 percent minority populations, concentrate most of their African-American and Latino citizens into highly segregated neighborhoods.[43] Affluent people who have stayed in central cities often send their children to expensive private schools that are generally unavailable to those of modest means.

The result has been what Jonathan Kozol called "savage inequalities." In contrast to the expansive facilities (good buildings, abundant libraries and computers), well-trained and well-rewarded teachers, and ambitious peers often found in affluent suburbs, many inner-city students have to cope with skimpy funding, decaying (sometimes dangerous) buildings, scarce supplies, burnt-out teachers, and segregated, demoralized fellow-students. Urban schools are often unhappy places. As Gene Maeroff, another sympathetic observer, has put it, the "dismal panorama" of urban schools leads to "withered hopes, stillborn dreams."[44]

The data are clear. Schools with high concentrations of poor students tend to have older buildings that are more in need of maintenance, less qualified teachers, less challenging and advanced curricula, fewer books, fewer computers, and fewer Internet connections. Many classes with high enrollments of poor students are taught by out-of-field teachers who lack training in the subject. This is especially true of English and science.[45] The question is what to do about unequal schooling.

Does Money Help?

One focus has been financial: the big differences between the levels of income and wealth in different school districts, which—when schools rely on local property taxes—translates into gross inequalities in the amount of money available to schools. It is hard to argue that schools with widely varying resources can provide equal educational opportunities for all the children in a given state. Indeed, in the 1971 *Serrano* case, the California Supreme Court declared that such inequalities among districts in the Los Angeles area violated the guarantee of equal protection of the laws under both the state and the federal constitutions.

After about 1950, the sharpest across-state differences in per-pupil spending, class size, teacher pay, and the like actually dropped somewhat, though they remain large (even after adjusting for price differences, in the mid-1990s New Jersey spent about twice as much per pupil as Utah did). Also, since *Serrano,* California and other states have taken measures to redress the most outrageous *within-state* differences among school districts. Most states now provide funding from general state revenues in ways designed to compensate somewhat for variations in local tax bases (some states like Massachusetts and Missouri, however, retain wide spending disparities). To a more modest extent, the federal government has helped as well, using Title I of the 1965 Elementary and Secondary Education Act to provide some $9 billion per year to schools in heavily low-income areas. This constitutes a small proportion of the schools' total revenues, and only a tiny fraction of the federal budget, but it makes a difference. Together, state and federal efforts have led to somewhat more equal per-pupil spending levels among school districts in each state.[46]

Progress toward more equal funding is certainly welcome. But it is important to see that even completely equal funding would not bring equal education or equal opportunity because it takes *more* effort and more money per pupil to educate disadvantaged students. Making up for early childhood deprivation, dealing with non-English speakers, providing special education for children with disabilities—these things are very expensive. Moreover, disadvantages within a school are cumulative. The quality of peer support and peer pressure has been shown to have very strong effects on educational achievement.[47] A student surrounded by eager, self-confident, proficient fellow-students simply has a much better chance to learn than one surrounded by the disadvantaged and discouraged. This is one reason why residential segregation is so pernicious. For these reasons, to provide disadvantaged students (and students surrounded by disadvantaged students) with equal chances for educational achievement requires not merely equal funding, but *compensatory* efforts involving more than equal resources.

Unfortunately, the post-*Serrano* drive for compensatory or at least equal educational resources has run into a surprising obstacle: the argument that money—or even the quality of schools themselves—does not really make any difference to educational achievement. It is said to be pointless to "throw money" at the problem. In recent years, this argument has been made with particular vigor by some who advocate a radical restructuring of education through vouchers or other forms of privatization. What should we make of it?

The "money doesn't matter" argument has roots in the first wave of systematic research, particularly the 1966 Coleman report on equality of educational opportunity, which concluded that the effects of money and of measured school inputs (facilities, curriculum, even teacher quality) had little or no impact on students' academic achievement. A host of subsequent studies have come up with conflicting estimates of the effects of school resources, often failing to find any statistically significant impact. As Larry Hedges and others have pointed out, however, the point is to calculate the *best* estimate of effects across a number of studies by some such technique as taking the *average* estimate—which is very large and positive.

Such estimates may be somewhat too large, due to publication biases (journals do not like nonfindings) and selection bias (parents who value education highly and help their children learn tend to choose to live in high-spending districts, making the spending seem responsible for success). Still, as schools have spent more money per pupil over the last two or three decades, the average achievement test scores of representative samples of students have mostly improved—though not by a lot, only for poor students, and about twice as much on math as reading. Estimates of spending effects based on changes over time, too, may be somewhat biased upward because parents' levels of education and income have risen (and the number of children per family has fallen), all tending independently to raise school achievement at the same time that school spending has risen.[48] On the other hand, to the extent that spending is concentrated in the neediest areas, we should not be surprised at a lack of positive correlation of funding levels with achievement.

The arguments continue. Gary Burtless's volume of essays on this issue pessimistically concluded that differences in school resources—while they may improve students' later earnings prospects—have essentially no effects on academic achievement, and that increased spending on school inputs has "not been shown to be an effective way to improve student achievement" in most instances.[49] We can agree that spending lots of money on schools is not a *sufficient* condition for improving achievement because it bound to matter exactly how the money is spent. Yet spending may well be a *necessary* condition for providing a good education. Surely a lack of habitable buildings, a dearth of reasonably paid teachers, or an absence of books and computers is not likely to advance educational aims. Surely it is easier to get excellent teachers if you pay them well. Research suggesting that *simply* "throwing money" at schools will not necessarily help should not be used as an excuse to deny books to the illiterate, to tolerate gross inequities, or to neglect the compensatory measures that are known to help poor students. Instead, questions about effects of money should encourage thinking about which factors matter most and where resources can have the most impact: perhaps in smaller class sizes, for example.

Segregation

It is easy to lose sight of one important fact that was emphasized in the Coleman Report and is agreed on by virtually all researchers: peers matter. Students are helped or harmed by the playmates, neighbors, and fellow-students who surround them. It follows inescapably that any educational system that segregates students by race, income level, or any other factor correlated with academic ability or achievement—any system that concentrates high-achieving students in some schools and low-achieving students in others—is bound to disadvantage the students who end up with below-average classmates. Besides affecting students' schoolwork and cognitive skills, such segregation is likely to create inequalities in self-esteem, access to interpersonal networks, and job prospects.[50]

In the case of race, the U.S. Supreme Court long ago ruled, in *Brown v. Board of Education* (1954), that state action deliberately bringing about racial segregation violates African Americans' rights to equal protection of the laws. Subsequent court decisions required states to dismantle segregation policies. The Civil Rights Act of 1964 put teeth into these decisions by denying federal aid (most notably under the subsequent Elementary and Secondary Education Act of 1965) to school districts that discriminate on the basis of race or other arbitrary grounds. Slowly, painfully, with much resistance and foot-dragging, formal legal segregation in the South was broken down. Black students were no longer forbidden to attend all-white schools, and single-race public schools were integrated, at least to a token extent.[51]

Almost immediately, however, private choices began to undo integration. Private, all-white "academies" were set up in the South to evade desegregation for those who could afford the tuition. In many parts of the country, there was "white flight": some parents chose residential locations (in lily-white suburbs, for example) partly to avoid sending their children to integrated schools. This did not always represent racism—some middle-class blacks fled as well. It sometimes represented "classism," a perceived self-interest in avoiding schools with many poor or disadvantaged students, for the reasons noted above. But the brutal fact of widespread *residential segregation,* regardless of motive, operated together with the long-standing system of *school attendance by location of residence* to reestablish segregated schools, not only in the South, but also in the cities and suburbs of the North. Douglas Massey and Nancy Denton speak of "American apartheid."[52]

Recognizing that residential segregation was perpetuating school segregation, and seeking to counteract it, the federal courts began ordering remedies like compulsory busing to non-neighborhood schools. The history of busing is painful to contemplate. There is some evidence that intelligently arranged busing can work well for students and gain acceptance by parents. But it does go against the obvious virtues of neighborhood schools (ease of transportation, encouragement of parental involvement, facilitation of after-school friendships). And fearful parents—their concerns sometimes inflamed by race-baiting politicians—created storms of protest and eventually forced the courts to retreat or legislatures to override busing plans. The result has been highly segregated schools, in which most minority students are surrounded mainly by minorities. In the mid-1990s, for example, some 73 percent of Hispanics attended public schools where more than half the students were Hispanic, and 65 percent of blacks attended public schools where more than half the students were black.[53] Segregation by income and socioeconomic status is also extreme.

As long as we insist on both freedom of residential choice and residentially based school attendance, our public schools are likely to be heavily segregated by race and income. The segregated students are going to be harmed as a result. As Orlando Patterson points out, one logical reaction to the rejection of busing is to address the underlying problem of residential segregation and to work seriously to integrate our neighborhoods.[54]

Integration can make a difference. Quasi-experimental data from the Gatreaux program in Chicago (in which some African-American public housing tenants were randomly assigned to new housing in the city and some to the higher-income, mostly white suburbs) indicate that the children of suburban movers were considerably less likely to drop out of school and more likely to take college-track courses. They were much more likely to attend college (54 percent to 21 percent) and to attend a four-year college (27 percent to 4 percent).[55]

But it is not easy to integrate with affluent whites on a large scale if they do not want to be integrated. The only other way to give disadvantaged students truly equal opportunities, in the sense of equal chances for high academic achievement, is to make special compensatory efforts. That means not merely providing resources equal to those in luckier schools and neighborhoods, but providing *superior* resources.

What Works

This question remains: what sorts of teaching, curriculum, school resources, and school organization actually work well? The Babel of conflicting theories and claims found in public debates, along with apparent swings and cycles of educational fashion ("phonics" versus "whole language," "the basics" versus "creativity," "standards" versus "flexibility"), sometimes seems to suggest that we do not know the answers. But in fact quite a lot is known about teaching and learning.

Some schools manage to succeed remarkably well even with quite unpromising student material. To take one inspiring example, the Central Park East elementary and secondary schools—"alternative" public schools in New York City's weakest district—serve a largely poor, black and Latino community and take students with low entering test scores. But they have achieved very high graduation rates, with only about 5 percent of students dropping out through the high school years (citywide, by contrast, there is a dismal 50 percent dropout rate before graduation), and remarkably high college attendance. Fully 90 percent of the graduates go on to college. The keys to success for these and many other "schools that work" seem to include vigorous, creative administrators with considerable freedom to run their schools; dedicated (though not necessarily overtrained) teachers; small schools (even if within a big complex) and reasonably small classes; extended contact between the same students and teachers; emphasis on creative achievements, rather than test scores; and, above all, a sense among students that the school is *theirs* to enjoy and be proud of.[56]

Statistical evidence on these matters is elusive for the reasons that plague much educational research and non-experimental social research generally: difficulty in measuring relevant variables and difficulty in specifying and estimating the complex, often reciprocal relationships among them. Selection bias is only one particularly vexing problem.[57] Most observers agree that good teachers are crucial, and many of us think we can tell a good teacher when we see one, but the quality of teaching or administering is not perfectly captured by quantitative measures like credentials or length of experience. Some terrible teachers are highly experienced burn-outs, and some of the best are eager young amateurs. Little surprise, then, that some quantitative studies find negligible (even apparently negative) effects of measured teacher education, administrative inputs, and the like.[58]

Certain quantitative studies, however, do single out particular ingredients in school success. John Chubb and Terry Moe, for example, noted—in a complicated analysis that seems to control for almost everything imaginable—that students who take "academic track," college-preparatory high school courses tend to have significantly greater gains in achievement than those who do not. The systematic "meta-analysis" of many studies seems to indicate that several factors have significant positive effects, including per-pupil expenditures (as noted above), small school size, small class size, and teachers' verbal ability, education, and experience. A meta-analysis of only the (more reliable) longitudinal studies found substantial positive effects for teacher experience, less robust results for teacher-pupil ratio (not quite the same thing as class size), and indications that teacher education makes a difference only in terms of possession or nonpossession of a master's degree.[59]

Experimental research in Tennessee schools has established that small class size is important, especially for first graders. This fits well with the Clinton administration's effort to provide federal funding for 100,000 new teachers.[60]

International comparisons, particularly with Japan, are also suggestive. There is considerable evidence that Japanese schools have been very successful in terms of graduation rates (91 percent of the population completes secondary school, more than in the United States or anywhere else), math and science skills, and a number of other accomplishments. Japan's success appears to be related to its strong emphasis on equality, cooperative learning, and emotional bonds. But it is not clear how much of this is transferable to the United States; Japanese society is quite homogeneous, and the Japanese culture encourages extremely strong commitment to child rearing and education.[61]

The question of what works in education leads us to the further question of how to design *processes* or structures to ensure that whatever works will eventually be widely implemented, even if we are not now sure exactly what it is. One possible process involves creating a variety of educational alternatives and letting parents and children choose among them.

Choice?

No educational issue caused more noise, confusion, and conflict during the 1980s and 1990s than the question of school choice and its relation to school quality and equity. The argument for choice—expressed as early as 1955 by Milton Friedman—has two main branches. First, as a matter of *liberty,* the argument claims that we ought to facilitate freedom of choice whenever we can, especially on a matter so important and so close to home and family as the schooling of our children. Second, the argument says that, as a matter of *efficiency,* we ought to let the powerful forces of market competition produce high-quality schools—sweeping away bureaucracies, teachers' unions, and rigid rules; letting creative entrepreneurs devise the best educational institutions they can; and letting consumers by their choices ensure that good schools flourish and bad schools fade away.[62]

Such arguments appeal to many Americans who are concerned about their own children's prospects or about the general quality of U.S. schools. Such worries were greatly magnified by fears of global economic competition and by the 1983 Carnegie report, *A Nation at Risk,* which deplored falling test scores and asserted that our public schools were failing. (Test scores for representative samples of students—as opposed to nationwide averages on Scholastic Aptitude Tests (SATs), which are confusing because they have reflected a changing and generally less able population of test takers over time—had actually begun to rebound from their decline just before the Carnegie report was issued.)[63]

Choice-based policy alternatives might conceivably include completely abolishing public schools and letting private markets do the job, but that idea has been rejected as too extreme (or at least not politically feasible) even by Milton Friedman. It would run into the objections noted at the beginning of this chapter by ignoring all the important aspects of education that involve externalities or equity, neither of which markets handle well. More plausible would be a system of government-provided *vouchers,* or portable scholarships, which parents and students could use at any school—public or private—that they wished to attend; both public and private schools could then compete to offer high-quality education and attract voucher-paying students.

Debates over vouchers quickly posed this question: just how good are private schools anyhow? In particular, how effective are Catholic parochial schools, by far the most common type of private schools, which have valiantly provided a church-subsidized education to many millions of disadvantaged inner-city children? If they can do a better job than public schools with similar or lesser resources, perhaps we should stop favoring the public schools with tax dollars and force them to compete on an equal basis.

Once again, scholarly research has provided less than definitive answers. One important study by James Coleman and his colleagues at the beginning of the 1980s found evidence of higher academic achievement—roughly one grade level higher—in basic cognitive skills (reading comprehension, vocabulary, and mathematics)—in Catholic schools than in public schools for students from comparable family backgrounds. Coleman also found higher aspirations for college, less segregation, and less rigid effects of family background in the Catholic schools. Minority and low-income students, in particular, did better than in public schools. But methodological problems seem to have inflated these estimates of differences. Coleman and associates did not correct for students' intellectual ability; when the same "High School and Beyond" data were reanalyzed with controls for students' abilities, as well as their family backgrounds, the differences in achievement between public and private high schools for all students turned out to be trivial. The apparent outcome effect of private schooling instead mostly reflected criteria for *selection* into those schools. Still, even with rigorous (perhaps excessive) statistical controls, *minority* students—though not whites—in Catholic schools appeared to have higher academic achievement than those in public schools, mostly as a result of a more demanding curriculum, with some effect of homework quantity and enrollment in college-prep programs. This finding, at least, seems to vindicate the widespread judgment of urban observers that Catholic schools, long barred from most public money for reasons of church-state separation, have still managed to do some outstanding work for the disadvantaged in inner cities.[64]

The somewhat equivocal state of evidence on private schools' effects has not been altered greatly by subsequent research. Chubb and Moe's *Politics,*

Markets, and America's Schools, for example, which became a favorite text of the choice movement, found that what the authors called "school organization" (a compendium of school, administrator, and teacher factors) affected high school students' achievement gains between their sophomore and senior years. It also found that "bureaucratic influence" in the form of constraints on administration and personnel from central offices or teachers' unions in turn had a substantial negative effect on "school organization," and that private school status was a major determinant of lack of administrative or personnel constraint.[65] But the overall amount of test gains being explained was quite small, each of the three effects noted above was small or moderate, and multiplying them by each other set up a very thin causal chain leading from private schools to test score gains.

There is some interesting evidence that the presence of private schools may actually tend to improve the quality of nearby *public* schools, presumably through competitive pressure. Public school achievement scores and college graduation rates appear to rise substantially (by about 8 percentile points) with a 10 percent rise in area private school enrollments. Public school spending per pupil stays constant, and there is little increase in public school segregation by race, income, or achievement (which, however, is already extremely high).[66]

The best evidence about the impact of private schools on their own students comes from a few small-scale voucher or scholarship programs in which disadvantaged students are given scholarships to attend private schools of their choice and the schools select among applicants by *lottery*. This sets up a classical experiment: the progress of the randomly chosen scholarship winners can be compared with the unsuccessful applicants left behind in public schools, who are presumably similar in all other respects. Preliminary findings from Milwaukee (with some imperfect lottery data) indicated that those who moved to private schools did no better than the others for the first two years—it may have taken time to adjust—but they then showed substantial gains in their third and fourth years. Early analysis of the New York City SCSF program indicated that the scholarship students at private schools (at least in the later grades) did somewhat better on math and reading test scores, and their parents reported a better school climate.[67] As such experiments proliferate, we will learn more about just who takes advantage of such opportunities and what the effects are.

One argument against tax-supported vouchers or scholarships that can be used in private (including religious) schools—and against similar measures like the Minnesota tax credit for educational expenses at either public or private schools—is that they improperly encourage sectarian religious instruction. The U.S. Constitution's First Amendment provision against the establishment of religion raises one set of legal issues, though some argue that they may not be insurmountable so long as aid is generally available and goes to religious schools only indirectly through private choices. Certain state constitutions have more stringent restrictions.[68] Aside from legalities, parents' rights to raise their children in whatever particular values they choose may conflict with the idea of inculcating a common, nationwide set of values. A related argument is that vouchers would undermine social unity and democratic citizenship training. But a possible counterargument is that tax support can and will bring with it substantial regulation of private schools to ensure common training, and that private schools are in fact *less* Balkanizing than public schools, at least in terms of racial and ethnic segregation.[69] In principle, voucher programs might be designed to maximize social diversity within schools—for example, by paying schools premiums for accepting disadvantaged and minority students or by requiring them to do so.

For us, a crucial question is whether widespread vouchers would undermine equality by allowing the most alert and best-prepared students to flee the public schools. That might leave behind the most disadvantaged children (with apathetic or disorganized parents), so that the public schools would face an even tougher job with fewer resources and less political support to do it with. One important empirical question, then, is exactly what sorts of students, under various plans, would in fact leave the public schools. A counterintuitive possibility is that not the best public school students but those in the *most trouble* may be first to leave when they are given a chance. Preliminary data from the New York SCSF program indicated that only 26 percent of the scholarship applicants were performing at grade level in reading and 18 percent in math, far below the 55 percent city average. On the other hand, first-come–first-served choice applicants in Indianapolis and San Antonio were above the norm for the city as a whole, suggesting that "creaming" was going on and that the public schools were being weakened.[70]

In order for voucher programs to increase rather than decrease equality, it would be necessary to ensure truly equal opportunity to participate. That would mean making the vouchers very generous for low-income students (covering full tuition plus incidental expenses, which is rarely done), conducting vigorous outreach to make sure everyone knows about the options, and giving schools strong incentives to accept the most disadvantaged (and most costly-to-deal-with) students. Moreover, it would be necessary to ensure that public schools have the resources—increased per-pupil resources—and the flexibility to deal with the students who stay, so that competition would invigorate rather than destroy the public schools. This is a tall order. Some voucher advocates seem uninterested in this sort of large public investment for equality, and more concerned with subsidizing the tuition bills of affluent parents who already send their children to private schools.

Of course, school choice can come in many forms other than vouchers for use in private schools. One little-studied kind of choice is that provided by multiple independent public school districts within a given metropolitan area. With multiple districts, some parents (those who can afford it) can choose among different public schools by choosing their place of residence. Some research indicates that the existence of multiple competing local school districts may cut per-pupil costs substantially, while causing small increases in student achievement and big increases in parental involvement.[71] But this works only if districts have substantial fiscal independence, and it is the very independence and multiplicity of school districts that exacerbates both residential and school segregation.

For many years, public school systems have also allowed for some choice through "magnet" and "alternative" schools, to which parents can voluntarily send their children. The number of such schools has grown markedly in recent years as several states (including Arkansas, Minnesota, and Massachusetts) broadened opportunities to choose them even when racial considerations were not involved. Beginning in Minnesota in 1991 and now in more than half the states, many "charter" schools have been set up. In charter schools, public or private groups contract with public school systems to deliver education meeting certain standards—but free of most of the usual rules and regulations—for a fixed per-pupil fee. Charter schools vary widely in who can run them, how many there can be, and how much autonomy they have. Arizona, for example, has allowed almost any group to charter schools and not limited the number, but many other states allow only local school districts to issue charters and/or restrict them in other ways. The evidence on performance of charter schools is sparse, for the usual methodological reasons and also because so many of them are new. Their effects so far appear to be limited by legislative restrictions (the result of political compromises) that restrict who can set up charter schools, how many there can be, how much autonomy they have from regulations and local district control, and whether full per-pupil funding follows children to them.[72]

Charter schools might potentially offer some of the benefits of choice and competition, while doing much better than most proposed voucher programs at combating poverty and inequality. Charters generally differ from vouchers in two key respects: charter schools are not allowed to charge tuition, so that they are equally affordable for all students, and they are not allowed to set admission standards (all applicants are admitted or given equal chances in a lottery), so that all students have equal access to them. This means that a bigger part of charter school funding is likely to help disadvantaged students. No public money goes to schools that exclude the disadvantaged through requirements of high tuition or high test scores, and no public money goes to pay the bills of affluent students already attending private schools.[73]

Two other differences between charters and vouchers are important, though less relevant to equality issues: (1) Charter school funding excludes public funding of schools with religious instruction—a crucial point when well over four-fifths of all U.S. private school students go to religious schools. (2) Charter schools have political accountability, both at the point of authorization and when their contract performance is reviewed. This may be important, since, at best, marketplace accountability for education is likely to operate slowly and imperfectly. A gallon of sour milk is fairly easy to notice and take back to the grocery store, but weak schooling of one's children may take longer to detect and cannot be returned. Charters are probably less vulnerable than voucher plans to charlatans or incompetents who would take the money now and fail later.

Training for Work

Job-related or *vocational* education and training are important for combating poverty and inequality. At the beginning of the twenty-first century, only about 28 percent of young American adults were completing four years of college, and many were not attending college at all (nearly 13 percent in fact were not even finishing high school).[74] Moreover, a bachelor's degree is not needed for the great majority of U.S. jobs. Now, and for the foreseeable future, the issue for many millions of people is not how to learn about topology or Bakhtin, but how to learn skills that they can use on the job.

Some of this occurs in high school; the old wood shop and metal shop courses have increasingly been supplemented or replaced by courses in the use of computers, business and accounting, food preparation, and the like.

Federal legislation has encouraged high schools to make their coursework even more relevant to practical work—and reduce dropout rates—by linking it to *apprenticeship* programs with local businesses. Apprenticeships, if more fully developed, have the potential to encourage disadvantaged young people to stay in school (reducing dropout rates and criminality) and raise their earning power, thus making a significant contribution to reducing inequality.[75]

Training programs specifically designed for disadvantaged young people have not always had outstanding success. Even the apparent achievements of the Job Corps (the average male participant three years out of the program worked for 63 percent of the year, 9 percentage points higher than a nonparticipant comparison group) have come under methodological suspicion. And those gains may have been restricted to the mid-1970s, when low-skill young people had better job opportunities. Generalized training does not help much, especially when jobs are scarce. Apprenticeships do help at training people for jobs that actually exist.[76]

We will have more to say about job training and retraining in the next chapter.

Higher Education

The role of higher education in equality and equal opportunity is complex. Practically everyone agrees that going to college—and, increasingly, to graduate school—is closely related to economic success. But by the time people reach college age, there are great and well-entrenched differences in their measured abilities and in their capacity to take advantage of higher education. These differences tend to be highly correlated with family background. Both for "meritocratic" reasons, therefore, and because of the great expenses that face students or parents under our tuition-based higher education system, most students in four-year colleges and universities are economically privileged. Most come from high-income families or have substantial resources of their own.

That is to say, higher education—which we think of as providing a great pathway for upward mobility and individual advancement, for realizing the American Dream—in some respects actually tends to *increase inequality* and to link unequal incomes closely to family background. In the early 1990s, for example, the average college graduate earned about 1.74 times as much as the average worker with only a high school diploma (i.e., about 75 percent more), up substantially from the 1.54 ratio in 1975[77] (recall the discussion in chapter 2). And the children of parents with incomes in the top tenth of the distribution were far more likely than those with parents in the bottom tenth to get that college degree. This is one reason that the income and the occupational prestige that children attain tend to reflect the social class of their parents. One study, for example, indicated that among white Americans, 59 percent of the sons of "upper white collar" fathers themselves got upper white collar jobs, whereas only 29 percent of the sons of lower manual workers and only 25 percent of the sons of farmers did so.[78]

Thus Americans coming from different family backgrounds have grossly unequal opportunities to get a higher education and the advantages it brings. Unless one believes that all achievement is heavily determined by genetic inheritance—and despite talk about the "Bell Curve," there are powerful reasons not to believe any such thing[79]—it is clear that this inequality of opportunity proceeds from social more than biological causes and that it could be much reduced by different social and economic arrangements.

Some kinds of government action in this area can help counteract inequality. Government programs that simply give general support to higher education (which, of course, may be worthwhile for other reasons) are likely, however—if they subsidize institutions that charge tuition or admit only the "most able" students—to end up exacerbating inequalities. This is probably true, for example, of taxpayer-subsidized four-year state universities, which mostly help the children of the relatively affluent to get ahead.[80] The unequalizing effect is even greater to the extent that higher education is just a "screening" or sorting device by which people purchase valuable credentials, rather than an actual contributor to increased productivity. We must therefore consider what kinds of effects higher education does in fact have or not have.

Effects of Higher Education

Few doubt that higher education has good effects; the question is precisely what sorts of effects and how big they are. Early efforts to estimate the "rate of return" to an individual's investment in college education (that is, the discounted impact on productivity and wages of an additional year of schooling) were methodologically naïve. In effect, they simply observed big earnings differences between people with different levels of formal education and attributed most or all of those differences to the effect of schooling. But, of course, such estimates tend to be inflated, since people who succeed economically for other reasons (inheriting mother's or dad's lucrative business, for example) are also more likely to go to college because their parents can afford to pay tuition. We know that a host of factors, notably including parents' income and education levels and children's early test scores, are strong predictors of *both* going to college and earning high incomes, but that does not mean that the college experience caused the earnings.

It is very difficult to sort these factors out through quantitative studies. Since no one is *required* to go to college (unlike high school), methodological problems due to selection bias are even worse than for studies of elementary and secondary education. Truly random experiments are next to impossible to carry out. Longitudinal (over-time) studies can help, but less than one might suppose; not only cross-sectional differences, but also changes over time can result from unmeasured background factors. Cross-sectional studies that try to get rid of spurious relationships through statistical "controls" for family background, innate ability, and the like can solve only part of this problem because the controls are always imperfect; often they altogether omit crucial factors like family aspirations and motivations.[81] Even studies of identical twins reared together and reared apart encounter difficulties because it is hard to measure and control for all possible similarities in the environments of twins who are reared apart.

Increasingly sophisticated studies have shown that the economic returns to higher education—despite their undoubted increase over the last couple of decades—are in fact substantially lower than earlier methods would indicate. Studies of the effect of different *qualities* of educational institutions are plagued by even worse methodological problems, since expensive private colleges and affluent students mutually select each other.[82] And even the latest estimates may be inflated if the "screening hypothesis" is correct: that people in effect buy college degrees as attractive credentials, which serve as costly signals to employers and are used to sort people into structurally unequal employment positions, rather than actually to increase their productivity. If the screening hypothesis in its most extreme form were totally correct (that is, if going to college actually added nothing at all to productivity), government investments in higher education not only would exacerbate inequality, but would utterly fail to increase national productivity as well. This extreme case seems unlikely, especially as applied to technical and professional training, but such reasoning does suggest skepticism about the extent to which hoped-for productivity gains from investment in higher education could justify concomitant increases in inequality. Why not go for *both* productivity and equality?

Higher education very likely has a number of non-economic benefits, including improvements in intellectual tolerance, esthetic sensibility, citizenship skills, and the like, although these are even harder to demonstrate than earnings effects.[83] To the extent that some of these, like citizenship, involve positive externalities or social rather than just individual benefits, there is an argument in favor of government help with providing them. Again, however, we would hope that this could be done in ways that advance equality as well as social efficiency.

Government Spending on Higher Education

The federal government devotes only a very small part of its budget (about $11 billion in 2000) directly to higher education, though if the increasing sums spent on student loans and on research done at educational institutions were included, the amounts would rival and even exceed the federal funds that are spent for elementary and secondary education. The bulk of the $11 billion in spending goes for student financial assistance. This includes Pell Grants for about 4 million needy students per year, some 76 percent of whom fall below 150 percent of the poverty level. Clearly this program significantly increases equality of opportunity, though the maximum grant of just over $3,000 is far from enough to pay for expensive private colleges, and the average grant is much smaller—on the order of $500. Many more low-income people could use help. Yet, at the end of the twentieth century, about two-thirds of all the direct student aid available in the country came from the limited federal grant and loan programs.[84]

In order to deal with imperfections in financial markets, the Department of Education oversees a system of guaranteed and direct student loans. About two-thirds of these loans are provided by banks and other private lenders, with repayment guaranteed under the Federal Family Education (FFE) loan program. Increasingly, however, the federal government itself also provides off-budget direct loans, which eliminate some of the paperwork, administrative costs, and credit restrictions of private lenders. Together, in 2000 federal direct and guaranteed loans amounted to about $41 billion and went to some 6.2 million students and their families. Most of these are middle-class people. (The Clinton administration was proud of reducing loan default rates to below 10 percent, from 22.4 percent in 1990, but this came at the cost of completely removing 1,700 schools from the program and rejecting about one-third of initial applications for loans—thus barring aid for some needy students.)[85]

There are also some substantial "tax expenditures" for higher education. These include the "HOPE" tax credit for up to $1,500 in college tuition and fees (worth nearly $5 billion in 2000), the Lifetime Learning Tax Credit for part-time as well as regular college expenses (worth just under $3 billion), and the deduction for education-related charitable contributions (about $3 billion). The first two of these are rather progressive, helping lower- to lower-middle-income people the most. The third, like most tax deductions, mainly benefits the affluent and institutions that they choose to support.[86]

Large and growing federal expenditures, amounting to perhaps $18 billion per year in the mid-1990s, go to colleges and universities for research. This spending is scattered among the budgets of several different departments and agencies, including Health and Human Services, Energy, the National Science Foundation, Defense, NASA, and Agriculture.[87] Since research has large positive externalities—a private sponsor of research, especially basic research, cannot usually hope to capture all its economic benefits—private markets tend to underproduce it. There is a good argument for government subsidy, both through the research spending mentioned here and through generous tax deductibility for private research efforts. But this does not usually increase equal opportunity. Much of the research money goes to elite universities, often expensive private ones, and tends to subsidize the instruction of the mostly affluent students there.

States spend considerably more on higher education than the federal government does, mainly on state-run universities and community colleges, where students' tuition does not cover full costs. Again, to the extent that most of the students come from relatively affluent families, this tends to increase economic inequality rather than decrease it. This is particularly true of the "flagship" state universities. The growing number of cheap, easily accessible community colleges, on the other hand, is a great help to those of modest background.[88]

The quality of American higher education is good to outstanding. And our colleges and universities have actually helped more with upward mobility than have those in many European countries. Still, access to U.S. higher education remains quite limited for young people from low-income families, as does access to top jobs. According to Thomas Dye, the majority of top U.S. leaders hold degrees from a very few (just twelve) prestigious private universities, where not many low-income students are able to penetrate. Holders of these prestigious degrees include 55 percent of top corporate leaders in industry, 50 percent in banking, 55 percent in insurance, and 61 percent in investment.[89]

Discrimination and Affirmative Action

One important aspect of equal access is the absence of *arbitrary barriers* to higher education. The *Brown* decision and subsequent constitutional law—together with the Civil Rights Act of 1964—have removed some of the most blatant formal and informal barriers. These once included the confinement of African Americans to institutions that were segregated by law, quotas that limited the number of Jews at many elite universities, and admission practices that refused to "waste" valuable college slots on women when they were expected to stay at home. Outside of a few private institutions dedicated mainly to serving particular groups—usually women, minorities, or particular religious denominations—both law and practice have nearly eliminated artificial barriers based on race, ethnicity, gender, religion, and the like. Those who can meet general admission standards and can pay the tuition are generally allowed in.

There, of course, is the rub. Members of groups with relatively low average incomes, such as African Americans, Native Americans, and Latinos, have a harder time paying tuition. Members of the same groups often fail to do well on the standardized tests that play such an important part in college admissions, partly because of past deprivation and partly because such tests give special advantages to members of the dominant white, Anglo culture. Yet there is abundant evidence that many students with shockingly low test scores can, if given the chance, do quite well in college. Not to give them the chance is to waste productive resources and to perpetuate inequality.

What to do? The obvious answer is some form of affirmative action. "Quotas" seem to be anathema to most Americans. Much more acceptable, however, is affirmative action that does not violate the sacred creed of admitting those who are academically "able," but that takes a broader view of ability than just test scores. Further, we can make special efforts to find such able students among minorities, and we can place a special value (in admission decisions) on promoting social diversity and equality—just as colleges have always put special value on athletic prowess, "well-roundedness," geographical diversity, alumni connections, and other nonacademic factors.

Affirmative action in college and university admissions has in fact accomplished a great deal for American society, expanding everyone's horizons and helping minorities and women—especially women—to train for and break into businesses and professions long barred to them.[90] Now more women than men go to college in the United States, and they generally get better grades. Yet women remain concentrated in certain traditional majors (education, English, nursing), and they still have far fewer faculty role models than men do. Women, like minorities, also have a harder time completing advanced degrees, in part because of the lack of mentors and role models.

Affirmative action in higher education, like busing in elementary and secondary education, ran into a firestorm of political opposition based on white males' fears of losing out, especially when jobs seemed generally scarce. Such fears were sometimes heightened by demagogic political rhetoric. Abandonment of affirmative action in places like the University of California system has led to alarming consequences, including the much-reduced presence (especially at the Berkeley campus) of black and Hispanic students—who represent large and rapidly growing fractions of that state's population. If we hope to become an integrated and just society and to advance equal opportunity, it will be necessary to reinvent affirmative action in some form. (Aiding the economically disadvantaged without reference to race or ethnicity can further economic equality, but not necessarily social diversity. Letting the top x percent of graduates from *every* state high school into the state universities can generally help somewhat with both.)

It will also be necessary to work harder, in elementary and secondary schools, to prepare low-income and minority kids for higher education. Informal evidence from the federally funded "Upward Bound" program indicates that this can be done. When minority and low-income high school students with no family history of going to college are given year-round help with SAT preparation, college applications, and the like, along with intensive summer classes (often on a university campus), they respond with very high rates of college attendance and graduation.[91]

The Politics of Education

In some respects, the politics of education in the United States is much like that of social insurance programs. Surveys have long shown that programs to improve education are highly popular among the citizenry as a whole, while certain business interests and conservative groups have resisted action at the federal level. As with Social Security and Medicare, the Democratic Party has been the chief innovator and supporter of federal education policies, such as the Elementary and Secondary Education Act of 1965, which was enacted as part of Lyndon Johnson's Great Society. The same is true of the Carter administration's establishment of a separate Department of Education, in order to focus attention on the issue. Republican representatives and presidents have mostly gone along only with reluctance, and many congressional votes on education have followed party lines; some right-wing Republicans continue to advocate abolishing the Department of Education.[92]

But in several respects, education politics is different. For one thing, many businesspeople and their Republican allies have accepted the argument that education is crucial to productivity and economic growth, especially in the globalized economy, and have therefore advocated more government activism in this than in other areas of social policy. George H. W. Bush, for example, sought to be known as "the education president," and the Republican Party at the beginning of the twenty-first century promoted a number of educational initiatives—generally insisting, to be sure, on control of money and standards by the states, rather than the federal government.

The very large role of *state* governments in education policy has pushed much of the political struggle into the fifty states, which are not merely small replicas of the national polity. States vary markedly from one to another in their ideological climate, in the power of interest groups, and even in the structure of government[93] (for a long time in Texas, for example, the powerful lieutenant governor played a central part in education policy). Factors unique to particular states can be critical. In California, both the big-owner-sponsored "property tax revolt" and resentment of immigration from Mexico contributed to the erosion of political support for public education that caused the state to cut education funding. (In per-pupil elementary and secondary school spending, California declined from eleventh in the country in 1959–60 to thirty-eighth in 1995–96.)[94] Those cuts in turn contributed to a sharp drop in school quality: a 1999 report showed that fourth-grade reading scores in California, an affluent and generally progressive state, ranked second from the bottom in the country as a whole.[95]

Local politics in local school districts also make a difference, for example, in school bond referendums. Public choice research has documented a tendency for citizens to vote their economic self-interests, so that substantial property owners (forming a high proportion of the electorate in these off-year, very-low-turnout elections) who have no school-age children have defeated many proposals to fund schools for other people's kids. Bond issues are particularly easy to defeat when super-majorities are required for approval. In decisions about curriculum, administration, and even the structure of schooling, an educational establishment—loosely consisting of superintendents and teachers, with backing from school boards—often resists major educational reforms.[96]

When politics has low visibility and deals are made out of the sight of ordinary citizens, as is often the case with state legislatures and local school boards, policies that the citizens dislike (or *would* dislike if they knew about them) can sometimes be pursued by narrow interests. These interests sometimes include education officials who are not held accountable, but they can also include groups like conservative Christian activists (who have helped elect school board members pursuing a religious fundamentalist agenda), teachers' unions, or (affluent) taxpayers' alliances. The only lasting remedy for low-visibility politics is to raise visibility. That means making a fuss, expanding the "scope of conflict," and increasing attention and voting turnout among ordinary citizens.[97]

Many critical decisions about education reform, vouchers, charter schools, and the like are made—and most funding is obtained—at the state and local levels, where the complexity and variety of politics guarantee that many different solutions will emerge. This leads to messiness; it can also license incompetence and promote economic and racial segregation and inequity. But decentralization does have the virtue, long expounded by advocates of federalism and separation of powers, of room for abundant experimentation and for other states and localities to emulate the experiments that work.

Education is an area in which the pressures of economic globalization may tend to work for an *increase* rather than a decrease in government action, in order to increase the productivity and competitiveness of U.S. workers. Similarly cities and states, rather than "racing to the bottom," may feel competitive pressure to upgrade their educational standards in order to attract industry and produce exports. An important question is whether or not policies that cost-effectively increase productivity will also increase equality. In some cases, there may still be a trade-off, and equity may need defenders.

Improving Education

We have argued that government has a central role to play in education and that more and better schooling is needed, especially for disadvantaged

Americans. If education is to enhance equal opportunity, the huge advantages of the luckiest children—born into affluent, ambitious, and nurturing families—need to be overcome at every level of schooling by greater efforts to improve the access and achievements of the less fortunate.[98]

At present, it is hard to argue with a straight face that the opportunities of America's children are anywhere close to equal. To be sure, it would probably not be feasible to ensure totally equal opportunity even under a restricted definition of that term, but considerable progress could be made without excessive cost.

One important step is to make sure that few children start out life with severe disadvantages. This means helping adults to avoid giving birth to unwanted children in bad situations. It also means fully funding Head Start and other preschool programs, as well as health and nutrition programs for children from the neediest families. High-quality day care should be provided free or at reasonable prices for all children who need it.

Another important step is to improve the quality of elementary and secondary education, devoting more resources to those who need them most. This means providing remedies or compensation for the evils of residential segregation: equalizing funding that is skewed by local property taxes, for example, and providing *more* resources per pupil to those in greatest need of help. It also means expanding school-to-work opportunities, job training and retraining programs, and (so that the middle-aged are not left behind) adult education. And it means restructuring schools for greater efficiency and effectiveness—perhaps harnessing the forces of competition among schools, but in a way that promotes equality for affluent and low-income children, rather than undermining it.

If more egalitarian policies were once instituted at the preschool, elementary, and secondary levels, meritocratic or ability-based admission to higher education would no longer so badly perpetuate intergenerational inequalities—*if,* that is, students of equal ability were actually given equal access to higher education, with enough scholarship help and other support to let all those qualified go to college. But we are a long way from either equal preparation or equal access. The persistence of gross inequalities of opportunity at all the earlier stages of life means that special efforts to ensure access to higher education are needed as well.

7

Jobs and Good Wages

The availability of good jobs at good wages is crucial. After people are educated and trained, they need the opportunity to put their skills to work and earn a satisfactory living. Only if everyone who is able to work can find an appropriate job, and only if *all* jobs pay decent wages, can there be an enduring solution to problems of poverty and inequality that maximizes individual freedom and self-fulfillment, while contributing to the general prosperity.

The number and nature of jobs and the pay that workers receive, of course, are largely determined in the United States by private markets. The economic demand for various kinds of labor, and the supply of people willing to do the work, together heavily affect how many people do what kinds of work and how much they are paid for it. This can have important benefits in terms of individual freedom and economic efficiency. Private labor markets allow workers wide choices among jobs, they encourage people to do work that is as productive as possible (and therefore pays well), and they encourage employers to make efficient use of labor.

Left to themselves, however, private labor markets also have a dark side. As we noted in chapters 2 and 3, they generally—perhaps inevitably—cause high levels of poverty and income inequality. In economic downturns, they often bring extensive unemployment. As we discussed, it is very hard to argue that the poverty, inequality, and unemployment are just or deserved. Nor are they required for the sake of efficiency. There are good reasons therefore to use employment-related government policies to reduce poverty and inequality. This chapter deals with a wide range of government policies that can and do affect the supply of jobs and the level of wages.

We begin with several things that government *must* do, but that it can do in various ways that either help or hurt with jobs and wages. Control of the money supply, for instance, which is accepted as a proper government function even by those who advocate minimal government, inescapably affects economic growth, inflation, unemployment, and therefore the extent of poverty and inequality; it can either promote high levels of employment or throw people out of work. The balance or imbalance between taxes and spending ("fiscal policy"), too, affects unemployment, inflation, and growth. Government taxation and spending—even if restricted to providing public goods like national defense that practically everyone supports—inevitably have an impact on what sorts of jobs are available and how much workers get paid. (Roughly one-fifth of all U.S. workers work for or under contract to government, so that their jobs and wages depend directly on government policy.) Foreign policies concerning international trade, investment, and immigration, which we will deal with toward the end of the chapter, also inevitably affect U.S. markets in labor and capital by shaping the nature and extent of competition from abroad.

In these and other respects, deep government involvement in our modern economy is inevitable. Given that inevitability, it would be strange to pay no attention to whether particular policies tend to increase or to decrease poverty and inequality. We argue that a conscious effort should be made to use expansive fiscal and monetary policy to stimulate the economy, increase employment, and raise wages; to provide public goods in ways that help workers; and to avoid—or compensate for—damage to jobs caused by international trade, investment, and immigration policies.

The chapter also addresses a number of additional kinds of public policies that can greatly help provide jobs and raise wages. Such policies include help with job training and placement, public service employment (perhaps guaranteeing a job to everyone, which we see as superior to the prison option), minimum wage laws, tax credits for low-income workers, encouragement of labor unions, and antidiscrimination measures.

Next the chapter turns to the politics of jobs and wages—in which conflicts between business and labor and between Republicans and Democrats are paramount, and the power of money in politics tends to impede egalitarian policies. We close with a brief summary of our ideas about how to improve jobs and wages.

Managing the Economy

The biggest single factor affecting short-term changes in poverty and inequality is whether the economy is in a state of boom or bust. When business is booming, employers eagerly chase after employees—even those with limited skills. Labor markets are tight, and wages rise, especially at the bottom of the income scale. Poverty and inequality are reduced. But when the *business cycle* moves on to recession or depression and the economy goes bust, the demand for labor drops, wages fall, people are laid off, and those on the bottom are fired first. Poverty and inequality increase.[1]

Unemployment and Inequality

One key indicator of trouble for those at the bottom of the income scale, then, is a high level of *unemployment*. The unemployment rate is officially defined as the proportion of "members of the labor force"—that is, all those who are either working or "actively seeking" work—that are not employed at a given moment. This official rate during the 1980s and 1990s varied from a high of 9.7 percent of the workforce, nearly eleven million men and women (in 1982), to a low of only about 4 percent, less than six million (in 1999), with several ups and downs in between. Those figures represent a lot of jobless people even at the best of times, and a tremendous number at worst.[2]

But the official unemployment rate understates the problem that people have finding jobs. For one thing, it disregards "discouraged" and "marginally attached" workers who want jobs, but have given up looking. In 1998, for example, even when the economy was doing well and the labor market was tightening up, the 6 million officially unemployed were joined by *4.8 million* others who said they wanted jobs. For another thing, the official statistics count as employment *any* work "for pay or profit," including part-time work. Someone who flips hamburgers part-time, at wages too low to support a family, is still counted as employed. Many millions of discouraged and *un*deremployed people add to the pain of official unemployment, especially in hard times.[3]

Moreover, the unemployment *rate* at one moment in time conceals the much higher *frequency* with which the average worker is hit with unemployment for some period during a given year. For example, if the unemployment rate averaged 8 percent throughout the year and if (on the average) each unemployed worker were out of a job for four months, then the unemployment frequency would be fully *24 percent.* That is, 24 percent of all workers, or about one-quarter of them, would suffer unemployment *at some point* during the year.[4] Frequency figures do better than rate figures at indicating the large number of working people affected by joblessness, but they are not generally reported.

The rate and frequency of unemployment tend to rise and fall over the years in a more or less periodic *business cycle.* Since World War II, each business cycle has averaged about five years from peak to peak, with about fifty months of economic expansion followed by about eleven months of contraction.[5]

When the unemployment rate rises, the number of discouraged workers and unwilling part-time workers also rises, wages tend to fall, and poverty and inequality increase. Rebecca Blank and Alan Blinder have estimated that a sustained 1 percentage point rise in the unemployment rate has generally resulted in a 1.1-percentage-point increase in the poverty rate. Similarly, James Tobin found that over half the variance in year-to-year changes in the poverty rate could be accounted for by changes in average real weekly earnings and changes in the unemployment rate (poverty rates within each state have been even more strongly related to state unemployment rates). Tobin also found that higher unemployment rates led to withdrawal from the workforce—more "discouraged workers"—especially among young black males.[6]

True, a dose of unemployment can be an effective tool for "worker discipline."[7] But so can serfdom or flogging. We could do just fine without it.

At the beginning of the 1990s, the United States had enjoyed nearly eight years of economic expansion, but low-income working people had been battered by fifteen years of increased international competition and stagnant or falling wages. Then their lot worsened further when the United States was hit by a rather short but deep recession. The July 1990 economic peak was followed by eight months of contraction. In 1992, the unemployment rate (which generally lags a bit behind gross domestic product or GDP trends) reached a cyclical high point of 7.5 percent of the actively-job-seeking workforce, nearly ten million people. About thirty-eight million people, nearly

15 percent of the entire U.S. population, had cash incomes that fell below the official poverty line. Black Americans were even worse off: fully a third of them (33.4 percent) fell below the poverty line. Poverty and inequality were both extremely high.[8]

At the end of the 1990s, by contrast, the United States was enjoying the heights of a long economic boom. In 1999, the unemployment rate dropped to about 4 percent. Poverty was still high but substantially reduced: only about 10 percent of the population fell below the poverty line. To be sure, inequality had continued to increase: in 1997, the lowest-income one-fifth of households were getting only 3.6 percent of the country's cash income, down a bit from their 3.8 percent in 1992, while the top 5 percent of households were getting fully 21.7 percent of all U.S. cash income—up nicely from 18.6 percent in 1992. The boom was definitely skewed. Still, people at the bottom of the economic heap were better off at the end of the 1990s than at the beginning, just as they are almost always better off at economic peaks than in business cycle troughs.[9]

Toward the end of every relatively long economic expansion, when stock market euphoria soars and exuberant fads like miniskirts run wild, some guru or another generally proclaims that "the business cycle has been repealed" and that the boom will go on forever. So far in the recorded history of capitalism, however, every economic boom has been followed rather shortly by a downturn. The question is just how quickly the downturn comes and how bad it is.

The federal government inescapably plays a part in these economic cycles of boom and bust. Especially important are two types of *macroeconomic* policy: *monetary* policy, concerning whether government provides a large or small supply of money and whether it sets interest rates low or high, and *fiscal* policy, which concerns the balance or imbalance between the amount of tax revenues and the level of government spending.

Fiscal and Monetary Policy

On one point practically all economists agree: how the government handles fiscal and monetary policy has a big effect on the economy. If expenditures far outrun revenues, for example, or if money is printed with abandon, too many dollars will chase too few goods, and there will be *inflation* (defined as a *general* increase in price levels, including wages).

Inflation does not necessarily have the deeply evil effects that have been drummed into the minds of many Americans. For low-income people, inflation is not nearly as bad as unemployment. According to one estimate, inflation tends to increase poverty by only *one-seventh* as much as an equivalent amount of unemployment does (that is, between 1959 and 1983, a 1-percentage-point increase in the inflation rate increased the poverty rate by only one-seventh as much as a 1-percentage-point increase in the unemployment rate did).[10] In fact, some people actually tend to gain from unanticipated inflation. This is particularly true of people with large fixed-dollar debts (farmers owing for seeds and planting expenses, for instance, or people with fixed-rate home mortgages who would like to pay back their debts with cheaper currency). Others—especially creditors like banks and bond holders—tend to lose from inflation. (The suffering "fixed-income retiree" is largely a myth, since stock dividends reflect inflation and Social Security benefits are automatically adjusted for it.) The economy as a whole may tend to grow faster when there is mild inflation. Still, a high level of unexpected inflation does definitely upset the certainty and ability to plan that is important for doing business and running family finances.[11]

On the other hand, if the government spends a lot less than it takes in in taxes, prints too little money, or sets interest rates too high, the decline in available funds to spend or invest will make business slow down. The economy will slip into *recession*, defined as a decline of economic output for at least two consecutive quarters of the year. The unemployment rate will rise, and many people will be hurt—especially those at the bottom of the economic heap.

Beyond these points of agreement, there is considerable controversy among economists concerning how business cycles work and what government should do about them. Some "monetarists" like Milton Friedman have advocated keeping budgets exactly balanced and calibrating the supply of money so that it grows at a steady rate: ideally the same rate at which economic production grows, no more and no less.[12] Other economists acknowledge that in the long run budgets should not get far out of balance and the money supply should roughly keep pace with production (wages, for example, should rise only with increased productivity). But they object that a rigid monetary policy would subject the economy to unnecessary booms and busts. Why not use monetary policy in a *countercyclical* fashion, they say, tightening money and raising interest rates in boom times if inflation becomes excessive, but loosening money and lowering interest rates to revive economic activity when times are bad? [13]

For decades after the experience of the Great Depression, when recovery from a devastatingly sharp drop in production and an extremely high unemployment rate (perhaps as high as 37.6 percent of the nonfarm workforce in 1933) [14] came only in response to government spending on domestic programs and massive deficit spending on World War II, nearly all U.S. economists and policy makers became "Keynesians." That is, nearly everyone accepted the theory of John Maynard Keynes that in bad economic times governments should use fiscal and monetary policies to stimulate demand and increase economic activity. [15]

With the advent of "stagflation" (simultaneously high unemployment and inflation) in the 1970s, however, many U.S. economists came to reject the correctness of the "Phillips curve" analysis that there is a trade-off between unemployment and inflation and to doubt the efficacy of government policy. Robert Lucas and others argued that the "rational expectations" of economic actors will take full account of what the government is doing and adjust in such ways as to counteract the effects. Any use of monetary or fiscal policy to try to counteract economic downturns, they claimed, will be futile and perhaps counterproductive. Governments can indeed create inflation, the argument goes, but they cannot do anything to smooth the business cycle or to lower unemployment below a fixed "natural" rate. [16]

But the early "rational expectations" models did not fare well, chiefly because they wrongly assumed that prices, wages, and employment levels can adjust instantaneously. Macroeconomic policy is not impotent. [17] Moreover, the fixed "natural" rate of unemployment (largely representing the bare minimum of "frictional" unemployment that workers are supposedly bound to undergo as they switch from one job to another) began to look less like a scientific law and more like an ideological effort to apologize for anti-worker, pro–bond holder, high-unemployment policies. In the face of improving economic realities in the 1990s, estimates of the allegedly "natural" rate kept being devised downward, from 6 or 7 percent to 5 percent and then just 4 percent. Workers are not inevitably condemned to high levels of unemployment. [18]

Even if there are indeed limits to what government stimulation of the economy can accomplish in the long run—that is, even if there may be little or no long-term trade-off between inflation and unemployment—*in the short run,* and probably the medium run, there is clearly a choice. Loose money and low interest rates do plainly tend to moderate economic downturns, whereas tight money and high interest rates do slow economic activity and hurt low-income people.

The generally tight money and high interest rates pursued by the Federal Reserve Board from the late 1970s to the mid-1990s, under the chairmanship of Paul Volcker and then Alan Greenspan, undoubtedly contributed to cutting the rate of inflation. So did the fiercely antideficit, budget-balancing fiscal policies of the post-Reagan period. These policies very likely did improve business confidence and increase profits. But they exacted large costs by keeping wages lower than they would otherwise have been and by exacerbating two steep and very painful recessions, in 1980–82 (with two troughs) and 1990–91. Those recessions, and two decades of balanced-budget constrictions on government spending, caused a great deal of unnecessary suffering among low-income people and the poor.[19] The low interest rates of the late 1990s finally began to turn things around.

In efforts to reduce poverty and inequality in the United States, there is clearly a place for monetary policies that stimulate rather than retard the economy, especially in times of economic downturn. James Galbraith, among others, has argued that the single most important statistical determinant of wage inequality is the rate of unemployment, and that efforts to deal with poverty and inequality should focus on macroeconomic policies designed to achieve full employment.[20]

Economic Growth

Economic growth can obviously be helpful for dealing with poverty. There is no guarantee that it will, as the skewed growth of the 1980s so painfully demonstrated. But a "rising tide" has the *potential* to "lift all boats"—not just the yachts—if we are careful to make sure that the benefits are widely shared and that not too many boats have serious leaks. Clearly, if there is more money and more goods to go around, there is less need for anyone to be poor.

Historically growth has indeed been associated with lower poverty rates and less inequality in wages and salaries. This is evident in Tobin's and others' findings that *rises in average wages,* as well as declines in unemployment, have been associated with declines in poverty rates—at least until the 1980s.[21]

This has been true partly because economic growth generally brings high demand for labor and hence higher wages, especially at the low end of the wage scale. But it has also been true because, *politically,* economic growth and prosperity make it easier to take equalizing or redistributive policy measures. Economic growth makes it possible to direct new resources toward low-income people without making anyone worse off than they were.

As we have seen, certain government policies can directly contribute to both equality and economic growth. This is true of fiscal and monetary policies that stimulate the economy. It is true of education and training programs that upgrade the skills of people who would otherwise suffer from very low incomes. And it is true of policies like the Earned Income Tax Credit (discussed below) that reward and encourage work effort by low-income people. It may also be true of certain kinds policies designed to encourage business in geographical areas where poverty is concentrated, through "enterprise zones," "community development," "urban empowerment zones," and the like. But it is not clear that these programs actually promote economic growth (the tax breaks, easy credit, relief from regulation, and the like may merely lure businesses from elsewhere)or that much of the largesse actually trickles down to the poor. As Rebecca Blank points out, it may often be more efficient to establish "mobility programs" that help poor people with information, personal networks, and transportation to get jobs elsewhere.[22]

Certain other growth-oriented government policies do not directly help reduce income inequality, but do not much worsen it either, and can be justified in terms of public goods or positive externalities. This is generally true of grant and contract support for basic research, which is crucial to growth, but which private markets tend to underproduce. It can also be true of tax incentives for industrial research and development and reasonable depreciation allowances for plants and equipment, which encourage the development of and investment in new, growth-producing technology. If such measures get out of control, however, as they did in the early 1980s, their exacerbation of inequality (producing profits for wealthy shareholders at the expense of ordinary taxpayers) can outweigh their value in contributing to economic growth.

Still worse are certain policies that are publicized as encouraging economic growth, but actually have little or no demonstrated impact on growth and greatly increase inequality. A further reduction of taxes on capital gains, for example, is a perennial favorite in some quarters. To cut those taxes from their already privileged level would undoubtedly encourage the liquidation of some long-held assets and might somewhat encourage future investment in growth-oriented stocks, but the chief effect would be to provide an enormous windfall for wealthy owners of corporate stock. As we noted in chapter 5 on taxes, there is no persuasive evidence that such a cut would significantly increase economic growth. The same is true of proposals to adopt a nonprogressive "flat" tax on incomes or to abolish estate taxes.

It is sometimes asserted that *any* major effort to equalize incomes, by any means, will hinder economic growth: that a high degree of inequality is inevitable if we want to pursue economic efficiency. But considerable cross-national evidence suggests that this is not so. A number of the fastest-growing countries in the world are in fact more egalitarian than the United States, and the statistical association between equality and growth is *positive,* not negative. Income equality can help growth because a broad sharing of income and wealth creates the extensive consumer demand that energizes production.[23]

Jobs and Spending on Public Goods

When governments spend money for goods and services, such spending generally has indirect effects on poverty and inequality. Exactly what sort of effects depends on how and by whom the goods and services are produced: whether they are capital- or labor-intensive, for example, and whether they are generally provided by high- or low-income people. Thus certain spending on health, education, or welfare may as a side effect provide income to impoverished parents who work at Head Start centers. Or, perhaps more typically, it may help middle-class teachers, social workers, or academic researchers (some critics of these programs have argued that their main political support in fact comes from the middle-class clienteles—an argument that cannot be dismissed out of hand). Medical care spending may sometimes enrich high-income physicians, the makers of expensive medical technology, the owners of pharmaceutical firms, and the like; some propoor regulations and legal remedies may do the same for the lawyers who litigate class-action suits. To the extent that they do so—a little-explored empirical question— the equalizing effects of those programs may be partly undercut.

Some of the biggest indirect effects of spending on poverty and inequality proceed from the substantial portion of the federal budget that goes to spending on the military, the environment, energy, science and technology, foreign affairs, and other areas involving more or less public goods.

Military Spending

During and just after the Korean War, national defense was by far the biggest thing that the U.S. federal government did. Military spending took up nearly 70 percent of the entire budget. This proportion has crept rather steadily downward ever since, however. It dropped to about 50 percent at the end of the 1950s and barely above 40 percent before the Vietnam War got under way. It rose a bit (to 45 percent) at the peak of the Vietnam War and then dropped rapidly to 30 percent shortly after Vietnam, to about 25 percent in the 1980s (with only a small upward blip during the Reagan years), and below 20 percent after the collapse of the Soviet Union and the end of the Cold War. The trend in military spending expressed as a proportion of GDP looks similar: from 14 percent in 1953 to 9.4 percent in 1968, 5.5 percent in 1974, 4.7 percent in 1979, about 6 percent in the 1980s, and less than 5 percent after 1991.[24]

By the beginning of the twenty-first century, military spending constituted just 16 percent of the federal budget (3 percent of GDP) and was projected to keep shrinking. Defense is no longer even close to the biggest function of the federal government; as we saw in chapter 4, that role has been taken over by social insurance programs like Social Security and Medicare. Still, the military outlays of more than $270 billion in 2000 were quite substantial. They were far greater, for example, than the federal education programs discussed in the last chapter or the job training programs discussed in this one. To most antipoverty programs, $10 billion (just 1/27 of the military budget) seems like a lot of money.

One may wonder whether such a substantial level of military spending still makes sense after the end of the Cold War, when actual or potential adversaries like Iraq, Serbia, and North Korea are minuscule by comparison to the United States. Even China and Russia put together could not remotely challenge U.S. military power if they felt inclined to do so. (In the mid-1990s, for example, Russia was spending only about $513 per person annually on the military, and China was only spending a tiny $53 per person, compared to the U.S. figure of $1,056. Russia's and China's military expenditures together summed to only $139.5 billion, about half of the U.S. $278 billion,[25] and their military technology was much inferior.) Perhaps we could spend less on the military and more on long-starved "discretionary" budget items for education and jobs.[26]

Quite aside from that, however, we can ask what indirect effects military spending has had on poverty and inequality. In one important respect, at least, military spending itself tends to *reduce* poverty and inequality in the United States. A substantial part of the military budget, close to one-third of it (about $80 billion in 2000) goes to pay for the salaries, benefits, and living expenses of about 1.4 million men and women in uniform and their families.[27] That is a lot of employees. The pay and benefits of an all-volunteer military supplement and compete with what is offered in the private sector, so that much of the money goes to people who would otherwise be earning lower wages in the civilian labor market. From this point of view, the U.S. military is a huge public service employment project, providing reasonable incomes—and valuable training—to many people who would otherwise be impoverished or barely scrape by. With its strict policies against racial discrimination, the military has provided particularly good opportunities not only to poor whites, but also to African Americans, Hispanics, and Native Americans. Many minorities—most dramatically represented by former Joint Chiefs of Staff Chairman Colin Powell—have been able to work their way into the top ranks on a merit basis without having to face the obstacles still found in much of the civilian world.[28]

To be sure, this is an odd sort of public employment program. If the military budget is larger than national security and international peacekeeping projects actually require, it would be more productive for society to pay these people to conserve national forests or to care for youngsters, rather than march around and practice marksmanship. (Of course, the military can do useful peacetime work like rebuilding bridges in hurricane-devastated Central America or catching drug smugglers, but this still represents a small part of its activity and may raise problems concerning professionalism and civilian control.) Still, the net effect of spending on military personnel is almost certainly to reduce poverty and to increase income equality in the United States. The *volunteer* system of military service, which ensures that pay must be high enough to attract enlistees, is crucial to this progressive effect. The compulsory draft system of the past amounted to a regressive tax—in wartime, a very bloody tax—that disproportionately fell on low-income and minority people.

Similar reasoning applies to the large part of the military budget (roughly another third of it) that goes for low-tech aspects of operation, maintenance, military construction, and procurement. Uniforms and food for the troops, barracks, and routine spare parts often involve labor-intensive production. When the military buys large quantities of such things, it tends to increase the demand for labor and thus (to a modest extent) raises the wages of low-income civilian workers.

No such egalitarian effect, however, results from the development and procurement of high-tech military *equipment,* especially the technologically sophisticated fighter-bombers, aircraft carriers, "smart" bombs, and nuclear missiles that tend to be highly promoted by defense firms and their allies in Congress. As the twenty-first century began, for example, the U.S. military was still pouring money into not-yet-successful anti-ballistic-missile defenses. It was buying Tomahawk missiles and smart bombs, new V-22 and Comanche helicopters, and (at $1 billion each) Aegis guided-missile destroyers. The separate armed services were eager to procure *three* different new fighter aircraft systems: the Navy's Super Hornets, the Air Force's F-22 Raptors, and the Joint Strike Fighter designed for all services (F-22s cost more than $300 million for each plane).[29] The manufacture of such weapons is relatively capital-intensive, relying on expensive computers, industrial plants, and machine tools. Much of the labor that goes into designing and building them comes from highly paid engineers, scientists, and technicians. When the defense budget creates demand for high-tech weaponry—often in excess of experts' and military leaders' assessments of needs—it increases the demand for and the salaries of a set of high-income workers, thus increasing income inequality.[30]

The "jobs" often touted as coming from military contracts tend to be jobs or profits for small numbers of politically potent people, including the owners of defense firms. By the late 1990s, for example, defense giant Lockheed Martin was spending about $1 million per year on campaign contributions; Northrop Grumman, Boeing, McDonnell Douglas, Raytheon, and Hughes Aircraft were also spending large sums to get procurement contracts.[31]

Peaceful Public Goods

A substantial part of the federal budget is spent on nonmilitary, more-or-less-public goods related to the environment, science and technology, energy, foreign policy, and so forth. It would be a tedious task to try to disentangle the many different employment effects of the bewildering array of programs, but some general observations can be offered.

In contrast to the employment of military personnel and the operation of social spending programs, many programs that provide nonmilitary public goods tend to channel benefits and income to people in the upper part of the income scale. This is true both of their employment effects and of their direct benefits. Even a "pure" public good would not necessarily be consumed or enjoyed equally by everyone. Since we seldom fund public goods through taxes based on individuals' preferences for those goods (it is rarely feasible to do so, even if we wanted to), some people get much more benefit or enjoyment from such goods than they pay for them in taxes. Others get much less. Often the winners are the well-to-do. And often the process of producing the goods, too, tilts toward upper-income people.

The acquisition and maintenance of national parks and other public lands, for example, provides the biggest direct benefits to middle- and upper-middle-income people who can afford to travel and enjoy them. And land acquisition, except perhaps in certain rare eminent domain cases, tends to give substantial compensation to large landowners and real estate developers (last-minute speculators seem to do particularly well). Research and development spending rather heavily flows to high-income scientists and engineers. The development of nuclear or fusion energy, new spacecraft, supercomputers, high-speed rail transportation, new navigational and communication systems, and so forth is unlikely to involve the employment of many low-income people.

None of this is to say that such spending is necessarily a bad idea. These programs should rise or fall chiefly on the strength or weakness of their rationales in terms of public goods or positive externalities. But in assessing what government does or should do about poverty and inequality, it makes sense to examine whether some programs have negative side effects on inequality. We can then consider efforts to minimize such effects or to compensate for them. In particular, if we find it easy to come up with many tens of billions of dollars in government spending for advanced military and civilian technology, we might want to find comparable funds to help educate all Americans and to help provide them with jobs at good wages.

Job Training and Placement

In a job-centered approach to poverty of the sort that we advocate, it is important to make special efforts to train disadvantaged adults and place them in jobs. Since 1961, several federal government programs have attempted to do this, but after a high point in the late 1970s, the level of commitment and funding fell. As of the mid-1990s, no more than 5 percent of those declared eligible actually got training (placement help has been more widespread). Most of the adult training programs, as well as about half of the youth programs, were combined under the Job Training Partnership Act (JTPA), the result of sharp cuts and program consolidations in 1982. JTPA was replaced starting in 2000 by the quite similar Workforce Investment Act (WIA).[32]

JTPA was—and WIA is—a joint public/private, federal/state/local program. The federal government provides most of the money: on the order of $3 billion per year, about one-third of it for adult training. The money is mainly given in block grants to the states. The states set up oversight and coordinating councils of various sorts, and local boards of public and private officials supervise activities carried out by both public and private training and educational institutions. JTPA as a whole served about one million people per year, roughly half of them adults, but most of them got very limited services: generally just job referrals and "how to look for a job" sessions. Only about 175,000 disadvantaged adults per year, under Title II-A, got some vocational training (about twenty weeks, on the average) in the form of free tuition at a local community college or technical school. Only about one-fifth of those people got work experience or on-the-job training; such arrangements dropped markedly after the 1980s, since few employers were willing to deal with less attractive workers in return for a small and temporary subsidy. Most of the training was for low-skill occupations that can at best produce only modest incomes.[33] The pattern for WIA is very similar. In 2000, it spent just under $1 billion to help about 380,000 adults with training, support, and job placement.[34]

Given the skimpiness of these programs, they have had surprisingly good effects. Women, in particular, show significant gains in employment and earnings with even minimal encouragement, perhaps because women trainees typically have little labor market experience and take good advantage of confidence-building and job-seeking tips. Men in these programs (many of them scarred by bad past employment experiences) generally gain less than women. But men's gains are still sufficient, especially in terms of employment stability rather than increased wages, to make the program worthwhile in cost-benefit terms. In 2000, about 65 percent of those who received services were expected to be working three months after leaving the program, with weekly earnings averaging about $360—substantially over the poverty line. A study of better-funded Comprehensive Employment Training Act (CETA) programs in the

1970s indicated that the employment and wage gains of those people who trained for more than forty weeks were six times as great as for those who trained for fewer than twenty weeks, suggesting (though not proving) that present training periods may be too short.[35]

The impact of currently available job training for disadvantaged adult men, then, is limited by pinched funding that restricts the number of people reached. Programs have not been well advertised, there is too little money to cover anywhere near all those eligible, and the 1982 elimination of stipends has made it hard for some trainees to afford sticking with the program. This has restricted what can be done for them: very brief training or none at all, and little work experience. Major expansion of this sort of program would not be cheap and would not be a panacea, but it could substantially improve the lot of many poor people. With much more intensive and long-term training, and with actual work experience, it could begin to qualify many people for jobs that could raise their families above the poverty line.

More generously funded—perhaps because it is chiefly a middle-class program—is the "Title III" segment of JTPA, now (under WIA) referred to as Dislocated Worker Employment and Training Activities. Title III spent about $1 billion per year to help workers who were dislocated or displaced by plant closings, job abolition, and the like due to import competition or other factors. According to Congressional Budget Office estimates, some *two million* American workers were displaced annually during the 1980s, often after many years of loyal service to the same employer. Job displacement seems to have continued subsequently at a substantial, though somewhat lower, rate. Not all these people are poor, of course; in fact, fewer than one-third of them are. Most have good skills, and many find new jobs quickly, especially when the economy is booming. Title III provided job search and relocation allowances, as well as weekly "trade adjustment" payments after unemployment insurance ran out, so long as the individual continued with certified training. Roughly half of the program enrollees received some training, which apparently paid off. In one year in the mid-1990s, when 188,000 people underwent training, 76 percent were placed in a job at the termination of training, and they had a wage recovery rate of 93.6 percent (that may be more a function of their preexisting skills than of the training, since those who skipped training did even better). Still, job displacement hurts. One source estimates that the displaced have suffered an average long-term loss of $80,000 in earnings, which it would take at least two years of retraining to make up.[36]

Again, the setup under the new WIA is much like that of the old JTPA. WIA's Dislocated Worker program spent about $1.6 billion in 2000 and reached about 840,000 displaced workers. The Clinton administration predicted that some 74 percent of those who received services would be working three months after leaving the program and that their wages would average 93 percent of the wages at their previous jobs.[37]

The federal-state Job Service, established back in 1933 and now known as the federal-state Employment Service, attempts to match employers with job seekers. A small proportion of these job seekers (about 2.9 million of 19 million per year served in the mid-1990s) are poor or "economically disadvantaged." State employment services get a little over $1 billion in federal funds per year for "One-Stop Career Centers" in perhaps 18,000 local employment offices. There is also increasing use of the Internet for bringing together job listings and job seekers through "America's Job Bank" and matching resumes and employers through "America's Talent Bank." These efforts are useful, but cannot perform magic. Jobs are often listed because they are hard to fill (i.e., not very desirable), and people apply because they are hard to place. Moreover, there have generally been many more seekers than jobs. In one month in the mid-1990s, the computerized Job Bank offered 400,000 job listings, but had 5.3 million applicant inquiries. Overall, during the same period, about one-third of all individuals who were referred were placed in employment, but this amounted to only 18 percent of all employment service applicants.[38]

Welfare to Work

Of particular importance in recent years have been efforts to get women "off welfare" (especially out of the former federal program of Aid to Families with Dependent Children, or AFDC) and get them to work. After a period of state-level experimentation, the 1988 Family Support Act required all states to run mandatory work placement programs for "work-eligible" AFDC recipients, under the federal JOBS (Job Opportunity and Basic Skills) program. Besides group work-preparedness sessions and assistance with job searches, these programs helped with transportation to job interviews and, in the case of successful job placement, extended Medicaid eligibility and provided child-care subsidies. They tried to centralize services, with a case manager helping each client overcome a variety of different obstacles to getting a job. For a few participants, some states also funded extensive training programs to complete a high school equivalency degree or post–high school training, but little money was available for this. Women assigned to the program were "required" to participate or be penalized by a reduction in AFDC benefits. But in fact enough money was provided for only about 600,000 of the five million AFDC women to get help.[39]

The evidence indicates that even minimal efforts along these lines produced employment and earnings gains among AFDC women, effects that lasted at least three years after completion of the program. A middle group of women who had acceptable literacy skills but who had been out of the labor market for a while benefited the most. Even from the narrowest cost-benefit perspective, these programs paid for themselves: costs were more than recovered through decreases in AFDC payments as the women worked more. Still, few women escaped poverty in this way; they typically gained only $150 to $600 per year on balance after subtracting the AFDC payments they gave up.[40] This illustrates a major theme of our book. Education and training programs cannot do much about poverty unless they ensure that the poor become qualified for reasonably high-paying jobs *and* that such jobs are widely available.

The 1996 legislation that abolished AFDC required that states involve a high percentage of their welfare caseload in work programs by early in the twenty-first century and that there be a fixed time limit for welfare benefits. The federal government helped out to a significant, though hardly lavish, extent. In 2000, about $1 billion was budgeted for grants to the states and local communities to help with job creation, job placement, job retention, and various postemployment support services. Small amounts were also spent to develop flexible transportation alternatives to get people to jobs, training programs, and child-care centers, and to provide housing vouchers to help some 75,000 welfare recipients to move closer to a new job or reduce a long commute. In addition, substantial tax credits were offered to employers, worth 35 percent (and in the second year, 50 percent) of the first $10,000 of wages paid to long-term welfare recipients.[41]

As of the end of the 1990s, the welfare rolls had been much reduced, and all reporting states had met the initial requirement that 25 percent of welfare recipients be engaged in work or training. (As we will see in the next chapter, however, exactly what happened to the former AFDC recipients, some of whom were stuck without either jobs or welfare, is more problematic.) The next requirement, that 50 percent of the welfare caseload be engaged in work or training by 2002, is expected to be more difficult to meet. It is also unclear how the states and Congress will respond when recessions create bigger public assistance caseloads and put heavy pressure on the system at the same time that state tax revenues decline.[42]

To the extent that welfare-to-work programs succeed in turning millions (roughly three million) of former welfare recipients loose on the job market, a troubling question arises: what effect will this new supply of labor have on the wages of low-skill Americans generally? The answer is not hard to discern. When the supply of something (e.g., labor) rises, its price (e.g., wages) tends to fall. As economist Robert Solow has put it, "Guess who pays for workfare?" His answer is that low-income workers will pay. Jobs will be scarce, and wages will tend to drop. Only if new jobs are created—through public service employment or employer incentives—and wages are subsidized (e.g., through the Earned Income Tax Credit) is this story likely to have a happy ending.[43]

Job training programs can work. The main problem has been meager funding.

Creating Jobs

Public Service Employment

What if, even after government has educated and trained workers, stimulated the economy, and purchased the usual range of public goods, private labor markets still do not provide enough jobs with good wages to eliminate poverty or reduce inequality? One possible answer is that *government* itself should directly provide jobs. At certain points in American history, this has actually been done, most notably with the Public Works Administration (PWA) and Works Progress Administration (WPA). The PWA and WPA rescued many unemployed people during the Great Depression of the 1930s, and they produced some enduring monuments (bridges, Diego Rivera murals, the Blue Ridge Parkway).[44] More recently the Comprehensive Employment Training Act (CETA) placed some of the unemployed—only about *one-twentieth* of them—in public service jobs early in the deep and discouraging recession(s) of 1980–82. CETA gave people jobs when they most needed work, and it appears also to have produced at least some modest long-run earnings gains.[45]

The usual objection, particularly from those suspicious of government in any form, is that "make-work" is inefficient; that what is produced is not worth the cost. It is not hard to find horror stories about lazy WPA workers or poorly run CETA programs that did not provide serious training and had unclear effects on participants' long-term labor prospects. Moreover, there can be political obstacles from local governments that do not want to partici-pate, public employees and private contractors who do not want to be dis-placed, and businesspeople who do not want wage rates driven up. For those reasons, political support and funding for CETA fell, and Democrats did not object much when CETA was completely abolished (only partly replaced by JTPA, without public service employment) under the Reagan administration in 1983.[46]

With careful program design, however, it should be possible to overcome these problems and objections. Local governments could be given incentives to participate, and unions could be reassured about effects on their members, by ensuring that public service employees do significant *new* work—such as repairing our crumbling infrastructure and cleaning up the environment—that would not otherwise be done. Workers can be assigned to nonprofit institutions, as well as government. The "not worth it" objection misses the point that if substantial productive work is done, it may be worth subsidizing wages at above-market rates, precisely in order to fight poverty and inequal-ity, while also getting valuable public goods produced for society as a whole. And any long-term gains in skills and private sector employability are a bonus. The main point is just to make sure that everyone has a job, especially during economic downturns.

Many other advanced countries have much higher proportions of their labor force working in the public sector than the United States does (at one point, Sweden's proportion was 33 percent, compared to 16 percent in the United States). And the pressures of economic globalization do not seem to have led to much retrenchment in this respect. Up to 1994, for example, Germany, Italy, the Netherlands, Denmark, and Belgium showed barely dis-cernible drops in the level of public employment; Sweden, one of the highest public employers in the world, declined by little more than one-tenth. Only the United Kingdom, in the grips of Thatcherism, experienced a large (29 percent) decline. Norway and Sweden, among other countries, have used their extensive public employment (as well as generous provision of child care, tax incentives, and other policies) to achieve particularly high labor force participation and employment among women.[47]

We may not wish to go as far in this direction as Scandinavia. Since the United States appears to have made the political decision that all able-bodied people must be required to work rather than receive welfare, however, it would seem to follow—unless we are totally heartless—that we should provide jobs for them that pay decent wages. So long as many of the poor continue to have limited skills, and so long as private labor markets put little value on their work (even onerous physical labor), public service employment looks like a serious option to consider. It would be especially useful to have a standby program in place with a quick trigger that would rapidly expand public service employment during recessions.

The Prison Option

While the United States has so far rejected the idea of extensive public service employment, we have drifted toward an alternative that seems odd, even bizarre: locking up large numbers of our poor people in prison.

By the end of the 1990s, we began to see the results of more than two decades of crusades against crime, with stricter laws, harsher sentences (including "three strikes and you're out" for life in many states, plus rigid federal guidelines[48]), and the building of many new prisons. The population of people in U.S. jails and prisons on any given day was rising toward *two million* people, almost *six times* as many as were incarcerated in 1972, before the prison boom started. The incarceration rate of 668 inmates per 100,000 U.S. residents (not far from 1 person out of every 100) had more than doubled since 1985 and stood as the highest in Western countries—very nearly the highest in the world, period. The U.S. incarceration rate is five to ten times as high as in the countries of Western Europe, about six times the rate in Canada, and twenty times as high as in Japan.[49]

Most prison inmates, of course, do not come from the upper crust of society. Most come from the bottom. Many are also members of ethnic or racial minorities. The number of African Americans in U.S. jails or prisons reached nearly *one million* in 2000, with approximately *one in ten* black men incarcerated. (Nearly one in seven black men loses the right to vote as a convicted felon.) The absolute numbers of jailed blacks and whites are roughly equal, which makes blacks more than *six times* more likely than whites to be held in jail. This disparity is related to more severe prosecution and sentencing, not just greater frequency or greater gravity of offenses.[50]

As a strategy for dealing with poverty, incarceration has several disadvantages. One is the sheer cost of prisons: about $50,000 or $60,000 per cell to build and perhaps $20,000 per inmate every year to maintain and operate.

Even college is usually cheaper. A lot of constructive antipoverty programs could be funded with the approximately $40 billion per year in state and federal money that is spent on jails and prisons.[51] Additional costs to society include the productive work that inmates are not doing. (To the extent that they work inside prison, they amount to something like slave labor, great for the profits of corporate contractors, but damaging to the wages of competing workers on the outside.[52] This problem might be solved by paying full wages, part for victim restitution and the rest going into blocked accounts until prisoners are released.) Also lost is the care that people in prison are not giving to spouses and children at home. But the biggest cost is the lifelong negative effect on people who go to prison. They are permanently branded as ex-cons, have bleak prospects of getting good jobs, and are trained in prison (by other inmates) mainly at more effective techniques of committing crimes. Rehabilitation is a lost dream, barely attempted and with little success. All in all, prisons are a very expensive option.

"But these are *criminals!*" you may say. "We want to be safe on the streets. Lock 'em up!" True, the great preponderance of inmates are guilty of crimes—though an alarming number of condemned men on Death Row have been proved innocent by DNA tests or by confessions from the real criminals, and minorities get executed more often than white perpetrators of similar crimes.[53] True also, the prison boom probably contributed to the steady decline in rates of virtually all kinds of crime, so that in the late 1990s those rates reached the lowest point since comparable statistics were first gathered in 1973 (other factors were important as well, however, including an improved economy, the aging population, the ebbing of the crack epidemic, and perhaps community policing).[54] A lot of violent crime is committed by a very few repeat offenders, and when they are locked up, the world is a pleasanter place.

Still, without being softheaded about crime, it is possible to be appalled by the extent of imprisonment in the United States. The combination of heavy spending on prisons and scant spending on antipoverty efforts seems to ignore the obvious point that crime is partly caused by poverty and by lack of legitimate economic opportunities. Antipoverty efforts can have positive side effects of reducing criminal activity—often more cost-effectively—while being more humane in the bargain. This becomes most obvious when we remember that most—more than two-thirds—of the two million inmates of jails and prisons are *not violent offenders* at all. Many, about one-third, are in for nonviolent property crimes like burglary, auto theft, fraud, or embezzlement. And an increasing proportion (about another third; half of all federal prisoners) are jailed for "victimless" or *consensual* crimes like the use or sale of "controlled substances" or, in the common parlance, drugs.[55] (Official language refers to "controlled substances" rather than "drugs" because of two awkward facts: some prohibited drugs are medicinally helpful, and the use of some harmful drugs like alcohol and tobacco is not criminalized.)

Drug offenses accounted for more of the 1980–96 increase in state prisoners than any other type of crime: 29 percent of the whole increase. To put it another way, drug offenders shot up from only about 7 percent of state prisoners in 1980 to about 30 percent in 1996. By the end of the 1990s, more than 400,000 Americans were in prison for drug offenses; they constituted a higher percentage of the population than those in prison for *all* crimes in England, France, Germany, and Japan combined. There are some puzzling disparities in the treatment of different drugs, such as crack versus powder cocaine (ghetto-dwelling crack users have been imprisoned much longer than upper-class cocaine sniffers) and marijuana versus alcohol, that do not seem much related to the harm they may cause. To the extent that we are determined to cut down drug use, it is well established that by far the most cost-effective way (and, again, the most humane way) to do so is through medical treatment. A RAND study estimated that a dollar invested in treatment programs would reduce U.S. cocaine consumption by about four times as much as a dollar invested in standard law enforcement techniques, and about *eight times* as much as the same expenditure on longer prison sentences for drug dealers. Treatment was estimated to have an even more dramatic advantage—ten or fifteen times the effectiveness of criminal justice measures—in reducing cocaine-related crime.[56]

The prison option seems inhumane, expensive, and ineffective. For many nonviolent (and some violent) offenders, close supervision, medical treatment, training programs, and public service employment would be superior.

Guaranteed Jobs?

A logical extension of the idea of public service employment is that government should *guarantee* jobs at reasonable wages for everyone, serving as employer of last resort when necessary. The Universal Declaration of Human Rights seems to embrace this idea when it asserts that everyone has the "right to work" (Article 23-1) and the right to "just and favourable remuneration

223

insuring . . . an existence worthy of human dignity" (Article 23-3). Opinion surveys provide some evidence that the idea appeals to the American public. Dozens of queries about whether the government should "see to it" that everybody can find a job, or whether government should "do more" to expand employment, have elicited support from about two-thirds of the public. And a specific question in the 1970s about passage of a "full employment bill in which the government guarantees a job to everyone who wants to work" won 60 to 66 percent support (the public is seldom given a chance to answer such questions).[57]

It may seem odd, therefore, that a job guarantee has not been prominent on the agenda of American politics, at least not since it was rejected as part of the Full Employment Act of 1946. But the reason is not hard to find: near-monolithic opposition by U.S. business interests, which have a great deal of political clout. Guaranteed work would substantially raise businesses' labor costs by eliminating the "reserve army of the unemployed" and ending the downward pressure on wages that is exerted by competition among under-employed or underpaid workers. That is presumably why the stock market reacts nervously to drops in unemployment rates, and why pundits sometimes decry wage gains as signifying "inflation." If the government guaranteed that everyone could have a job and earn a good wage, all employers would have to pay wages at least as high as the guaranteed level in order to attract employees.

By the same token, of course, such a guarantee would go a long way toward eliminating poverty. It would have a profound equalizing effect on the distribution of income. It is hard to imagine any other measure that would have comparable effects, other than a high level of guaranteed *income* regardless of work (a measure with less economic appeal and considerably less political appeal to Americans). As we recover from the antigovernment rhetoric of recent years, there are some signs that policy makers' receptiveness to the idea of guaranteed work may be increasing. Articulate advocates include William Julius Wilson, Sheldon Danziger, and Peter Gottschalk.[58]

Raising Wages

The point is not only to make sure that everyone able to work has a job, but also to be sure that everyone is *paid adequately* for working; that, for example, millions of working people no longer fall below the poverty line. Stimulation of the economy and the provision of well-paid public service jobs can help raise wage levels. So can a range of other government policies, from minimum wage laws to low-income tax credits, encouragement of trade unions, and laws against job or wage discrimination by race, gender, age, or other arbitrary characteristics.

Minimum Wage Laws

If the private labor market produces extremely low wages and a high degree of inequality, one thing government can do is simply *require* that all workers be paid at least a specified minimum amount per hour. Since the Fair Labor Standards Act of 1938, federal legislation has in fact mandated such a "minimum wage" requirement. The federal minimum wage has gradually covered an increasing proportion of the nonsupervisory workforce: now about nine out of ten such workers, although some ten million people, in retail, service industries, and agriculture, are still not covered.[59]

Generations of economists have argued that high minimum wage requirements are likely to have a counterproductive effect. The standard argument asserts that if employers are forced to pay more than market-based wages for low-skill workers (that is—assuming a marginal product theory of wages— more than their work is worth), then the employers simply will *not hire* such workers. Instead of raising the wages of the lowest-income workers, the argument goes, minimum wages will throw them out of jobs and increase unemployment.

But research by David Card and Alan Krueger has cast considerable doubt on this conventional wisdom. Using careful econometric techniques to examine what happened when state minimum wages were raised in New Jersey and California and when the federal minimum was raised in 1990– 91, they found that unemployment did *not* appreciably rise.[60] This suggests that minimum wage laws, within a reasonable range, can actually help low-income wage earners without the negative side effects that were once thought inevitable.

Reacting to the old economic arguments—and perhaps also to retail, fast-food, and other businesses' strong feelings about the matter—Congress has generally set the minimum wage at a very low level, seldom above 50 percent of the median wage in the country. That way few workers are actually affected by it. Congress has also been slow to increase the level of the minimum wage to keep up with inflation. During the 1980s, the minimum stayed fixed at a dismal $3.35 per hour, while the cost of living rose 40 percent. To put it another way, the inflation-adjusted value of the minimum wage dropped by nearly one-third. In 1981, a full-time, year-round worker at the minimum wage earned just enough to support a family of three right at a poverty-line level, but by 1989, the income of the same worker and family had fallen to only 70.5 percent of the poverty line. (A family of four was even worse off, at 55 percent of the poverty line.) A series of small minimum wage increases after that did little more than keep even with further increases in the cost of living, so that many families with only a single, full-time minimum wage worker were left in poverty. Only toward the end of the 1990s, as the federal minimum wage rose to $4.75 (1996) and $5.15 (1997)—still rather meager levels when the median wage in the country for full-time workers was around $10—did it begin to make up some of the ground lost in the 1980s.[61]

While the federal minimum wage was stagnating in the early 1990s, several states enacted more generous minimum wages of their own. A "living wage" movement also has prevailed in a number of cities, including Baltimore, New York, Los Angeles, Chicago, Boston, and Milwaukee. The idea of the "living wage"—advocated by Joel Rogers and the New Party, among others—is to ensure that workers in firms contracting with local governments pay wages sufficient for a decent standard of living. San Jose, California, for example, in 1998 adopted what was then the nation's highest "living wage" on record, requiring that service workers under new city contracts be paid at least $9.50 per hour plus health benefits. That was nearly double the federal ($5.15) or state ($5.75) minimum wage at that time. Since a city or other government body is not obliged to make a profit, its taxpayers and voters are free to pay city employees as high wages as they want to pay. In the long run, though, high wage costs (in San Jose's case, the first-year cost was estimated at only $350,000 for about 720 workers) might provoke taxpayer resistance or encounter budget constraints and cause some reduction in employment. Even the public sector is not immune to effects from the labor market. Still, for the particular set of workers contracting with governments, this has been an encouraging trend.[62]

Whether they are enacted at the federal, state, or local level, however, minimum wage and "living wage" requirements are likely to play only a part in dealing with poverty and inequality. If they were set high enough to substantially redistribute incomes, there could be significantly negative effects on employment and economic growth. Only within the modest ranges that have been tried in recent decades can we be sure that minimum wages make a positive contribution to the average incomes of poor Americans. Minimum wages are most effective as complements or "companion tools" along with other programs that fight poverty. In 1997, for example, a full-time minimum wage worker who supported a family of four earned (at that year's $5.15 rate) $10,300 for the year. She or he could also receive the maximum Earned Income Tax Credit of $3,560 and Food Stamps worth $2,876, while paying $788 in payroll taxes. The family's net income would then just barely exceed the applicable poverty line of $15,600—no princely sum, but maybe enough to get by.[63] Minimum wage laws also work best when other measures are used at the same time to keep the general level of wages high.

Earned Income Tax Credit

As the above example suggests, the Earned Income Tax Credit (EITC) is very important in helping workers at the bottom of the economic scale to earn a minimally satisfactory income around the poverty line or not far below. This is one income-transfer program that follows eminently conservative economic principles, because it provides a strong incentive to work. Only working people get the credit, and the more they earn (up to a point), the more they get. The EITC was established in 1975 and was expanded markedly in 1993, with substantial bipartisan support; it weathered attacks by right-wing congressional Republicans in the mid-1990s.[64]

The EITC is only loosely attached to the federal income tax; it is a *refundable* credit. Either it can be subtracted from taxes due (in a lump sum in April or by "reverse withholding" throughout the year) or, if it exceeds tax liabilities, it can be taken as a check from the government. Workers with dependent children get most of the benefits, a significant limitation of the program. The size of the credit varies, depending on the number of children and the level of earnings. As an individual goes to work and earns the first few thousand dollars of income, each dollar earned is supplemented by as much as a 40 cent credit (less with fewer children), providing a strong incentive to enter the labor market and earn some income. As earnings increase, the percentage credit declines, and after earnings reach a certain level, the total dollar amount of the credit stays constant. At still higher earning levels, the total credit is gradually reduced, reaching zero for earnings above about $30,000. In 2000, some twenty million families received credits averaging

$1,644 each. The maximum credit was about $4,000—enough to make quite a difference to low-income families.[65]

Studies indicate that the EITC does in fact encourage poor people to work.[66] These effects could probably be increased further if potential recipients were clearly told exactly how the credit supplements each dollar they earn, so that they would not think of it as just another feature of the tax system. The lump-sum way in which most people get the credit sometimes creates difficulties, since it does not add to monthly income that can be used to pay for rent and groceries. But some recipients apparently like the forced-savings aspect of getting a big one-time payment that they can use for major debt payments or big-ticket purchases.

The EITC has become one of the largest and most important antipoverty programs in the United States. In 2000, it involved $27 billion in outlays plus $5 billion in "tax expenditures" (foregone tax revenues), for a total of $32 billion.[67] This made it substantially bigger than the $21 billion Food Stamp program, let alone the many very small antipoverty programs we have been discussing. But given its sound, work-oriented economic basis and its crucial role in helping the working poor, the size of the EITC remains rather modest. This is especially so when its $32 billion is compared to the roughly $270 billion spent on the military or the $1,800 billion total federal budget. For those who want to reduce poverty and inequality, while encouraging all able-bodied people to work, expansion of the EITC to give more help to people without children and to offer more substantial benefits should be a top priority item.

Encouraging Labor Unions

Historically a very important force for higher wages among workers has been organized labor. In Europe—and, to a significantly lesser extent, in the United States—trade unions have used collective bargaining, backed by the threat of strikes, to drive wages upward.

One function of unions is to force employers to pay wages above what an unconstrained labor market, with individual workers competing against each other, would otherwise dictate. The idea that unions could have the power to do this, through cooperation and solidarity among many workers, drives some businesspeople and economists apoplectic. Isn't free individual competition desirable under all circumstances, among workers just as among businesses? Doesn't competition lead to efficiency? Why should workers and their unions be allowed to engage in "collusion" or to exert "monopoly power"? Why should they be permitted to prevent the forces of competition from driving their wages down to whatever level is set by supply and demand? [68]

But this objection to unions and collective bargaining ignores issues of equity and justice. It focuses only on efficiency, treating labor as a commodity to be bought and sold in the marketplace just like any other commodity. Do we really want workers' jobs and incomes to be determined in the same way that the price of a candy bar or a CD is determined, even if that creates a lot of poverty and inequality? Working men and women are, before anything else, human beings. There are many reasons—some of them mentioned in chapters 2 and 3—for insisting that human beings' incomes not be driven purely by the market. Unions can help ensure that workers get wages sufficient to make a decent living.

In any case, pressuring wages upward is not the only thing that unions do. As Richard Freeman points out, unions also provide important collective goods that are valuable to workers and management alike. Unions can help keep a peaceful and orderly workforce, improve the efficient organization of the workplace, and ease transitions to new technology or shifts in investment from one industrial sector to another.[69] In Germany and in Scandinavia, for example, powerful unions have helped lead to some of the highest wages in the industrialized world, along with very low strike rates, a high level of technological innovation, and robust economic growth. This has happened in different ways. Sweden, for example, has had a very high union density (some 75 percent of all Swedish workers were already unionized in the 1970s, and the figure rose to 91 percent in the 1980s) and, until recently, a system of centralized wage setting. Germany's "co-determination" of wages, on the other hand, proceeded from unions' control over plant politics, rather than high overall union density.[70] Either way, however, workers prospered, and so did the countries as a whole.

The situation in the United States has always been somewhat different. Various factors—including the ethnic, linguistic, and racial Balkanization of U.S. workers, their disenfranchisement, unusually strong business opposition, and an inhospitable legal and political system—prevented a strong, progressive, and unified U.S. trade movement from emerging in the late nineteenth century as it did in Europe.

American workers were divided by ethnic and racial rivalries that employers could exploit (with African-American strikebreakers who had been excluded from unions, for example). The workforce consisted largely of immigrants, many of whom were not permanently settled in the United States, were hard to organize, and were denied the right to vote. Winner-take-all rules for the presidency and congressional districts, together with working-class disenfranchisement, discouraged establishment of a workers' party. Alexander Keyssar has documented immigrants' unsettled residential status (some 50 percent of Italian and Eastern European immigrants went back and forth between the United States and Europe) and their lack of voting rights: in some working-class wards in 1896, fewer than 15 percent of adults—30 percent of men—had the right to vote. Business- and professional-led movements to restrict voting through difficult registration processes and the like could be sold to middle-class natives on grounds that immigrants were "uncivilized" and not literate in English. Partly as a result of workers' disenfranchisement, the U.S. political system—and especially the legal system—was largely hostile to organized labor.[71]

The progressive and inclusionary Knights of Labor grew rapidly, but then was crushed in the 1880s. The craft-based American Federation of Labor (AFL), which after the 1890s (discouraged by political and legal hostility) moved in a bread-and-butter, keep-our-own-gains, exclusionary direction, overcame competition from the more socially and politically activist Industrial Workers of the World. In the 1930s, the relatively progressive Congress of Industrial Organizations (CIO) made considerable progress organizing workers in industrial plants and giving labor a political voice. Automobile and steel plants were unionized after hotly contested and sometimes bloody strikes. But this process largely stopped with World War II antistrike provisions, the failure of "Operation Dixie" in the South, the Cold War purge of leftist union leaders (some of labor's most vigorous organizers), and the 1956 merger of the AFL and CIO. The merger seemed to take steam out of the CIO's organizing and political activism, leaving Walter Reuther's United Auto Workers nearly alone on the mild Left.[72]

All these elements contributed to a postwar settlement in which business accepted existing unions and paid reasonably good wages and benefits, so long as management control was not challenged and a large segment of the workforce was left un-unionized. Even at their peak in the mid-1950s, however, U.S. unions never organized much more than one-third of the workforce. The stage was set for later trouble: a steady decline in coverage to a level below 14 percent of the workforce by the end of the twentieth century—not enough to have a major impact on wages outside a few industries.

Government policy at the state and federal levels has played an important part in the long-term weakness and the recent decline of U.S. labor. During the nineteenth century, for example, court orders and injunctions (based on the idea that unions "interfere with trade" or "deprive people of property" without due process of law) discouraged unionizing and broke up strikes, as did local police and even National Guard troops.[73] True, federal legislation in 1914 and in 1935 (the Wagner Act or National Labor Relations Act) did legitimate and ease collective bargaining, giving workers the legal right to choose unions in elections supervised by the National Labor Relations Board (NLRB). This somewhat facilitated the CIO's unionization of heavy industries in the late 1930s. But there remained large gaps of unorganized workers, especially in the South, where "Operation Dixie" was stopped cold. Later, state "Right-to-Work" laws (which forbid the closed-shop contracts that overcome the free-rider problem by requiring workers to join unions) consolidated antiunionism in the South. That left the South as an attractive destination for employers fleeing the North to avoid unions. The Taft-Hartley Act of 1947 tipped the balance of federal policy against unionization. The Landrum-Griffith Act of 1959, passed amidst highly publicized union corruption scandals, went still further in that direction. In the 1970s and 1980s, the forces of low-wage global competition severely undercut unions' ability to strike or organize. The job was finished by a fierce employer offensive against unions, aided by the Reagan administration.[74]

By the end of the 1980s, U.S. labor unions were extremely weak and disorganized; they stemmed the tide only in the 1990s, under new and more vigorous leadership that emphasized organizing low-income, minority, and women workers, especially in service, temporary, and government jobs.

Antiunion attitudes are widespread in the United States, even among liberals—many of whom were offended during and after the Vietnam War by the stodgy, prowar, antiblack, and antifeminist union leadership that had been left in charge after the Cold War purges of the left wing. Those attitudes, as well as the power and hostility of business, the frequent unfriendliness of government, and factionalization among workers, have operated so strongly and for such a long time that it is hard to imagine a feasible pathway to a strong and united U.S. labor movement like those in many European countries. (Unions in Europe have themselves come under increasing pressure as a result of global wage competition, but union density, coverage, concentration, and authority have actually remained fairly stable. The U.S. decline of unions, to such an extreme low point, is quite unusual.[75])

Still, measures that encourage rather than discourage unionization can make a significant contribution to reducing poverty and inequality. At the beginning of the twenty-first century, the newly energetic AFL–CIO was beginning to make some progress. Most gains in unionization came among workers in small- and medium-sized workplaces, often with women and minorities and with service workers who are not vulnerable to competition from low-priced imported goods (home-care workers in Los Angeles County, telephone operators, restaurant employees, medical assistants). "Union Summer" seminars and hands-on organizing activities got enthusiastic young people involved.[76] We will have more to say about unions below, in connection with international economic policy.

Preventing Discrimination

Income inequality among different social groups is exacerbated by employment discrimination based on race, gender, religion, ethnicity, or other arbitrary factors. The many-decades long exclusion of African Americans from many kinds of jobs and professions caused many of them to be relegated to much lower incomes than they would otherwise have enjoyed—a blatant violation of equal opportunity. When blacks migrated to northern cities from the South, for example, they—unlike practically all immigrant groups—were prevented by discrimination (and later by deindustrialization) from establishing low-skill labor niches that could be used to work themselves and their children upward to college educations and socioeconomic success.[77] Discrimination against women long barred them from most professional and business careers and kept their wages low.

Government policy has been slow to redress these inequalities. Indeed, state and local Jim Crow laws in the South gave many racist practices the force of law. Similarly, some legislation ostensibly designed to "protect" the supposedly frail females of the species in fact operated to bar women from jobs they were willing and able to perform.[78] Only with the 1964 Civil Rights Act did the federal government make a substantial effort to fight racial and other discrimination in the workplace, chiefly through the Equal Employment Opportunity Commission (EEOC). But the EEOC has had its ups and downs. It has never been amply funded, and it seemed to lapse into near-total inactivity during its Clarence Thomas–led years in the 1980s. EEOC complaints of discrimination take a long time to process and rarely result in relief. On the other hand, more and more private antidiscrimination lawsuits have been filed under a number of different statutes and have revolutionized the law on workplace discrimination, sexual harassment, and the like.[79]

Social movements and broad societal changes have had profound effects on hiring and wage discrimination. Many factors—the civil rights movement and women's movement that got under way in the 1950s and 1960s, the post-birth-control-pill influx of women into the workforce (labor-force participation by married women jumped from 30.5 percent in 1960 to 61.1 percent in 1996[80]), legislation and court decisions, and heightened consciousness of the problem—together led to considerably less overt discrimination in hiring and pay. This does not mean that wages for equal work are now equal, though it is hard to be precise about exactly how unequal they are. Women, who once averaged only 59 cents in wages for every dollar that men earned, still average only about 75 cents on the dollar. Much of that gap cannot be explained by differences in the work done. As Ellen Goodman has noted, for example, there is a gender gap between the wages of male and female bartenders of about $50 per week, a gap for reporters and editors of about $163 a week, and a gap for accountants of about $200 per week. There is still considerable distance to go in enforcing existing antidiscrimination and "comparable worth" laws.[81] And few women have reached top management positions.

Nor does the progress to date mean that there is full parity among equally qualified candidates in hiring. As in the area of education, for two or three decades affirmative action hiring policies helped many well-qualified people, especially middle-class and upper-middle-class women, to get jobs they never would have attained without employers making special efforts to find and evaluate them. Affirmative action was important for overcoming the habits of using old-boy networks and biased hiring criteria. But the partial rollback of affirmative action policies—less severe, to be sure, than in education—has set back equal hiring in a number of fields, particularly for African Americans and Latinos.

International Economic Policy

In the increasingly globalized world economy, U.S. policies that regulate international economic relations have more and more important effects on poverty and inequality within the United States. Even if there is a net gain for the parties to each private international transaction (usually that is why people trade), it does not follow that *everyone* in both countries is better off.

When we import goods from abroad manufactured by low-wage labor, for example, the direct buyers and sellers gain; American consumers also clearly benefit, as do those who make the goods that we export in return. But U.S. workers trying to compete with the imported goods may lose jobs or suffer drops in wages. As we discussed in chapters 2 and 3, many U.S. workers, especially those with already low incomes, may now be outcompeted by hundreds of millions—even billions—of workers abroad with similar skills who are willing to work for 40 or 50 cents an hour.

This problem has worsened as transportation has become cheaper, as political barriers like the walls around the former Communist bloc have fallen, and as the volume of trade has accelerated. (Trade still involves a smaller part of the U.S. economy than in the small, close-together countries of Europe; U.S. imports amount to something on the order of only 20 percent of GDP, while the ratios for Belgium, the Netherlands, the Scandinavian countries, and Germany are 60 percent or higher. But U.S. trade involvement doubled in about two decades.[82]) The problem for low-income U.S. workers is also worsened as cheaper and quicker communications and the elimination of political barriers have greatly increased capital mobility. United States companies and investors can close their U.S. factories and build plants abroad, taking advantage of cheap foreign labor and sending the products back to the United States, undercutting the wages of competing U.S. workers. Even American service workers, whose products are inherently local and not subject to competition from imported goods, are exposed to some wage and employment pressure from immigration of foreign workers who are willing to work for wages that are low by U.S. standards.

Free Trade

For two hundred years and more, leading economists like Adam Smith, David Ricardo, and their neoclassical successors have insisted that free trade is invariably a good thing. After all, voluntary economic transactions will not take place unless they make both parties better off. Even if certain third parties apparently suffer, it is not hard to prove mathematically—within the context of economic models based on certain apparently reasonable assumptions—that *in principle* the net gains from trade are generally sufficient to make everyone better off, if those gains are just distributed properly.[83] So why would anyone oppose free trade?

The answer, of course, is that the gains are *not actually* distributed properly, in all cases, unless special measures are taken to do so. A free market, left to itself, does not necessarily take care of this. Free-market transactions can produce uncompensated losers.[84] If free trade leads to increased poverty and inequality in the United States, therefore, it is natural to look to government to help out. This means either modifying free trade or (better) using the gains from trade to compensate those who are hurt by it.

Ever since the passage of the Reciprocal Trade Act in 1934, the U.S. government—led by the executive branch under Democratic and Republican presidents alike—has worked to increase free trade on a bilateral (two-nation) basis. With various trading partners, we have mutually lowered tariffs and quotas and then applied the same measures to other countries under "most favored nation" provisions. In recent decades, U.S. presidents of both political parties, including Carter, Reagan, Bush, and Clinton, vigorously pursued free-trade policies under the rubric of the General Agreement on Tariffs and Trade (GATT). GATT was a 1948 international treaty that led to various "rounds" (including the lengthy, 1986–94 "Uruguay round") of multicountry reductions in tariffs, quotas, and other barriers. In 1995, a new international agreement established the World Trade Organization (WTO), which has carried this process still further by institutionalizing a method of resolving trade disputes that is binding on individual countries. The WTO can actually override national legislation that it sees as restraining trade.[85]

There remain significant barriers—especially nontariff barriers—to international trade, including ostensibly "voluntary" limits on exports to the United States that the United States has imposed on Japan, China, and other countries. But the overall trend has been toward lower and lower barriers, especially for goods not dominated by a single producer interest. Obstacles to trade have been reduced even more sharply within regional trading blocs like the countries signing the North American Free Trade Agreement (NAFTA) or the European Union.

The drops in tariff barriers, together with improved transportation and the opening of nearly all countries to Western markets, has meant an enormous increase in imports. Just between 1982 and 1992, for example, the real value (adjusting for inflation) of U.S. imports doubled, from $257 billion to $545 billion. And by 1998, the value of imports nearly doubled again, to about $1,050 billion.[86] In the manufacturing sector, the "trade content" (total imports plus exports as a percentage of gross national product) soared from

17.5 percent in 1960 to 26.6 percent in 1970, 56.8 percent in 1980, and 64.4 percent in 1987. In the ten industries with the largest growth of import share of sales from the 1960s to the mid-1980s, import sales reached fully 73 percent of domestic sales on average.[87]

The flood of imports has enabled American consumers to buy cheap automobiles from abroad, first from Germany and then from Japan and Korea; inexpensive clothing and toys from China; and high-quality, low-priced electronic goods from Japan and then Southeast Asia (most trade, however, is still with Canada and Western Europe). And the income from those exports has allowed the exporting countries to buy U.S. grain, computer chips, and jet aircraft, adding to the wealth of all countries concerned. But this same trade has not been kind to U.S. workers who made cars, clothing, toys, or consumer electronics goods. Many companies pressured these workers into accepting lower wages and benefits, or closed U.S. factories altogether. The econometric evidence is convincing: the surge of imported manufactured goods contributed to the protracted, substantial drop after 1973 in the wages of most American workers, and to the marked increase of income inequality. In the ten industries with the largest growth of imports from the 1960s to the mid-1980s, for example, employment fell by fully 56 percent.[88]

This is sometimes referred to as a "transition problem": as imports undercut certain kinds of production in the United States, we may "simply" need to shift workers to other industries, particularly to those in which we have a comparative advantage and can produce exports. According to this line of thinking, all that U.S. workers need to do is to retrain, to make the transition to new kinds of work. To some extent, government policies like the "trade adjustment" measures described above have in fact assisted some workers with such transitions.

For many workers, however—especially older workers who spent most of their lifetimes working hard on assembly lines—retraining is no simple matter. They cannot suddenly become computer programmers or financial analysts. Nor is it easy to move to another city or state. It takes trade-displaced workers longer than others to find something new. In the 1990s economic boom, most displaced workers were eventually able to find *some* sort of job, but it was often a low-level service job that paid less than they used to make.[89] This is not, as the word "transition" implies, a short-term problem; it is a long-term problem—sometimes lifelong—that government has not yet done a lot to address.

What to do? Protectionism—raising new barriers against trade—is probably neither feasible nor desirable. The mainstream economists are right: free trade is potentially good for everyone. To realize that potential, however, requires that government help those who are injured by trade. It would be difficult to ferret out and precisely compensate each individual injury. Beyond short-term trade adjustment and retraining, therefore, it makes sense to design universal policies so that *no one* in American society is denied the benefits of general prosperity. Such policies would include facilitating long-term education, training, and retraining; providing sufficient and nonstigmatizing income support when necessary; and, most important, ensuring—through minimum wages, earned income tax credits, public service employment, and the like—that *all* people who work full-time receive a decent income.

In addition, specifically *international* policies short of protectionism can make a substantial difference. If the United States insists on decent wages, working conditions, and environmental protection in the countries and industries that we trade with, the sharpness of import competition will be blunted somewhat. The price of imported goods will tend to rise and displace fewer comparable U.S. goods and workers, while many (though not all) people abroad will benefit as well. Some measures of this sort have been undertaken in connection with international agreements like NAFTA, but they have so far not been vigorously enforced. And the WTO actually works *against* environmental or occupational health and safety restrictions, which are often argued to be restraints on free trade. Remedies of this sort will require political struggle.[90]

Capital Mobility

Like international trade in goods and services, the movement of capital (investment money) from one country to another has vastly accelerated. The development of instantaneous electronic communication, together with the dropping of political barriers, has permitted billions of dollars to be sent instantly to virtually any country of the world for use in building new industrial plants and making other investments. In the 1980s, China (particularly the coastal provinces) became increasingly open to U.S. investment, and the fall of the Soviet Union at the end of that decade opened Eastern Europe and Russia to U.S. investment as well. NAFTA in the early 1990s helped accelerate the already thriving U.S. investment in Mexico (though the peso crisis temporarily dampened it). Even bigger investments in Europe and Canada expanded rapidly as well.[91]

By the beginning of the twenty-first century, foreign investment *in* the United States (amounting to more than $200 billion per year) regularly exceeded investment *by* Americans abroad; in fact, the U.S. net investment position was well over a *negative* $1 *trillion* ($1,000 billion).[92] Still, U.S. companies and individuals had enormous investments abroad, which already in the mid-1990s were worth about $3 trillion. About $1 trillion of that represented "direct foreign investment" in plants, equipment, and the like. Both amounts had more than tripled since 1980.[93] As with trade, most U.S. foreign direct investment is in Europe ($300 billion total as of 1994), Latin America ($115 billion), and Canada ($73 billion). But total direct investment in the Asia and Pacific region had already reached $114 billion in 1994 and was rising rapidly.[94] Many U.S. manufacturing companies (clothing and shoe manufacturers, for example) that once operated almost entirely in the United States now operate almost entirely abroad, taking advantage of cheap labor, easy transportation and communication, and the lack of trade or investment barriers.[95]

The effects on poverty and inequality of capital mobility are similar to the effects of free trade. Indeed, some economists who resist the idea that free trade by itself hurts low-income American workers nonetheless acknowledge that the flight of business abroad is likely to have that effect.[96] When U.S. plants move to India or China, the American workers who used to operate them are left in the lurch and face lengthy, even lifelong, "transition" problems, while other U.S. workers in the same sector face a new flood of inexpensive imports. The lowered "value" (i.e., market value) of these workers' work, which we sometimes refer to as "unskilled" simply because it is no longer paid well, is not intrinsic to the work itself; it results from globalizing trends that in turn have a lot to do with conscious policy choices.

United States government policies have increasingly facilitated the free movement of capital, working to open up investment opportunities abroad. But little has been done about the negative side effects. The solution is not to try stuffing the genie of globalization back into the bottle—a counterproductive and almost certainly futile endeavor. (Controls on huge, speculative money flows can make sense, however, as Malaysia demonstrated in the late 1990s when its ban on quick removal of capital largely spared it from the "Asian financial crisis" that devastated many other countries.) Rather, the main solution is to help train or retrain workers for jobs at which the United States has the best comparative advantage and, at the same time, to pursue employment policies that give *all* workers—however modest their tasks— incomes that provide a reasonable standard of living.

In addition, the regulation by U.S. law or international agreement of U.S.-owned facilities abroad, to require acceptable wages and working conditions and environmental protection, can (by increasing foreign labor costs) somewhat blunt the force of wage competition. This can slow the erosion of U.S. wages and give U.S. workers more time to adjust. Government policies have so far done little along this line, however. More progress has been made by activist nongovernmental organizations (NGOs)—with help from publicity by Bob Herbert and others—boycotting and pressuring particular U.S. firms like The Gap and Nike to reject child labor and sweatshop conditions in their own or their suppliers' factories abroad. Under such pressure, some firms have not only changed their own practices, but also lobbied for more general regulation so they will not suffer competitive disadvantages. In that context, the Clinton administration facilitated some industrywide agreements on child labor. A number of corporations have also signed on to broad "sustainability" agreements to provide good working conditions abroad.

Immigration

The immigration of workers from abroad constitutes a third major element of economic globalization. When low-wage workers immigrate to the United States, the effects on U.S. poverty and inequality tend to be similar to the effects of low-wage imports or the flight of capital to low-wage countries. But there are certain important differences that on balance have made this a less severe problem. On the negative side, immigrants, unlike imported goods, can compete directly with the most *locally provided* and geographically bound services (health care, gardening, janitorial work) that are not threatened by imported goods. Also, immigration tends to be tightly concentrated geographically, clustered in "gateway cities" like Miami, New York, and Los Angeles, where immigrants have sometimes constituted one-quarter or more of the workforce. But the magnitude of immigration, even in areas of high concentration, has generally been much less than the magnitude of imports within particular industries, so that the impact on wages has probably been less.[97]

The 1970s and 1980s saw a big upsurge in immigration to the United

States. About 4.5 million immigrants were officially counted by the Immigration and Naturalization Service (INS) in the 1970s and 5.9 million in the 1980s, up from just 2.5 million in the 1950s and 3.3 million in the 1960s. Those are official figures; if estimates of illegal immigration are added, the totals were perhaps 5.8 million immigrants in the 1970s and 8.4 million in the 1980s, constituting approximately 26 percent and 38 percent, respectively, of U.S. population growth over those two decades. In contrast with earlier immigration, few of these migrants came from Europe; most arrived from Asia (nearly 40 percent in the 1970s and about 50 percent in the early 1980s) or Latin America (about 35 percent in both decades). Most had limited skills and were prepared to work for low wages. The number of illegal immigrants from Mexico was far less than xenophobic alarmists claimed in the media at that time—the actual total residing in the United States in 1980 was more nearly two million than the alleged ten or twelve million—but that number was still significant.[98]

The upsurge of immigration in certain areas did apparently depress the wages of other current immigrants, cut the wages of earlier waves of immigrants, and (to a modest extent) undermine the wages of young black and Hispanic Americans with whom immigrants tended to compete for work. But these effects were small, mainly because even in the ten highest immigrant-concentration metropolitan areas, the immigrants constituted only some 20 percent of the workforce on the average (in Miami, though, they reached 41 percent). Neither the employment nor the wages of less educated black and white natives worsened noticeably. There were even some signs that employment grew more rapidly in low-wage industries in those areas and that less-skilled natives moved into better jobs. Immigrants' downward pressure on wages may have been offset by the increased demand for goods and services that immigrants create, by their complementarity with native workers, and by a tendency for fewer than usual native workers to move into areas with many immigrants.[99]

This limited effect reflects the fact that the United States has never pursued anything like completely free immigration in the same way that it has facilitated free trade and capital mobility. To be sure, immigration law changes in 1965 did permit the immigration surge and did shift it toward low-skill workers, to the detriment of low-wage American workers. But a number of more recent measures like the restrictive 1986 immigration act, higher expenditures on border controls, and possibly the denials of various social benefits to resident aliens acted to stem the flow.

We must not forget the important long-run economic and social benefits from immigration, including the energy and cultural diversity that immigrants bring to us and the new or inexpensive goods and services they provide (largely, to be sure, for middle- and upper-middle class people: cheap taxicabs, gardening, day care, and house cleaning). Without question, too, immigration improves life for most immigrants and very modestly reduces *world* poverty.[100] Given these benefits, we may well consider the limited costs to low-income Americans to be acceptable, particularly if those costs are mitigated by the kinds of policies advocated in this book. It does not by any means follow, however, that egalitarians should advocate a substantially higher level of immigration than at present. That would very likely have sharply negative effects on low-wage Americans and would bring aspects of a third-world economy to the United States without much improving the lot of the rest of the world's billions of poor people.

Job Politics

By far the most important factor in the politics of employment and wages is the great power of business (or, more broadly, capital), as compared to the power of labor.

Business versus Labor

In virtually all the policy areas we have discussed, from macroeconomic policy to spending on public goods, job creation, minimum wages, immigration, and international trade and investment, the interests of business owners and managers partly conflict with the interests of labor. Workers want high wages, but to most businesses, wages are just "labor costs." In order to maximize profits, businesspeople want low costs, including low wages and low taxes.

To be sure, this conflict is not absolute; workers would lose if they wrecked the firms that employ them, and businesses often gain from measures that help their workers—as some employers are able to perceive. (Peter Swenson argues that active support by some businesspeople, and acquiescence by many, was crucial in constructing the Swedish welfare state, as well as U.S. social programs.[101]) But clearly most workers want better wages and more government benefits than most employers want to give them. The relative political power of business and labor therefore has much to do with what sorts of policies are enacted.

Just as organized labor in the United States is very weak in the marketplace, it is also weak politically. Now covering less than 15 percent of the workforce, U.S. unions have a smaller political role than they did at the time of the New Deal or the Great Society. They do not enjoy the numbers of members, the dues and political war chests, or the close connections with politicians that are needed for political influence. As we have repeatedly emphasized, U.S. unions do not wield anything like the power of organized labor in most other advanced industrial democracies.[102]

Business, on the other hand, is politically very powerful. A very large part of the interest group universe in Washington consists of lobbyists from business and the professions, including the Business Roundtable, the National Association of Manufacturers, the U.S. Chamber of Commerce, associations representing specific industrial sectors, and individual firms—especially corporations from the Fortune 500. Multibillion-dollar corporations can easily afford to invest a few millions in politics. They can maintain permanent Washington offices, hire the most expensive lawyers, fly politicians around in private planes, buy expensive political advertising, and create bogus "grassroots" campaigns that may influence public opinion as well as legislators' votes.

A careful compilation of 1997 lobbying expenditures by the Center for Responsive Politics, for example, showed that nearly all the top spenders were business firms or business associations. Philip Morris alone spent $15.8 million, making it #2 on the list—closely followed by Bell Atlantic ($15,672,840), the Chamber of Commerce of the United States (about $14 million), General Motors ($11 million), Boeing ($10 million), the Edison Electric Institute ($10 million), Pfizer ($10 million), the American Automobile Manufacturers Association ($10 million), and the Business Roundtable ($9 million). Only two labor organizations showed up on the entire list of 100 top lobbying spenders: the AFL–CIO, at #76 (just $3 million for the whole federation), and the United Auto Workers, way down at #96 (spending just $2.5 million).[103]

Similarly, campaign contributions to candidates and political parties come much more heavily from business than labor. The political action committee (PAC) contributions that the media often focus on are somewhat misleading in this respect. They represent only a small fraction of all political money, and they make unions look stronger than they are because PACs are the main channel for union money (lists of contributions from the top ten or top twenty PACs generally show about half of them to be labor union PACs). Business gives much more of the hard-to-trace "soft money" that goes to parties, rather than candidates. Still, during the 1997–98 electoral cycle, clearly corporate-related PACs—excluding trade association and apparently "nonconnected" PACs—spent $138 million, compared to labor PACs' $98 million.[104]

Little wonder, therefore, that wage and employment policies in the United States have tended to tilt in favor of business rather than labor. As Richard Freeman puts it, U.S. workers operate under "different rules." Compared to the situation in much of the industrialized world, American workers have regularly been afflicted with less favorable macroeconomic policies, less public employment, less friendly labor-management regulation, and the like.[105] Policy outcomes got worse for workers as organized labor became economically and politically weaker, reaching a nadir in the 1980s. Policies turned a bit more worker-friendly as the labor movement showed signs of revival in the late 1990s.

Political Parties

Historically the Democratic Party has generally been more supportive of pro-worker wage and employment policies than the Republican Party. Democratic presidents and congressional majorities originated and expanded most of the prolabor policies we have had, including the National Labor Relations Act of 1935, public service employment, and the federal minimum wage. Congressional roll call votes on employment- and wage-related issues regularly divide along party lines. In the House of Representatives, especially, ideological polarization has sharply increased since the mid-1970s, so that now there is virtually no overlap between the two parties. Nearly all the most "moderate" Republican representatives are more conservative than the most conservative Democrats.[106] This sharp increase in the party polarization of Congress apparently reflects greater influence by ideologically committed activists in the party primaries that pick candidates, together with greater precision in drawing House district boundaries for "safe seats," in which the nominees nearly always win.

The reason for the basic party division is clear enough. At least since the New Deal, the Republican Party has been more closely linked to business groups, and the Democrats closer to labor, in terms of their crucial activists and money-givers. For a time, in fact, organized labor was so intertwined with the Democratic Party and so important to it that J. David Greenstone saw labor as virtually a part of the party.[107] It is still true that most labor money goes to the Democrats, while most business contributions go to the Republicans. PAC contributions are fairly accurate indicators in this respect. In the 1997–98 electoral cycle, for example, corporate PACs gave $53 million to Republicans, but only $25 million to Democrats, while labor PACs gave an overwhelming $41 million to Democrats and only $4 million to Republicans.[108] Firms among the top political spenders typically gave 60 to 100 percent of their campaign contributions to Republicans. (Philip Morris, for example, gave 79 percent of its $2.5 million to Republicans; Bell Atlantic gave them 65 percent of its $1.3 million and Boeing 62 percent of its $1.3 million.)[109]

But the situation is more complicated than that. As Thomas Ferguson and others have shown, the Democratic Party has never relied solely on its mass base among unionized workers and racial, ethnic, and religious minorities (or, more recently, women). A critical part of the Democratic Party coalition has always consisted of *major investors,* particularly from internationalist, capital-intensive business and financial firms. The business part of the Democratic coalition was critical in obtaining the free trade–oriented Reciprocal Trade Act of 1934 and in limiting several prolabor aspects of the New Deal. It became increasingly important in subsequent years as the strength of labor declined. Some liberal supporters of Bill Clinton were startled, after his 1992 victory, when the new administration set aside issues of economic expansion or wage improvement and made free trade (NAFTA and then the WTO) its top priority. But the crucial role of Goldman Sachs and other firms in providing the money needed to win, and the appointment Robert Rubin, Goldman Sachs's former chairman, as secretary of the treasury, provided early signs that the Clinton administration agenda had roots in business as well as—even in opposition to—labor.[110]

Economic Growth and International Competition

Without doubt, there are structural constraints on U.S. wage and employment policies. If U.S. wages were pushed too high, whether by minimum wage laws, wage subsidies, public service employment, or other means, foreign-based firms would be able to produce much cheaper goods and flood U.S. markets; there would be a high level of unemployment, and economic growth would slow or stop. Some of the European countries that have achieved high wage levels, such as small and highly export-dependent Sweden, have encountered problems of this sort. But high productivity can justify high wages, and the comparative evidence suggests that there is still substantial leeway for the advanced industrial countries to pay their workers well.[111] The United States, with its huge domestic market, could presumably choose to treat its workers even better.

In any case, fortunately, the United States is very far from being pinched by these constraints. Our policies have been so persistently unfriendly to labor that it would be possible to do a significant turnaround without serious ill effects. This is particularly true since certain prolabor policies by their nature tend to *help* rather than hurt economic growth. Such is the case, for example, for macroeconomic policies that stimulate demand, so long as inflation is not allowed to get out of control. It is true of training and retraining programs that increase the employability and productivity of labor. And it is true of carefully targeted wage subsidies like the Earned Income Tax Credit that increase employment and work effort.

Improving Employment and Wages

At the center of any successful strategy to reduce poverty and inequality in the United States must be the provision of full employment at good wages. It is essential to ensure that as many Americans as possible are well trained to work, that all who are able to work can find a job, and that all jobs pay decent wages.

A number of policy changes could help achieve these goals. Macroeconomic monetary and fiscal policy could be used more extensively (though still within limits) to stimulate the economy, rather than restrict it. Public service jobs could be provided when too few jobs or too low wages are available in the private sector; they could, in effect, guarantee a job to everyone who needs one. This would be a profoundly important policy change. Training and placement programs, if expanded, could do much more to help those with limited skills and those who are displaced by imports or stuck on welfare to train for productive work. An adequate minimum wage, together with a more substantial Earned Income Tax Credit, could ensure that everyone who works makes a living wage. Broadened and better-enforced antidiscrimination measures could eliminate irrational and wasteful barriers that keep people out of jobs they can ably fill. And laws and international agreements that require good working conditions and environmental protection abroad could blunt or slow some of the most injurious side effects of free trade and investment flows.

Perhaps most important is to put together a combination of minimum wage laws, public jobs, and earned income tax credits such that everyone who works can earn a living above the poverty line. Our society insists, not unreasonably, that it is the duty of every able-bodied person to work. When people carry out that duty, we might well consider it a reciprocal obligation of society to ensure that their work brings with it a decent standard of living.

Is this politically feasible? We will never know unless we try. Political feasibility can change if citizens get active and if the lineup of political forces can be altered. Measures that facilitate the organization of labor or that limit the impact of businesses' (and others') money in politics, for example, would tend in the long run to facilitate policy shifts favorable to full employment, higher wages, and less poverty.

8

"Safety Nets" and Basic Needs

The term "safety net" has been widely used at least since the early 1980s to refer to programs designed to help needy people with essentials like food, housing, medical care, and basic income maintenance. In this chapter, we discuss those topics one at a time, noting the skimpiness of—and restricted eligibility for—most of the programs that actually help the poor (larger food and housing programs have benefited the well-to-do). We then analyze the sometimes-nasty politics of antipoverty policy. Finally, we argue in favor of a general right to the essentials of life, returning to the social insurance logic that has animated much of the book.

First, however, the term "safety net" itself is worth brief examination. It evokes a rather specific metaphor concerning the nature of poverty and how we should deal with it, a metaphor with distinct—and perhaps unfortunate—political implications.

Circus Imagery versus Economic Rights

The language of "safety nets" apparently refers to an old-fashioned, three-ring circus, in which daring acrobats perform gymnastic feats on a high wire or trapeze far above the ground. In the rare event of a fall, an acrobat plunges toward earth—but is not smashed to death. Instead, just before hitting the ground, he or she is caught by a strong net. The crowd gasps with relief.[1]

As applied to poverty, this image seems to imply that all Americans are or should be highly skilled acrobats, unafraid of dizzying heights, willing to risk near-death experiences for the entertainment of others. Implicitly the metaphor dismisses the importance of mundane, noncircus work. It takes for granted that we all have high-wire skills or access to the specialized training needed to acquire them. It ignores the values of security and stability that are so important to many people, and it slights the idea of social insurance designed to prevent or mitigate, rather than dramatize, near-death falls. The "safety net" image does have the virtue of encouraging skillful, hard work, and of suggesting that falls from the heights are mostly beyond an individual's control: even the most agile may occasionally slip. But it implies, quite contrary to evidence and experience, that falls are nearly always *temporary* (acrobats quickly climb right back up) and that falls are very *rare*. Moreover, accompanying language often indicates that we should only help these rare victims of accident, the "truly needy"—excluding the allegedly numerous fakers or sluggards who have not really tried to be acrobats at all.

Thus the safety net image suggests that true poverty is temporary and rare. It implies that we need not worry much about expensive government programs of social insurance, education and training, job creation, or wage support. It suggests that plenty of highly paid acrobat jobs are available and that all of us are—or should be—ready to take them. All government needs to do is provide a sturdy but very cheap net to break the occasional fall.

Are we making too much of a simple phrase? Perhaps. Metaphors are susceptible to multiple interpretations, depending on context. Their effects are hard to untangle; some metaphors become "frozen" and slip by the casual listener, causing no awareness or impact at all.[2] But the terms of public discourse do matter. A widely used image like the "safety net" may unconsciously affect how we feel about poverty, unless we make a conscious effort to think through the implications. It is important to reflect on the nature of prevailing political language and think beyond it.

As we see it, government can and should deal with poverty and inequality in much broader ways than merely putting up a cheap rope net. Indeed, if government does all the things discussed in earlier chapters—provide social insurance against old age or illness or disability, help educate and train and otherwise enable people to work productively, ensure that jobs are available at good wages, and tax incomes fairly—there should be rather little need for the sort of last-minute, emergency rescues that the "safety net" image evokes.

No matter how well education and job programs are designed, however, some people will probably not be reached. To use a quite different metaphor, they will "fall through the cracks": a metaphor that suggests the desirability of standing on a solid floor, rather than balancing on a thin, swaying high wire. We advocate filling in the cracks. A wealthy country like the United States can easily afford to provide a solid floor for everyone. It can guarantee a set of basic necessities, including food, housing, and medical care, which all Americans can rely on even if they are not able or willing immediately to climb back up to the high wire. And there is no need to impose unpleasantness, stigma, or a near-death experience on those who make use of such a guarantee.

We believe that the idea of guaranteeing basic necessities to everyone follows logically from the broad concept of social insurance that we outlined in chapters 3 and 4. Much of people's fate is beyond their control. A sense of common humanity suggests that every person should be insured against disastrous misfortune of any kind, whether it arises from accident, disease, or a disadvantage based on genetic inheritance or deficient upbringing. This can be done without undermining individual responsibility or the obligation to work when able to do so.

In a highly individualistic and legalistic society like that of the United States, it probably makes sense to think in terms of *rights* to basic necessities: rights to minimal standards of food, housing, medical care, and perhaps income. We will return to the idea of such rights at the end of this chapter.[3]

Food

One of the most basic human needs is for adequate nutrition. This is so obvious, and malnutrition or starvation is so shocking, that even the most strict proponents of self-reliance generally hesitate to deny help to the hungry. Practically everyone acknowledges that government should help provide food to those who lack it.

Hunger and Malnutrition in America

Back in 1967, many Americans were surprised to discover the existence of widespread malnutrition and hunger in the United States. In that year, Senators Joseph Clark and Robert Kennedy, travelling to the Mississippi Delta for congressional subcommittee hearings, visited the shack of Annie White and found that her two-year-old daughter was numb, unresponsive, and starving. So were the children of many poor Delta farm workers who had been displaced by mechanization or cutbacks in cotton planting and were getting no government help. A year later the Citizens Board of Inquiry reported in *Hunger USA* that at least *ten million* Americans suffered from hunger and malnutrition. It identified 256 "hunger counties" (mostly in the South), where 40 percent or more of the people were poor, less than one-quarter of the poor participated in welfare or government food programs, and the postnatal mortality rate was at least twice the national average. A startling number of Americans suffered from beriberi, kwashiorkor, or marasmus, diseases normally associated with malnutrition in the third world. The CBS documentary "Hunger in America" further dramatized this issue and increased public awareness.[4]

A lot has changed since 1967. Outright starvation has become quite rare in the United States, in good part as a result of government action—particularly a much-expanded Food Stamps program. But in the mid-1990s, about 5 percent of U.S. households still reported that they sometimes or often did not have enough to eat.[5] Malnutrition remains a problem, especially among poor people who cannot afford to buy or store expensive fresh vegetables or low-fat, high-protein foods. Many people do not take advantage of food help to which they are entitled, either because officials discourage them or because a stigma of dependency is still associated with it.

Agricultural Subsidies and Commodities Distribution

In the past, U.S. government spending on food and agriculture often had little to do with providing adequate nutrition to low-income people. Most of it went to agricultural subsidies designed to *increase* food prices (costing consumers more) and to bolster farm incomes by restricting production or purchasing surpluses. A substantial amount of money is still devoted to this purpose. In 2000, for example, the federal government spent about $12 billion on "farm income stabilization" for growers of corn, wheat, rice, cotton, soybeans, and other crops. In addition, the federal government directly gave or guaranteed about $18 billion in loans, including some $2 billion in "marketing loan" payments, which are made when commodity prices fall below a certain level (in effect, this guarantees a minimum price for major commodities). And "milk marketing orders" keep milk prices up through government enforcement of minimum prices, while tariffs and quotas on imports of cheap foreign sugar and other commodities keep those prices artificially high.[6]

Even if we set aside the traditional Jeffersonian claims that small farmers embody special social and political virtues (do they, really?), there is a respectable social insurance argument for helping family farms: otherwise, they could unfairly be wiped out by misfortune with bad weather or pests. Private loan and insurance markets cannot adequately deal with such risks. The problem of moral hazard, for example, prevents lenders or insurers from counting on the full value of likely future farm production, since even a slight slackening of effort by a farmer might allow future profits to slip away or might let serious losses occur. (By the same token, of course, any government insurance program must also be wary of moral hazard). In recent years, especially since the passage of the 1996 Federal Agriculture Improvement and Reform Act ("FAIR"), crop subsidies and planting restrictions have been reduced in favor of more market-oriented, insurance-based programs. The federal government now spends about $1.5 billion per year for free insurance against catastrophic crop loss and subsidized insurance against the risk of lost revenue. This insurance covers some 65 to 70 percent of the eligible agricultural land.[7]

Despite warm and fuzzy rhetoric about family farms, however, most of the government help in fact goes to large agribusinesses. One reason is simply that not many family farms remain. The total number of farms in the United States declined from a peak of 6.8 million in 1935 to only 2 million in the mid-1990s, and just 63,000 big farms now produce more than half of all the value of agricultural output in the United States. Direct government payments are proportionally higher for small farms (providing about 24 percent of cash farm income for the smallest farms and only 2 percent for the largest). But the more land and the more crops a farmer has, the bigger the *total dollar* benefits tend to be. In the mid-1990s, small farms—that is, the 89 percent of U.S. farms that accounted for only about one-quarter of total production—averaged only $1,666 each in direct government payments, while the top 3 percent of farms averaged well over $10,000 each.[8] And the tilt toward big, high-income agribusinesses is much greater when we take account not only of direct cash payments, but also of the many government measures designed to keep prices high. The higher the volume of a farm's sales, the bigger the profit gained from high prices. High corn prices bring a lot more money to multibillion-dollar Archer Daniels Midland (a big political money-giver) than to 160-acre Farmer Jones.

It is not easy to calculate exactly how much in total government subsidies and elevated prices goes to farms of different sizes (moreover, neither the farmers nor the Department of Agriculture seems particularly eager to publicize this information). Charles Schultze's classic study remains one of the best. In 1969, according to Schultze's calculations, the 7 percent of farms with the highest incomes got about 40 percent of all the benefits from farm commodity programs. The top 19 percent of farms got nearly 63 percent of all benefits.[9] Despite the passage of time and changes in the programs, it remains true that most agricultural help goes to support the profits of corporations and high-income landowners—many of whom are sufficiently big and diversified to insure themselves without government help.

The first major federal program designed to help the hungry with food was the "commodities distribution program," initiated as part of the New Deal response to the Great Depression of the 1930s. This program, operating through county welfare agencies, gave poor people some of the food commodities that the government had purchased in order to keep prices up: flour, cornmeal, dried milk, rice, and occasional butter and cheese; then, under Presidents Kennedy and Johnson, as many as fifteen different foods.[10]

Commodities distribution did a great deal of good, preventing starvation and adding protein to many poor people's diets. But the coverage was very incomplete. Many counties did not participate at all. Others, especially in the rural South and the Midwest, distributed food in the winter to keep the agricultural labor force alive, but then stopped doing so during the rest of the year in order to force people to do farm labor at low wages (sometimes just $3 per day in the mid-1960s). Moreover, neither the quantity nor the variety of distributed commodities was sufficient to provide a balanced diet. No meat and no source of vitamin C were included. The U.S. Department of Agriculture in the early 1960s found, for example, that many Blackfoot Indians of Montana, who depended on the commodity distribution program for survival, were suffering from inadequate nutrition. For years, the agriculture committees of Congress, dominated by segregationist Southern Democrats who wanted to keep poor blacks in their place and by conservative Midwestern Republicans opposed to government help for the poor, kept the commodities program skimpy. It existed only as an offshoot of the subsidies designed to help farmers and was not allowed to interfere with the availability of low-cost agricultural labor; it was even subordinated to overseas sales and "Food for Peace" aid abroad that brought in revenue to the U.S. Treasury.[11]

The Food and Nutrition Service of the Department of Agriculture currently runs several successors to the old commodity distribution program, through which it purchases commodities "to remove surpluses from the marketplace" (i.e., to subsidize farmers) and then distributes them to various special groups. These include the school lunch, school breakfast, women-infants-and-children (WIC), day care center, and summer food programs described in chapter 6. They also include smaller nutrition programs for the elderly, soup kitchens and shelters, Native Americans living on reservations, and disaster relief agencies.[12]

Food Stamps

The closest thing to a guarantee of any necessity in the United States is now provided by the Food Stamps program, which allows most needy people to obtain coupons that can be redeemed at most grocery stores for food supplies (*not* for cigarettes, liquor, household products, or hot ready-to-eat food). It is a means-tested program. Individuals and families are eligible only if their gross monthly incomes fall below a certain figure that depends on family size ($1,783 for a family of four in 1999). Their net incomes after certain deductions, including costs of dependent care, must also fall below a threshold figure, as must their total savings and other resources excluding a home and an inexpensive car. Once people are eligible, they can receive coupons worth the "maximum allotment" for their household size minus 30 percent of their net monthly income.[13] That is, Food Stamp benefits decline as incomes rise; they are supposed to make up whatever portion of the "maximum allotment" of food expenses cannot be covered by 30 percent of the family's net income.

In 2000, the federal government spent about $21 billion on Food Stamps, which paid for an average of about $75 worth of food monthly for some 20 million people. In theory, at the end of the twentieth century the Food Stamps program guaranteed that a family of four—between its own income and the coupons—could purchase at least the "maximum allotment" of $419 worth of food per month: that is, $105 per person per month.[14] That comes out to a little more than $1 per meal for each family member—definitely not enough for haute cuisine, but probably enough to avoid serious malnutrition for those able to plan, purchase, store, and prepare food very thriftily. (Many poor people, however, lack access to the supermarkets and freezers that are key to economical food preparation).

The Food Stamps program was originally enacted in 1964, when liberal Northern Democrats in Congress pressured conservative Southerners and Midwesterners to accept it in return for votes for wheat and cotton subsidies. The program was then expanded moderately during the Johnson years (LBJ, bogged down in the expense of the Vietnam War, resisted any major expansion) and more substantially under President Nixon, who roughly doubled average benefits in a two-year period. Initially many counties opted out or skimped on Food Stamps, just as they had done with commodities distribution. But after the Nixon expansions, the program became firmly established as a national entitlement, with universal eligibility criteria, defined benefits available everywhere in the country, and mandatory funding by Congress. Although average benefits barely kept up with inflation during the 1970s and 1980s, the program gradually grew into one of the largest U.S. antipoverty measures.[15] Some 90 percent of Food Stamps benefits have gone to people below the poverty line, significantly supplementing their incomes and making a substantial difference in their lives. The program has grown especially large during and after economic recessions, when the need is greatest, reaching a peak of 27.4 million participants—one of every ten Americans—in March 1993.[16]

For a time, Food Stamps stood as a truly comprehensive U.S. antipoverty program—in fact, the *only* such program. Every poor person was eligible— male or female, working or not, able-bodied or disabled, citizen or resident alien, married or single, parent or childless. Recently, however (especially in the course of the 1996 restrictions on "welfare"), this comprehensiveness was abandoned. Benefit levels were cut, work requirements were imposed, most legal immigrants were banned from receiving Food Stamps, and able-bodied childless adults were limited to three months of assistance during a thirty-six-month period.[17] From the point of view of basic rights to food, this was a step backward.

Without question, Food Stamps and the smaller federal antipoverty food programs, including WIC and school lunches, have made a difference. They have in effect substantially raised the total incomes and living standards of poor people. A Field Foundation team of doctors revisiting poor areas in 1977 found "far fewer" grossly malnourished people than they had in 1968. A variety of more recent studies have established that families on Food Stamps spend more on food than they get in coupons (that is, the stamps really go for needed food); those families buy more food in total and have better availability of nutrients. Rebecca Blank wrote (before the late-1990s cuts took effect, to be sure) that "evidence of severe malnutrition-related health problems has almost disappeared in this country. The primary reason is Food Stamps."[18]

At the same time, we noted above that in the mid-1990s about 5 percent of U.S. households still reported that they sometimes or often did not have enough to eat. A different Census survey found in 1998 that 3.6 percent of all households had experienced "hunger," defined as the inability to obtain enough food at least occasionally. This proportion was down a bit from the 3.9 percent level of 1995, but it still amounted to nearly ten million people, over one-third of them children. A more broadly defined "food insecurity," involving limited or uncertain access to food, was suffered by a much larger and rather alarming 10.2 percent of all U.S. households.[19]

One reason that hunger and food insecurity persist in the United States is that Food Stamps benefits are so limited. Another is that participation in the program has never been nearly complete among those who are eligible. Many people (especially those with relatively higher incomes and hence lower benefits) do not find the food coupons worth their cost in terms of the hassles of filling out applications, going through interviews, undergoing intrusive means testing, reporting household circumstances monthly or whenever things change, and suffering scornful looks and loss of self-esteem in the grocery store line. One study done shortly after the expansion of the program found that only 40 percent of those eligible participated. Participation rates rose as information spread and eligibility was made automatic with receipt of Aid to Families with Dependent Children (AFDC) or Supplementary Security Income (SSI), so that over two-thirds of the poor received Food Stamps in 1993. But Food Stamps never came to be seen as a natural, normal recourse for people unable to afford good nutrition. The 1996 abolition of AFDC made this worse: many poor people lost their automatic eligibility for Food Stamps and were discouraged by officials from applying or simply not informed that they could. Largely as a result, Food Stamp use plunged from nearly twenty-eight million people in 1994 to just nineteen million in 1998.[20]

Shame and disrespect are often associated with the use of Food Stamps, especially in middle-class neighborhoods, where disparaging remarks are sometimes made when food coupons are used at the checkout counter. Americans' insistence on self-reliance and their distaste for dependency, laziness, or "freeloading" has, in the case of Food Stamps, been exacerbated by politicians' and pundits' inflammatory rhetoric about "fraud, waste, and abuse." Even a president of the United States, Ronald Reagan, passed along apocryphal anecdotes about deadbeats illegally using Food Stamps to buy gin.[21]

Administrative costs have in fact been somewhat higher for Food Stamps than for other antipoverty programs: about 12.2 percent of total program costs, compared to 11.7 percent for AFDC, 6.7 percent for SSI, and 4.0 percent for Medicaid. But little, if any, of this represents "waste"; it is the inevitable result of requiring complicated means-testing for a population of applicants with a high turnover rate. The administrative costs are roughly comparable to those of private insurance companies and private charities.[22] They could be cut if a more universal program were adopted.

As to fraud and abuse, close scrutiny of error rates at the beginning of the 1990s indicated that overpayments did represent a higher proportion of total benefits paid for Food Stamps (about 8 percent) than for AFDC (5 percent), SSI (3.5 percent), or Medicaid (3 percent), apparently because Food Stamp eligibility and benefit rules are so complex. But the total was hardly enormous, and increasingly strict federal standards, better quality control by states, and the implementation of electronic processing have caused payment errors to plummet. Less than half of such errors appear to be due to misinformation provided by clients; most are the responsibility of administrators. The extent of actual fraud is difficult to determine; guesses range up to $1 billion per year, about 4 percent of total program dollars. Most fraud involves unscrupulous grocers who buy food coupons at a deep discount— often just 50 percent of value—from recipients (including substance abusers) who are desperate for quick cash; the grocers then redeem them for full value. That is, the thieves are mostly grocers, not the poor. The increasing use of electronic benefit transfer (EBT), in which beneficiaries use a card similar to a bank card, rather than coupons, is expected to reduce this problem further. As with other in-kind programs (especially Medicaid and housing), money could be saved by closer monitoring of vendors and providers, rather than recipients.[23]

Those who look seriously at Food Stamps and other antipoverty programs now see little reason to obsess about "fraud, waste, and abuse." Unfortunately, however, inflammatory anecdotes and negative imagery linger in the public memory, and the push to get people off welfare and onto work has confused and intimidated many needy people. The stigma associated with Food Stamp use, together with eligibility hassles and low benefit levels, remains a significant barrier against an effective right to adequate nutrition.

Soup Kitchens and Private Charity

Those who entertain the hope that private charity, rather than government programs, might be sufficient to deal with poverty and inequality sometimes point to soup kitchens and food pantries run by volunteers and private charities.

It is true that many thousands of dedicated volunteers in hundreds of communities devote a great deal of time and energy to feeding the neediest Americans, and that a number of grocery chains, food wholesalers, and other businesses generously provide free food. These are some of the volunteerist "thousand points of light" which President George H. W. Bush once praised. We should be proud of them and should participate as much as possible.

Soup kitchens, where anyone who shows up can get a hot meal, are especially helpful for people who are too disorganized or demoralized—sometimes because of mental illness, drug addiction, or alcoholism—to work, to undergo training, or even to apply for SSI, public aid, or Food Stamps. The existence of substantial numbers of such people, of course, points toward the need for much deeper intervention in their lives—help with overcoming addiction, getting organized for training and work, or finding long-term care. Unless and until we do a much better job of such intervention, however, there will be a substantial need for easy-to-get emergency food.

At the same time, it would be a serious error to imagine that private charities can on their own take care of this emergency food problem, let alone the much broader problem of ensuring adequate nutrition for all Americans. For one thing, very little of Americans' charitable donations reaches low-income families. As of the early 1990s, perhaps just $12 billion, 10 percent of the roughly $111 billion in annual tax-deductible gifts to philanthropic organizations, did so. Most charitable giving goes to support religious worship, private schools, the arts, the environment, and medical research. The $10 to $15 billion of total private contributions to the poor is dwarfed by government help, which is some twenty times as great. Indeed, many private charities are able to operate only with help from public funds. The largest charities have gotten about one-fifth to one-quarter of their money from government, and the government share for those providing emergency food and shelter to the poor has typically been higher: for Catholic Charities USA, it was 65 percent. If government help were eliminated, it is almost inconceivable that private charity could fill the gap.[24]

The post-1996 purge of state and local welfare rolls further strained private charitable resources by causing a sharp rise in charitable food lines at the same time that crucial donations of food were declining. (Seekers of food increased by 50 percent in Arizona between 1993 and 1998, for instance, even while the overall economy was improving.) Second Harvest, the main hub for large-scale food donations—which at the end of the 1990s distributed food to a network of soup kitchens and food pantries that served more than $1 billion worth of food per year to some twenty million Americans—found that it would have to double the flow of food in order to supply everyone seeking help. But over a three-year period, food donations instead actually fell by 10 percent, largely because grocery manufacturers were moving toward policies of "zero defects" and were developing new markets for formerly unsaleable food that had once been given to the poor. In 1998, half the food charities in New York City reported that they were forced to cut the size of food servings at least part of the year.[25]

The Right to Eat

It would not be difficult to implement an effective right for every American to get enough nutritious food to eat. We have the money to do it. Food Stamps could be made more generous: why not at least $1.50 per person per meal, rather than $1? The comprehensiveness of the program could be restored: why an arbitrary cutoff for the childless after three months? And stigma could be reduced by moving rapidly to less visible (and cheaper-to-administer) credit cards, rather than coupons,[26] as well as changing the tone of public discourse. Little, if anything, is gained by making people suffer for their acceptance of publicly provided food. Work incentives are already strong and can be made stronger by improving training, job opportunities, and wages. Unnecessary pain and social divisiveness represent real losses.

The most dramatic way to end the stigma and to clearly establish a right to food would be to abolish the expensive and demeaning means-testing associated with Food Stamps, making the program truly *universal*. Simply issue *everyone* in the country a credit card worth a certain amount of food purchases per month. True, this would mean initially giving a government benefit to many who do not need it, but that is the point. Those people would just be getting some of their tax money back (at little administrative cost) in the form of a food card, to establish the principle that they, like everyone else, are entitled to a minimal supply of food. To make aid universal, rather than graduated according to income, would actually *increase* work incentives for many low-income people by ending the high tax on earned income that is implicit in the sharp means-tested reductions in Food Stamp benefits as earnings rise.[27]

Universality and flat benefits can generally reduce the perverse work disincentives associated with means-tested programs. True, high *levels* of such benefits would tend to relax the financial pressure on the needy to take extremely low-paying jobs. But other measures we have recommended, such as widespread training, job creation, and a higher minimum wage, would mostly remove the need for such pressure: nearly everyone would have the capacity, motivation, and opportunity to do meaningful work for a good wage. Universal food cards, designed to meet one of the most basic human needs, are worth thinking about even by those opposed to unrestricted guaranteed incomes.

Housing

Another basic human need is for shelter. Everyone needs a place to sleep that is warm and dry, protected from rain, snow, and cold; a place that is secure against interlopers, where personal property is safe and there is a modicum of privacy. But the United States has not moved anywhere close to guaranteeing suitable shelter to all its citizens. The chief reliance is on private markets to produce and distribute housing, with substantial subsidies to the middle and upper-middle classes, but only limited assistance for the poor.

Private Markets and Middle-Class Subsidies

Most U.S. government efforts related to housing have *not* involved (and, unlike the case of food, still do not involve) meeting basic needs of low-income people. Instead, most of the money has gone to subsidies for the construction and ownership of middle-class homes. Henry Aaron's pathbreaking study at the beginning of the 1970s, for example, showed that the biggest government housing programs were tax breaks for home owners. The Internal Revenue Code allows large deductions from taxable income of local property tax payments and interest paid on home mortgages. It also excludes "imputed rent" (the value of living in an owner-occupied home) from taxable income, even though imputed rent is income derived from wealth just like a stock dividend or bond interest. Aaron found that in 1966 these provisions saved home owners about $7 billion—roughly one-sixth of the total income taxes they paid that year—and that the bulk of the benefits went to the middle and upper-middle classes.[28]

These tax provisions still constitute the biggest government housing programs. In 2000, the Treasury gave up about $55 billion in revenue because of mortgage interest deductibility, over $19 billion as the result of the deductibility of state and local property taxes, and nearly $19 billion because of the exclusion from taxation of capital gains on most home sales.[29] Even disregarding the huge amount of taxes not collected on imputed rent (an amount that is much harder to calculate), this adds up to a total of some $93 billion. Ninety-three billion dollars! A staggering amount of money. Not only does it dwarf what is spent on all propoor housing programs, but also it is nearly twice what is spent on such programs plus Food Stamps and WIC taken together. The vast bulk of these tax subsidies goes to middle- and upper-middle-class people, with the highest benefits accruing to the wealthiest. Few poor people own homes. The deductions and exclusions are worth most to people with the highest incomes.

Aaron found that the next largest housing programs were FHA (Federal Housing Authority) and VA (Veterans Administration) mortgage guarantee and insurance programs, which have economic effects that are complicated, but do not do much to redistribute income. Historically the FHA and VA, together with federal highway programs, have greatly subsidized the growth of suburbs that are mostly middle class and lily white. They have helped many working-class people. But they have not done much for the rural or urban poor.[30] These programs remain large: in 1998, the FHA, VA, and smaller U.S. Department of Agriculture (USDA) programs guaranteed or issued a total of about $150 billion in new loans for some 1.7 million housing units. The total loans outstanding at the end of the twentieth century amounted to nearly $700 billion. Again, very few of the recipients were poor. The chief exception is that the USDA Rural Housing Service provides some direct loans to low-income rural residents, but this is a very small program; it and the moderate-income rural program together covered only about 57,000 homes in 1998.[31]

Public Housing and Rental Assistance

Government help with housing for low-income people comes in two main forms: conventional "project" public housing, and—increasingly—subsidies for renting privately owned rooms or apartments. But both types of aid are quite limited and do not reach a high proportion of poor people. According to one estimate, only 22 percent of all poor families receive housing assistance.[32]

Public housing now seldom resembles the notorious, dilapidated high-rises full of gangs and drugs that once helped convince outraged citizens that government could do nothing right. Indeed, the federal budget document for fiscal year 2000 boasted of plans to demolish 100,000 of the worst remaining units by 2003.[33] Today most of the 1.4 million or so public housing units are in low-rises located outside of city centers. Increasing efforts have been made to include as tenants families that derive most of their income from work, who constituted 37 percent of tenants in 1999 and about 43 percent in 2000: these people presumably provide stability and role models for others.[34]

Perhaps the chief problem with public housing today is simply lack of units to meet the demand. The public housing operating fund of the U.S. Department of Housing and Urban Development (HUD) spent only about $2.9 billion in 2000, down from $3.1 billion in 1998; the public housing capital fund spent only about $3.2 billion. Many people wait in vain to get public housing. In 1998, the average waiting time nationally was eleven months. For the largest public housing authorities, the average wait was nearly three years (thirty-three months), up sharply from an already high twenty-two months two years earlier. And in several major cities, waiting times were even longer: five years in Washington, D.C., and Cleveland, six years in Oakland, and a staggering eight years in New York City.[35] Obviously most applicants give up long before they get in.

As the emphasis has shifted away from public housing, more federal money now goes to the roughly 1.8 million low-income households who get subsidies attached to privately owned multifamily housing projects, and the roughly 1.6 million who get rental vouchers.[36] Vouchers can in theory be used anywhere; this has the advantages of dispersing the poor among stable neighborhoods, giving them free choices of where to live, and stimulating the private housing market to meet their needs. The rental voucher program is potentially superior to public housing.

Despite the solidly conservative, market-based rationale of the voucher program, however, its funding has been pinched, particularly after the 1995 Gingrich-led Congress imposed a freeze on new vouchers. (In addition, the requirement that vouchers be used only in "Section-8 eligible" dwellings that are up to code has created an opportunity for landlords, especially in higher-income communities, to refuse to apply for certification and therefore be "unable" to accept vouchers. Others "opt out" of their contracts.[37]) As a result of limited funding, the average waiting time for a housing voucher nationally is even longer than the wait for public housing. In 1998, it was twenty-eight months. In Memphis and Chicago, the average wait for voucher assistance was five years, in Houston seven years, in New York City eight years, and in Los Angeles and Newark ten years.[38] Again, of course, most applicants give up.

The federal government also grants a relatively modest amount of tax credits (about $3.3 billion in 2000) to developers who construct or renovate rental housing guaranteed to help low-income tenants for at least fifteen years.[39]

Total government spending on public housing, rental subsidies, and other housing aid for low-income people amounted to about $29 billion in 2000: a substantial amount, yet much less than that devoted to middle-class subsidies and not enough to reach most low-income people. The combination of private housing market activity, government spending, and government tax subsidies clearly does not guarantee satisfactory housing for all Americans. According to HUD, in the mid-1990s, an all-time high of 12.5 million people faced "worst case" housing needs. These people lived in severely substandard housing or had to pay more than one-half their income for rent, while rents were rising rapidly and the stock of affordable housing was declining.[40] Other Americans are altogether homeless.

Homelessness

The most dramatic evidence of the failure of federal housing programs to reach everyone is the presence, especially in big cities, of homeless people. On any given night, many Americans sleep in vehicles, tents, boxes, caves, or boxcars, as well as in more conspicuous places like park benches or doorways, on subway grates, or under bridges.

The number of homeless people in America is hard to assess. It depends heavily on definitions and methods of study, both of which are politically contested. In the United States (in contrast to Britain and Canada, for example), the official definition for a long time was quite narrow, initially encompassing only people on the streets or in emergency shelters and later broadening marginally to include people in welfare hotels and temporary or transitional housing. Advocates for the poor like the National Coalition for the Homeless have promoted a broader conception of homelessness, emphasizing vulnerability and risk and including the "invisible homeless," who tend to be missed in studies.[41]

Even using a narrow definition, however, there are many homeless people in America. At the beginning of the 1980s, during a sharp recession when the problem first won public attention, activists' guesses of two to three million homeless were probably inflated, but HUD's cautious figure of 250,000 to 350,000 was troubling enough. In his scrupulously careful analysis, Christopher Jencks estimated that there were about 350,000 narrowly defined, "visible" homeless Americans during a given week in March 1987, and about 400,000 during a comparable week the following year. About half of them stayed homeless for more than a year, but turnover was so high among the others that roughly *1.2 million* adults became homeless at some point during a given year in the late 1980s. The number of homeless has vastly increased—tripled or quadrupled—since 1980. It may have dipped a bit by 1990, but then rose during the recession at the beginning of the 1990s.[42]

Because homelessness is a temporary condition for most people, very large numbers of Americans experience it at one time or another. The Clinton administration estimated that perhaps *seven million* people experienced homelessness sometime during the latter half of the 1980s. A survey of the national population in the mid-1990s found that 6.5 percent of the respondents, representing fully *twelve million* adults nationwide, had experienced homelessness at some point in their lives.[43] The problem clearly continues. Toward the end of the twentieth century, the U.S. Conference of Mayors reported that in thirty cities about one-quarter (26 percent) of all requests for emergency shelter went unmet, due to lack of resources, even though shelter capacity had more than doubled over the previous decade.[44]

Who are the homeless? It depends partly on how you define the population and where you look.

The stereotype says that homeless people are alcoholic, drug-addicted, and/or mentally ill single men, unable to work, with a history of institutionalization in hospitals and jails. A substantial number of the homeless people on any given night do fit this description, especially in urban shelters and among the long-term homeless who are in the most desperate trouble and require special attention. Most clinicians who have examined homeless people have concluded that about one-third suffer from severe mental disorders. Recent research, however, suggests that the figure for the whole homeless population may be more nearly 20–25 percent, and that perhaps only 5–7 percent of homeless persons with mental illness require institutionalization; most could live in the community with supportive housing options. Surveys during the early 1980s typically found that about one-third of the homeless had serious alcohol problems, and Jencks estimated that in 1991 one-third of all homeless single adults used crack cocaine regularly (of course, these groups overlap). Again, however, recent research suggests that these rates may have been overestimated; among all single adults who are homeless in a year, perhaps fewer than one-third have a current addiction of any sort.[45]

Without question, one significant factor in rising homeless rates has been the "deinstitutionalization" movement, which began as a commendable civil libertarian effort to end the involuntary commitment to mental institutions, the "warehousing," of people who were capable—with community support and newly developed medications—of living reasonably normal lives. By about 1975, however, when the number of patients in state mental hospitals had already plummeted from 468 per 100,000 adults to only 119, things got out of control. Fiscal austerity and budget cuts began to push many seriously ill and even dangerous people out onto the streets, at the very same time that nursing homes were squeezed financially and other support for the poor was drying up. (In the early 1980s, for example, the Reagan administration purged the Social Security disability rolls of many seriously disabled people. Jencks calls this brief but shameful episode "one of the low points of modern American social policy.")[46] Little of the community support and careful tracking that the deinstitutionalization movement had envisioned ever materialized. Many of the homeless today are people who should be getting professional care for mental illness, but have no way to do so.

At the same time, it is all too easy to overstate the importance of this side of homelessness or to confuse causes with effects. Mental disorders and substance abuse can themselves be caused or worsened by homelessness and by the economic and social disasters that precipitate it. These conditions do not necessarily in and of themselves lead to homelessness (rich alcoholics rarely end up on the streets), and they are by no means intractable. With the right medication, counseling, social support, and opportunities, many alcoholics, drug abusers, and mentally ill people can get organized and live productive lives. Human beings are amazingly resilient.[47]

In any case, the homeless by no means all fit the stereotype. They are a diverse lot. Minorities (especially African Americans) are disproportionately represented, but not overwhelmingly so; while about half the homeless in big cities are black, most of the rural homeless—an important and under-studied group—are white. Most homeless adults are men, but the number of women is substantial and probably increasing. In New York City, women and female children at one point constituted about 46 percent of the home-less, and women probably make up a majority of the at-risk population vul-nerable to homelessness.[48]

A major cause of homelessness among women and children is repeated physical or sexual abuse, which can lead to sudden, unplanned, desperate flight with no clear destination. More than 40 percent of homeless women have reported abuse by a spouse or partner. These terrified and demoralized people need special women's shelters that can conceal their location, keep out unwanted male visitors, give them a feeling of safety and supportive com-munity, and provide an array of services: counseling, training in parenting and job skills, child care, and the like. Their children, whose schooling is usually interrupted and whose physical and emotional health is damaged (they are sometimes subjected to violence by mothers who were themselves mistreated by fathers, husbands, or boyfriends), also need special help.[49]

Further, the homeless include teenage runaways—some 59,000 at the be-ginning of the 1990s—mostly refugees from family breakups or victims of physical, sexual, or emotional abuse. Homeless teenage girls, often neglected by social service agencies, are easy prey for criminals and are some fourteen times as likely as their peers to get pregnant (about one in three does so). Some of them, battered by sexual abuse, hooked on drugs or alcohol, and having attempted suicide at least once, resort to prostitution, drug dealing, or shoplifting to get by. Again, obviously, these girls need specially de-signed help.[50]

But the homeless also include military veterans (perhaps one-quarter to one-third of all the homeless), some of them aging Vietnam vets suffering from posttraumatic stress disorder who have lost touch with the extensive system of veterans' social services. And the homeless include some new im-migrants who could not find work or got fired, speak little English, fear the authorities, and have no family or neighborhood network to fall back on. There are also increasing numbers of frail—often disabled—old people, mostly women who outlived their husbands and could not maintain their dwellings.[51]

This disparate collection of homeless people has two main things in com-mon. First, despite recent sharp increases in the number of homeless families with children, the vast majority of homeless adults (perhaps 97 percent of them[52]) are without a spouse or partner. Thus they lack the most intimate and loving kind of personal support. Second, nearly all of the homeless are desperately poor. A focus on individual characteristics of the homeless tends to obscure the fundamental economic fact that the number of poor Americans has risen or stayed about constant at the same time that the number of cheap housing units has shrunk drastically and rents have gone up sharply. Many millions of people are highly vulnerable to homelessness because they are spending more than half their incomes on housing. According to the National Low Income Housing Coalition, at the end of the 1990s in the median state a minimum wage worker would have had to work *eighty-seven each week* in order to afford a two-bedroom apartment for 30 percent of his or her income, which is the federal definition of affordable housing.[53]

In addition to high housing costs, then, the main causes of homelessness are much the same as the causes of poverty generally. These include our failure to educate and train all Americans for productive work, the shrinking of jobs at good wages for the less skilled—due in part to competition from low-wage imports and immigrants—and especially our failure to remedy this situation by providing jobs at good wages or adequate rental vouchers.

Shelters

The problem of homelessness has been worsened by the destruction of cheap rental units, including single-room occupancy (SRO) hotels. This often resulted from public policies, including restrictive zoning, burdensome building codes, and urban renewal–style bulldozing to make way for freeways, shopping centers, and luxury condos. Much of the destruction occurred in the 1960s and 1970s. Subsequently, when the demand for cheap shelter surged, the supply was limited, and rental rates soared—pushing many people over the line into homelessness.[54]

The chief response to homelessness in the United States has been to provide emergency shelters. Most of the money (perhaps two-thirds of it) comes from public funds, under the federal Homeless Relief Act (or McKinney Act) of 1987, which provides some $1 billion per year, plus various state and municipal programs. But most shelters are staffed and administered by nonprofit charitable agencies of various types, ranging from traditional religious missions—where attendance at sermons may be compulsory—to broad-range secular coalitions and groups that focus on specific clienteles like alcoholics or battered women. Shelters run the gamut from the purely public (several cities, including New York, run their own shelters) to the purely nonprofit/charitable, with every sort of mixture in between.[55]

Emergency shelters have a mixed record. On the one hand, they do provide a roof (and, in many cases, meals) for people who would otherwise be very badly off. The nonprofit organizations and volunteers, as well as public funders, deserve a lot of credit for this. On the other hand, especially in the typical shelters designed for single men, conditions are often primitive—sometimes just rows of beds with no privacy, no sense of belonging, few services, only short-term stays, and enforced absence during the day—so that men are forced to wander the streets.[56] There is little sense of participation or control. Some homeless people prefer sleeping outdoors to putting up with these conditions. Shelter policies sometimes seem dominated by fears that men will settle in and become dependent for a long time.

But this is not the only model. At least since the mid-1990s, there has been a trend toward providing more comprehensive services and longer-term, "transitional" housing. Family-oriented shelters tend to be smaller and more supportive and to provide some privacy. Shelters for battered women increasingly offer an array of services and a small-community atmosphere for extended periods of time. Cooperative group homes and "half-way houses" (though often fiercely resisted by local home owners and excluded by law from many communities, especially when they house recovering alcoholics or drug addicts) can provide pathways to permanent homes. And daytime "drop-in" centers help fill the daylight-hour void for shelter residents, sometimes offering free or inexpensive sandwiches and coffee, a warm place to get out of the weather, laundry facilities, free clothing, counseling and referrals, a telephone and mail drop, and a chance to socialize. But funding is often precarious.[57]

As long as there are substantial numbers of homeless Americans with major mental health, addiction, and spousal abuse problems, shelters (especially shelters that offer comprehensive services) are going to be needed. They deserve more public support. The chief alternatives are not attractive: hospitals, which are extremely costly, or *prisons,* which presently provide expensive, dead-end shelter for nearly two million people, many of them guilty of nothing but victimless crimes like drug use (recall the discussion in chapter 7).

Affordable Housing and Self-Help

Policies to help hundreds of thousands or millions of basically healthy people actually to get homes of their own, however, would have to involve creating more inexpensive housing and/or assisting more with rent payments. Having a place of one's own is a precious thing—for privacy and respite, for protection of self and possessions, and (not least) for receiving mail and listing an address on job applications. A cot in a New York armory just does not do it. As Vaclav Havel has observed, a home is "an inseparable element of our human identity." It is a major contributor to self-respect and a productive life. It provides a connection to the community and often a link to family and previous generations.[58]

A mid-1990s newspaper ad by Almost Home, a business coalition for supportive housing, pointed out that permanent homes are not only better for people than shelters, but also cheaper. In New York City at that time, according to the ad, a psychiatric hospital bed cost $113,000 a year, a prison cell cost $60,000, and a shelter cot cost $20,000—but a permanent home and supportive services cost only $12,500.[59]

One side of the affordable housing equation involves getting people more money or vouchers to pay for housing that currently exists. The measures we have discussed for upgrading people's skills and bolstering jobs and wages, as well as providing better social insurance for those who cannot work, would go a long way in this direction. A further important step would be to greatly increase the size and reach of housing vouchers and/or general income support. As the Center on Budget and Policy Priorities points out, it makes particular sense to expand efforts like those of Connecticut and New Jersey to assist former welfare recipients with housing so that they can live near their work and afford new employment-related expenses.[60]

The other side of the equation involves construction of adequate but simple, inexpensive housing. Increasingly governments (especially *city* governments) and nonprofit organizations have moved in this direction. Boston, San Francisco, Seattle, Washington, D.C., and other cities have worked deals with developers that permit downtown commercial projects to go ahead in return for construction of low-income housing and related facilities in low-income neighborhoods. Pittsburgh has built SRO housing with help from state and local governments, private corporations, and federal tax credits. Chicago has renovated foreclosed buildings and offered easy second mortgages and rent subsidies for residents. Corporate participation can be crucial.[61]

Many of the most promising affordable housing projects have been devised at the grassroots level and involve substantial self-help in planning and operation. Self-help is not easy, since the homeless tend to be transient, inexperienced in decision making, and awkward at working with people. It requires time, flexibility, and (ideally) assistance from committed, full-time community organizers. But a key factor in the success of projects for the homeless appears to be the degree of power and control that they themselves exercise. Many residents have built their own housing, particularly in rural areas where land and materials are cheap, building skills are common, and regulations do not get in the way. In cities, low-income residents can often be involved in renovation projects, particularly when there is help from government and from nonprofits like the Enterprise Foundation or Habitat for Humanity.[62]

Self-help is superior to the patron-client relationships that sometimes damage efforts to help the poor. Gerald Daly quotes a formerly homeless person living in a supportive SRO on the telling distinction between a paternalistic "case manager" and a helpful "service coordinator." He notes the value of advocacy and administration by the poor themselves, rather than by high-income professionals who may be out of touch. Self-help gives residents a stake in success, a voice in design and management decisions, and practice at useful skills, while increasing the chance that projects will have features that the residents actually want and need.[63]

Medical Care

Good health, like adequate food and shelter, involves basic human needs. The idea of social insurance applies with particular force to illness, injury, or disability, which can capriciously strike anyone through no fault of her or his own. Taken to its logical conclusion, social insurance reasoning suggests that we should think in terms of a *right* to medical care for all Americans.

The Uninsured and the Untreated

As we saw in chapter 4, however, the United States is very far from guaranteeing such a right. Medicare helps greatly with medical care for the *elderly,* but has been beleaguered by privatizers and budget cutters. Medicare also suffers from conspicuous gaps, most notably its lack of coverage for prescription drugs, which has only very recently begun to be addressed. And it has offered less and less adequate reimbursement for care, so that some providers (especially health maintenance organizations or HMOs) have dropped out of the program and abandoned their elderly patients.

The system of employer-provided health insurance has broken down, as more and more employers cut costs by sharply restricting programs or eliminating them altogether. And freestanding health insurance (plagued by the adverse selection problem) has become unaffordable to millions and completely unavailable to many people with "preexisting medical conditions"—precisely the sort of hazard that social insurance is supposed to protect us against. As the twenty-first century began, the United States was moving toward having *forty-five million* people (about one-sixth of the population) with no medical insurance at all.

Lack of insurance does not usually result in death from untreated disease or injury. Only the most callous hospital emergency rooms turn away acute cases, and hospitals can get in legal trouble for doing so. (They may, however, be required only to "stabilize" emergency patients and then feel free to discharge them. Such "patient dumping" by private hospitals imposes extra costs on public institutions. It can be a problem for patients in a place like El Paso, which is some eight hundred miles from the only fully state-funded indigent care center in Texas, the University of Texas medical branch in Galveston.)

Much more common is a tendency for people to put off or skip trips to the doctor over "minor" or endurable problems and then to rush to the emergency room—a very expensive source of care—when the pain becomes too great or a critical bodily function is lost. (Untreated asthma, for example, can become life-threatening.) Thus lack of medical insurance worsens the tendency of the U.S. medical care system to slight *preventive* medicine; to neglect inexpensive, ongoing care; and instead to wait until medical problems are far advanced and cause unnecessary pain and expense. The tilt toward the well-insured wealthy also distorts our health system away from basic care and toward elective procedures like plastic surgery—liposuction, breast enhancement, hair plugs, and the like.

Lack of comprehensive health insurance exacerbates inequality in the United States. It creates a special sort of poverty by letting middle-class people be hit capriciously by enormous financial burdens that exhaust their economic resources. Only then—and only for some people—does Medicaid, with its off-putting aura of a program reserved for the poor, take up the remaining burden of unpaid medical bills.

Medicaid

Medicaid (which, again, must be distinguished from the Medicare program for the elderly) is a means-tested "safety net" medical program for some but not all of the poor. It is a very large program, jointly run by the federal and state governments, that in 1998 covered about thirty-three million Americans at a cost of $101 billion (57 percent of the total) from the federal budget and $76 billion from the states. The federal contribution was expected to grow to about $115 billion in 2000 and to continue to grow by nearly 8 percent per year for the next several years.[64]

Numbers like that make Medicaid by far the largest program in the United States exclusively targeted to the poor. It is also one of the fastest-growing federal government programs. For example, *six times* as much money was spent on Medicaid in 1995 as in 1980. Most of this increase was due to the overall rise in medical care costs, but spending almost doubled in inflation-adjusted dollars. Most of the increase has resulted from rising costs for the disabled and elderly, who require very expensive, long-term, continuous care, and for whom there are few feasible or humane ways to cut costs.[65]

Medicaid has made a substantial difference to low-income households. Since it was established in 1965, poor people have received more medical care, and their health has steadily improved. Infant mortality among poor mothers has declined, life expectancies have increased, and the incidence of various infectious diseases has gone down (true, poor people are still at higher risk of medical problems than higher-income people are). As Rebecca Blank notes, a variety of studies have linked these improvements directly to the creation and expansion of Medicaid. When Medicaid was extended to all poor and near-poor pregnant women and children, for example, there were substantial reductions in both infant mortality and low birth weights (children's health did not immediately improve, however, apparently because many newly eligible children were not enrolled).[66]

Contrary to some anecdotes and public imagery, Medicaid is also a generally efficient program. Its administrative costs have amounted to only about 4 percent of benefit payments, a very low figure that partly reflects the very high average benefit levels (in contrast to Food Stamps or AFDC, for example), the continuing nature of much eligibility, and the automatic exten-sion of eligibility from other programs. Overpayments are also relatively small, amounting to perhaps 3 percent of benefits in the mid-1980s and prob-ably less since then. The extent of actual fraud is hard to determine; as with Food Stamps, however, most of any fraud enriches vendors or providers, not the patients.[67]

None of this, however, means that Medicaid constitutes anything like uni-versal health insurance, or even that it covers all of the poor. For one thing, states are required to extend eligibility only to certain narrowly defined groups of people: poor women and children (at one time, this automatically included all AFDC beneficiaries) and the elderly and disabled who are poor enough to receive SSI. Some thirty-five states also extend coverage to the "medically needy," but about 29 percent of the poor and 28 percent of the near-poor are not covered by Medicaid or any medical insurance.[68] For an-other thing, many services are not covered or are covered for only a limited time. And reimbursement rates to providers have been cut, so that many physicians and institutions refuse to participate in the program.

Moreover, as we noted in chapter 4, the bulk of Medicaid benefits now go to people who are "poor" only in a particular sense. They go to elderly and disabled people who were once middle class, but who have been brought down by medical afflictions (and whose middle-class children would pre-sumably otherwise be paying for them). According to the federal budget document for fiscal year 2000, the elderly and disabled made up less than a third of Medicaid beneficiaries, but they accounted for almost two-thirds of all the program's spending. Medicaid is now the largest single purchaser of nursing home and other long-term care services, and it covers almost two-thirds of all nursing home residents in the United States.[69] Thus Medicaid has evolved into a largely middle-class program, but a stigmatized and in-complete program, while it also fails fully to serve low-income and poor people.

Universal Health Care

Why not establish a *right* to medical care without stigma or economic desti-tution? Why not set up a universal health care system, in which everyone is covered regardless of economic resources or previous medical history? As we suggested at greater length in chapter 4, one good way to do so would be to follow the Canadian model of unified, government-guaranteed medical insurance for everyone, with government-negotiated care standards and reimbursements to private providers. The evidence from other countries indicates that such a system could save on administrative costs, reduce waste, and be much cheaper overall than the present U.S. system, while providing better than the present level of care for most people. Within such a universal insurance system (or, for that matter, even within a socialized medical system like Britain's), the affluent could, if they wished, still pursue elective procedures and multiple specialists of their choice; the U.S. advantages in technical innovation and specialization could be maintained. But everyone would get access to basic care.

A universal health care system could be designed to encourage the development of cheap, quick-care clinics in neighborhoods that now lack medical facilities. By relying on negotiated reimbursements, rather than fee-for-service medicine (and perhaps by imposing modest co-payments to discourage unnecessary use), it could keep costs down, provide incentives for efficient care giving, and put new emphasis on preventive care. At the same time, its single-payer structure would help avoid the competitive squeeze on quality of care that is currently plaguing HMOs. Together with the programs that we have described to ensure adequate nutrition and child care, such a system could help prevent a number of illnesses that are relatively cheap and easy to avoid, but that presently blight people's lives and cost many billions of dollars per year.

Income Maintenance

To a number of economists and others, the best way to combat poverty seems obvious: give poor people money. Abolish the complicated tangle of targeted cash and in-kind benefit programs; set up a simple, cheap-to-administer, comprehensive system of "family allowances," "negative income taxes," or "income support payments" to everyone in need, and let them spend this money as they choose on food, shelter, or anything else. Let poor people maximize their satisfaction for each dollar spent, and let private markets respond by providing whatever people will pay for.

But this does not appear to be the American Way. We insist that every able-bodied person should work. As that lively public philosopher James Carville has remarked, "My momma, who is known to most of Louisiana as Miss Nippy, informed my nephew that there were only two acceptable activities for a human being between the ages of five and sixty-five: being in training for a job or having a job." Most progressive Americans agree with Carville that work and training for work are core values, that "the most sacred thing you can render in this world is your labor," and that government should focus on promoting work and training for work.[70]

In this context, U.S. policy makers have sought to restrict cash payments to narrow categories of the "truly needy," who are unable to earn adequate incomes for reasons clearly beyond their control. The main steps—rather halting steps—toward general income support divorced from work have involved in-kind help with the basic necessities of food and medical care. Even there, exhaustive efforts have been made to ensure that such help is strictly confined to basic necessities, not "wasted" on anything frivolous or entertaining. A hint that some degenerate might contrive to use Food Stamps to get a drink of alcohol can turn people against the entire program. There is even grumbling about ice cream and potato chips. American social policy has a distinctly Puritan side.

We will suggest, now that our review of U.S. government policies dealing with poverty and inequality is nearly complete, that it is time to revisit and rethink the concept of a universal guaranteed income. Even within a work-centered philosophy, a broad view of social insurance and a sense of common humanity point toward a system of comprehensive income maintenance that would guarantee a very modest but decent standard of living for every American, without shame or stigma. At the same time, we will argue that cash support cannot solve all problems and, further, that there is some merit to focusing instead on comprehensive and universal provision of basic needs.

"Welfare"

In the past, the main cash-assistance program for nonelderly poor people in the United States was Aid to Families with Dependent Children (AFDC), commonly known as "welfare."[71] AFDC had its origins in the Social Security Act of 1935 as an effort to help widows and their children. It expanded steadily and then doubled between 1967 and 1972, to cover a quite different population: young abandoned or (less often) never-married mothers. AFDC encountered storms of controversy and criticism, suffered budget cuts and erosion of benefit levels, and was finally abolished as a federal entitlement in 1996. It was replaced by Temporary Assistance for Needy Families (TANF), which now provides block grants to the states.[72]

AFDC provided monthly cash payments primarily to single mothers with income and assets below specified levels and with children under age eighteen living at home. In the mid-1990s, nearly *one-ninth* of America's children, 9.3 million of them, participated during the average month. AFDC was a federal *entitlement* program—that is, benefits were guaranteed to all eligible people who applied. The federal government paid more than half (about 55 percent) of the costs and imposed some regulations, but states and counties operated the program, and the separate states could each determine their own benefit and eligibility levels, which varied widely. In 1994, for example, Connecticut paid $680 per month to a family of three with no other resources, while Mississippi paid only $120—a mere 13 percent of the poverty level. This difference was much greater than the variation in cost of living.[73]

Contrary to political rhetoric about "runaway welfare costs," AFDC was always a very small program. In 1995, just before its abolition, it took up only 1.1 percent of the federal budget, far less than the 5.8 percent going to Medicaid, let alone the much larger amounts devoted to the middle-class elderly through Medicare's 10.2 percent of the budget or Social Security's 21.8 percent. (According to Rebecca Blank, 40 percent of all means-tested "public assistance support" at that time went to the just 10 percent of the poor who were elderly or seriously disabled.) Nor were the benefit levels in most states ever very generous. During the 1970s and 1980s, benefits were deeply cut or eroded by inflation. Adjusting for inflation—using constant 1994 dollars—the median state in 1970 had paid $792 per month for a mother with three children, but in 1993, it paid only $435—a punishing 45 percent cut. The average monthly AFDC payment fell to just 38 percent of the official poverty threshold.[74]

AFDC or "welfare" became the most hated and denigrated of all antipoverty programs, as exemplified and inflamed by President Reagan's references to "welfare queens," who supposedly lived in luxury on payments fraudulently obtained under multiple names. (Such cases were quite rare and were vigorously prosecuted. A much more frequent—and morally more ambiguous—sort of "fraud" was failure to report outside earnings. Low AFDC benefit levels made outside earnings essential to survival, but to report those earnings would result in losing every penny earned, since equal amounts would be taken away in AFDC benefit reductions.[75])

Opponents of the program also claimed that it discouraged work by women who ought to be out in the labor market, rather than staying at home with young children; that it discouraged marriage and encouraged childbearing by poor and unmarried people who should not be having children;

and that it developed cycles of dependency, in which children and grandchildren of welfare mothers lived on the dole. Opposition was reinforced by racism-tinged stereotypes of AFDC mothers as predominately African-American and as lazy and sexually promiscuous. (Most were actually white, many were eager to work, and their sexual behavior did not differ markedly from that of their peers.) Also damaging to AFDC were fiscal austerity, an unwillingness to support the poor among working people who were themselves struggling economically, and some politicians'—mostly Republicans' and Southern Democrats'—discovery that welfare was a marvelous "wedge" issue for splitting support away from liberal Democrats.[76]

AFDC did in fact provide some perverse financial incentives. Under federal mandates, a woman lost a dollar in benefits for every dollar she earned working (after deducting some work-related expenses). In effect, this imposed a nearly 100 percent tax on earnings, which was bound to discourage work at least somewhat—particularly in combination with the implicit taxes built into Food Stamps and other means-tested programs, as well as low minimum wage levels and scanty job opportunities. (Similarly, after an initial fifty-dollar threshold, each dollar paid in child support by an absent father was subtracted from the mother's AFDC benefits, weakening a father's incentive to pay or a mother's to collect.) Further, the focus on single parents—at one time involving surprise inspections to make sure that no unreported man was lurking around the house—presumably discouraged low-income people from forming and keeping stable families; the 1988 requirement that all states run at least some programs for married couples never fully overcame this.[77] Remarkably, however, the impact of these poorly designed provisions of AFDC was not in fact very great.

The cross-state evidence indicates, for example, that AFDC payments had little or no impact on rates of out-of-wedlock childbearing. Low-income single white women may have had a slight tendency to have more children where AFDC benefits were high, but African-American women showed no such tendency at all. This is consistent with other patterns. Over time, as AFDC benefit levels fell, U.S. out-of-wedlock births *rose,* rather than the opposite. This increase occurred throughout the income distribution, not just among poor people who had access to AFDC. And the rate of out-of-wedlock births (and especially of teen pregnancies) was *higher* in the United States than in other countries with much more generous welfare benefits. Moreover, quite contrary to the "welfare brood" image, the average size of

AFDC families steadily declined, to a moderate 2.8 people in 1995. The alleged "fertility effect" of AFDC, then, was small or nonexistent.[78]

On the other hand, AFDC does seem to have had a significant "independence effect": when benefit levels were higher, more women who had children tended to leave their parents' homes and set up their own households.[79] It is hard to be sure whether the independence effect was good or bad: whether, when they chose to leave, these women were fleeing tight quarters and abusive or interfering relationships, or whether they were missing out on supportive assistance in mothering. Absent clear evidence on this point, the independence effect does not seem to have amounted to a seriously negative impact of AFDC.

Nor is there much to the oft-asserted claim that AFDC created "dependency," either over recipients' lifetimes or across generations. In the first place, many—perhaps one-third—of the women eligible for AFDC did not use it at all, presumably because of hassles and stigma. Most who did use it got off fairly quickly: nearly two-thirds of them within two years. Only a tiny 7 percent of recipients stayed on welfare continuously for ten years or longer. True, many women cycled in and out, with nearly one-quarter of AFDC recipients receiving benefits for ten or more years over their whole lifetimes, and this accounted for a large share of the total benefits paid. But the very fact of cycling in and out tended to refute the notion that AFDC was addictive. So did recipients' evident distaste for the program ("Anyone on public aid, they been treated like dogmeat," commented one), their clear willingness to accept jobs or training when available, and the decision of many eligible people not to take AFDC benefits at all.[80]

The substantial number of long-term recipients of AFDC can easily be accounted for without any notion of addiction or dependence, simply by the fact that they were extremely disadvantaged. Most (nearly three-quarters) lacked high school diplomas, most lacked extensive job experience, many had two or more small children with no child support from the father, and many suffered from health problems. In a labor market increasingly unfriendly to less-skilled people, these women were bound to have trouble finding and keeping adequate jobs.[81]

Similarly, no notion of habitual dependency is required in order to understand the perpetuation of poverty across generations. Though children of poor women were much more likely than others to themselves be poor and to receive AFDC, only somewhere between one-quarter and one-third in fact did so. And this resulted chiefly from having disadvantages similar to those of their mothers—little education, childbearing at a young age, low occupational aspirations. When these factors were statistically controlled for, there was only a small residual tendency for daughters of AFDC women to themselves use AFDC. In short, the much-ballyhooed idea of welfare dependency rested more on myth and ideology than on fact.[82]

What about work incentives? A substantial body of research has compared work behavior in high- and low-benefit states and analyzed negative income tax experiments. These studies—exhaustively reviewed by Robert Moffitt, Philip Robins, Sheldon Danziger, and others—indicate that with higher AFDC benefits women did tend to work a bit less, but only a bit: perhaps only about two hours less per month for each $100 increment in monthly benefits. That is, when AFDC benefits were $200 per month higher in Indiana than in Mississippi, Indiana recipients may have worked about forty-eight hours less in the course of a full year. Since these people generally got very low wages, the total value of work lost was quite small. On a nationwide basis in 1993, according to Rebecca Blank's figures, if all AFDC payments had been entirely eliminated, the resulting increased work effort would have produced only an average $337 increase in annual income—hardly enough to shout about.[83]

The small magnitude of work disincentive effects becomes even clearer when it is contrasted with the ameliorative effects that AFDC had on poverty. Again according to Blank's figures, the average "poverty gap" for single-mother families in 1993 was $6,670: that is, their total incomes, including AFDC payments, fell below the official poverty line—itself quite low—by an average of $6,670. But if the AFDC payments had been entirely eliminated and their increased work efforts taken into account, the average poverty gap would have amounted to a substantially bigger $8,940. Thus the $337 worth of foregone work might be viewed as a cost, a rather moderate cost, of reducing the average AFDC recipient's poverty by $2,270. But there is more to it than that because not all of the $337 should really be viewed as a cost. Many of these women did valuable unpaid work caring for their preschool children when they did not have to work full-time outside the home, a point sometimes missed by enthusiasts of family values.[84]

It is also important to see that even a decrease in work effort of this modest size is not inherent in cash income-maintenance programs per se, but largely resulted from the poor design and the stinginess of AFDC. The key to avoiding work disincentives is to reduce payments only *gradually* with increased earnings, so that the implicit tax on earnings is much less than 100 percent. (The EITC, for example, does this. In 1997, the credit for workers raising one child rose with income until it reached a level of $2,210 for people earning between $6,500 and $11,500; it then declined very gradually and did not completely vanish until income reached $25,500.[85])

The rub, of course, is that such a program is necessarily more expensive; it requires making some payments to the merely poor and to people of low incomes, not only to the totally destitute. But the United States can afford such expenditures. And we believe that the side effect of helping low-income as well as destitute people would be altogether a good thing.

Work and Temporary Assistance

The 1996 legislation abolishing AFDC and substituting TANF (Temporary Assistance for Needy Families), however, went in a quite different direction. Rather than providing more generous income supplements and work incentives, it focused on trying to *force* people to move from welfare to work.

TANF ended the legally guaranteed federal entitlement to aid and broadened the already substantial state discretion concerning eligibility and benefit levels, including the nature and amount of cash, in-kind, or work-related benefits. The federal government now gives the states block grants—about $17 billion worth in 2000—and mandates that they meet certain standards of performance. States must require work or enrollment in training programs after two years on assistance, impose five-year lifetime limits on aid to any one individual (20 percent of the caseload can be exempted), and get adults into work activities in at least 25 percent of the families on welfare, with the 25 percent figure (liberalized for states with big drops in their welfare rolls) increasing by 5 percent per year until reaching 50 percent in 2002. TANF also required unmarried minor parents receiving aid to live under adult supervision, tightened eligibility for children's disability benefits, permitted states to deny aid to most legal aliens, mandated substantial help with child care, sharply cut Food Stamps and child nutrition, and made a variety of other policy changes—most of them involving benefit cuts.[86]

Some states, led by Wisconsin (whose Governor Tommy Thompson had pioneered several welfare law changes), entered into the new policy with gusto. Many pursued a "work first" strategy, helping recipients look for work and pushing them to take any job they could find by cutting off payments when some sort of employment turned up. Some states relied mostly on compulsion, imposing shorter time limits than the federal requirement and strongly discouraging all applicants for aid. Other states gave extensive help with counseling and training, transportation to work, child care, and the like.[87]

In one key respect, at least, the policy change was a spectacular success: the number of welfare recipients dropped sharply, by 38 percent (4.6 million people) in just two years after the August 1996 signing of the bill. By the beginning of 1999, in fact, there were only 7.6 million welfare cases nationwide, the lowest figure in thirty years and little more than *half* of the 14.1 million in January 1993. Moreover, all 36 states reporting data indicated that they met the 1997 target of having adults working in at least 25 percent of the families on welfare. As detailed reports from individual states began to trickle in, it became clear that many former welfare recipients—perhaps half to two-thirds of them—were finding work. Massachusetts, for example, reported that 71 percent of people who got off and stayed off welfare reported a year later that someone in their household was working, and 86 percent said their families were at least as well off as in their welfare days (this, however, was based on a study of just 210 households that were probably better off than those who declined to be interviewed). Michigan, too, found that about two-thirds of former welfare recipients were working.[88]

At the same time, many of the jobs taken by former welfare recipients proved to be only temporary and/or to provide much less income than needed to support a family. Scrutiny of the Massachusetts report, for example, revealed that only slightly more than half of former welfare recipients had family income from earnings after a year and that about one-quarter of those who left welfare got back on it. Other states showed similar patterns, with 24 percent returning to welfare within three months in Michigan, 19 percent in Maryland, and 38 percent in New Jersey. What would become of these people when time limits eliminated the welfare option? And what happened to the "missing in action"—the roughly one-fifth to one-quarter of former welfare recipients who were *neither* working nor back on welfare? How were they getting by? [89]

An analysis of twenty-one state reports found that most former welfare recipients, even those who were working, were still poor; many had trouble paying for food and utilities. Pamela Loprest's systematic Urban Institute study of early welfare-leavers found that about one-third were back on welfare within a year or two. About 25 percent of those who stayed off welfare had no one in the family working, one-third had to skip meals or cut back on food, and 39 percent reported that there was at least one time in the year when they were unable to pay rent, mortgage, or utility bills. A study by the Children's Defense Fund and the National Coalition for the Homeless found that only a small fraction (8 percent) of former welfare recipients' new jobs paid above-poverty wages—most paid far below—and extreme child poverty was increasing even at a time of economic expansion. [90]

In any case, the early successes of welfare reform reflected the booming late-1990s economy, with the unemployment rate around 4 percent, the lowest level in thirty years. Tight labor markets meant that former welfare recipients had a relatively good chance of finding a job. Moreover, the earliest cuts in welfare rolls were the easiest; those still remaining on welfare were likely to have the biggest disadvantages—the least formal education or job experience and the most illness, substance abuse, mental disturbances, and the like. To get those people to work would be much harder. And the long-term results of the policy changes would be evident only when a serious recession came, throwing former welfare recipients (the first to be fired) out of work at the same time that state programs were squeezed by drops in tax revenues.

The effort to get people off welfare and onto work has the great potential merit of contributing to people's long-term productivity, self-sufficiency, and self-esteem. To accomplish this in a way that actually reduces U.S. poverty and inequality, however, it is essential to ensure that jobs are available at good wages that will actually lift people out of poverty. This requires measures of the sort that we discussed in chapter 7 on jobs and wages: good macroeconomic policy, a substantial minimum wage, a broadened Earned Income Tax Credit (fully helping adults without children as well as those with), and probably some government job creation—especially for those with the most limited skills. The neediest Americans, including former welfare recipients, also require special help with education and training, housing, transportation to work, child care, and the like. In the short run, all this may well be more expensive than simply handing out cash assistance. But the investment is worthwhile. Further, income maintenance will be needed for those who cannot or should not work even with all this help. At minimum, former welfare recipients should not be intimidated or deceived out of obtaining the Food Stamps or SSI benefits that they have a right to. The point of genuine welfare reform is not to shame or punish, but to help.

Guaranteed Income?

We have already mentioned some of the arguments in favor of providing a guaranteed minimal level of income in cash. Such a program would be cheap to administer; writing checks to everyone costs less than providing services or enforcing complex eligibility rules. It would eschew paternalism and maximize free choice by the recipients. It would rely on markets, rather than bureaucracies, for efficient provision of the things that recipients need. Perhaps most important, a guaranteed income could be cast as a *universal* program that goes to everyone. People with high incomes would eventually get much or all of their benefits taxed away, but at least initially they could get the same check or credit as everyone else. And everyone would share the equal guarantee of a minimum income if things go wrong. This means that shame and stigma could be avoided. A legal and moral *right* of everyone to such an income could be established.[91]

Some of the standard objections to such a plan seem to us not to be compelling. The costs, for example, can be made to look enormous by talking about the huge "Treasury transactions" involved,[92] but much of any money that went to high-income people as grants would come back in taxes. The traditional American fear that people would slack off and not bother to work—never backed by much evidence—loses most of its remaining force if, as we urge, plentiful jobs are made available at good wages so that everyone has the opportunity, as well as the financial incentive, to work. Thus we believe that the idea of a guaranteed income, at a level just sufficient for a family to maintain an adequate but modest standard of living—and with the benefits gradually taxed away as income from other sources goes up—is worth another look. Just because an idea seems revolutionary does not mean it is necessarily a bad one, or even that it cannot be politically feasible.

At the same time, guaranteed cash incomes do have at least one serious weakness: free choice in the use of cash will not inevitably maximize the well-being of all poor people. A drug addict or alcoholic, for example, cannot be counted on to spend his or her money on detoxification, rather than a fix or a drink. A person with limited skills will not always invest scarce cash in education and training. A disorganized or demoralized parent may not put aside enough money for his or her child's food, medical care, or education. In such cases, there is an argument for providing needed goods and services in kind, rather than cash.[93]

It is mainly for this reason that we lean away from guaranteeing cash incomes and toward guaranteeing the right to certain essential goods like food, shelter, and medical care, while also offering special programs to help children, train the unskilled, treat substance abusers and the mentally ill, and the like. Either way, however, we believe that the most crucial measures for reducing poverty and inequality in the United States are those that help provide jobs for all workers at good wages.

Politics: The War against the Poor

In many respects, the politics of "safety net"–type programs resembles the politics of other policy areas we have discussed. Democratic (at least Northern Democratic) politicians have tended to favor these programs, while most Republicans generally oppose them. Most antipoverty programs were originated and expanded under Democratic presidents—particularly Franklin D. Roosevelt and Lyndon B. Johnson—while efforts to cut and retrench have generally come from Republicans like Ronald Reagan and the Newt Gingrich–led Republican Congress of 1995–96. Votes in Congress tend to divide sharply along party lines.[94]

The Nixon administration, which helped expand Food Stamps and proposed an ambitious guaranteed income program that it called the Family Assistance Plan (FAP), represents a partial exception to this tendency. But the politics of FAP in fact tends to confirm the general pattern because the opposition that killed it consisted of legislators taking their traditional partisan positions—Republicans thinking the benefit levels too high and Democrats thinking them too low.[95]

The lineup of interest groups is generally familiar as well. Labor unions (allied with the Democrats) support many antipoverty programs, while most business and financial interests (allied with the Republicans) usually oppose them. But the balance of interest group forces is even more antiegalitarian in this case than usual. To unions, antipoverty measures are only a secondary priority; they are primarily concerned with their own members' wages and working conditions. Most other groups that are liberal on various issues—trial lawyers, retired people, the entertainment industry, even women's groups—do not share identical interests with the poor. Poor people themselves—especially children—obviously lack resources; they do not have millions of dollars to give to election campaigns, and they are usually unorganized. Their interests must often be articulated—if at all—by racial and ethnic organizations, by big-city mayors, or by sympathetic middle-class people in certain churches and small groups like the Children's Defense Fund or the National Coalition for the Homeless. Only occasionally have poor people themselves risen up and demanded government help.[96]

This is one of the cases, therefore, in which the old pluralist myth of "balanced" interest groups is most obviously false. Poor and low-income Americans do not have Philip Morris or General Motors on their side, or even the relatively liberal Goldman Sachs investment firm. The Center for Responsive Politics (CRP) calculates that in the most recent election cycle for which large individual political contributions can be combined with political action committee (PAC) contributions (1991–92), business outgave labor by a factor of *7 to 1*. Of the 1,197 PACs that gave $20,000 or more to members of Congress, *not a single one* represented poor people, the unemployed, the underemployed, the homeless, or tenants of public housing. In the CRP's tabulation of the top ninety-three industries and interest groups that made election contributions in 1997–98, retired people came out fairly well (#2 on the list), and various unions and socially liberal organizations showed up among the much more common business firms and associations, but *no* explicitly propoor organization or coalition appeared at all.[97] Little wonder that we have reasonable social insurance programs for the elderly and the middle class, but no guaranteed minimum standards of food, shelter, and medical care for everyone.

There is a further reason. The politics of poverty is also distinguished by what Herbert Gans has called a "war against the poor." Wars against the poor or the "underclass" periodically erupt with venomous rhetoric and angry emotions.[98] Hostile condemnation of "handouts," "freeloaders," "welfare queens," and "Food Stamps for gin" does not generally originate in corporate boardrooms (though it can sometimes help advance corporate agendas). It often springs from, or at least resonates with, the feelings of hard-pressed small businesspeople and workers, especially when economic times are tough. And it reflects certain themes deeply embedded in American values and American political culture, particularly our cult of self-reliance and our extreme individualism.[99] Fears of being taken advantage of by lazy, shiftless, and greedy people who can be defined as "others" in terms of race, ethnicity, or gender lurk within the hearts of many Americans. These fears can be inflamed and exploited by demagogues in ways that are not characteristic of most other advanced countries. Clearly racism, rooted in our history of slavery—as well as sexism toward poor women—plays a part.[100]

Yet the role of the more usual political forces even in these wars should not be discounted. Antipoor rhetoric has been translated into respectable intellectual terms ("dependency," "disincentives," "fertility effects") and has been widely publicized, only with help from lots of money flowing to scholars and popularizers from right-wing foundations and think tanks like Scaife, Hoover, and Heritage, whose funding comes mostly from conservative businessmen.[101] And recent poverty wars may also have reflected the major structural factor that has so altered American politics in general: the pressure of increased global economic competition, which made the costs of antipoverty spending seem more troublesome to business—at least until federal budget deficits turned to surpluses.

Some of the most rapid progress for poor and low-income people has occurred when they have organized themselves into social movements, thrown a little fear into the hearts of politicians, and overcome the usual forces of opposition.[102] One hopes that future progress will not require the galvanizing force of a major depression. Far better if affluent Americans, luxuriating in their recent gains, voluntarily decide to share a bit.

The Right to Basic Necessities

In speaking of "rights," we have in mind not God-given or "natural" rights of the sort that were revealed or advocated in the eighteenth century, but rather rights that are created by human beings for human purposes. We believe that adequate food, shelter, and medical care are just as important to people's lives as are the constitutional rights that Americans are so fortunate to enjoy, such as freedom of speech and freedom of the press. Perhaps, in fact, economic needs should have priority. Free speech is not of much use to people who are homeless, desperately ill, or starving. "Freedom to" live a decent life surely should, in our view, have at least equal priority with the "freedom from" government tyranny that is guaranteed by our Constitution. To speak of economic rights, in the context of the uniquely legalistic American society, is simply to emphasize the importance of the material world and to insist that rights to cooperative help with material life deserve equal priority with individualistic rights to be left alone.

Franklin D. Roosevelt spoke of "freedom from want" as one of the Four Freedoms to spread throughout the world. The Universal Declaration of Human Rights, adopted by the United Nations General Assembly in 1948, puts it clearly. According to Article 25-1, "Everyone has the right to a standard of living adequate for the health and well-being of himself and of his family, including food, clothing, housing and medical care and necessary social services. . . ."[103]

To guarantee basic economic rights to all Americans would greatly reduce U.S. poverty and inequality, producing the many benefits noted in chapter 3: a better sense of community, harmony, and social stability; more nearly equal opportunity; more complete human development and fulfillment of potential; more human happiness or satisfaction. As we have suggested, such a guarantee also follows logically from the idea of social insurance, because it insures everyone against the myriad factors—accidents of birth, upbringing, life experience—that can deprive people of necessities. If we have enough imagination and empathy to see that we ourselves might have suffered (or might in the future suffer) in the same way as the poor— there but for the grace of God go we—then we ought to favor such comprehensive insurance.

With an annual gross domestic product of well over $8.5 billion—about $31,000 per person, or close to $85,000 per household—at the beginning of the twenty-first century,[104] the United States can clearly afford a few thousand dollars worth of help to each of those Americans whose incomes presently fall far below that figure and who lack minimum standards of medical care, housing, or food. Such a *guarantee* would apply equally to everyone, but of course the *cost*—the actual resources expended—would be far less than the guarantee level multiplied by the number of people in the country because most people already do much better than the modest minimum level.

Implementation would not be very difficult. No adequate system of health care can be truly cheap or simple, but universal health insurance could be made far less expensive and less complex than the present bizarre and incomplete tangle of private and public programs. To guarantee adequate food and shelter would be easy. Every month, for example, each American household—rich, poor, or in between—might simply receive a coupon or a credit on its Food Card for an amount of money reflecting the household's size that could be spent (for food only) at grocery stores or restaurants. And each household might also get a monthly housing voucher or credit on a Housing Card good for rent or mortgage payments. Since everyone would receive and use these benefits, no stigma could attach to their use. But since their value would be reported as income and taxed accordingly—at higher rates for people with higher total incomes—the actual net benefits could be distributed quite progressively.

Yes, technical details would have to be worked out: how to minimize paperwork and administrative expenses, for example, while certifying and monitoring grocers and landlords. (Presumably the purchase of alcohol and cigarettes would be excluded; otherwise, why not just mail a check and call it a guaranteed income?) Yes, shelters, soup kitchens, and special medical treatment would still be needed for the few unable to navigate the guarantee system. And yes, the political barriers are formidable; we would not expect such guarantees to be enacted by the U.S. Congress tomorrow. But there is no harm in pointing out the direction in which policy should go or in working to achieve it.

9

Conclusion

At the beginning of this book, we asked what, if anything, government can do about poverty and inequality. Our answer is clear: government can do a great deal. It can do so while preserving other things we value, including liberty, economic efficiency, and general prosperity.

Persistent poverty and a high level of income inequality in the United States cast a dark shadow over our otherwise great achievements. When (as chapter 2 showed) about one-fifth of American children live in families with incomes below the poverty line, when the top fifth of families receive about half of all the income in the country but the bottom fifth get less than 4 percent of it, something is seriously wrong. No doubt a substantial degree of inequality would be tolerable, so long as the lot of those on the bottom was satisfactory and steadily improving. But that has not been the case. Inequality has increased sharply over the past three decades, with big gains for the wealthy, while most people's incomes stagnated or declined. We are troubled by the extraordinary extent of disparities in income and wealth, by the persistence of absolute poverty, and by the fact that many millions of working people have to struggle desperately in order to make ends meet.

Such extensive poverty and inequality waste lives and cause unnecessary suffering. They limit freedom. They prevent full individual development, impair a sense of community, upset social stability, make a mockery of the idea of equal opportunity, and unnecessarily reduce human happiness.

Private markets and free-enterprise capitalism, for all their virtues, plainly do not themselves keep the levels of poverty and inequality within acceptable bounds. Even to the extent that markets accurately reward individual skills and efforts—and the most eloquent defenders of markets admit that they do not invariably do so—huge inequalities in "rewards" cannot be considered fair or just. Many factors that lead to high or low incomes are beyond individuals' control. To a great extent, they reflect happy or unhappy chance, the results of nature, nurture, and social arrangements: the fortune or misfortune of genes, upbringing, parents, peers, good breaks, catastrophic accidents, economic fluctuations, global trends.

Nor is poverty or extreme inequality necessary in order to motivate people to learn, to work hard, and to do their best. Duty, pride, love of family, aspirations for achievement, and self-fulfillment are excellent motivators. We do not need to use unlimited greed or fear of starvation. Given encouragement and opportunities—the opportunities are crucial—the vast majority of people will work hard and productively.

There are many reasons therefore to think that governments *should* act to reduce poverty and inequality, if they can do so in ways that do not entail too many costs: without too much inefficiency, for example, and without seriously infringing on individual liberties. Our review of the evidence indicates that government *can* in fact do so. The old canard that governments cannot do anything right is simply not correct. Nor is the newer claim that globalization renders national governments completely impotent. Yes, globalization does exert pressure against certain types of egalitarian programs, but those pressures are much less overpowering than is often supposed. Some important kinds of egalitarian programs (investment in education, for example; childhood health and nutrition; income supplements for low-wage work) actually can confer global competitive advantages, rather than disadvantages. Yes, it requires creativity and care to design programs to maximize their effectiveness, while minimizing red tape and bureaucratic interference. But such creativity and care are well within the reach of our experts, political leaders, and citizenry.

Right now, in fact, the U.S. federal, state, and local governments *do,* in many efficient and effective ways, contribute to the reduction of poverty and inequality. At the same time, there remains much more that can and should be done. To make further progress requires recognizing and surmounting certain political and economic obstacles.

Programs That Work

As we saw in chapter 4, U.S. social insurance programs, which offer certain kinds of protection that private insurance markets cannot provide, make very significant contributions to reducing poverty and inequality. Social Security in particular—the very foundation of American social policy—does more than any other government program to keep people's incomes above the poverty line. Without Social Security old age benefits, many more millions of elderly Americans would be poor, as many millions were before the enactment and expansion of the program.

That great reduction in poverty has been accomplished with a high degree of efficiency. Social Security's administrative costs amount to only about 1 percent of total payments. The poverty reduction has been achieved through a near-universal system of forced savings linked to work, in which people contribute while they are working and then quite properly feel entitled to benefits when they retire. The antipoverty effects are real; payroll contributions to Social Security have not merely replaced private savings that would have occurred without the program.

To be sure, Social Security is largely a middle-class program designed to smooth out individuals' earnings over their life cycles and to prevent disastrous losses of income upon retirement. It only modestly reduces inequality between the lifetime earnings of high- and low-income people. True also, the long-term financial health of the program will probably require some new resources, but those can be obtained relatively easily through such methods as extending the payroll tax to higher incomes, drawing on general tax revenues, and/or investing some tax revenues in higher-yield securities. The chief challenge for Social Security right now is simply to keep the program intact against forces working for benefit cuts or destructive privatization schemes.

Similarly, U.S. social insurance programs do a reasonably good job of helping Americans who have severe disabilities that prevent them from working. Together with the Americans with Disabilities Act's legal provisions for nondiscrimination and mainstreaming, the benefits of Social Security's Disability Insurance (DI) and Supplemental Security Income (SSI) have helped most gravely disabled Americans to avoid impoverishment.

Again, the Medicare program for the aged, despite its gaps in coverage, has greatly helped the elderly with medical expenses and (together with

Medicaid) has prevented millions of people from sinking into poverty under the weight of bills for hospitals, doctors, and nursing homes. Although Medicare's scope and efficiency could be bettered by a universal health insurance system, the first task for the twenty-first century is simply to augment its financial resources and protect the program from benefit cutting or privatizing.

We saw in chapter 5 that it is possible to operate a fair tax system that sets tax rates according to ability to pay and reduces the inequality of after-tax incomes. A progressive personal income tax—at one time reviled as a form of "communism"—can accomplish those aims, as is clear from several periods of our history. It can do so at rather low administrative expense (vigorous enforcement efforts more than pay for themselves, though anti-government legislators have cut back enforcement in recent years) and without serious negative effects on work efforts or savings.

The income tax is also a useful vehicle for what may be the most effective of all work-encouraging antipoverty programs, the Earned Income Tax Credit (EITC). The refundable EITC has brought the total earnings of millions of low-wage workers close to or just above the poverty threshold. The EITC puts some reality behind the all-too-facile American promise that everyone who works hard can get a decent income. It does so in a way that is cheap to administer, reduces income maintenance expenses, and encourages increased work effort, thus increasing economic output and helping rather than hurting the United States in global competition.

In education and training, too, as we saw in chapter 6, various U.S. government policies have enjoyed a great deal of success: considerably more success than they are usually given credit for. It is fashionable to disparage the U.S. system of public elementary and secondary education as ineffective, internationally inferior, and perhaps hopeless. But this trashing—sometimes inflicted by armchair critics who are less than fully committed to a multicultural, egalitarian society—ignores the awesome magnitude of the tasks we want our schools to perform. It slights the schools' real achievements in accomplishing those tasks. We ask our public schools to teach everyone the basics, to socialize children of diverse cultural and linguistic backgrounds, to cope with economic and racial segregation, and to make up for absent or neglectful parents, all while working with limited amounts of unequally distributed money. The federal Elementary and Secondary Education Act has provided important resources for poor students and poor school districts.

With federal government help, the system of higher education, too, has done a great deal of excellent teaching and research and has provided pathways to upward mobility for many Americans of modest background. Educational opportunities are certainly not equal for all Americans, and much needs to be done to improve this situation, but our educational system has the potential—to some extent already realized—to build up nearly everyone's skills and talents.

Several programs specifically designed to help educate and train the disadvantaged have demonstrated the capacity to do so. Head Start, despite surprisingly pinched funding, has helped prepare millions of poor children for school. Childhood health and nutrition programs provide some of the food and medical care that is essential for the development of sound minds in sound bodies. Special education helps many disabled children to acquire cognitive and social skills and the ability to function in mainstream society. Vocational education, apprenticeships, retraining, and welfare-to-work programs (particularly those that offer help with day care and transportation, as well as job training) have all demonstrated the capacity to prepare even severely disadvantaged Americans for useful work. Some of these programs require a substantial investment of resources in each trainee, but the trainees and society as a whole generally get good returns on the investment in terms of lifelong reductions in income maintenance payments, increased productive work, and more fulfilling lives.

As indicated in chapter 7, U.S. public policies have fallen considerably short of the ideal of providing jobs for everyone at good wages. Yet here, too, effective policy tools are available and have been successful when used. The trick is to use them. When the U.S. Congress, the president, and the Federal Reserve Board encourage economic growth through moderately expansive fiscal policies and low interest rates, for instance, the economy does tend to grow, unemployment falls, and the lowest-wage workers do better. (On the other hand, obsession with deficits and inflation has sometimes led to excessively tight money and unnecessarily steep recessions, in which low-income workers have suffered most.) Job creation through public service employment, when tried, has worked fairly well, and it could easily be made to work better. The minimum wage (when set at a reasonable level and not allowed to fall behind increases in the cost of living), together with the EITC, does a great deal to make sure that all work is rewarded by a living wage. Antidiscrimination laws and regulations have helped reduce employment discrimination based on arbitrary factors like race and gender.

Conclusion

United States government policies have even successfully provided at least one important part of a minimal standard of living. As we saw in chapter 8, the Food Stamps program, our only near-comprehensive effort to provide an essential good to everyone in need, has sharply reduced the extent of hunger and malnutrition in America from the outrageously high levels that existed in the 1960s. Weathering years of ideological attacks and misleading rhetoric, Food Stamps have accomplished this very important task with limited and declining levels of fraud and with administrative costs that are reasonable, given the difficulty of determining eligibility and enforcing complex rules (some administrative costs could be saved by simplifying the rules and making Food Stamps universal). The much smaller and more grudging program of rental vouchers, and the experience of other countries like Canada with universal health insurance, makes clear that governments also have the capacity—not yet realized in the United States—to provide everyone with the basic necessities of shelter and medical care.

Amid the antigovernment rhetoric of the 1980s, John Schwarz wrote *America's Hidden Success,* documenting a number of important accomplishments of U.S. social programs.[1] Yet the false images and outrageous assertions of government failure that Schwarz chronicled have proved surprisingly persistent—even as both the need for government action and the accomplishments of government have grown. We see no reason at all to despair about the capacity of governments to deal with the problems of poverty and inequality. The challenge is to make better use of that capacity.

What Remains to Be Done

Throughout this book, we have suggested ways in which programs could be expanded, modified, fully funded, or replaced in order more effectively to deal with poverty and inequality. We will not repeat all those suggestions here. Instead, we will highlight four general strategies. Each strategy draws on a number of different government programs, puts those programs into coherent relationships with each other, and suggests promising directions for policy change. These strategies are closely related to several of the approaches that we outlined in chapter 3 and elsewhere: advancing equal opportunity, investing in human capital, ensuring that jobs are available at good wages, providing social insurance, redistributing income, and providing basic necessities.

Preparing People for Work

One fundamental strategy is to *help everyone develop the skills, knowledge, motivation, and physical capability for productive work*. Work should be the cornerstone of efforts to deal with poverty and inequality. Work is central to self-esteem and self-fulfillment. It produces the valuable goods and services that are needed for healthful and satisfying lives. The value of an individual's work will, and should, generally have a substantial relationship to the income received by that individual and her or his family.

A crucial way to reduce poverty and inequality, therefore, is to make sure that very few people are unable to work and that as many people as possible acquire high-level skills and work capacities that are close to those of the most talented and energetic members of society. In a largely market-driven economy, where financial rewards partly reflect the value of what people produce, it would be difficult to proceed very far toward income equality without first working toward more equality of productive capacity.

The strategy of preparing people for work has profound implications for a wide range of government policies, starting at the very origins of people's lives. It suggests, for example, that we need to reduce the chances that children will be born with preventable disabilities or that they will suffer from life-constricting malnutrition, violence, emotional damage, an intellectually deprived home life, or inferior schools. To put it in positive terms, we need to try to ensure that children are born to healthy, loving, and nurturing parents who (along with peers and schools) will provide emotional support, intellectual stimulation, and opportunities for healthy growth and learning.

The excruciating problem is that there are now severe inequalities among the parents, peers, and neighborhood schools that will play critical parts in developing the work capacities—or incapacities—of future citizens. Inequalities among parents, communities, and schools are likely to produce highly unequal work capacities, and highly unequal incomes, in the next generation of children. This means that government policies need not only to try to reduce the inequalities among parents and neighborhoods and schools—a formidable and very long-range task—but also to *compensate* for persistent inequalities in children's environments. They need to work from an early age to help provide the nutrition, health care, nurturing, intellectual stimulation, and teaching that children in deprived families and deprived communities may otherwise miss.

Conclusion

As we saw in chapter 6, there is a very long way to go. Major policy changes are needed before all American children have anything close to equal opportunity to develop high-level work skills and capacities. A really thoroughgoing approach would probably have to include the economic as well as racial desegregation of all U.S. communities and neighborhoods, so that rich and poor people live together and all their children have equal chances to profit from interaction with the most advantaged peers and schoolmates. But such desegregation may not be feasible. It would go directly contrary to the preferences of most high-income people and many in the middle class; it would run up against the sharply income-segregating tendency of private housing markets and the long-term refusal of U.S. public policy to intervene.[2]

If we continue to refuse to undo the economic apartheid that so strongly tends to perpetuate inequalities, it is important to have open eyes about the consequences. If we want to reduce inequalities without tackling residential segregation by economic class, major compensatory efforts will be needed. For example, to bring schools located in poor neighborhoods (where each student generally needs much more help and attention) up to the quality of schools located in affluent suburbs will require not just equal resources, but *more* resources for each child. Such schools will require not just equal salaries for teachers, for example, but substantially *higher* salaries, in order to encourage the best educators to accept the challenge.

In any case, it is clear that many public policies will have to be changed if we are to move toward the goal of equal preparation for work. The highly successful Head Start program should be further enriched and extended to many more preschoolers, including younger children as well as the many who are now eligible but not funded. Family planning, and health and nutrition programs for children and pregnant women, should be expanded so that children are not born into hopeless situations—and so that the situations that children are born into are not hopeless. The successful vocational education, apprenticeship, job training, and retraining programs need to be expanded. Most important, American public schools—critical foundations for any effort to equalize education and training—should be further strengthened, especially in lower-income communities. They need more resources, better leadership, perhaps carefully designed competition among schools (e.g., charter schools), and special attention to the cognitive skills and information-processing technology that are so highly valued in today's economy.

Ensuring the Availability of Jobs at Good Wages

Even if everyone is willing and able to work, neither poverty nor inequality can be much reduced if people cannot find jobs that pay them enough to live on. The second main strategy for government policy therefore is to try to *ensure that everyone able to work has a job, that the net incomes from all jobs are sufficient for a decent standard of living, and that the net incomes of the highest- and lowest-paid workers are not excessively unequal.* Our focus is on *net* disposable incomes, after all taxes and government transfer payments, because government can use tax and transfer policies to supplement low wages up to an acceptable level and to redistribute part of the highest incomes. Government can also manage the economy so as to raise the level of private wages, and can provide well-paying public service jobs. No one of these approaches is sufficient by itself. All are needed.

Here, too—as we saw in chapter 7—much remains to be done, including making sure that the gains won in good economic times are not squandered in harder times. The benign late-1990s macroeconomic policy of low interest rates, which encouraged substantial economic growth and rising wages, should be continued or restored. Public service employment, usually neglected in boom times, should be in place at all times for those who cannot find private jobs and should be kept available on a standby basis for quick expansion during economic downturns. It would not be difficult to keep an administrative structure in place, along with a prioritized list of public projects to activate in hard times. There are plenty of unmet needs: maintaining and expanding public parks, renovating slum housing, creating works of art, upgrading rapid transit, fixing urban school roofs, blazing forest trails, building and expanding branch libraries. Funding could be automatically triggered by a downturn in economic indicators, and projects could be activated in order of priority.

In both good times and bad, we should encourage, rather than discourage, labor unions and collective bargaining. It is also important to use the twin tools of minimum wage laws and the Earned Income Tax Credit to keep workers' net wages from falling to unacceptably low levels. In order to accomplish this, the minimum wage, which finally began to creep upward in the middle and late 1990s after two decades of decline in value, should be set at a substantial level—perhaps a bit more than one-half of average wages. The minimum wage should automatically rise as workers' productivity increases. The EITC, which is very important for supplementing the incomes of low-wage workers, should be increased so that it, together with the minimum wage, assures that no full-time worker falls below the poverty line. The arbitrary and unconscionable exclusion of childless workers from full EITC benefits should be ended.

Another important policy change related to net wages would be to make taxes more progressive, as discussed in chapter 5. In particular, higher amounts of income should be made subject to Social Security payroll taxes (a measure that would greatly enhance the financial health of the Social Security system), and personal income tax rates should be increased on the highest incomes. Since the 1980s, the wealthiest Americans have enjoyed an amazing bonanza of rapidly rising salaries and extraordinary capital gains. Between January 1980 and the end of the 1990s, for example, the average value of blue-chip stocks increased by about *1,200 percent*—that is, stocks became worth about *thirteen times* as much. At the same time that the average worker's wages were stagnating, in other words, a wealthy investor who simply held onto his or her stocks (but spent the dividends) became about thirteen times as wealthy as before. One hundred thousand dollars became *one million,* three hundred thousand dollars.[3] The most affluent Americans can afford to share some of those gains, through higher taxes, in order to help people the boom left behind. This could be accomplished by some combination of eliminating unjustified deductions, more fully taxing capital gains, and imposing higher marginal tax rates on the highest levels of ordinary income.

Providing Social Insurance

Even when people are well educated and well trained, even when they have jobs at satisfactory wages, they may still suffer grievous economic hardship and be thrown into poverty if they are not protected against disasters or dislocations that can make them stop working: grave illness, a disabling accident, unemployment, old age. Only government-provided social insurance can protect everyone against these risks and against the even more devastating misfortunes that curtail their ability to learn or work in the first place. The third major strategy, therefore, is to *provide social insurance against accidents of birth or upbringing, against the major hazards of everyday life, and against the costs of retirement.*

In chapter 4, we discussed the need to defend and strengthen Social Security's retirement and disability benefits. Fortunately, despite much apocalyptic talk, the financing of the Social Security system can be bolstered relatively easily by using any of several new revenue sources—such as applying the payroll tax to high incomes as well as low, investing Trust Fund receipts in equities, and/or using general tax revenues. Individuals can also be encouraged to save more, to the benefit of the overall economy as well as themselves, by establishing universal government-subsidized savings accounts that stand outside the Social Security system and supplement rather than supplant it.

Health insurance is a more difficult issue. One reasonable approach would be to start by bolstering Medicare and Medicaid with new revenues and extending them in certain crucial ways, while relying on managed care to contain costs. (Medicare should cover prescription drugs, for example, an improvement that was beginning to be discussed at the time of this writing; the reach of Medicaid could be broadened so that it is seen as an entitlement for everyone under heavy pressure from medical bills, rather than just the poor.) A superior approach, however, which would be far cheaper, more efficient, and more just than the present system, would be to establish universal health insurance, in which all Americans are covered by a single (government) payer. The present failure of the United States to provide any health insurance at all for some forty-five million of its citizens, a failure that is unique among advanced countries, is scandalous.

Unemployment Insurance (which a Massachusetts governor once called an "economic impossibility") already helps somewhat at smoothing out the incomes of laid-off workers in cyclical industries and protects many people against the harshest effects of recessions and depressions. The main improvements needed are to raise the skimpy level of benefits and to provide for automatically extending the duration of payments during economic downturns, so that millions of unemployed workers do not run out of benefits and get condemned to destitution for reasons completely beyond their control.

But we see the concept of social insurance as going beyond these standard categories of insurance against illness, disability, retirement, and unemployment. We see it as extending also to protection from *any* loss, proceeding from *any* cause, of basic necessities like food, shelter, and medical care.

Guaranteeing the Basic Necessities of Life

Once as many Americans as possible have been helped to be physically fit, well educated, and established in well-paying jobs, the need for "safety nets"—or, better, solid floors of subsistence below which no one is allowed to fall—should be much reduced. But some people will undoubtedly still lack basic necessities. No matter how carefully education, employment, and standard social insurance programs are designed, they are likely to miss some people who need help. Yet the idea of social insurance, fully considered, suggests that *all* conceivable destitution-producing hazards should be insured against, and that we should think in terms of a *right* to basic necessities of life. For this reason, the fourth major strategy is to *guarantee everyone a minimally satisfactory amount of food, shelter, medical care, and perhaps cash income.*

For the reasons discussed in chapter 8, we are ambivalent about guaranteeing a cash income. That would not necessarily be the most efficient or effective way to help some of the people who are in greatest need. Still, the simplicity, ease of administration, and freedom-enhancing aspects of the idea make it worthy of serious consideration. The prosperity of the U.S. economy and the high level of average wages (particularly after the implementation of our other suggestions) would counteract any danger that the existence of a guaranteed minimal income would seduce many people into quitting work and living on the dole. The rewards of working and earning a much higher income, together with the self-fulfillment and social approval that working brings, would be sufficient to ensure that very few would voluntarily rely solely on the guarantee. The relatively few unfortunate people whose temporary or longer-term circumstances put them outside the reach of other programs do deserve help.

If the American public and U.S. policy makers continue to reject the idea of a guaranteed cash income, many of the same objectives can be accomplished—perhaps somewhat more cheaply and efficiently, and with less chance of facilitating dependency on drugs or alcohol by those who are susceptible to addiction—by providing essential goods and services, rather than cash. It would not be at all difficult to design programs to do this, building, for example, on our experience with Food Stamps and rental vouchers. A *universalized* system of food coupons or credit cards *for everyone*—along with similar shelter coupons or cards good for rent and mortgage payments, and perhaps medical insurance cards as well—could efficiently and effectively guarantee the provision of these basic necessities to all Americans.

In order to make this work, the benefits should be *universal.* If we decide that minimal food, shelter, and medical care are *rights* to which everyone is entitled, we will be able to get rid of any damaging and unnecessary scorn, stigma, or unpleasantness associated with having to exercise those rights. We can distribute the benefits in equal amounts to everyone, letting millionaire CEOs as well as low-paid clerks pay restaurant and home mortgage bills in this way. Then we can tax these benefits, along with other income, on a progressive scale (that is, we can take a portion of affluent people's benefits back in taxes). That would—at a moderate administrative cost—help those in need without demeaning and expensive means tests. It should go a long way toward restoring civility, respect, and a sense of shared community among all Americans. And the cost would be only a small fraction of our roughly $85,000 in annual gross domestic product per household.

Overcoming Political and Economic Obstacles

We are convinced that government can and should do a great deal more about poverty and inequality. Large majorities of citizens agree with many of the measures we have recommended and are willing to pay the taxes needed to fund them. So why haven't they already been enacted? Why does so much remain to be done?

The evidence—including cross-national evidence—indicates that the answer of despair, that global competition or other structural economic factors make it impossible to enact egalitarian policies, goes much too far. If we design policies carefully and pay attention to their international implications, we can cope with the forces of globalization. Certain *political* obstacles to egalitarian policies are more troubling, however. In order to proceed very far in reducing poverty and income inequality, we may first have to reduce the political inequalities that tilt our policy-making system against the interests of low- and middle-income people.

Coping with Globalization

Without question, the forces of economic globalization, including free trade, cheap communication and transportation, capital mobility, and (to a lesser extent) immigration, have put downward pressure on the incomes of low-wage American workers, by throwing them into fierce and often losing competition with much-lower-paid workers abroad. Globalization contributed to the discouraging, two-decade-long wage stagnation and the sharply increased degree of inequality that remains with us today.

Without question also, globalization makes it more difficult for government to carry out certain kinds of tax and regulatory policies that raise the costs of doing business. Taken to the extreme, burdensome taxes or regulations that lack offsetting, positive effects on production could make U.S. goods and services noncompetitive and could chase capital and manufacturing plants—even, conceivably, business executives and wealthy investors—out of the country to locations abroad.

But the evidence we have reviewed indicates that fears about these pressures have been greatly overblown. The rhetoric of globalization has served more as an ideologically driven *excuse* than as a compelling reason to oppose egalitarian policies. For one thing, some of the most devastating wage-reducing impacts of globalization appear to have run their course, by largely shutting down U.S. "rust belt" manufacturing activities that proved much cheaper to conduct in low-wage countries. This has been extremely painful for the workers involved, who need and deserve government help to adjust. But it has certainly not meant the end of work in America. Transportation costs and geographic proximity still matter; the enormous U.S. domestic market provides substantial advantages for factories and workers located in the United States. So long as immigration is kept within reasonable bounds, this market will support decent wages for many lower-skill workers in manufacturing and especially in service industries. Also, it has become clear that the relatively high educational levels of the U.S. workforce, our technological strengths, our transportation and communications infrastructure, our reliable legal system, and our political and economic stability (all sorely lacking in many third-world countries) give the United States major competitive advantages in producing and selling many goods and services to the world. The specter of U.S. wages falling to 50 cents an hour in order to compete with Chinese workers is only a specter. If worldwide wage rates do indeed converge toward each other, the resulting equilibrium wage—to be reached only many years in the future—is likely to be much closer to that of the present-day United States than to that of India.

Moreover, egalitarian government policies need *not* hinder American business in world competition. In many cases, such policies can help rather than hurt the overall competitive strength of our economy. One notable example is that of health, nutrition, and early-learning programs for children, which are extremely cost-effective in cutting welfare costs and helping to develop a new generation of Americans who are healthy, well adjusted, and productive over their whole working lifetimes. More broadly, increased investment in education and training—emphasizing information-age learning, especially among the most disadvantaged members of the population—

would almost certainly yield rich dividends in future productivity gains by an increasingly skilled workforce. Another important example of an egalitarian program that contributes to economic production is the Earned Income Tax Credit, which, while significantly raising the incomes of low-wage workers, reduces welfare costs and increases economic output and the long-term productiveness of people by encouraging them to work. Many job-training and welfare-to-work programs have similarly positive effects on the economy.

To be sure, minimum wage laws and the EITC could, if they were set too high, raise the wage floor above the value of the work that some workers do, imposing net costs on the economy. But it may be necessary and possible to pay relatively small costs of this sort for the sake of ensuring that all able-bodied people can work at a decent wage. Moreover, as Germany's and Sweden's "active labor market policies" have demonstrated, the enforcement of uniformly high wage levels can give employers strong incentives to increase productivity and to invest in technology, rather than sweating their workers.

It is easy to underestimate the wide range of egalitarian programs that in fact help rather than hurt the economy, because it is easy to miss ways in which their societywide benefits facilitate doing business in the United States. Reducing poverty-related crime, moving homeless panhandlers off the streets and into homes of their own, improving the morale and cooperativeness of low-paid workers, and improving the sense of community and the feeling that we all get a fair shake can improve life for managers and owners, as well as workers. The economic effects of increased good feelings and a heightened sense of community are hard to measure, but these intangibles surely tend to increase workers' productivity. Surely they also help keep executives and investors happily located in the United States, rather than fleeing abroad.

To be sure, some kinds of egalitarian programs, particularly those that can be plausibly characterized as purely paying for "consumption," rather than investment in human capital, may impose net burdens on the U.S. economy. At first glance, this seems likely to be true of programs like Social Security retirement benefits and Medicare and Medicaid payments for the elderly, which constitute such a large portion of our federal budget. The elderly, at or near the end of their working careers, cannot be expected to respond with greatly augmented future productivity. This (plus the programs' large budget share) is undoubtedly one reason that Social Security,

Medicare, and Medicaid have been subjected to such loud and determined attacks by businessmen and others who say that, for reasons of international competitiveness, they want to cut government taxes and spending.

But even here the pressures of global competition can easily be overestimated. The assurance of future help in their old age surely contributes to workers' morale and productivity during their wage-earning years. In any case, if these government programs were abolished, much of the cost of supporting retirees and sick old people would actually remain the same, unless we turned to a massive and rather grisly policy of euthanasia—that is, unless we started killing off the elderly. The bulk of the costs would simply be shifted to emergency public aid or to retirees' children, most of whom would not stand idly by while their parents perished or became destitute.

Some expenses of programs for the elderly can be reduced without substantially cutting the incomes or degrading the living conditions of old people. We can, for example, further encourage (not coerce) work from older people who are able and willing to do it. We can utilize managed medical care— while avoiding cuts in quality—and can skip expensive life-prolonging procedures that people do not want to suffer through. We can encourage and support home care when costly nursing home beds are not needed. Most fundamentally, we can adopt national health insurance, which the Canadian and European experiences have shown to be cheaper as well as better than our current muddled health care system.

With respect to care for the elderly, the competitive pressure from advanced industrial countries—which are still the most relevant international competitors in most economic sectors—is considerably tamed by the fact that *all* such countries appear to have made the decision to stand by their older citizens and keep substantial retirement and medical benefits in place. All in all, fortunately, international competition is consistent with simple human decency. We need not throw our older citizens out in the cold.

Highly progressive taxes, particularly those that reduce corporate profits, may be relatively vulnerable to competitive forces. High corporate income taxes, for example, which tend to cut the profits of corporations and reduce the rate of return to capital, undoubtedly encourage investments and multinational corporations to flee abroad and/or to conceal their profits in other countries. It is largely for this reason that corporate income taxes have been cut in many countries around the world, and it may not be feasible to restore them. But this does not mean that progressive taxation is impossible.

Progressive *personal income taxes,* unlike corporate taxes, are imposed on individual human beings who cannot so easily run away out of the country. In order to do so, they would have to lose proximity to the friends, homes, communities, cultural and recreational attractions, and amenities that make up a big part of what they enjoy in life. Most American citizens, including rich and successful executives and investors, are not about to leave the United States. They may not like high taxes (though some, as a matter of fact, seem quite willing to return to society part of the abundance with which they have been blessed), but they will put up with taxation. A progressive income tax—considerably more progressive than we now have—is economically feasible and would help moderate the upper extremes of the income distribution, as well as providing the revenue needed for egalitarian spending programs.

Finally, a number of *international policies* can do a great deal to blunt the inequality-producing effects of global economic competition on U.S. wages. Despite all the cultural and other benefits that immigration brings, it is still important to keep the magnitude of immigration by low-wage workers under control. It is also important to resist the importation of ultra-low-cost goods produced by poorly paid or unpaid workers, especially small children, prisoners, and slaves. We should insist that industries abroad—particularly, but not only, plants owned by or under contract to U.S. multinational firms—pay their workers adequate wages, permit them to organize unions, provide safe and healthy working conditions, and not damage the local or world environment. Such measures would help the environment and improve the lot of many people abroad, while reducing the downward pressure of imports and capital flight on U.S. wages and loosening competitive constraints on U.S. public policy.

Given the size and importance of the U.S. market, some of these international policies can be implemented unilaterally by the United States simply by regulating what can be imported here and what U.S. investors are allowed to do abroad. In order to enact such policies, however, it will be necessary to overcome the undemocratic decision-making processes and the free-trade-over-everything ideology of the World Trade Organization, which has the power to veto U.S. laws and regulations.

Worker-friendly international environmental and labor measures will generally be far more effective if they are implemented on a *worldwide* basis, so that no manufacturer or producer anywhere on the globe, and no individual country, can profit by destructively exploiting workers or the environment. This will require all-nation, truly global international treaties and agreements, designed to minimize conflicts between developing and developed nations, under the rubric of the United Nations or other international organizations. International treaties that set world standards (calibrated to each country's current economic capacity) for safe and healthy working conditions, for stringent environmental protection, and for adequate minimum wages could go a very long way toward helping the United States and other advanced countries reduce their own levels of poverty and inequality. Global problems require global solutions.

Political Reform

None of our suggestions can be implemented, however, unless the U.S. political process allows it. We have noted that large majorities of American citizens favor a number of public policies that would be very helpful in further combating poverty and inequality. And—contrary to a great deal of antitax mythology—majorities are willing to pay more taxes to fund these programs. But our political system does not always respond to the wishes of the majority. Sometimes the preferences of ordinary citizens are neglected in favor of the demands of organized interest groups, corporations, major investors, and affluent people who do not mind a high degree of inequality. To enact some of the policies we have recommended therefore may require changes in the political system so that the power of big money is reduced and the power of ordinary citizens is increased.

Most obviously, we cannot expect the U.S. Congress or the president always to respond to ordinary citizens if most of those citizens cannot or do not vote. In some cases, our politicians do not have to fear being thrown out of office even if they blatantly ignore what most Americans want. Our turnout rates, on the order of only half of the citizenry for presidential elections and barely over 35 percent for off-year congressional elections,[4] are among the lowest in the world. Our "class bias" in voting and our depressed level of participation by lower-income citizens are unmatched by any other advanced country.

Some simple remedies are available. We could, like most other countries, make voting registration the responsibility of the state, rather than individual citizens, automatically registering all adults. Or we could at least make it much easier for individuals to register by expanding the use of postcard registration, facilitating absentee voting, distributing easy change of address forms, and the like. We could, like nearly all the rest of the world, hold our elections on holidays, so that potential voters are not pinned down at work. We could permit voting from home, by mail. We could better publicize exactly where people should go to vote and make sure that everyone has a voting place within easy walking distance of home. Harder, but also important, would be to make sure that the choices offered by parties and candidates are sufficiently clear and attractive that they make people *want* to vote.

The class bias in participation—which much reduces the political power of lower-income Americans—goes well beyond the bias in who votes. Most important, in our wide-open-to-money political system, those who have more money naturally tend to invest more of it. National survey data indicate, for example, that more than *nine times* as many people with family incomes over $75,000 as with incomes below $15,000 gave money to political parties and candidates, and that the average contributions from high-income givers were nearly four times as big. The average high-income person therefore gave about *thirty-five times* as much political money as the average low-income person.[5] The biggest election money of all, huge contributions for "issue advocacy" ads, "soft money" to the parties, and large "bundled" contributions to candidates, comes mostly from big corporations and the most affluent Americans. The main thrust of lobbying activity, too, reflects the wishes of corporate and moneyed America.

Although some scholars shy away from saying so, there can be little doubt in any reasonable observer's mind that all this money, lavished on both political parties (though especially on the Republicans), tends to push U.S. policy making in antiegalitarian directions. Most candidates who get elected—indeed, most who even get the chance to run a serious (i.e., expensive) campaign—take policy stands that are acceptable to people with a lot of money. Most officials who want to stay in office pay special attention, and grant special access, to individuals and corporations with a lot of money.

Whatever a majority of Americans may want, therefore, the extraordinary power of money in American politics makes it hard to enact a number of policies that could significantly reduce poverty and inequality.

The U.S. Supreme Court has made it harder to remedy this situation by rather oddly ruling (in *Buckley v. Valeo,* 1976) that to spend political money on issue advocacy is to utter "speech" that is protected by the First Amendment to the Constitution. (Perhaps it is actually not so odd that the Court—

itself a product of money-infected political processes and, for most of U.S. history, a particularly conservative institution—has acted to defend the political power of moneyed interests.) One important political and legal task therefore is to make sure that Justices are appointed who will reverse this profoundly antidemocratic and antiegalitarian ruling. But even in the meantime, it would be possible to enact important reforms that would significantly slow down the runaway power of money. Right away we could restrict the size and the "bundling" of individuals' contributions to candidates. We could eliminate the grossly abused, unrestricted "soft" money given to parties; end the tax-deductibility of businesses' lobbying expenses; require more full public disclosure of political contributions; and substitute public money for private.

The conundrum, of course, is how to reform political inequality while working within a political system that itself is built on that same political inequality. Moneyed interests and the politicians they help put in office bitterly resist any measures that would reduce their political influence. Powerful forces from outside politics-as-usual—especially strong and noisy citizens' movements—may be needed in order to break through the self-sustaining status quo and to insist on reform.

Fortunately the corrupting power of political money has become so clearly evident to most Americans, and has been the focus of such vigorous efforts by citizens' movements, public interest groups, and a few courageous politicians, that serious political reform now seems possible. Only when it occurs is there likely to be full opportunity to carry out a systematic, wide-ranging effort to bring U.S. poverty and inequality down to acceptable levels. Every citizen who wants to reduce economic inequality would be wise also to work against political inequality.

Government for the People

We believe that the chief purpose of government is to pursue policies hat benefit all its citizens. All Americans should be able to enjoy what Lincoln called government *for the people*. We have argued that government for the people entails, among other things, policies that greatly reduce the extent of poverty and economic inequality. And we maintain that such policies can be efficient, effective, and freedom-enhancing, rather than wasteful or freedom-reducing.

As our discussion of political reform indicates, however, a government that fully works *for* the people probably must also be government *by* the people. Only citizens themselves can be trusted, in the long run, to favor and push for the policies that would benefit them most. The democratic ideal implies that each citizen should have equal political power, an equal political voice. Unless this ideal of equal political power is realized in fact, unless the disproportionate influence of corporations, the affluent, and well-organized special interests is curtailed, it will be extremely difficult to deal effectively with the problems of poverty and inequality.

NOTES

Chapter One

1. Bluestone 1994. Christopher Jencks (personal communication, December 1999) points out that the apparent decline in real incomes may be partly or wholly an artifact of a failure of the Consumer Price Index to reflect improvements in the quality of goods and services. But *inequality* clearly did increase.

2. Ladd and Bowman 1998, 105–8, 83–84, 102, 109–10. On all four of these items, the sharpest drops in confidence occurred in the 1968–74 period. The "waste a lot of money" response, for example, jumped from 47 percent in 1964 to 74 percent in 1974 (p. 102). See Lipset and Schneider 1983.

3. See Page and Shapiro 1992, chap. 4; Free and Cantril 1968.

4. Miller (1974) argues that the late-1960s upsurge in distrust resulted in substantial part from dissatisfaction with the policy alternatives that parties and politicians offered to deal with major social problems. On negativity in the mass media, see Patterson 1993.

5. See Osborne and Gaebler 1993; Holzer and Callahan 1998. We will see that some types of competition can have unfortunate effects on poverty and inequality.

Chapter Two

1. U.S. Bureau of the Census 1975, 8, 12, 139, 224. The per capita GNP figures, in constant 1958 dollars, are based on the Kendrick-Kuznets estimates (p. 224; see the note on p. 216).

2. Ibid., 55, 224. Levy (1998, chap. 2) gives a concise picture of family income and consumption patterns at the end of the 1940s.

3. Median family income figures, derived from the Current Population Surveys of the Bureau of the Census, are given in Levy 1998, 27, 34, 50. Levy converted them to constant 1997 dollars using the Bureau of Labor Statistics chain-weighted personal consumption expenditure (PCE) deflator. This deflator avoids the overstatements of inflation that appear to exist in the more familiar Consumer Price Index and produces higher estimates of postwar growth in purchasing power (see pp. 6–7). Still, social changes toward smaller family units in recent decades may lead family income statistics to understate gains enjoyed by the average family member. See also our caveats, below, concerning reliance on purely monetary measures of income or gross domestic product (GDP).

4. Levy 1998, 50.

5. In the spring of 1999, per capita GDP was $32,309.40, based on an annualized, seasonally adjusted GDP of $8,808.7 billion (revised) in the first quarter of 1999 and an estimated residential population of 272,636,000 in June 1999. U.S. Department of Commerce, Bureau of Economic Analysis web site, "National Accounts Data," based on the GDP news release of June 25, 1999 (visited 8/10/99); U.S. Department of Commerce, Bureau of the Census web site, "Monthly Estimates of the United States Population: April 1, 1980 to June 1, 1999," from the Population Estimates Program of the Population Division (visited 8/10/99).

6. If the $8.8 trillion GDP noted above had been equally shared among 102.5 million households (the number counted in the 1998 Current Population Survey), each household—including unrelated individuals as well as families—would have received $85,939. The national savings rate was then about 6.5 percent of GDP (U.S. Office of the President 1999, 71–72), or $5,586 per household, which would leave $80,353 available for consumption by each household after subtracting savings by households, businesses, and governments.

7. United Nations Development Programme (UNDP) 1999, 134–37. These "Purchasing Power Parity" comparisons are much more accurate than comparisons based on monetary exchange rates (see p. 248).

8. Nelson (1996) and Rosenberg (1982) analyze the sources of economic growth, emphasizing technological progress. North (1966) emphasizes the importance of property rights and national integration.

9. See Handlin and Handlin 1969; White 1991, esp. pt. II.

10. See Schor 1992.

11. A crisp critique of the defects of the GDP measure and a sketch of the alternative "GPI" are given in Halstead and Cobb 1996. See Cobb, Halstead, and Rowe 1995; Breslow 1996. The United Nations Development Programme (e.g., UNDP 1999) takes account of life expectancy and education levels, as well as GDP per

capita, in assessing the level of "human development" in many countries of the world.

12. See Case and Fair 1999, 235–44.

13. See Blaug 1996, chaps. 8–11.

14. The assumption of declining marginal returns to labor, which is quite reasonable (it makes sense that at some point additional labor and production would not be worth their cost; otherwise, factories would expand infinitely), is also essential in order to ensure that there exists a theoretical equilibrium.

15. Theories of "optimal" savings rates and of links between profit and savings levels are notoriously mushy.

16. Nelson (1996, chaps. 1–3) emphasizes the impossibility of sorting out the separate contributions of labor, investment money, technology, and other factors in a production process that is integral and interactive.

17. One should be very cautious, however, about any notion that genetically inherited intelligence substantially determines incomes, even in the "information age." Levy (1998, 113–17) reports Thomas Kane's finding that IQ, as measured by the Armed Forces Qualification Text (AFQT), could account for less than 12 percent of the variance in annual income in a set of twenty-five- to thirty-three-year-old workers in 1990. Even that estimate probably overstates the effect of intelligence on earnings because the AFQT is partly based on general knowledge that is affected by education, as well as heredity. The same data set was used in a misleading fashion in *The Bell Curve,* by Herrnstein and Murray (1994), to make the opposite point.

18. Kuttner 1996, esp. chap. 3.

19. On inheritance and inequality, see Brittain 1978, which notes (p. 88) that inheritance has a "strong role" in causing an unequal distribution of wealth.

20. Galbraith 1998, 13–14.

21. Wolff 1995, 7. See also Wolff 1998.

22. Levy 1998, 19. Government payments account for about 10 percent and dividends, interest, and rents another 10 percent. (The Census, however, does not include capital gains, so that income from capital is understated in these figures.) Galbraith (1998, 82–83), using the more accurate national income accounts, rather than Census survey data, shows wages, salaries, and proprietors' income as constituting just 67 percent of personal income in the 1990s, with government transfers accounting for 16.5 percent, interest 13 percent, dividends 3.3 percent, and rents well under 1 percent. (Again, capital gains are excluded from the data.)

23. A compelling analysis of the importance of such external factors that affect wages, along with a trenchant critique of the marginal product theory, is given in Galbraith 1998.

24. Jencks et al. (1972, esp. 8–9, 228) emphasize the role of luck in producing income inequality. Jencks et al. (1979, 306–11) note difficulties in conceptualizing

and measuring the importance of luck. Granovetter (1995) points out the crucial importance of personal networks in getting a job. On personal networks among elites, see also Dye 1986, esp. chaps. 6, 7.

25. Jencks et al. 1972, 213–16. The 75 percent figure for income advantage is based only on father's education and occupational status. If mother's education and occupation, as well as total family income, were taken into account, the estimated advantage of coming from the most privileged families would be somewhat greater. Jencks et al. (1979, chap. 3) and Solon (1999) report even stronger effects of family background. Tilly (1998) emphasizes the importance of social networks, including those based on families, in perpetuating all forms of inequality.

26. Jencks et al. (1972, 214–15) themselves called their estimate of a 75 percent family-based upper-middle-class advantage "trivial" in light of the fact that the richest fifth of all men made at least 650 percent more than the poorest fifth. They noted (p. 237 fn. 23) that Blau and Duncan (1967, app. H) found that the status of a father's occupation accounted for only about 15 percent of the variance in the status of a son's occupation. But Jencks et al. (1979, 81, 292) found that family background as a whole accounted for about 48 percent of the variance in young men's initial occupational status and about 22 percent of the variance in earnings. The more recent sibling correlations reviewed by Solon (1999) indicate that about 40 percent of the variance in the permanent component of U.S. men's earnings (logged) is generated by variation in the family and community background factors shared by siblings.

27. Jencks et al. 1972, 216, 236–37 fn. 22.

28. U.S. Bureau of the Census 1999b, "Poverty," vi, 1, A-3.

29. The U.S. Bureau of the Census (1999b, "Poverty," viii, B-2) presents a graph and a table on the number in poverty and the poverty rate from 1959 through 1998.

30. Blank 1997, 5, 13–17, 22–23. Blank tabulated most of her data on the poor from the March 1994 Current Population Survey. The duration of poverty was calculated from the Panel Survey of Income Dynamics (PSID) interviews of 1980 through 1992. Blank 1997, 295–96 fn. 2, 8. The U.S. Bureau of the Census (1999b, "Poverty," vi–vii) gives quite similar—though less complete—data on characteristics of the poor in 1998.

31. Harrington 1962.

32. Blank 1997, 14–18.

33. Ibid., 8, 13–18.

34. A concise account of the official poverty measure and its imperfections is given in Blank 1997, 9–12. A much more exhaustive treatment, with recommendations for changes, is provided by a National Research Council report (Citro and Michael 1995). See U.S. Bureau of the Census 1999b, "Poverty," A-2, A-3, and the lucid discussion of measurement issues in Atkinson 1998. The U.S. Bureau of the Census (e.g., 1999a, 48–49) reports on "Money Income in the United States" conve-

niently analyze the distribution of income under some eighteen different income definitions—with and without various taxes, transfer payments, and special sources of income. We will make use of this in discussing inequality, below.

35. Smeeding 1992. See Danziger and Gottschalk 1995, 61.

36. UNDP 1999, 149–50. The figures refer to proportions of the population falling below 50 percent of median adjusted disposable personal income. On Switzerland, see Katzenstein 1984.

37. Ehrenreich 1999.

38. Data for 1994 from Numbers News web site, William P. O'Hare, "A Shocking Rise in Working-Poor Families," June 1996 (visited 8/17/99).

39. Child Trends web site, Richard F. Wertheimer, "Working Poor Families with Children," February 1999, 4 (visited 8/17/99).

40. Mishel et al. 1999, 189–91. This is a comprehensive and very useful source on the state of working Americans, updated annually for a number of years.

41. See Sennett and Cobb 1972.

42. Sen 1997, 212–13.

43. Citro and Michael 1995. See Easterlin 1974.

44. U.S. Bureau of the Census 1999a, "Money Income," xv.

45. Ibid., xv, B-6.

46. Levy 1998, 2 fn. To be sure, some very low-income people understate their incomes (particularly from illegal sources) as well.

47. U.S. Bureau of the Census 1999a, "Money Income," B-6.

48. Danziger and Gottschalk 1995, 44–47, 52–54.

49. The controls for family size mentioned above help establish this point, as does the analysis in Danziger and Gottschalk 1995, chap. 5.

50. See Danziger and Gottschalk 1995, esp. chap. 7.

51. Anderson et al. 1999. See also "The best . . . and the rest," *Economist,* May 8, 1999, 3–20.

52. Dow Jones web site.

53. Hacker 1997, esp. 27, 66–71 and chaps. 4, 5.

54. U.S. Bureau of the Census 1999a, "Money Income," xv, B-6. Gini coefficients and their underlying Lorenz curves are explicated both graphically and mathematically in Lambert 1993.

55. Braun (1997, 118–21) summarizes data on inequality in Organization for Economic Cooperation and Development (OECD) disposable household incomes from an exhaustive study reported by Atkinson, Rainwater, and Smeeding (1995a, 1995b).

56. Braun 1997, 118, from Atkinson, Rainwater, and Smeeding 1995a, 1995b.

57. Braun (1997, 106–7) presents Gini coefficients from a much broader range of countries (less reliably calculated, however) than those encompassed in the OECD studies, based on World Bank and International Labor Organization data.

58. UNDP 1999, 148–49.

59. See Reynolds and Smolensky 1977; Musgrave, Case, and Leonard 1974; Page 1983, chap. 4.

60. Unfortunately definition #4 does not include imputed rent on equity in one's home, which the Census adds only in definition #15, while also including government transfers and subtracting taxes. And, of course, no such measure can eliminate the indirect effects of government macroeconomic policies, minimum wages, labor-relations policies, public goods spending, or a host of other government influences on supposedly "private" wages and salaries.

61. U.S. Bureau of the Census 1999a, "Money Income," 48–49. We cannot be sure how big an effect government had, both because we cannot identify and sub-tract out all government effects on "pregovernmental" income and because, in the absence of government action, individuals' behavior—and their "pregovernmental" income—would undoubtedly have been different.

Chapter Three

1. Hobbes 1996 [1651].

2. Locke 1952 [1690], 25. Wolin (1960) emphasizes Locke's key role in the development of liberalism.

3. Smith 1976 [written 1766–76], esp. IV-iii-a, IV-ix, V-i.

4. See Horwitz 1977, 1992; Trachtenberg 1982, chap. 3.

5. See Grossman and Adams 1996.

6. Friedman's list of "don'ts" includes agricultural price supports, tariffs, rent control, the minimum wage, industrial regulation, the Social Security old age and retirement program, professional licensing, public housing, a peacetime military draft, national parks, and toll roads (1962, 35–36). Friedman's work was heavily influenced by the Austrian school of procapitalist, antigovernment theorists, including Ludwig von Mises (1951 [1922]) and Friedrich Hayek (1994 [1944]), whose *Road to Serfdom* remains an important text for libertarians. See also Nozick 1974.

7. D. Friedman 1973, 1.

8. Smith 1976 [written 1766–76], esp. I-x, V-i.

9. Pigou 1952 [1920, 1932], esp. pt. II, chaps. 2, 9, 11, 20.

10. Musgrave and Musgrave (1980) discuss public goods in the context of the "allocation" function of government.

11. Samuelson 1955, 1956. See Musgrave and Musgrave 1980, chaps. 3, 4.

12. Ronald Coase and others have asserted that unaided private entrepreneurs have in fact built lighthouses, but the historical evidence appears to refute this proposition. British entrepreneurs were assisted by funds from government-enforced col-

lection of port tolls, government-granted monopolies, and the like. See van Zandt 1993.

13. See Musgrave and Musgrave 1980, chap. 4.

14. See Barr 1993, 1998.

15. See Wolf 1993.

16. Milton Friedman does not go this far, but some of his disciples do.

17. Musgrave and Musgrave (1980) call this the "stabilization" function of government.

18. Macroeconomics textbooks differ from one to another and tend to change their tunes over time in response to economic events. Contrast, for example, the enthusiastic Keynesianism and pro–full employment attitude of Baumol and Blinder (1997) with the skepticism and strongly anti-inflation stand of Gordon (1990).

19. See Begg 1982; Miller 1994.

20. See Eisner 1994.

21. Friedman 1962, 164–65, 191–92.

22. Musgrave and Musgrave (1980) call this the "distribution" function of government. Most non-economists refer to "redistribution."

23. Bentham 1970 [1789, 1823]. The ordinalist posture of neoclassical economics, which insists that positive economic theory can be built on purely ordinal preference rankings and without making difficult interpersonal comparisons, in no way contradicts the necessity for considering interpersonally comparable cardinal utilities in any serious treatment of ethical questions.

24. See Page 1983, chap. 1. An early version of the utilitarian argument for income equality can be found in Sidgwick 1907 [1893]. Sidgwick is excerpted in Phelps 1973, chap. 8, which explores several alternative conceptions of justice.

25. Hobbes 1996 [1651], chap. 30.

26. Quoted in Myrdal 1971, 15. See also Tawney 1961 [1931].

27. Beecher and Bienvenue 1971, 139–50.

28. Rawls 1971.

29. See Rousseau 1977 [1754]; Sidgwick 1907 [1893].

30. Okun 1975. Any trade-off between equality and efficiency would also affect the extent of equalization under Rawls's maximin criterion.

31. Our thinking about different approaches has been influenced by Marmor, Mashaw, and Harvey (1990, chap. 2), who distinguish among "behaviorist," "residualist," "social insurance," and "egalitarian populist" conceptions of social welfare programs and characterize the U.S. hybrid as an "opportunity-insurance" state.

32. E.g., Friedman 1962, 191–92.

33. Bowles and Gintis (1998) convincingly argue that, for these and other reasons, "asset-based redistribution" is generally superior to income transfers.

34. Blank 1997, 145–51.

35. See Groves 1974; Pechman 1987.

36. A focus on the extent of inequality in net "postgovernment" incomes is characteristic, for example, of Musgrave and Musgrave's (1980) analysis of the "distribution" function.

37. Garfinkel, Hochschild, and McLanahan 1996.

38. Congressional report cited in Osborne and Gaebler 1993, 206, 220, 381, 382.

39. Orfield et al. 1984.

40. Jencks et al. 1979; Solon 1999.

41. Giddens 1994, 192–93.

42. Reich 1991. See also Becker 1993. Investment in the human capital of low-income people is a particularly sustainable variety of the "asset-based redistribution" espoused by Bowles and Gintis (1998).

43. See Herzenberg, Alic, and Wial 1998.

44. Wilson 1996; Blank 1997; Danziger and Gottschalk 1995.

45. Galbraith 1998.

46. See Amenta 1998.

47. Csikszentmihalyi (1990) argues that it is in challenging work that we have the most *fun*.

48. Streeck 1992, chap. 1.

49. Marmor, Mashaw, and Harvey 1990. Nicholas Barr (1993, 1998) gives a lucid economic analysis of the arguments for social insurance. See also National Academy for Social Insurance web site. For the situation in other countries, see Titmuss 1970 and Esping-Andersen 1990.

50. See also Marmor, Mashaw, and Harvey 1990, chap. 5.

51. On the very American fear of encouraging laziness or immorality, and its consequences in pinched social policy, see Skocpol 1992; Trattner 1999; and Katz 1990. A striking manifestation of such fear is Murray 1984.

52. The "globalization ends the nation state" literature is canvassed in Garrett 1998, chap. 1. See Albert 1993; Sassen 1996; Blecker 1999; Economic Policy Institute web site.

53. Borjas (1990) argues that immigrants create jobs, start new business, and have little negative impact on natives' wages or local government resources.

54. For an example of premature pessimism along these lines, by one of the present authors, see Page 1997. Rifkin (1995) may likewise be overly pessimistic about the technological revolution.

55. In the advanced industrial countries of Western Europe, globalization has clearly hurt labor unions by ending labor-market centralization (Pontusson and Swenson 1996; Western 1997, chaps. 9–11). That in turn has weakened one pillar of support for European social welfare states and has allowed some Social Democratic parties to toss social democracy overboard (see Kitschelt 1994). Still, Pierson (1994)

points out that dismantling a welfare state is much harder than creating it. Among other things, beneficiaries become constituencies. Garrett (1991) argues that exposure of a country to international economic pressures actually creates popular demand for welfare state measures; Iversen and Cusack (1999) make a similar argument concerning deindustrialization rather than international exposure.

Even if globalization weakens the political support for welfare states, it is much less clear that it makes welfare state measures impossible to afford so long as productivity remains high. Then it is possible to compete either on the low road (cheap goods) or on the high road (high quality) (Boix 1997). As Garrett and Lange (1991) and Weiss (1998) argue, so long as there is no big budget deficit, it is possible to have a welfare state (i.e., one proportional to the economy). Service-based economies (as the United States has increasingly become) are even less exposed to international competition and have more flexibility.

In the 1990s reversals and retrenchments of the most extensive welfare states, those in Scandinavia, specific macroeconomic policy measures, rather than the welfare state itself, appear to have been at fault (Huber and Stephens 1998).

56. Persson and Tabellini 1994. This article gives more empirical support to the finding of a negative correlation (both cross-sectional and time series) in democracies between growth rates and inequality than it does to the particular causal mechanisms posited, which involve political interference with property rights and investment returns. See also Institute for Public Policy Research work cited in *Economist,* November 5, 1994, 21. Atkinson (1999, 184–87) judges the aggregate evidence on economic growth and the size of welfare states to be inconclusive; different programs and institutional structures have different effects.

57. Additional barriers to the enactment of egalitarian policies may be found in the U.S. system of separation of powers and federalism (which provides multiple veto points), in the Supreme Court and legal system, and in the peculiar apportionment of the U.S. Senate. For comparative overviews of this type of political resistance to egalitarianism, see Steinmo and Watts 1995 and Immergut 1992.

58. Yeric and Todd (1996, 98) report 1992 National Election Study (NES) data on these issues.

59. Verba, Schlozman, and Brady 1995, 190; U.S. Bureau of the Census web site (visited 11/1/99). See Piven and Cloward 1989; Teixeira 1992, chap. 3.

60. Dunn and Slann 1994, chap. 9.

61. Single-member districts and plurality, "winner-take-all" voting encourage a two-party system because only a single party can win any representation in a given district and only one other party—over the long term—can mount a plausible challenge to win a plurality against it.

62. Downs 1957, 39 and chaps. 8, 14.

63. Lijphart 1994, 6–7.

64. Stephens (1979) emphasizes the critical role of labor-backed Social Democratic parties in developing European welfare states. This point is reinforced by Huber, Ragin, and Stephens (1993).

65. Rosenstone and Hansen 1993. Piven and Cloward (1989) note that in 1984 the Democrats—despite a golden opportunity—decided not to spend money registering low-income voters (chap. 6, esp. p. 188). Intensive efforts to do so by nonprofit "New Politics" groups were then counteracted by Republican and Religious Right registration of millions of new higher-income and conservative voters. Piven and Cloward also point out that official election commissions have frequently used a number of techniques to obstruct efforts at low-income registration (pp. 195–200).

66. Burnham 1970; McGerr 1986; Keyssar 2000. Piven and Cloward (1989, chaps. 2, 3) discuss the mechanisms of electoral demobilization and the scholarly controversies over these matters.

67. Rosenstone and Wolfinger's (1978) careful analysis of the 1972 presidential election indicates that registration laws reduced turnout by about 9 percentage points, with most of the impact occurring among people with little formal education and low incomes.

68. Census survey data indicate that 63 percent of professional people and 59 percent of managers, but only 34 percent of service workers and 23 percent of laborers, voted in 1994 (Rothman 1999, 134).

69. Verba, Schlozman, and Brady 1995, 190.

70. Ibid., chap. 15, esp. pp. 417, 441, 444.

71. Sabato and Simpson 1996.

72. McChesney 1997; Sorauf 1988.

73. Shuldiner 1999 is an exceptionally useful compilation of lobbying expenditures and campaign contributions by firm and industry. See Schlozman and Tierney 1986; Heinz et al. 1995. West and Loomis (1998) analyze media campaigns.

74. Olson 1965.

75. Schattschneider 1960, 35. Contribution data from the Center for Responsive Politics (Makinson 1997), reported in Marger 1999, 350.

76. In races for the House of Representatives, Jacobsen (1978) argued that only challengers for House seats benefit from money; Green and Krasno (1988) maintain that incumbents benefit as well.

77. Hall and Wayman 1990.

78. Lohmann 1998.

79. Schattschneider 1935; McConnell 1966; Gibbs 1991. See also Cox and Skidmore-Hess 1999. Outstanding journalistic work includes Drew 1998, 1999.

80. Ferguson and Rogers 1996; Edsall 1984; Saloma 1984; Stefancic and Delgado 1996.

81. Information about the Indian Law Resource Center from Alexandra Page (personal communication, 8/11/99).

82. The idea of a policy zigzag around a trend line moving toward popular policies is implicit in Sundquist 1968.

83. Aldrich 1995. Implicit collusion between the two parties may be necessary for this to happen. See Wittman 1973; Simmons 1992.

84. McClosky et al. 1960; Poole and Rosenthal 1997; Hibbs 1987, 1994; Sundquist 1968.

85. Heard 1960, chaps. 5–7, esp. pp. 120–29.

86. Ferguson 1995, chaps. 2, 4. Peter Swenson (1997), who argues that some businesses joined Roosevelt's "cross-class alliance" for domestic economic reasons (advantages against less liberal competitors), does not alter the basic point that a segment of business support was crucial to the New Deal and the Democratic Party.

87. Webber and Domhoff 1996.

88. Quadagno (1994) emphasizes the continuing importance of racism in blocking egalitarian programs.

89. A wealth of information on the occupational backgrounds and business connections of high executive-branch officials is gathered together in Burch 1980, 1981. On McCloy, see Bird 1992.

90. Ferguson and Rogers 1981, 1986. On the absence of any substantial rightward shift in public opinion, see Page and Shapiro 1992, chap. 4.

91. Ferguson 1995, chaps. 5, 6, and Conclusion; see also Lewis et al. 1996, esp. 34–73. The Democrats' move toward more conservative positions on certain social issues, however, put them in closer touch with the views of ordinary citizens; see Page and Shapiro 1992, chap. 3.

92. Woodward 1994; Reich 1997.

Chapter Four

1. A concise analysis of the economic theory of insurance is given in Barr 1993, chap. 5 and pp. 126–28, 194–99, 227–29, 294–302, or comparable sections of Barr 1998. Lubove (1968) chronicles the rise in the United States of social insurance ideas and policies as advocated by I. M. Rubinow and others. See also Marmor and Mashaw 1997.

2. U.S. Office of Management and Budget 1999, 358 [hereafter cited as *U.S. Budget FY00*]. See Howard 1997, 21.

3. *U.S. Budget FY00,* 36, 333–39, 347. Figures are estimated outlays for fiscal year 2000, including both discretionary and mandatory expenditures. Percentages are based on total estimated outlays of $1,766 billion.

4. *U.S. Budget FY00,* 35–38, 253–55; U.S. Social Security Administration press release, October 19, 1999. See Levitan, Mangum, and Mangum 1998, 63: in 1995, the average retiree got $722 per month; widows and widowers of covered workers got $673; widowed mothers and orphans got a little under $500.

5. *U.S. Budget FY00,* 359. See Howard 1997, 20 and chaps. 2, 6.

6. *U.S. Budget FY00,* 37–38; U.S. Office of the President 1999, 156.

7. U.S. Federal Old-Age and Survivors Insurance and Disability Insurance Trust Funds, Board of Trustees 1999, 2 [hereafter cited as *OASDI Trust Fund Report 1999*].

8. Figures refer to 1996. U.S. Office of Management and Budget 1998, 229 [hereafter cited as *U.S. Budget FY99*].

9. Levitan et al. 1998, 59, 63–64. This textbook provides a wealth of information about poverty-related government programs.

10. Ibid., 63.

11. U.S. Congressional Budget Office 1998, 11–13. These estimates are found in fourteen cross-sectional studies. Estimates from time series and cross-national studies are widely inconsistent and fraught with conceptual problems.

12. See Costa 1998.

13. Benjamin Friedman (1988, chap. 3) notes that the link between changes in incomes and changes in savings is not rigid: the Reagan tax cuts of the 1980s, for example, did *not*—contrary to heady predictions—cause any great influx of cash to personal savings or investment.

14. Calculated from *U.S. Budget FY00* (p. 253) estimates for 2000 of $473 billion in Social Security tax receipts, $57 billion in interest credits, and $405 billion in spending. Later estimates by the Office of Management and Budget and the Congressional Budget Office indicated that the year 2000 Social Security surplus would be considerably larger, approximately $144 or $155 billion. Calculated from figures reported in *USA Today,* July 2, 1999, 4.

15. Levitan et al. 1998, 26–27, 64. The U.S. Bureau of the Census web site (visited 7/3/99) produced a striking graph of poverty rates by age from 1959 to 1997, showing a steep drop in poverty among the elderly between 1959 and 1975.

16. U.S. Bureau of the Census web site graph on "Poverty: 1959–1997."

17. Blank 1997, 228. Neither Blank's book nor most other analyses of poverty spend much time exploring the central role of Social Security, however, presumably because of scholarly division of labor.

18. Levitan et al. 1998, 61–62. Figures are for 1994. "Very-low-income" workers were defined as those earning only 45 percent or less of average wages; "high-income" workers were those earning the maximum taxable Social Security wage or more.

19. The redistributive effects of Social Security are also complicated by spousal benefits and by differing life expectancies, which prevent some people from collecting their full share of benefits. Lower-income people, for example, tend not to live as long as high-income people and often do not collect as many years of retirement benefits.

20. Page 1999.

21. U.S. Social Security Administration press release, October 19, 1999; *U.S. Bud-*

get *FY00*, 359–60. The tax expenditure figure includes benefits to survivors and dependents, as well as retirees.

22. See Steuerle 1997, 249.

23. One of the most noisy and persistent critics of Social Security has been investment banker Peter G. Peterson (e.g., 1988). See Skidmore 1999.

24. Useful demographic and historical data are presented, though in unnecessarily alarmist fashion, in Schieber and Shoven 1999.

25. A crisp, brief statement to this effect by a leading Social Security expert is Aaron 1999.

26. Baker and Weisbrot 1999 and Skidmore 1999, lively and readable sources on Social Security generally, emphasize this point.

27. OASDI Trustees Report, 1998, from web summary. The 2020 turning point assumes "intermediate" economic forecasts and includes interest on the fund, as well as payroll tax income. The U.S. Social Security and Medicare Board of Trustees' 1999 status summary (1999, 7) puts this date at 2022.

28. OASDI Trustees Reports 1998, 1999.

29. To judge whether and to what extent Social Security surpluses have been saved actually requires a hypothetical exercise: what *would* various other taxing and spending programs have looked like if the Social Security surpluses had not existed? It is very hard to know.

30. See Marmor, Mashaw, and Harvey 1990, chap. 5.

31. The seventy-five-year "actuarial deficit" for OASI was estimated at 1.7 percent of payroll and for DI at .36 percent (U.S. Social Security and Medicare Boards of Trustees 1999, 7).

32. The exact figure is 68 percent (U.S. Social Security Advisory Board 1998, 26).

33. See Ball 1998; Aaron and Reischauer 1998. U.S. Social Security Advisory Board 1998, 25–26, presents a very useful table estimating what proportion of the projected seventy-five-year Social Security deficit would be eliminated by various different measures.

34. Page 1999.

35. Michael Boskin, National Association for Social Insurance (NASI) web site briefing, 10/98, 2, notes that the projected 2:1 "dependency ratio" of just two workers to support each retiree (down from 4:1 or 5:1 some decades ago) is nothing compared to Germany's expectation of a 1:1 ratio. Even the expected decline in the U.S. ratio is partly misleading, since it ignores the greater past prevalence of dependents *other* than retirees, especially small children. Hargreaves (1999) reports projections that 36 percent of Germany's population will be over age sixty by 2040 and will (under current law) take up fully 18.4 percent of German gross domestic product (GDP) in pensions, compared to 11.1 percent at present.

36. Barr 1993 or 1998, chaps. 5, 9.

37. Some partial privatization plans, like that of Schieber and Shoven (1999),

would protect the poor by maintaining minimal fixed public benefits and by subsidizing their private investments. But such plans involve heavy administrative costs (see below). They may not be politically feasible because they do not cater to the self-interest or greed of some of the most enthusiastic privatizers, who do not care much about poor or low-income people. And any privatization plan that involves moving to a fully funded system must face very high transition costs, which entail steep, probably unpalatable, tax increases.

38. According to the "Gordon formula," the long-run real return from stocks should be about 4.0 percent or 4.5 percent (starting from 1999 stock market values), rather than the often-assumed 7 percent. This suggests the market would have to decline some 35–45 percent before it began to achieve the 7 percent return (Diamond 1999, 2–3).

39. See James et al. 1999. Thanks to Ben R. Page of the Congressional Budget Office.

40. For vigorous, concise arguments for and against a particular privatization plan, see Kotlikoff and Sachs 1999 and Aaron 1999.

41. *U.S. Budget FY00,* 36, 338–39) (estimates for 2000).

42. In 1995, the average disabled worker got $682 per month, compared with retirees' $720; spouses and children of the disabled averaged only $164 and $183, respectively (Levitan et al. 1998, 63).

43. See Barr 1993 or 1998, chaps. 5, 8.

44. Levitan et al. 1998, 66–68.

45. Ibid., 67; *U.S. Budget FY99,* 230–32; U.S. Social Security and Medicare Boards of Trustees 1999, 2.

46. Levitan et al. 1998, 66.

47. Lubove 1968, 53–55.

48. 1996 figures, from Levitan et al. 1998, 96–98.

49. 1993 figure, from ibid., 97.

50. *U.S. Budget FY00,* 336.

51. *U.S. Budget FY99,* 235–36.

52. Ibid., 236, 315.

53. U.S. Social Security Administration press release, October 19, 1999.

54. Blank 1997, 103–4; Levitan et al. 1998, 85, 87.

55. *U.S. Budget FY99,* 224, 312.

56. Dobelstein 1996, 149–50; Levitan et al. 1998, 93; Swenson 1997.

57. Levitan et al. (1998, 94–96) document the erosion of UI between 1971 and the mid-1990s.

58. Ibid., p. 95.

59. Dobelstein 1996, 150–51; Levitan et al. 1998, 93–94.

60. Levitan et al. 1998, 94–95; *U.S. Budget FY99,* 224.

61. Levitan et al. 1998, 94–96.

62. Marmor et al. 1990, 192, 199; Flora and Heidenheimer 1981.

63. According to the Census Bureau, in 1998, 44.3 million Americans, or 16.3 percent of the population (47.5 percent of the working poor and about one-third of the poor generally), lacked health insurance. *New York Times,* October 4, 1999, 1, 24.

64. Marmor et al. 1990, chap. 6, esp. pp. 175–76, 199–201; Himmelstein and Woolhandler 1994, 118 (the strikingly lower U.S. satisfaction with health care is documented on p. 117). Cross-national comparisons for later in the 1990s are quite similar: *OECD in Figures,* Paris, 1999, 8–9; Anderson and Poullier 1999.

65. See Starr 1982.

66. See Marmor 1973. Patel and Rushefsky (1995, chap. 4) give a good overview of Medicare. They calculate that in 1963 only 54 percent of the elderly had hospital insurance (p. 80).

67. Patel and Rushefsky 1995, 80; see Moon 1996a, 1996b.

68. HCFA web site, "Brief Summaries" (visited 8/14/98); *U.S. Budget FY00,* 334.

69. U.S. Social Security and Medicare Boards of Trustees 1999, 2, summarizes the earnings bases and tax rates for OASDI and Medicare.

70. Patel and Rushefsky 1995, 80–81, drawing on John T. Petrie, "Overview of the Medicare Program," *Health Care Financing Review,* 1992 annual supplement, 1–12.

71. Patel and Rushefsky 1995, 80–82), again drawing on Petrie.

72. Medicare web site (visited 7/3/99); Patel and Rushefsky 1995, 83–84.

73. Moon 1996b, 51; Patel and Rushefsky 1995, 85–87. Pamela Farley Short and Jessica Primoff Vistnes, "Multiple Sources of Medicare Supplementary Insurance," *Inquiry* 29 (Spring 1992): 42, gives data on the upper-income tilt of Medigap insurance coverage.

74. Moon 1996b, 53.

75. Jacobs 1995.

76. *U.S. Budget FY99,* 221.

77. Marmor et al. 1990, 179; HCFA web site (visited 6/98); Patel and Rushefsky 1995, 89–91. The comparisons with total health expenditures are taken from Katharine R.Levit et al., "National Health Expenditures, 1993," *Health Care Financing Review* 16 (Fall 1994): 285. In 1996, Medicare served about 14 percent of the U.S. population and paid out $167 billion, about 45 percent of all U.S. personal health care expense (U.S. Health Care Financing Administration 1998, 22, 34).

78. Marmor et al. 1990, 179–80, using data from the 1988 *Statistical Abstract of the United States.* They point out, however, that Medicare and Medicaid cannot bear all of the blame for medical inflation, since medical prices were already growing much faster than the Consumer Price Index before 1965. The gap actually narrowed somewhat during several years after 1965.

79. Marmor et al. (1990) note that to eliminate all moral hazard in the insuring

of modern medical care is all but impossible; to completely prohibit health insurance, on the other hand, would be a "cure worse than the disease" (p. 186).

80. Moon 1999, 1–2, 6.

81. Marmor et al. 1990, 186–87; Kilborn 1998, 1, 16.

82. Patel and Rushefsky 1995, 91–94; Pear 1998a, 1, 10. Robert Pear, "Clinton to Announce Help as H.M.O.'s Leave Medicare," *New York Times,* October 8, 1998, A20.

83. Weissert and Weissert (1996, 288–91) consider this a case study in how one determined legislator can get good things done. Patel and Rushefsky (1995, 95–96) are more skeptical of the impact.

84. Marmor et al. 1990, 202–9; Himmelstein and Woolhandler 1994, 92–145.

85. Patel and Rushevsky 1995, 96–98.

86. Ibid.; U.S. Department of Health and Human Services 1996, 180–81.

87. Patel and Rushefsky 1995, 99.

88. Leuchtenberg 1963, esp. 127.

89. Marmor 1973, 68.

90. Poole and Rosenthal 1997.

91. Page and Shapiro 1992, 118–21; Page 1999; Jacobs and Shapiro 1998.

92. Page and Shapiro 1992, 129–32; Kohut 1998, 40–42; Himmelstein and Woolhandler 1994, 255–63.

93. West and Loomis (1998) give a particularly telling account of how moneyed interests influence public debate through direct issue advocacy.

94. Kingdon 1984, 46–53; Birnbaum 1993.

95. Western 1993, 267, 274–76. See Wallerstein 1999. Western (1998) argues that unions thrive when workers are insulated from competition with each other.

96. Korpi 1983; Stephens 1979; Esping-Andersen 1990; Sassoon 1996.

97. See Skocpol 1992; Lubove 1968, esp. 28.

98. See Goldfield 1989.

99. Ferguson 1984; Swenson 1997, 2000; Jacoby 1993. See also Domhoff 1990, 1996.

100. Quadagno 1988, 181–82. On the disorganization of the U.S. working class, see also Bridges 1986 and Shefter 1986.

101. Quadagno 1988, 186–88.

102. Mettler 1998.

103. See Skocpol 1992. The U.S. Chamber of Commerce, which mostly represents small and labor-intensive firms, has been particularly adamant in opposition.

104. Himmelstein and Woolhandler 1994, 111.

105. Starr 1982; Weissert and Weissert 1996, chap. 3.

106. Harris 1966. Marmor (1973) tends to minimize the effect of the AMA.

107. Ferguson and Rogers 1981, 1986.

108. Edsall 1984; Saloma 1984.

109. Hacker 1997.

110. Jacobs and Shapiro 2000; West 1998, chap. 4; Center for Public Integrity

1994. Skocpol (1997, esp. 173–78) blames the Clinton plan's demise on "Reagan's revenge": the legacy of debt, deficit cutting, and distrust of government. We would add that the right turn by business was probably the chief influence underlying each of these factors.

111. See the AARP web site.

112. Huber and Stephens (1998) argue that this sort of labor market rigidity, rather than excessive welfare-state generosity, caused problems for Social Democratic states of Europe in the 1990s.

113. In the Clinton health reform case, Greer (1998) argues that some businesses that "should" have welcomed the plan turned against it not because of ideology, but because of the usefulness of privately provided health benefits as personnel recruitment and retention mechanisms. Others (e.g., Cathie Jo Martin [2000]) emphasize that narrow opposition could easily prevail within fragmented business associations.

114. *U.S. Budget FY99,* 226. 1995 Census data indicated that 26 percent of $388 billion in social insurance expenditures and 56 percent of $78 billion in means-tested expenditures helped cut the "poverty gap": the aggregate extent to which incomes fell below the official poverty line.

115. Marmor et al. 1990, 203.

116. Fuchs 1998 [1974]; Marmor et al. 1990, chap. 6.

117. Marmor et al. 1990, 205; Himmelstein and Woolhandler 1994, 92–119.

118. Himmelstein and Woolhandler 1994, 269–88. Hacker (1998) points out that current stakeholders have to get something and that the longer we wait for reform, the harder it is to achieve.

119. Fuchs 1998 [1974], 37–38. In 1997, the U.S. infant mortality rate of 7 per 1,000 live births was much lower than it had been in 1970 (when it was 20), but it remained significantly higher than in virtually all other advanced countries (United Nations Development Programme 1999, 168).

120. "Big Increase Reported in Tobacco Lobbying Costs," *San Francisco Chronicle,* October 30, 1998, A10, based on a report by Public Citizen.

121. We cannot, however, be sure that the problem is temporary; the "dependency ratio" may remain high into the future.

122. See Barr 1993, 196–97.

123. United Kingdom 1942, 163.

124. Rawls 1971.

Chapter Five

1. U.S. Office of Management and Budget 1999, 29–30 [hereafter cited as *U.S. Budget FY00*].

2. Metcalf 1996, 62.

3. Locke 1960 [1690], 327.

4. Lindahl 1958 [1919]. A crisp account of alternative theories of just taxation is given in Musgrave 1996.

5. There is, however, a good efficiency argument for basing some taxes on benefits received ("users' fees") *after* other taxes have helped achieve a more equal distribution of income.

6. See Vickrey 1945; Rawls 1971.

7. Mill 1923 [1848], bk. 2, chap. 1, secs. 1, 8; bk. 5, chap. 2, sec. 2. See Groves 1974, 26–38.

8. Edgeworth 1925, 106–7, 117. See Groves 1974, 54–63. Under Edgeworth's assumptions, minimum total sacrifice is equivalent to equal *marginal* sacrifice, which has come to be the version of "equal sacrifice" most accepted by economists.

9. Pigou 1920, esp. 60, 76. See Groves 1974, 64–73. The assumption of similar utility functions is most plausible with respect to a single society like the United States, not the whole world.

10. A particularly incisive and influential critique is Blum and Kalven 1953.

11. Ordinal measurement involves only rank orderings (x is "preferred to" y, or the opposite), whereas cardinal measurement deals with the magnitude of differences (x costs $10 more than y or is 15 degrees Celsius warmer than y). For most purposes, modern economic theory works with ordinal preferences.

12. In policy debates, economists sometimes acknowledge that ordinalist economic theory is largely impotent to assess considerations of distributive justice, but then talk as if equity considerations are therefore irrelevant and need not be considered. This incorrect inference can lead to an exclusive emphasis on efficiency and a disregard for equity.

13. To reward *claims* of special capacities for enjoyment would create incentives to misrepresent such capacities and would encourage waste and greed.

14. Edgeworth 1925, 117. See Groves 1974, 55. If people had increasing rather than declining marginal utility for money, we would expect to observe a variety of bizarre behavior, including a tendency for people to gamble away most or all of their incomes for low probabilities of extremely high gains.

The optimal extent of progressivity does become sensitive to the shape of utility functions when possible trade-offs with economic production are taken into account.

15. Browning and Johnson 1984. See Burtless 1996b.

16. Hausman 1981b; Burtless 1981. See also Hausman 1981a.

17. Pechman 1987, 76–77, 122, 147–51.

18. Slemrod 1996, 6. See Slemrod 1992, 250–56.

19. Burtless 1987.

20. Triest 1996, 139–43.

21. Ibid., 143–59.

22. Burtless 1996b, 170–71.

23. OECD, *Economic Outlook* no. 65, June 1999. Figures are estimates for 2000

of general government current receipts as a percentage of nominal gross domestic product (GDP).

24. Most recent literature on European social welfare states emphasizes cuts, not the still quite high levels compared to the United States. But see Huber and Stephens 1998. Steinmo (1995) argues that U.S. taxes are inefficient and too low relative to these other countries because of the fragmentation of U.S. government institutions—particularly reliance on a decentralized Congress, rather than the executive.

25. Quinn 1997; Swank 1992, 1996.

26. The income tax enacted during the Civil War was only temporary, and the tax enacted in 1894 was declared unconstitutional in the *Pollock* case of 1895. Brownlee 1996, 29, 38–39; Blakey and Blakey 1940, chaps. 1–3.

27. Pechman 1987, 313–14. Brownlee (1996) gives a concise analytical history of tax policy and an excellent bibliographical review.

28. Pechman 1987, 313–14; Brownlee 1996, 89–100.

29. Pechman 1987, 117–20.

30. Pechman 1977, 350.

31. Ibid.

32. Pechman and Okner 1974, 59 (incidence assumptions "1c" and "3b").

33. Pechman 1987, 313; Steuerle 1992.

34. Pechman 1985, 77, 78, 91, 88, 80, 87; see also 69–70. It is essential to substitute the revised tables at the end of the book. See Pechman 1986.

35. Kasten, Samartino, and Toder 1996, 18, 29–33. See the comments by William Gale and others (Slemrod 1996, 51–58).

36. Brownlee 1996, 51.

37. Pechman 1987, 302–5, 321–22.

38. Pechman 1987, 157–62.

39. Goode 1951, 71–72. See Pechman 1987, 141–45.

40. Harberger 1962.

41. Pechman 1987, 144.

42. Harberger 1983.

43. The "double taxation" argument asserts, reasonably enough, that corporate income is taxed twice: both to the corporation as a legal entity and (in the form of dividends and capital gains) to corporate shareholders as individuals. The most important question, however, is how big a bite is taken by the two taxes together. Since the effective rates of both the corporate and the personal income taxes are quite low—and since corporations enjoy many special legal privileges—complaints about double taxation are largely specious.

44. Pechman 1987, 145.

45. Tanzi 1995, 113, drawing on Jorgenson and Landau 1993. For many purposes, it is important to combine corporate taxes with personal taxation of income from corporate sources (as these scholars do) because countries high in one are often low

in the other. As we have noted, however, corporate taxes may be more vulnerable to global economic competition. Tanzi (p. 116) notes the worrisome "fragility" of King-Fullerton estimates, but they appear to be the best available.

46. Pechman and Okner 1974, 59.

47. Pechman 1985, 78, 91, 88, 80.

48. Fullerton and Rogers 1993, 6, 37–38, 180–84.

49. The "full integration" solution is not without practical problems, however. See Pechman 1987, 179–88.

50. Some economists argue that the "employers'" share is shifted forward to consumers. If so, the tax is still quite regressive; see Pechman 1987, 220–21.

51. Survey by the Swedish Employers' Confederation, reported in *Economist,* May 27, 1995, 98.

52. Payroll taxes take very little from the lowest-income people, who have little or no income from which employers can withhold those taxes. Their government benefits are not subject to payroll taxes; neither are any earnings from the underground economy. But slightly higher-income workers are hit hard by payroll taxes.

53. U.S. Social Security Administration press release, October 19, 1999.

54. Pechman and Okner 1974, 59, 61; Pechman 1985, 77, 78, 91, 88, 80; Pechman 1987, 220. Only in 1985, during the peak effectiveness of Reagan tax and welfare policies, were payroll taxes regressive throughout the income range.

55. Fullerton and Rogers's result does not capture the effect of the income cap; it depends mainly on the presumed shifting to consumers (which means that poor non–wage earners pay some of the tax) and on the fact that low-income groups take a lower fraction of their endowments as leisure, therefore paying relatively less endowment tax (the null model against which Fullerton and Rogers calculate incidence) than payroll tax (1993, 5, 37, 176–78).

56. Automatic adjustments of payroll tax "caps" cannot much affect relative progressivity because they merely keep up with average wage increases; they do not extend the tax to higher-income fractions of the population.

57. U.S. Social Security Advisory Board 1998, 26.

58. The conclusion that payroll tax surpluses were used for general revenue purposes depends on hypothetical reasoning: that other spending would not have been as high without the surpluses. Even though Social Security was supposedly "off budget," its surpluses were counted in order to make budget deficits look smaller than they would otherwise have been. This presumably reduced pressure to cut other spending.

59. *U.S. Budget FY00,* 30; see our figure 5.1.

60. Institute of Economic Affairs (United Kingdom) data reported in *Economist,* September 19, 1998, 124.

61. Pechman 1987, 200. See Pechman and Okner 1974, 59, 61; Pechman 1985, 77, 78, 91, 88, 80.

62. Poterba 1989; Fullerton and Rogers 1993. See Metcalf 1996 and the critique by Menchik in Slemrod 1996, 94. Lifetime incidence calculations either rely on consumption as a proxy for income (which assumes flawless working of the lifetime income hypothesis) or rely on panel data that are seriously incomplete— ignoring appreciation of assets and transfers by gift and bequest, for example, thus understating the total incomes of high-income people and overstating tax progressivity.

63. If we acknowledge that some people gain special pleasure from living and working in familiar places, we may want to treat the inheritance of certain *tangible* goods like houses and farms more permissively. (Under current law, fewer than one in twenty farmers in fact leaves a taxable estate, and ongoing family businesses are given special breaks.) Except for these cases, however, the oft-mentioned concern that high inheritance taxes can force liquidation of assets seems misplaced. The notion that it is fair to let people pass what they have accumulated on to their children does not hold up well if we focus on fairness to the living, rather than to the dead; its main support is the anticipation and incentive argument mentioned in the text.

64. Citizens for Tax Justice 1998. Nominal rates in the mid-1980s ranged from 18 to 50 percent (Pechman 1987, 335).

65. 1995 Internal Revenue Service data reported in Citizens for Tax Justice 1998, 3.

66. Pechman 1987, 238–39, 351, 390.

67. See ibid., 240–52. Nielson (1985) documents the general weakness of connections between the donors who give foundation money and the staff members who spend it.

68. U.S. Bureau of the Census web site, "National Totals of State and Local Tax Revenue" (visited 7/11/99). See Metcalf 1996, 60–62.

69. See Aaron 1975, 18–55; Mieszkowski 1972, 1967. Metcalf (1996, 65) offers a brief account.

70. Pechman and Okner 1974, 59 (variant "1c").

71. Pechman 1985, 77, 78, 91, 88, 80 (variant "1c"). The 1970 findings are given on p. 78 and those for 1985 on p. 80.

72. Fullerton and Rogers 1993, 6, 37, 178–80.

73. Smith 1999.

74. Barlett and Steel 1994, chap. 8, esp. p. 323; Aaron 1975, 12–17, 56–70.

75. U.S. Bureau of the Census web site, "State Government Finances," July 11, 1997. This figure combines $147 billion in general sales taxes with $69 billion in selective (excise) taxes.

76. Pechman and Okner 1974, 59 (both variants "1c" and "3b").

77. Pechman 1985, 77, 78, 91, 88, 80.

78. Fullerton and Rogers 1993, 5, 36, 174–76.

79. The Federation of Tax Administrators found that in 1996 twenty-four states exempted food and twelve states did not.

80. Metcalf 1996, 71–74, 82 (these are "consumption base" figures).

81. See the comments on Metcalf, particularly those by Sheffrin, Menchik, and Musgrave, in Slemrod 1996, 93–94.

82. Citizens for Tax Justice 1996. Data are for 1995.

83. Metcalf 1996, 61–62.

84. *World Almanac 1999* (Mahwah, N.J.: Primedia Reference, 1998), 161. See Gold 1991.

85. Metcalf 1996, 74–77, 82.

86. Peterson 1981.

87. Metcalf's (1996, 82–83) argument that on a lifetime basis the sales tax is equally as progressive as the income tax is not persuasive because of the defects in his study noted in our discussion of the sales and property taxes.

88. Pechman and Okner 1974, 49.

89. Pechman 1985, 77, 78, 91, 88, 80. The 1985 estimates are given on p. 80.

90. Johnson and Lav 1997.

91. Fullerton and Rogers 1993, 36, 38, 184–86.

92. Shapiro and Greenstein 1997.

93. See Slaughter 1986.

94. Brownlee 1996, chap. 1.

95. This emergence of "democratic-statist" tax regimes in response to national emergencies is the main theme of Brownlee 1996. Hansen (1983) emphasizes the role of critical elections, which sometimes—though not always—were associated with these crises. See Brownlee 1996, 39–40 fn. 25. Witte (1985), while stressing the incremental nature of most tax changes, notes that substantial increases in progressivity arose from wars and crises.

96. See Goodwyn 1978; Hofstadter 1963.

97. Brownlee 1996, 47–100. As Leff (1983, 1984) points out, however, the redistributive policies of the New Deal were limited and often just symbolic.

98. Witte 1985, chaps. 7–12.

99. Howard 1997, esp. chap. 9.

100. King 1993. See Mellon 1924.

101. Martin 1991.

102. Birnbaum and Murray 1988; Martin 1991.

103. See Schattschneider 1960.

104. Keene 1983; Page and Shapiro 1992, 160–66. Witte (1985, chap. 16) emphasizes the limits to the American public's expressed desires for redistribution.

Since the concept of progressivity is difficult for most people to understand, abstract survey questions about it tend to be quite misleading. See Roberts, Hite, and Bradley 1994.

105. Barlett and Steel 1994, 338–39.

Chapter Six

1. Education is a major determinant of different individuals' social mobility. See Marger 1999, chap. 6, which puts this into the context of accidents of birth and changes in the opportunity structure.

2. Reich 1991. An eloquent brief plea for improving U.S. education, tempered by concerns about the job market, is Zinberg 1993.

3. We will discuss the "screening" hypothesis further below, in connection with higher education.

4. U.S. Department of Education, National Center for Educational Statistics 1999, 11, tbl. 1 [hereafter cited as U.S., NCES 1999].

5. Hassel 1998, 45.

6. U.S., NCES 1999, 11. For a cross-national view, see Heidenheimer, Heclo, and Adams 1990, chap. 2.

7. Some countries (e.g., Germany) have succeeded in giving employers strong incentives to train their workers by limiting workforce mobility and making it very hard to fire employees. See Streeck 1992, chap. 1. Herzenberg, Alic, and Wial (1998) suggest ways to translate these employer incentives to the U.S. service sector.

8. Kaestle 1983.

9. Tuition at heavily subsidized Catholic schools averaged $1,628 for elementary grades and $3,643 for secondary; the figures for non-Catholic religious schools were $2,606 and $5,261, respectively. U.S., NCES 1999, 73.

10. On the U.S. history, see Kaestle 1983. For a comparative, cross-national view, see Wilensky and Lebeaux 1965, chap. 3. Insightful explorations of the economic theory of education are given in Barr 1993 or 1998, chap. 13, and Poterba 1996.

11. Barr 1993, 337; contrast the broader view on p. 147.

12. Barr 1993, 147. See the several concepts of equal opportunity in Roemer 1996, 163–64, 263–315.

13. On the importance of intrinsic motivation, see Hatano and Inagaki 1987.

14. A broad view of equal opportunity, with some kinship to our own, but with deeper philosophical foundations, is Levine 1998.

15. See Fishkin 1983, which argues that broadly construed equal opportunity is incompatible with the autonomy of families.

16. Leung (1999, 244) links this to the Confucian idea that everyone is educable, even perfectible.

17. Levitan et al. 1998, 148, 173, 150; Bergmann 1996, 117. See "Facts in Brief" at the Alan Guttmacher Institute (AGI) web site, agi-usa.org. Hollander (1996, 29–30) documents the sharp rise in births to separated and unmarried (again, this does not mean *never*-married) women up to the early 1990s, when the rate stabilized and then began to decline.

18. Levitan et al. 1998, 147–53. More than half (55 percent) of the 939,000 teenage pregnancies in 1994 ended in births, two-thirds of which were unplanned. AGI web site, "Facts in Brief," 4 (visited 7/18/99).

19. Alan Guttmacher Institute 1997, 1, 7, 9. See Levitan et al. 1998, 150–51; Frost and Bolzan 1997.

20. Levitan et al. 1998, 150–51. By 1994, 6.6 million women received contraceptive services annually through some 7,122 publicly subsidized clinic sites. These services were estimated to help women avoid some 1.3 million unintended pregnancies per year, which prevented the number of U.S. abortions from being 40 percent higher and saved about $3 in Medicaid costs for every public dollar spent on contraceptive services (Alan Guttmacher Institute 1997, 2–4).

21. Levitan et al. 1998, 148, 152–53. On public opinion concerning abortion, see Page and Shapiro 1992, 63–64, 105–10.

22. Levitan et al. 1998, 157–58.

23. Ibid., 158–60; Blank 1997, 122–23.

24. U.S. Office of Management and Budget 1999, 82 [hereafter cited as *U.S. Budget FY00*]. One barrier to improvement has been the practice of subtracting 100 percent of the child support that is received from public aid payments, so that the children often gain nothing from improved enforcement. This also reduces the incentives of fathers to pay and of mothers to pursue them.

25. Blank 1997, 163–64.

26. *U.S. Budget FY00*, 92. See Levitan et al. 1998, 137.

27. Levitan et al. 1998, 116–17; Blank 1997, 166. More recently the Mississippi threshold has improved somewhat to 42 percent of the poverty line, while Alabama (23 percent), Texas (26 percent), and Virginia (31 percent) fall miserably far below it. U.S. Department of Health and Human Services 1996, sec. 8, tbls. 8–17.

28. Levitan et al. 1998, 117–18.

29. Ibid., 136–37; Blank 1997, 164 fn. 46, 47.

30. Levitan et al. 1998, 136; Blank 1997, 164.

31. *U.S. Budget FY00*, 78, 233; Levitan et al. 1998, 161–63.

32. Barnett (1998) reviews the literature. See also Blank 1997, 178–80; Wilgoren 1999.

33. Bergmann 1996, 132; see Levitan et al. 1998, 227.

34. Levitan et al. 1998, 163. Barnett (1998, 8) notes that fewer than half the children *eligible* for Head Start (under rather narrow eligibility criteria) are served by the program. Bergmann (1996, 123) estimated that her ambitious proposal for all-day, year-round day care for children under six would cost $36 billion. That would be a substantial sum, but not much compared with a $300 billion military budget or compared to the proposal's benefits.

35. *U.S. Budget FY00*, 358, 76–77. In that budget, it was proposed to extend bene-

fits of the child care tax credit up to incomes of $59,000. See also Levitan et al. 1998, 156–57.

36. *U.S. Budget FY00,* 76–77. Federal child care grants were cut and consolidated into a single block grant in 1981 and languished for some time afterward. See Levitan et al. 1998, 154–56.

37. Bergmann 1996; Boocock and Larner 1998; Gustafsson and Stafford 1998; Frank 1996.

38. U.S., NCES 1999, 98, 170. The states' share of school financing varies widely, from 74 percent in New Mexico down to just 7 percent in New Hampshire, where 87 percent of the money comes from local or intermediate sources.

39. Katz (1987, chap. 1) gives a concise account of the origins of U.S. public schools. For more detail, see Kaestle 1983.

40. See Coleman 1968. At best, however, this was a *local* equality, with different localities varying widely in resources.

41. Katz 1987, chap. 2; Coleman 1968.

42. Jackson 1985, esp. chaps. 11, 12.

43. Massey and Denton 1993;, Farley and Fry 1994. See Coleman 1981.

44. Kozol 1991; Maeroff 1988.

45. U.S., NCES 1999, 477. In 1990–91, 33 percent of students in high-poverty-enrollment English classes, but only 16 percent in low-poverty classes, were taught by teachers who had not even minored in a related field. Figures for science were 29 percent and 12 percent, respectively. U.S., NCES 1996, 16–18.

46. Burtless 1996a, 1–2, 14; *U.S. Budget FY00,* 64–65.

47. See Steinberg, Brown, and Dornbusch 1996.

48. Hedges and Greenwald 1996; Jencks 1996.

49. Burtless 1996a, 40. Burtless suggests that in the past, at lower spending levels, additional money mattered more—that is, that marginal returns have declined. Heckman, Layne-Farrar, and Todd (1996) call into question even the apparently well established finding that school resources improve students' later earnings prospects.

50. See Steinberg, Brown, and Dornbusch 1996.

51. Rosenberg (1991, pt. 1) presents considerable evidence that significant school desegregation occurred only after the 1964 act.

52. Massey and Denton 1993.

53. *USA Today,* May 12, 1994, 2A.

54. Patterson 1999.

55. Rosenbaum 1995, 242.

56. Meier 1995, esp. 16. See Wood 1992.

57. For example, the success of Central Park East may possibly be overstated due to selection bias if unusually high-aspiration parents and students tend to apply. But the likelihood of this is reduced by the fact that most applicants have had disadvan-

taged backgrounds and very low test scores and that applicants have been admitted by lottery, rather than letting the schools "cream" the best applicants. See Meier 1995, 19, 28.

58. See, e.g., Hanushek 1996, 54. In apparent contradiction to Hanushek's text, however, his table indicates positive effects of per-pupil expenditures, teachers' experience, and perhaps also teachers' salaries.

59. Chubb and Moe 1990, 92–95; Hedges and Greenwald 1996, esp. 84–87. Note that meta-analyses assuming "fixed effects" should be distinguished from those based on superior "random effects" models.

60. Mosteller 1995; *U.S. Budget FY00,* 66.

61. See Stevenson and Lee 1998 and the comments by Lewis and Rohten.

62. See Friedman 1962, chap. 6; Friedman and Friedman 1980, chap. 6.

63. See Jencks 1996, esp. 93–94; Stedman 1998.

64. Coleman (1981) gives a succinct summary and reflection on his study; Keith and Page (1985) critique it.

65. Chubb and Moe 1990, 126, 129, 138, 152, 154, 160, 302.

66. Hoxby 1998, 148. It is hard to know whether all relevant variables have been controlled, however, in analyzing these cross-sectional, aggregate data.

67. Peterson 1998, 22; Greene, Peterson, and Du 1998; Peterson et al. 1999. Focusing on broader nonlottery data from the Milwaukee program, Witte (1993) reported unimpressive early results. Witte (1999) acknowledges some success in Milwaukee, but warns that large-scale voucher programs could undermine equal education and harm the poor. For a lucid brief in favor of school choice, see Peterson 1999.

68. See Gilles 1998 for a provoucher reading of the federal issues and Viteritti 1998 on state constitutions. At the time of writing, the Cleveland voucher program was under challenge in the federal courts.

69. Contrast Gutmann 1987, 70, with Peterson 1998, 22–23.

70. Peterson 1998, 26.

71. Hoxby 1998, 144–45.

72. Hassel 1998a, 1998b. See Hill, Pierce, and Guthrie 1997.

73. See Hassel 1998b.

74. U.S., NCES 1999, 17, 20. Figures refer to twenty-five- to twenty-nine-year-olds in 1997.

75. See Lerman 1996. Eleanor Page (personal communication) reports that vocational programs at Evanston High teach useful skills, but have problematic effects on racial separation.

76. Lerman 1996, 141–42.

77. Bowen 1997, xi (1992 figure).

78. Rothman 1999, 192. Among African Americans, the comparable figures were just 37 percent, 18 percent, and 10 percent, respectively.

79. Gould 1981 is a classic refutation of the contention that some sort of unidimensional "intelligence" is inherited; it exposes the shoddy and sometimes fraudulent science behind this idea. Fischer et al. (1996), among others, have demolished the "Bell Curve" arguments of Herrnstein and Murray (1994).

80. See Hansen and Weisbrod 1969.

81. The 1997 forward to Bowen 1997 [1977], xi–xiv, is particularly trenchant on these methodological problems. Jencks et al. 1979, however, which may still be the best study of this type, found that college (though not high school) education had nearly as powerful a measured effect on status and earnings after extensive controls as before (chap. 6 and pp. 223–29).

82. See Bowen 1997 [1977], xiv.

83. Bowen 1997 [1977] remains a magisterial survey.

84. U.S., NCES 1999, 397, 414; *U.S. Budget FY00,* 229, 329; U.S. Office of Management and Budget 1998, 207 [hereafter cited as *U.S. Budget FY99*].

85. *U.S. Budget FY00,* 70, 230, 330.

86. Ibid., 69, 228, 257.

87. U.S., NCES 1999, 419.

88. See Hansen and Weisbrod 1969.

89. Dye 1995, 171.

90. See Bell 1996; Curry and West 1996.

91. Timothy Page (personal communication from Finland, 11/24/99).

92. Page and Shapiro 1992, 49–50, 132–34; Sundquist 1968; Poole and Rosenthal 1997.

93. Daniel Elazar (1966) emphasized the major institutional and cultural differences among states.

94. Calculated from U.S., NCES 1999, 182. See Smith 1999.

95. *Los Angeles Times,* March 5, 1999, A1.

96. Hess 1999. Of course, the educational establishment tends to resist bad, as well as good, proposed "reforms."

97. See Schattschneider 1960.

98. See Myrdal 1971, chap. 3.

Chapter Seven

1. See Baumol and Blinder 1997, 116–24.

2. U.S. Office of the President 1998, 368–69; U.S. Bureau of Labor Statistics (BLS) web site (visited 9/99).

3. BLS web site, *Monthly Labor Review* daily update, April 26, 1999 (visited 7/25/99). In June 1999, when the official unemployment rate (U-3) was 4.5 percent, the rate including all marginally attached and discouraged workers (U-5) was 5.3 percent. The rate including the marginally attached plus those employed part-time for

economic reasons (U-6) was 7.9 percent. BLS web site, Table A-8, "Range of Alternative Measures of Labor Utilization" (visited 7/25/99). Figures are not seasonally adjusted.

4. See Keyssar 1986, esp. chap. 3 and pp. 356–58.

5. National Bureau of Economic Research (NBER) web site, "U.S. Business Cycle Expansions and Contractions" (visited 8/10/99).

6. Blank and Blinder 1986, 185–88; Tobin 1994, 155–62. See Galbraith 1998, chap. 8.

7. See Shapiro and Stiglitz 1984.

8. U.S. Office of the President 1999, 368, 366. See Mischel, Bernstein, and Schmitt 1999, an outstanding, annually updated report on the state of working America.

9. U.S. Bureau of the Census web page, Table H-2, "Share of Aggregate Income Received by Each Fifth and Top 5 Percent of Households (All Races): 1967 to 1997" (visited 7/25/99).

10. Blank and Blinder 1986, 185–88.

11. See Baumol and Blinder 1997, 124–35. Barro (1997, esp. chap. 3) finds high inflation to be related to slower growth across countries, but this finding is by no means universally accepted.

12. Friedman 1968, esp. 16.

13. See Mankiw 1998, esp. 13, 456 ff.

14. U.S. Bureau of the Census 1975, pt. 1, p. 126. Other calculations put the 1933 unemployment rate at 24.9 percent, still a very high figure (Goldfield 1997, 181). See Leuchtenburg 1963.

15. On the reception of Keynesian ideas in the United States and Europe, see Hall 1989.

16. See Gordon 1990, 197–202, on rational expectations models and their weaknesses.

17. Blanchard (1997, 610–21) presents a capsule history of macroeconomic theory. Blanchard maintains that a "core" consensus accepts the rational expectations assumption, but does not rule out inflation/unemployment trade-offs or the effectiveness of policy measures.

18. A particularly scathing theoretical and empirical attack on the idea of a "natural" rate of unemployment (sometimes known as a "non-accelerating inflation rate of unemployment" or "NAIRU") is Galbraith 1998, chap. 10. For contrary views, see Gordon 1990, 11–13, and Blanchard 1997, 307–11 (which, however, allow for extensive changes in such a rate).

19. Greider (1987) gives a critical account of the politics and economics of the Federal Reserve Board, suggesting that bankers run the Fed in their own interests.

20. Galbraith 1998, esp. 145, 267–68.

21. Tobin 1994, 155–56. Blank (1997, chap. 2) points out that, contrary to the

usual pattern, aggregate economic growth in the 1980s and early 1990s did not reduce poverty.

22. Blank 1997, 127–32; Levitan et al. 1998, 213–16. On the politics and economics of Community Development Block Grants (which emphasize social services, rather than business growth, and which have not always gone where the poor people are), see Rich 1993.

23. See chapter 3. To be sure, Barro's (1997) longitudinal study of about one hundred countries found that higher levels of "nonproductive" government spending were associated with slower growth, but this spending measure excluded education (pp. 13, 26). (Indeed, more schooling of the population was associated with faster growth [pp. 13, 19].)

24. U.S. Office of Management and Budget 1999, Historical Tables, 103–9 [hereafter cited as *U.S. Budget FY00*].

25. *Statistical Abstract of the United States 1997*, 861. The $6 billion per year spent by North Korea (sometimes touted as the major new U.S. enemy), amounted to only 1/46 of U.S. expenditures.

26. See the web sites of the Council for a Livable World, Business Leaders for Sensible Priorities, and (for excellent charts and graphs) the National Priorities Project.

27. *U.S. Budget FY00*, 152, 315. The $80 billion figure includes $75.4 billion for personnel and $3.7 billion for family housing.

28. On the other hand, the preponderance of lower-class and minority people in the military is considered by some observers to be troubling and unfair. See Dorn 1989, esp. chap. 7 by Charles Moskos and chap. 11 by Roger Wilkins.

29. *U.S. Budget FY00*, 155–56.

30. Nor do the "spinoffs" from exotic new weapons generally contribute much to growth of the civilian economy. See Alic et al. 1992. Markusen et al. (1991) analyze the economics and geography of U.S. military spending.

31. *New York Times*, March 15, 1998, WK3.

32. *U.S. Budget FY00*, 231–32; Levitan et al. 1998, 176–77. A useful compendium of programs related to training, public-sector employment, support services, and job placement is given on pp. 178–79 of Levitan et al. 1998.

33. Levitan et al. 1998, 178, 180–81; Blank 1997, 118.

34. *U.S. Budget FY00*, 232.

35. Levitan et al. 1998, 181–82; Blank 1997, 176–77; *U.S. Budget FY00*, 232.

36. Levitan et al. 1998, 178, 195–97.

37. *U.S. Budget FY00*, 231–32.

38. Ibid., 232, 329; Levitan et al. 1998, 200–202.

39. Blank 1997, 119, 174–75; Levitan et al. 1998, 192–94. See Burtless 1998.

40. Blank 1997, 175–76.

41. *U.S. Budget FY00,* 80–82. See Levitan et al. 1998, 195; Blank 1997, 119–20.

42. Pear 1998b.

43. Solow 1998; Solow et al. 1998; Burtless 1998.

44. Amenta 1998. See Patterson 1981, 63–67, 186–87. Goldfield (1997, chap. 6, esp. pp. 204–5) points out that racial discrimination was rampant in New Deal work relief programs.

45. Barnow 1987. See Blank 1997, 120; Bassi and Ashenfelter 1986, esp. 147–48.

46. Blank 1997, 121; Bassi and Ashenfelter 1986, 149. See the bar graph of spending trends in Levitan et al. 1998, 177.

47. Clayton and Pontusson 1998, esp. tbl. 7; Esping-Andersen 1990, esp. 202, 158. Of all twenty-nine OECD countries, only five (Australia, Iceland, Switzerland, Japan, and New Zealand) have public employment percentages below that of the United States (Feigenbaum et al. 1999, 13). On the preponderance of women in the United Kingdom's private service sector and (with better pay and benefits) in Scandinavia's public services, see Klausen 1999, 268–69.

48. See Stith and Cabranes 1998.

49. Butterfield 1999; *Economist,* March 20, 1999, 30–31. Already in 1996, a much higher 5.5 million adults were under "correctional supervision," about two-thirds of them under probation or on parole. U.S. Bureau of Justice Statistics 1999, 2. According to Mauer (1999, 23), the U.S. incarceration rate is the highest among all industrial states except Russia.

50. *San Francisco Chronicle,* March 8, 1999, A9; Butterfield 1999. *The Economist* (March 20, 1999, 31) commented that U.S. drug laws "seem aimed directly at blacks," with sentences *100 times* as great for ghetto-prevalent crack as for upper-middle-class powdered cocaine. See The Sentencing Project web site (visited 11/13/99).

51. Mauer 1999, 81.

52. Hightower 1998; Lafer 1999.

53. Capital Punishment Information Center web site (visited 11/13/99). See Protess and Warden 1998.

54. U.S. Bureau of Justice Statistics web site, "Criminal Victimization 1998," July 1999, 1 (visited 7/25/99); Massing 1998.

55. U.S. Bureau of Justice Statistics 1999, v, 13. See The Sentencing Project web site, "Drug Policy and the Criminal Justice System" (visited 11/13/99).

56. U.S. Bureau of Justice Statistics 1999, 13; *Economist,* March 20, 1999, 30; Caulkins et al. 1997. See Massing 1998.

57. United Nations General Assembly 1948, 134; Page and Shapiro 1992, 24, 121–23. The unfortunate National Election Study question that lumps "and a good standard of living" together with a job guarantee regularly finds more respondents placing themselves on the opposition than the supportive end of a 7-point scale, presumably because of opposition to guaranteed *income,* rather than guaranteed work. Page and Shapiro's (1992, 122) comment that support for guaranteed work

has been "limited to special situations" does not seem well supported by the data they present.

58. Wilson 1996, 225–38; Danziger and Gottschalk 1995, 168–74. Specific proposals vary. Danziger and Gottschalk suggest a slightly *sub*minimal wage for all but inner-city youth, and a cautiously experimental start-up (1995, 171–72).

59. Levitan et al. 1998, 205–9; Blank 1997, 114–16.

60. Card and Krueger 1995.

61. *Statistical Abstract of the United States 1997,* 433; Levitan et al. 1998, 205–6. See Economic Policy Institute web site, which gives current- and constant-dollar values for the minimum wage from 1960 onward (visited 7/27/99), and the BLS web site.

62. Pollin 1998; Henneman 1998. See Schuman 1998. The living wage also protects city *employees* from the danger that their jobs will be "contracted out" to low-wage private firms.

63. Levitan et al. 1998, 207–8; Blank 1997, 114–16.

64. Blank 1997, 111–14. See Scholz 1993–94; Hoffman and Seidman 1990.

65. *U.S. Budget FY00,* 81, 249; Blank 1997, 111–13.

66. Blank 1997, 113; Dickert et al. 1995.

67. *U.S. Budget FY00,* 338, 359, 360 fn. 4.

68. For a vehemently antilabor perspective, see Green 1996.

69. Freeman 1994, esp. chap. 1.

70. Stephens 1979, esp. tbl. 4.8; Western 1993, 267; Thelen 1991. See Katzenstein 1985.

71. Ostreicher (1988) discusses divisions among workers. Keyssar (2000) emphasizes working-class disenfranchisement. Forbath (1991) and Hattam (1992) stress the critical role of courts and the legal system. Goldfield (1997) focuses on racial conflict. On general issues of "American Exceptionalism," see Lipset 1996.

72. See Foner 1955, 1962, 1965.

73. McCloskey 1994, chaps. 5, 6; Hattam 1992; Forbath 1991.

74. See Goldfield 1987.

75. Golden, Wallerstein, and Lange 1999. See Locke, Kochan, and Piore 1995. But as Wallerstein (1999) shows, centralized wage bargaining is crucial to relatively equal pay for workers. Sweden abandoned its centralized wage-setting system, largely under pressure from both capital and labor in the export sector, where high union wages threatened to undercut Sweden's international price competitiveness (Pontusson and Swenson 1996). For a very pessimistic view on the prospects for workplace democracy in core countries, see Greenberg 1999.

76. The AFL–CIO web page "work in progress" feature gives regular updates on organizing successes, and its "union summer" location tells about young people's involvement in such efforts as the organization of New Orleans hotel and restaurant employees (visited 7/26/99). See Nissen 1999.

77. Model 1993.

78. Skocpol 1992; Mishel, Bernstein, and Schmitt 1999.

79. See Mayer and Abramson 1994, esp. 143.

80. *Statistical Abstract of the United States 1997,* 404.

81. Goodman 1999a. The AFL–CIO web page feature on women and equal pay extensively documents gender inequalities. See also Evans and Nelson 1989; Nelson and Bridges 1999.

82. McKeown 1999, 13.

83. See, e.g., Ethier 1995; Wong 1995. In the event of external economies of scale and imperfect competition, however, trade will not necessarily increase welfare, even theoretically.

84. The notion that an "efficiency gain" is necessarily a welfare gain, even without actual compensation, violates economists' strongest ethical principle—namely, Pareto optimality—because changes that increase efficiency often make someone worse off.

85. WTO web site, "WTO in Brief" (accessed 7/26/99). Goldstein (1993) gives a useful account of U.S. trade policy.

86. U.S. Office of the President 1999, 355. Figures are in chained 1992 dollars. Goldstein (1993, 163) presents a table showing drops in average U.S. tariff rates and corresponding rises in imports (especially in the early years) between 1934 and 1991.

87. Abowd and Freeman 1991, 8, 24.

88. Ibid., 24.

89. Herzenberg et al. 1998, esp. 30–31, 175–83; Abowd and Freeman 1991, 25.

90. Internet activism may be key. See, for example, the Global Trade Watch, associated with Public Citizen.

91. Capital outflows to Canada amounted to about $6 billion in 1994 and over $10 billion in 1998. The figures for Mexico were $4.5 billion in 1994, but only $2.5 billion in 1998. U.S. Bureau of Economic Affairs (BEA) web site (visited 8/25/99).

92. BEA web site, news releases of June 9 and June 30, 1999 (visited 7/26/99).

93. *Statistical Abstract of the United States 1996,* 787. In the year 1998 alone, there were about $122 billion in new U.S. direct foreign investments. BEA web site (visited 8/25/99).

94. *Statistical Abstract of the United States 1996,* 791.

95. See Greider 1997; Longworth 1998.

96. In classical trade models, trade and factor mobility are perfect substitutes for each other. Wong (1995), however, specifies theoretical conditions under which this does not hold. Trade and factor mobility may have somewhat different effects on factor price equalization if there are national external economies of scale, if there is monopolistic competition with differentiated products, or if there are oligopolistic industries (e.g., pp. 6–8). This is a maze within which the unwary can easily get lost. See Ethier 1995, esp. chap. 10. For an early model, see Stolper and Samuelson 1941.

97. Abowd and Freeman 1991; Bartel and Koch 1991.

98. Abowd and Freeman 1991, 4, 6, 21; Borjas, Freeman, and Lang 1991.

99. Abowd and Freeman 1991, 22–24; LaLonde and Topel 1991; Card and Altonji 1991. Wilson (1987, 34, 78, 189–91) notes that some African Americans resent immigrants, particularly Korean shopkeepers in ghettoes.

100. For a glowing account of the benefits of immigration, see Millman 1997.

101. Swenson 2000. See Domhoff 1996.

102. See Freeman 1994, esp. chap. 1; Golden et al. 1999.

103. Center for Responsive Politics (CRP) "opensecrets" web site, "Influence Inc.: Top Spenders" (visited 7/27/99). The list of the top 100 lobbying spenders included a few other nonbusiness organizations, such as the American Medical Association (#1 at $17 million, and no particular friend of the blue-collar worker), the Christian Coalition (#13), and—well down the list—the Seniors Coalition (#26) and the American Association of Retired Persons (#28).

104. U.S. Federal Election Commission (FEC) web site (visited 7/26/99). On the Center for Responsive Politics' list of top "soft money" contributors to the national parties in 1993–94, sixteen of the first twenty listed were business firms, headed by Amway, Philip Morris, and Archer Daniels Midland. Three were labor unions, and one was an Indian tribe interested in casino gambling. CRP web site, "Soft Money in the 1993–994 Election Cycle" (visited 8/26/99).

105. Freeman 1994. See Lindblom 1977 on the "privileged position" of business, giving what Block (1977b) would classify as a structural argument. Our account of business influence (emphasizing differences between the United States and other capitalist countries) is more instrumental than structural.

106. McCarty, Poole, and Rosenthal 1997, 14–16; Poole and Rosenthal 1997, chap. 4. See Mahood 2000.

107. Greenstone 1977. For a more recent view, see Dark 1999.

108. FEC web site (visited 7/26/99). These figures nicely express a crucial fact about American politics: organized labor depends almost exclusively on the Democrats, but the Democrats do not depend exclusively on labor.

109. CRP web site (visited 7/27/98).

110. Ferguson 1995. As we noted in chapters 3 and 4, controversies over the particular makeup and motivations of the Democrats' business backers are less important to our point than the fact that backing by a segment of business has been crucial for the party. On the Clinton administration, see also Woodward 1994 and Reich 1997.

111. Garrett 1998.

Chapter Eight

1. A number of interesting insights into this imagery (not all of them reflected here) were offered by 1998–99 fellows at the Center for Advanced Study in the

Behavioral Sciences, including Manny Schegloff, Dan Segal, John Gumperz, Don Lamm, Jeff Alexander, Alex Keyssar, and Bill Deverell.

2. Schegloff and Segal emphasize these points.

3. The emphasis on individualistic "rights" is chiefly an Anglo-American phenomenon. In most of Europe, the guarantee of basic human needs is justified in terms of national solidarity or concern for all citizens as a "family."

4. Kotz 1971, esp. chaps 1, 3, 7.

5. Bauman 1998, tbl 1. The hunger figure for 1995 was 4.8 percent. Bauman used Census survey data to validate a composite measure of material hardship based on questions introduced by Mayer and Jencks. For evidence of extensive hunger during the 1980s, when the value of Food Stamps and Aid to Families with Dependent Children (AFDC) benefits had eroded, see Physicians Task Force on Hunger in America 1985. A good discussion of the contemporary hunger problem and solutions to it is Eisinger 1998.

6. U.S. Office of Management and Budget 1999, 197, 200, 322, 323 [hereafter cited as *U.S. Budget FY00*]; U.S. Department of Agriculture web site, "Final Regulatory Impact Analysis of Federal MMO Consolidation and Reform" (a murky document indeed) (visited 8/99).

7. *U.S. Budget FY00,* 200.

8. U.S. Department of Agriculture, Economic Research Service 1998, 7–9, 20, 27.

9. Schultze 1971, 29, 30.

10. Kotz 1971, 47–49.

11. Ibid., 23, 44, 48.

12. USDA Food and Nutrition Service (FNS) web page, "Food Distribution" (accessed 8/9/99); *U.S. Budget FY00,* 335.

13. FNS web site, Food Stamps "Income Chart," "Deductions," "Resources," "Allotment Chart," "Benefits" (visited 8/9/99).

14. *U.S. Budget FY00,* 248, 337; FNS web site, "Allotment Chart," updated October 1998, effective through September 1999 (visited 8/9/99).

15. Steiner 1971, chap. 6; MacDonald 1977, esp. 7, 10–11; Blank 1997, 106, 107.

16. Levitan et al. 1998, 132; *U.S. Budget FY99,* 225.

17. Levitan et al. 1998, 134–35; FNS web site, "Facts about the Food Stamp Program," 2, and "Work and Aliens" (visited 8/9/99).

18. Blank 1997, 162–63.

19. FNS web site, Office of Analysis, Nutrition, and Evaluation, "Measuring Food Security in the United States: Household Food Security in the United States, 1995–1998 (Advance Report—Summary)," July 1999 (visited 8/9/99).

20. MacDonald 1977, chap. 6; Blank 1997, 106; Revkin 1999b, 1999c; Murray 1999.

21. See Green and MacColl 1983.

22. Blank 1997, 168–69.

23. Blank 1997, 170–72. EBT must be implemented carefully. Early reports about the Citicorp system in New York, for example, found welfare recipients without access to most ATMs, unable to check their credit level, and subject to onerous special fees (Barstow 1999).

24. Blank 1997, 202–3. Blank (pp. 203–7) discusses evidence that public spending does displace some transfers between families and some charitable giving. But she points out the enormous and highly unlikely upsurge in donations that would be required to replace government aid, and urges public-private complementarity and partnership.

25. Revkin 1999a, 1999c.

26. The Clinton administration reported some progress in this direction, though between 1998 and 2000 it projected an increase only from 36 to 42 percent in the proportion of states using EBT to issue Food Stamp benefits. *U.S. Budget FY00*, 248.

27. The subtraction from maximum food stamp allotments of 30 percent of net earnings amounts to a 30 percent marginal tax on such earnings, in addition to payroll taxes and nondeductible work expenses.

28. Aaron 1972, 53–59.

29. *U.S. Budget FY00*, 356.

30. Aaron 1972, chap. 5.

31. *U.S. Budget FY00*, 205–6.

32. Blank 1997, 109.

33. *U.S. Budget FY00*, 207. Oddly that document said almost nothing else about public housing and did not indicate whether or how the demolished units would be replaced. We have relied below on the slightly more informative fiscal year 1999 budget.

34. U.S. Office of Management and Budget 1998, 189 [hereafter cited as *U.S. Budget FY99*]; Blank 1997, 109.

35. *U.S. Budget FY00*, 335; U.S. Department of Housing and Urban Development (HUD) web site, "Waiting in Vain: An Update on America's Rental Housing Crisis," revised June 30, 1999 (visited 8/9/99).

36. *U.S. Budget FY99*, 189.

37. Blank 1997, 110. In 1998 alone, 13,000 opted out, according to HUD, "Waiting in Vain."

38. HUD, "Waiting in Vain."

39. *U.S. Budget FY00*, 207. See *U.S. Budget FY99*, 190.

40. *U.S. Budget FY00*, 335; HUD, "Waiting in Vain."

41. Daly 1996, 7–9; National Coalition for the Homeless 1999a.

42. Jencks 1994, 2–3, 7, 13, 17–18. Jencks's definition (p. 7) of the homeless included everyone who slept in a public place or a shelter (including welfare hotels) during a given week, but excluded hundreds of thousands in jails, detoxification centers, or mental hospitals, as well as teenage runaways and children in foster care.

Jencks's figures were largely based on a reweighting and recalculation of data reported by Martha Burt.

43. Link et al. 1995.

44. U.S. Conference of Mayors 1998.

45. Jencks (1994, 24, 41, 43) reports the higher rates of mental illness, alcoholism, and crack addiction; Koegel et al. (1996) and the National Coalition for the Homeless (1999b) report the lower ones.

46. Jencks 1994, chap. 3, esp. pp. 29, 37.

47. See Goodwin 1981; Daly 1996.

48. Daly 1996, 20–22; Jencks 1994, 22; National Coalition for the Homeless 1999b. Daly 1996, which compares U.S. homelessness to the more humane situations in Britain and Canada, is also notable for its accounts of the experiences of homeless people themselves and for its striking photographs that give homeless people human faces.

49. Daly 1996, 134–36.

50. Ibid., 136–37.

51. Ibid., 140–44; National Coalition for the Homeless 1999b. See the National Coalition for the Homeless web site for further information on veterans, victims of domestic violence, people afflicted with addictions or mental illness, homeless families with children, and other specific groups.

52. Jencks 1994, 22.

53. National Coalition for the Homeless 1999b, 3. The vignettes in Snow and Anderson 1993 (e.g., pp. 46–55) suggest that many people in America are just a paycheck or two away from the ditch.

54. Jencks 1994, chap. 6.

55. Daly 1996, 174–81, 202.

56. Daly 1996 (e.g., pp. 153–55 on New York's notorious "welfare hotels" of the 1980s). Snow and Anderson (1993, chap. 3) describe shelters that accommodate, or preach, or profit, but do not solve homeless people's problems.

57. Daly 1996, 160–61, 204–5.

58. Daly 1996, chap. 8, "More Than Just a Roof." Havel is quoted on p. 149.

59. Daly 1996, 150.

60. Center on Budget and Policy Priorities 1998, 10–12.

61. Daly 1996, 182, 224.

62. Daly 1996, chap. 11, esp. pp. 210, 225, 230, 233.

63. Ibid., esp. 195–99, 224–31.

64. *U.S. Budget FY00,* 237–38, 333.

65. Blank 1997, 108, 272–73.

66. Ibid., 165–66.

67. Ibid., 167–73.

68. Ibid., 108; Levitan et al. 1998, 111–12; Wolfe 1996, 1.

69. *U.S. Budget FY00,* 237–38.

70. Carville 1996, xvii.

71. As noted in chapter 4, Social Security gives substantial cash assistance to the *elderly* poor, and Supplemental Security Income (SSI) helps impoverished elderly and disabled people.

72. U.S. Department of Health and Human Services 1996, sec. 8; Levitan et al. 1998, 69–80; Blank 1997, 98–103.

73. U.S. Department of Health and Human Services 1996, sec. 8; Levitan et al. 1998, 79, 70, 71; Blank 1997, 100.

74. Blank 1997, 86–88, 100–101; Levitan et al. 1998, 71.

75. Edin and Lein 1997. See Green and MacColl 1983 and the inspiring portraits of struggling welfare mothers in Zucchino 1997.

76. Gilens (1999) demonstrates the critical influence on antiwelfare sentiments of racism as well as the feeling that the poor are "undeserving"; he links these attitudes to media stereotypes. Kinder and Sanders (1998, chaps. 7–9) highlight racist tactics in election campaigns.

77. Blank 1997, 303 fn. 13, 101–2. Levitan et al. (1998, 76, 73, 78, 72) provide some qualifications to these points.

78. Moffitt 1992, esp. 31; Blank 1997, 149–50; Levitan et al. 1998, 73.

79. Blank 1997, 151.

80. Ibid., 102–3, 153, 157. See Bane and Ellwood 1994, chap. 3.

81. Blank 1997, 154–56; Levitan et al. 1998, 79.

82. Blank 1997, 151–57.

83. Moffitt 1992; Robins 1985; Danziger et al. 1981; Blank 1997, 146–47. We arrived at the $337 figure by subtracting the third line of Blank's table 4.2 from the second line.

84. Blank 1997, 147. The $2,270 figure results from subtracting line 1 of Blank's table 4.2 from line 3.

85. Center on Budget and Policy Priorities web site, "EIC Benefits for Tax Year 1997 at Various Income Levels" (visited 8/5/99).

86. U.S. Department of Health and Human Services web site, "Comparison of Prior Law and the Personal Responsibility and Work Opportunity Reconciliation Act of 1996" (visited 8/9/99); Levitan et al. 1998, 81–83; *U.S. Budget FY00,* 248.

87. Trutko et al. (1999) indicate that supportive services under welfare-to-work grants got under way more slowly than anticipated. From the Urban Institute web site (visited 11/16/99).

88. Seelye 1999; Pear 1998b; Associated Press 1999; Goldberg 1999a.

89. Goldberg 1999a, 1999b.

90. Associated Press 1999; Loprest 1999, pp. 6, 9, 20, charts 1, 5, tbl. 4; Children's Defense Fund and National Coalition for the Homeless 1998.

91. On the merits of universal versus means-tested programs, see Garfinkel 1982 and Skocpol 1995, chap. 8.

92. Hubert Humphrey, for example, attacked George McGovern's demogrant proposal in these terms in the 1972 presidential primaries.

93. A similar objection applies to Ackerman and Alstott's (1999) otherwise admirable proposal to give a large cash "stake" to every American at age twenty-one.

94. Rushevsky and Patel 1998; Sundquist 1968.

95. Moynihan 1973.

96. See Imig 1996;, Skocpol 1995, Conclusion; Piven and Cloward 1977.

97. Center for Responsive Politics web site, "Myth 2: The Special Interests Balance Each Other Out," and "Who Paid for This Election? Summary; Industry/Interest Group Contributions in 1997–98" (obtained 7/29/99 and 8/5/99, respectively).

98. Gans (1995) documents recent wars of words against the poor, including tendentious use of the dubious term "underclass." On that concept and its relation to reality, see Jencks and Peterson 1991; Jencks 1992; and Katz 1993.

99. Katz 1996; Skocpol 1992.

100. See Gilens 1999; Kushnick and Jennings 1999.

101. See Smith 1991.

102. Piven and Cloward 1971, 1977.

103. Franklin D. Roosevelt, annual message to Congress, January 6, 1941, in Rauch 1957, 272–75; UN General Assembly 1948, 135.

104. The gross domestic product stood at $8,538 billion, in annual terms, in the third quarter of 1998 (U.S. Office of the President 1999, 356), when the U.S. population was about 270 million.

Chapter Nine

1. Schwarz 1988 [1983].

2. Even if extensive economic and racial desegregation of neighborhoods is not feasible, some measures can be taken to ameliorate segregation—enforcing measures against discrimination in housing sales and rentals, for example, and ensuring that rental vouchers can be used everywhere. More equal incomes, too, would greatly reduce the stratification of neighborhoods. In addition, the crippling effects of housing segregation on Americans' information about each other can be at least somewhat counteracted by college-age internships to different neighborhoods, volunteer programs to disadvantaged neighborhoods (e.g., Americorps), and the like.

3. Based on Dow Jones Industrial Average closing values of 824.57 on January 2, 1980, and 10,655.15 on August 10, 1999. The New York Stock Exchange (NYSE) composite index rose nearly as rapidly: from 60.69 on January 2, 1980, to 648.13 on June 30, 1999, making it nearly *eleven times* as high. Figures from NYSE online and Dow Jones online.

4. The turnouts of the U.S. voting-age population in presidential years 1988, 1992, and 1996 were only 50.1 percent, 55.1 percent, and 49.1 percent, respectively. In off-

years 1986, 1990, and 1994, the turnouts were a miserable 36.4 percent, 36.5 percent, and 38.8 percent, respectively. Information Please web site, based on data from Federal Election Commission (visited 8/10/99).

5. Just 6 percent of low-income people said they gave money (an average of $86 each), while 56 percent of high-income people gave an average of more than $322 each. (Contributions by the few respondents with incomes over $125,000 averaged $1,183, but they have conservatively been counted in the $322 group.) Verba et al. 1995, 190, 192.

REFERENCES

Aaron, Henry J. 1972. *Shelter and Subsidies: Who Benefits from Federal Housing Policies?* Washington, D.C.: Brookings.

———. 1975. *Who Pays the Property Tax?* Washington, D.C.: Brookings.

———. 1999. A Bad Idea Whose Time Will Never Come. In *Controversies in American Public Policy,* ed. John Hird and Michael Reese, 217–23. New York: St. Martin's/Worth.

Aaron, Henry J., and Joseph A. Pechman, eds. 1981. *How Taxes Affect Economic Behavior.* Washington, D.C.: Brookings.

Aaron, Henry J., and Robert D. Reischauer. 1998. *Countdown to Reform: The Great Social Security Debate.* New York: Century Foundation Press.

———, eds. 1999. *Setting National Priorities: The 2000 Elections and Beyond.* Washington, D.C.: Brookings.

Abel, Andrew B., and Ben S. Bernanke. 1998. *Macroeconomics.* 3rd ed. Reading, Mass.: Addison-Wesley.

Abowd, John M., and Richard B. Freeman, eds. 1991. *Immigration, Trade, and the Labor Market.* Chicago: University of Chicago Press.

Abowd, John M., and Thomas Lemieux. 1991. The Effects of International Competition on Collective Bargaining Outcomes: A Comparison of the United States and Canada. In Abowd and Freeman (1991, 343–67).

Ackerman, Bruce A., and Anne Alstott. 1999. *The Stakeholder Society.* New Haven, Conn.: Yale University Press.

References

Alan Guttmacher Institute. 1997. Title X and the U.S. Family Planning Effort. From website, agi-usa.org.

Albert, Michel. 1993. *Capitalism against Capitalism,* trans. Paul Haviland. London: Whurr.

Aldrich, John H. 1995. *Why Parties? The Origin and Transformation of Political Parties in America.* Chicago: University of Chicago Press.

Alic, John A., Lewis M. Branscomb, Harvey Brooks, Ashton B. Carter, and Gerald L. Epstein. 1992. *Beyond Spinoff: Military and Commercial Technologies in a Changing World.* Boston: Harvard Business School Press.

Altonji, Joseph G., and David Card. 1991. The Effects of Immigration on the Labor Market Outcomes of Less-Skilled Natives. In Abowd and Freeman (1991, 201–34).

Amenta, Edwin. 1998. *Bold Relief: Institutional Politics and the Origins of Modern American Social Policy.* Princeton, N.J.: Princeton University Press.

Anderson, Gerard F., and Jean-Pierre Poullier. 1999. Health Spending, Access, and Outcomes: Trends in Industrialized Countries. *Health Affairs* 18(3).

Anderson, Sarah, John Cavanagh, Ralph Estes, Chuck Collins, and Chris Hartman. 1999. *A Decade of Executive Excess: The 1990s.* Washington, D.C.: Institute for Policy Studies.

Anyon, Jean. 1980. Social Class and the Hidden Curriculum of Work. *Journal of Education* 162:67–92. Reprinted in Kretovics and Nussel (1994, 253–76).

Arnold, R. Douglas, Michael J. Graetz, and Alicia Munnell, eds. 1998. *Framing the Social Security Debate: Values, Politics, and Economics.* Washington, D.C.: National Academy of Social Insurance.

Associated Press. 1999. Most Leaving Welfare Remain Poor. *San Francisco Chronicle,* May 12, A6.

Atkinson, A. B. 1998. *Poverty in Europe.* Malden, Mass.: Blackwell.

———. 1999. *The Economic Consequences of Rolling Back the Welfare State.* Cambridge, Mass.: MIT Press.

Atkinson, Anthony, Lee Rainwater, and Timothy Smeeding. 1995a. Income Distribution in Advanced Economies. Working Paper no. 120. Syracuse, N.Y.: Syracuse University.

———. 1995b. *Income Distribution in OECD Countries.* Paris: Organization for Economic Cooperation and Development.

Baker, Dean, and Mark Weisbrot. 1999. *Social Security: The Phony Crisis.* Chicago: University of Chicago Press.

Ball, Robert M., with Thomas N. Bethell. 1998. *Straight Talk about Social Security.* New York: Century Foundation Press.

Bane, Mary Jo, and David T. Ellwood. 1994. *Welfare Realities: From Rhetoric to Reform.* Cambridge, Mass.: Harvard University Press.

References

Barlett, Donald, and James Steel. 1994. *America: Who Really Pays the Taxes?* New York: Simon & Schuster.

Barnett, W. S. 1998. Long-Term Effects on Cognitive Development and School Success. In Barnett and Boocock (1998, 11–44).

Barnett, W. Steven, and Sarane Spence Boocock, eds. 1998. *Early Care and Education for Children in Poverty.* Albany: State University of New York Press.

Barnow, Burt S. 1987. The Impact of CETA Programs on Earnings: A Review of the Literature. *Journal of Human Resources* 22(2): 157–93.

Barr, Nicholas. 1993. *The Economics of the Welfare State.* 2nd ed. Stanford, Calif.: Stanford University Press.

———. 1998. *The Economics of the Welfare State.* 3rd ed. Stanford, Calif.: Stanford University Press.

Barro, Robert J. 1997. *Determinants of Economic Growth: A Cross-Country Empirical Study.* Cambridge, Mass.: MIT Press.

Barstow, David. 1999. ATM Cards Fail to Live Up to Promises to Poor. *New York Times,* August 16, 1, 21.

Bartel, Ann P., and Marianne J. Koch. 1991. Internal Migration of U.S. Immigrants. In Abowd and Freeman (1991, 121–34).

Bassi, Laurie J., and Orley Ashenfelter. 1986. The Effect of Direct Job Creation and Training Programs on Low-Skilled Workers. In Danziger and Weinberg (1986, 133–51).

Bauman, Kurt. 1998. Direct Measures of Poverty as Indicators of Economic Need: Evidence from the Survey of Income and Program Participation. Technical Working Paper no. 30. Washington, D.C.: Population Division, U.S. Bureau of the Census.

Baumol, William J., and Alan S. Blinder. 1997. *Macroeconomics: Principles and Policy.* 7th ed. Fort Worth, Tex.: Dryden Press.

Becker, Gary Stanley. 1993. *Human Capital: A Theoretical and Empirical Analysis, with Special Reference to Education.* 3rd ed. Chicago: University of Chicago Press.

Beecher, Jonathan, and Richard Bienvenue. 1971. *The Utopian Vision of Charles Fourier.* Columbia, Mo.: University of Missouri Press.

Begg, David K. H. 1982. *The Rational Expectations Revolution in Macroeconomics: Theories and Evidence.* Baltimore: Johns Hopkins University Press.

Bell, Derrick. 1996. *Faces at the Bottom of the Well.* New York: Basic.

Bentham, Jeremy. 1970 [1789, 1823]. *An Introduction to the Principles of Morals and Legislation,* ed. J. H. Burns and H. L. A. Hart. London: Althone.

Bergmann, Barbara R. 1996. Child Care: The Key to Ending Child Poverty. In Garfinkel, Hochschild, and McLanahan (1996, 112–35).

Bird, Kai. 1992. *The Chairman: John J. McCloy and the Making of the American Establishment.* New York: Simon & Schuster.

Birnbaum, Jeffrey H. 1993. *The Lobbyists: How Influence Peddlers Work Their Way in Washington.* New York: Times Books.

Birnbaum, Jeffrey H., and Allan S. Murray. 1988. *Showdown at Gucci Gulch: Lawmakers, Lobbyists, and the Unlikely Triumph of Tax Reform.* New York: Random House.

Blakey, Roy G., and Gladys C. Blakey. 1940. *The Federal Income Tax.* New York: Longmans, Green.

Blanchard, Oliver. 1997. *Macroeconomics.* Upper Saddle River, N.J.: Prentice-Hall.

Blank, Rebecca M. 1997. *It Takes a Nation: A New Agenda for Fighting Poverty.* Princeton, N.J.: Princeton University Press.

Blank, Rebecca M., and Alan S. Blinder. 1986. Macroeconomics, Income Distribution, and Poverty. In Danziger and Weinberg (1986, 180–208).

Blau, Peter, and Otis Dudley Duncan. 1967. *The American Occupational Structure.* New York: Wiley.

Blaug, Mark. 1996. *Economic Theory in Retrospect.* Cambridge, England: Cambridge University Press.

Blecker, Robert. 1999. *Taming Global Finance.* Washington, D.C.: GPI.

Block, Fred L. 1977a. *The Origins of International Economic Disorder: A Study of United States International Monetary Policy from World War II to the Present.* Berkeley: University of California Press.

———. 1977b. The Ruling Class Does Not Rule: Notes on the Marxist Theory of the State. *Socialist Revolution* 7(3): 6–28.

Bluestone, Barry. 1994. The Inequality Express. *American Prospect* 20 (winter): 81–93.

Bluestone, Barry, and Bennett Harrison. 1982. *The Deindustrialization of America.* New York: Basic.

Blum, Walter J., and Harry Kalven, Jr. 1953. *The Uneasy Case for Progressive Taxation.* Chicago: University of Chicago Press.

Boix, Charles. 1997. *Political Parties, Growth and Equality.* Cambridge: Cambridge University Press.

Boocock, S. S., and M. Larner. 1998. Long-Term Outcomes in Other Nations. In Barnett and Boocock (1998, 45–76).

Borjas, George. 1990. *Friends or Strangers.* New York: Basic.

Borjas, George J., Richard B. Freeman, and Kevin Lang. 1991. Undocumented Mexican-Born Workers in the United States: How Many, How Permanent? In Abowd and Freeman (1991, 77–100).

Boston Globe. 1999. Number of Blacks in Jail Rising Toward 1 Million. *San Francisco Chronicle,* March 8, A9.

Bowen, Howard R. 1997 [1977]. *Investment in Learning: The Individual and Social Value of American Higher Education.* Baltimore: Johns Hopkins University Press.

References

Bowles, Samuel, and Herbert Gintis. 1998. *Recasting Egalitarianism: New Rules for Communities, States and Markets.* New York: Verso.

Braun, Denny. 1997. *The Rich Get Richer.* 2nd ed. Chicago: Nelson-Hall.

Breslow, Marc. 1996. Is the U.S. Making Progress? Unlike the GDP, a New Measure Says "No." *Current Economic Issues,* 4th ed. (March/April), Article 1.

Bridges, Amy. 1986. Becoming American: The Working Classes in the United States before the Civil War. In Katznelson and Zolberg (1986, 157–96).

Brittain, John A. 1978. *Inheritance and the Inequality of Material Wealth.* Washington, D.C.: Brookings.

Browning, Edgar K., and William R. Johnson. 1984. The Trade-Off between Equality and Efficiency. *Journal of Political Economy* 92:175–203.

Brownlee, W. Elliott. 1996. *Federal Taxation in America: A Short History.* New York: Cambridge University Press.

Burch, Philip H., Jr. 1980, 1981. *Elites in American History.* 3 vols. New York: Holmes & Meier.

Burnham, Walter Dean. 1970. *Critical Elections and the Mainsprings of American Politics.* New York: Norton.

Burtless, Gary. 1981. Comment. In Aaron and Pechman (1981, 76–83).

———. 1987. The Work Response to a Guaranteed Income: A Survey of Experimental Evidence. In Munnell (1987, 22–52).

———, ed. 1996a. *Does Money Matter? The Effect of School Resources on Student Achievement and Adult Success.* Washington, D.C.: Brookings.

———. 1996b. Comments. In Slemrod (1996, 170–75).

———. 1998. Can the Labor Market Absorb Three Million Welfare Recipients? *Focus* (University of Wisconsin-Madison Institute for Research on Poverty) 19(3): 1–6.

Butterfield, Fox. 1999. Number of Inmates Reaches Record 1.8 Million. *New York Times,* March 15, A14.

Card, David, and Alan B. Krueger. 1995. *Myth and Measurement: The New Economics of the Minimum Wage.* Princeton, N.J.: Princeton University Press.

Carville, James. 1996. *We're Right, They're Wrong: A Handbook for Spirited Progressives.* New York: Random House.

Case, Karl, and Ray Fair. 1999. *Principles of Economics.* 5th ed. Upper Saddle River, N.J.: Prentice-Hall.

Caulkins, Jonathan P., C. Peter Rydell, William L. Schwabe, and James Chiesa. 1997. *Mandatory Minimum Drug Sentences: Throwing Away the Key or the Taxpayers' Money?* Santa Monica, Calif.: RAND Corp.

Ceglowski, Deborah. 1998. *Inside a Head Start Center.* New York: Teachers College Press, Columbia University.

Center for Public Integrity. 1994. *Well-Healed: Inside Lobbying for Health Care Reform.* Washington, D.C.: Center for Public Integrity.

Center on Budget and Policy Priorities. 1998. Reinvesting Welfare Savings: Aiding Needy Families and Strengthening State Welfare Reform. March 30. From CBPP web site (visited 8/3/99).

Children's Defense Fund and National Coalition for the Homeless. 1998. *Welfare to What? Early Findings on Family Hardship and Well-Being.* Washington, D.C.: Children's Defense Fund and National Coalition for the Homeless.

Chubb, John E., and Terry M. Moe. 1990. *Politics, Markets, and America's Schools.* Washington, D.C.: Brookings.

Citizens for Tax Justice. 1996. State & Local Taxes Hit Poor & Middle Class Far Harder Than the Wealthy. Press release. June 26.

———. 1998. Want to Slash Taxes on the Wealthy? Repeal the Estate Tax. *CTJ Update,* March, 1–3.

Citro, Constance F., and Robert T. Michael, eds. 1995. *Measuring Poverty: A New Approach.* Washington, D.C.: National Academy Press.

Clayton, Richard, and Jonas Pontusson. 1998. Welfare-State Retrenchment Revisited: Entitlement Cuts, Public Sector Restructuring, and Inegalitarian Trends in Advanced Capitalist Societies. *World Politics* 51(1): 67–98.

Cobb, Clifford, and John B. Cobb, Jr. 1994. *The Green National Product.* Lantham: Human Economy Center.

Cobb, Clifford, Ted Halstead, and Jonathan Rowe. 1995. *The Genuine Progress Indicator: Summary of Data and Methodology.* Lantham: Human Economy Center.

Coleman, James S. 1968. The Concept of Equality of Educational Opportunity. *Harvard Educational Review* 38:7–22. Reprinted in Kretovics and Nussel (1994, 18–31).

———. 1981. Quality and Equality in American Education: Public and Catholic Schools. *Phi Delta Kappan* 63:159–64. Reprinted in Kretovics and Nussel (1994, 228–38).

Cook, Fay Lomax. 1979. *Who Should Be Helped? Public Support for Social Services.* Beverly Hills, Calif.: Sage.

Cook, Fay Lomax, and Edith J. Barrett. 1992. *Support for the American Welfare State: The Views of Congress and the Public.* New York: Columbia University Press.

Costa, Dora L. 1998. *The Evolution of Retirement: An American Economic History, 1880–1990.* Chicago: University of Chicago Press.

Cox, Ronald W., and Daniel Skidmore-Hess. 1999. *U.S. Politics and the Global Economy: Corporate Power, Conservative Shift.* Boulder, Colo.: Lynne Rienner.

Csikszentmihalyi, Mihaly. 1990. *Flow: The Psychology of Optimal Experience.* New York: Harper & Row.

Curry, George, and Cornel West, eds. 1996. *The Affirmative Action Debate.* Ann Arbor: University of Michigan Press.

Daly, Gerald. 1996. *Homeless: Policies, Strategies, and Life on the Street.* New York: Routledge.

Danziger, Sheldon, and Peter Gottschalk. 1995. *America Unequal.* Cambridge, Mass.: Harvard University Press.

Danziger, Sheldon, Robert Haveman, and Robert Plotnick. 1981. How Income Transfers Affect Work, Savings, and the Income Distribution: A Critical Review. *Journal of Economic Literature* 97(3): 975–1028.

Danziger, Sheldon H., Gary D. Sandefur, and Daniel H. Weinberg, eds. 1994. *Confronting Poverty: Prescriptions for Change.* Cambridge, Mass.: Harvard University Press.

Danziger, Sheldon H., and Daniel H. Weinberg, eds. 1986. *Fighting Poverty: What Works and What Doesn't.* Cambridge, Mass.: Harvard University Press.

Dark, Taylor E. 1999. *The Unions and the Democrats: An Enduring Alliance.* Ithaca, N.Y.: Cornell University Press.

Dewey, John. 1916. *Democracy and Education.* New York: Macmillan.

Diamond, Peter A. 1999. *What Stock Market Returns to Expect for the Future?* Chestnut Hill, Mass.: Center for Retirement Research at Boston College.

Dickert, Stacy, Scott Houser, and John Karl Scholz. 1995. The Earned Income Tax Credit and Transfer Programs: A Study of Labor Market and Program Participation. In *Tax Policy and the Economy,* vol. 9, ed. James M. Poterba. Cambridge, Mass.: MIT Press.

Dobelstein, Andrew W. 1996. *Social Welfare Policy and Analysis.* 2nd ed. Chicago: Nelson-Hall.

Domhoff, G. William. 1990. *The Power Elite and the State: How Policy Is Made in America.* New York: Aldine de Gruyter.

———. 1996. *State Autonomy or Class Dominance? Case Studies on Policy Making in America.* New York: Aldine de Gruyter.

Dorn, Edwin, ed. 1989. *Who Defends America? Race, Sex, and Class in the Armed Forces.* Washington, D.C.: Joint Center for Political Studies Press.

Downs, Anthony. 1957. *An Economic Theory of Democracy.* New York: Harper.

Drew, Elizabeth. 1998. *Whatever It Takes: The Real Struggle for Political Power in America.* Updated ed. New York: Penguin.

———. 1999. *The Corruption of American Politics: What Went Wrong and Why.* Secaucus, N.J.: Carol Publishing Group.

Dunn, Charles, and Martin Slann. 1994. *American Government in Comparative Perspective.* New York: HarperCollins.

Dye, Thomas R. 1986. *Who's Running America? The Conservative Years.* 4th ed. Englewood Cliffs, N.J.: Prentice-Hall.

———. 1995. *Who's Running America?* 6th ed. Englewood Cliffs, N.J.: Prentice-Hall.

Easterlin, Richard A. 1974. Does Economic Growth Improve the Human Lot? Some Empirical Evidence. In *Essays in Honor of Moses Abramovitz,* ed. Paul David and Melvin Reder. New York: Academic Press.

Edgeworth, F. Y. 1925. *Papers Relating to Political Economy.* London: Macmillan.

References

Edin, Katherine, and Laura Lein. 1997. *Making Ends Meet: How Single Mothers Survive Welfare and Low-Wage Work.* New York: Russell Sage.

Edsall, Thomas Byrne. 1984. *The New Politics of Inequality.* New York: W. W. Norton.

Ehrenreich, Barbara. 1999. Nickel-and-Dimed: On (Not) Getting By in America. *Harpers Magazine,* January, 37–52.

Eisinger, Peter K. 1998. *Toward an End to Hunger in America.* Washington, D.C.: Brookings.

Eisner, Robert. 1986. *How Real Is the Federal Deficit?* New York: Free Press.

———. 1994. *The Misunderstood Economy: What Counts and How to Count It.* Boston: Harvard Business School Press.

Elazar, Daniel Judah. 1966. *American Federalism: A View from the States.* New York: Crowell.

Esping-Andersen, Gosta. 1990. *The Three Worlds of Welfare Capitalism.* Princeton, N.J.: Princeton University Press.

Ethier, Wilfred J. 1995. *Modern International Economics.* 3rd ed. New York: Norton.

Evans, Sara M., and Barbara J. Nelson. 1989. *Wage Justice: Comparable Worth and the Paradox of Technocratic Reform.* Chicago: University of Chicago Press.

Farley, Reynolds, and William H. Fry. 1994. Changes in Segregation of Whites from Blacks: Small Steps toward a More Integrated Society. *American Sociological Review* 59:23–45.

Feigenbaum, Harvey, Jeffrey Henig, and Chris Mamnett. 1999. *Shrinking the State: The Political Underpinnings of Privatization.* New York: Cambridge University Press.

Ferguson, Thomas. 1984. From "Normalcy" to New Deal: Industrial Structure, Party Competition, and American Public Policy in the Great Depression. *International Organization* 38:41–92. Reprinted in Ferguson (1995, 113–72).

———. 1995. *Golden Rule: The Investment Theory of Party Competition and the Logic of Money-Driven Political Systems.* Chicago: University of Chicago Press.

Ferguson, Thomas, and Joel Rogers, eds. 1981. *The Hidden Election: Politics and Economics in the 1980 Presidential Campaign.* New York: Pantheon.

———, eds. 1986. *Right Turn: The Decline of the Democrats and the Future of American Politics.* New York: Hill and Wang.

Fischer, Claude S., Michael Hout, Martin Sanchez Jankowski, Samuel R. Lucas, Ann Swidler, and Kim Voss. 1996. *Inequality by Design: Cracking the Bell Curve Myth.* Princeton, N.J.: Princeton University Press.

Fishkin, James S. 1983. *Justice, Equal Opportunity, and the Family.* New Haven, Conn.: Yale University Press.

Flora, Peter, and Arnold Heidenheimer, eds. 1981. *The Development of Welfare States in Europe and America.* New Brunswick, N.J.: Transaction.

References

Foner, Philip S. 1955, 1962, 1965. *History of the Labor Movement in the United States.* 4 vols. New York: International Publishers.

Forbath, William E. 1991. *Law and the Shaping of the American Labor Movement.* Cambridge, Mass.: Harvard University Press.

Frank, Robert H. 1996. Consumption Externalities and the Financing of Social Services. In Fuchs (1996, 175–90).

Frank, Robert H., and Philip J. Cook. 1995. *The Winner-Take-All Society: Why the Few at the Top Get So Much More Than the Rest of Us.* New York: Penguin.

Frede, E. C. 1998. Preschool Program Quality in Programs for Children in Poverty. In Barnett and Boocock (1998, 77–98).

Free, Lloyd A., and Hadley Cantril. 1968. *The Political Beliefs of Americans.* New York: Simon & Schuster.

Freeman, Richard B., ed. 1994. *Working under Different Rules.* New York: Russell Sage.

Freeman, Richard B., and Lawrence F. Katz. 1991. Industrial Wage and Employment Determination in an Open Economy. In Abowd and Freeman (1991, 235–59).

———. 1994. Rising Wage Inequality: The United States vs. Other Advanced Countries. In Freeman (1994, 29–62).

Friedman, Benjamin M. 1988. *Day of Reckoning: The Consequences of American Economic Policy under Reagan and After.* New York: Random.

Friedman, David. 1973. *The Machinery of Freedom.* New York: Harper.

Friedman, Milton. 1962. *Capitalism and Freedom.* Chicago: University of Chicago Press.

———. 1968. The Role of Monetary Policy. *American Economic Review* 58(1): 1–17.

Friedman, Milton, and Rose D. Friedman. 1980. *Free to Choose.* New York: Avon.

Friedman, Milton, and Anna Jacobson Schwartz. 1963. *A Monetary History of the United States, 1867–1960.* Princeton, N.J.: Princeton University Press.

Frost, Jennifer J., and Michele Bolzan. 1997. The Provision of Public-Sector Services by Family Planning Agencies in 1995. *Family Planning Perspectives* 29(1): 6–14.

Fuchs, Victor R., ed. 1996. *Individual and Social Responsibility: Child Care, Education, Medical Care, and Long-Term Care in America.* Chicago: University of Chicago Press.

———. 1998 [1974]. *Who Shall Live? Health, Economics and Social Choice.* Expanded ed. River Edge, N.J.: World Scientific.

Fullerton, Don, and Diane Lim Rogers. 1993. *Who Bears the Lifetime Tax Burden?* Washington, D.C.: Brookings.

Galbraith, James K. 1998. *Created Unequal: The Crisis in American Pay.* New York: Free Press.

References

Gans, Herbert J. 1995. *The War against the Poor: The Underclass and Antipoverty Policy.* New York: Basic.

Garfinkel, Irwin, ed. 1982. *Income-Tested Transfer Programs: The Case For and Against.* New York: Academic.

Garfinkel, Irwin, Jennifer L. Hochschild, and Sara S. McLanahan, eds. 1996. *Social Policies for Children.* Washington, D.C.: Brookings.

Garrett, Geoffrey. 1998. *Partisan Politics in the Global Economy.* New York: Cambridge University Press.

Garrett, Geoffrey, and Peter Lange. 1991. Political Responses to Interdependence: What's Left for the Left? *International Organization* 45(4): 539–64.

Gibbs, David N. 1991. *The Political Economy of Third World Intervention: Mines, Money, and U.S. Policy in the Congo Crisis.* Chicago: University of Chicago Press.

Giddens, Anthony. 1994. *Beyond Left and Right.* Stanford, Calif.: Stanford University Press.

Gilens, Martin. 1999. *Why Americans Hate Welfare: Race, Media, and the Politics of Antipoverty Policy.* Chicago: University of Chicago Press.

Gilles, Stephen G. 1998. Why Parents Should Choose. In Peterson and Hassel (1998, 395–407).

Gold, S. 1991. Changes in State Government Finances in the 1980s. *National Tax Journal* 64:1–20.

Goldberg, Carey. 1999a. Most Get Work after Welfare, Studies Suggest. *New York Times,* April 17, 1, 11.

———. 1999b. Welfare's Missing in Action. *New York Times,* May 2, WK4.

Golden, Miriam, Michael Wallerstein, and Peter Lange. 1999. Postwar Trade-Union Organization and Industrial Relations in Twelve Countries. In Kitschelt et al. (1999, 194–230).

Goldfield, Michael. 1987. *The Decline of Organized Labor in the United States.* Chicago: University of Chicago Press.

———. 1989. Worker Insurgency, Radical Organization, and New Deal Labor Legislation. *American Political Science Review* 83(4): 1257–82.

———. 1997. *The Color of Politics: Race and the Mainsprings of American Politics.* New York: New Press.

Goldstein, Judith. 1993. *Ideas, Interests, and American Trade Policy.* Ithaca, N.Y.: Cornell University Press.

Goode, Richard. 1951. *The Corporation Income Tax.* New York: Wiley.

Goodman, Ellen. 1999a. Paycheck Gender Gap. *San Francisco Chronicle,* March 16, A19.

———. 1999b. Working Moms Do No Harm. *San Francisco Chronicle,* March 4, A23.

Goodwin, Donald W. 1981. *Alcoholism: The Facts.* Oxford: Oxford University Press.

References

Goodwyn, Lawrence. 1978. *The Populist Moment.* New York: Oxford University Press.

Gordon, Robert J. 1990. *Macroeconomics.* 5th ed. New York: HarperCollins.

Gould, Stephen Jay. 1981. *The Mismeasure of Man.* New York: W. W. Norton.

Granovetter, Mark S. 1995. *Getting a Job: A Study of Contacts and Careers.* 2nd ed. Chicago: University of Chicago Press.

Green, Donald Philip, and Jonathan S. Krasno. 1988. Salvation for the Spendthrift Incumbent: Re-estimating the Effect of Campaign Spending in House Elections. *American Journal of Political Science* 32:884–907.

Green, Mark, and Gail MacColl, with Robert Nelson and Christopher Power. 1983. *There He Goes Again: Ronald Reagan's Reign of Error.* New York: Pantheon.

Green, Max. 1996. *Epitaph for American Labor: How Union Leaders Lost Touch with America.* Washington, D.C.: AEI Press.

Greenberg, Edward S. 1999. Workplace Democracy in the Core Countries: Problems and Prospects. Paper delivered at the annual meeting of the European Consortium on Political Research, Mannheim, Germany, March 26–31.

Greenberg, Stanley B., and Theda Skocpol, eds. 1997. *The New Majority.* New Haven, Conn.: Yale University Press.

Greene, Jay P., Paul E. Peterson, and Jiangtao Du. 1998. School Choice in Milwaukee: A Randomized Experiment. In Peterson and Hassel (1998, 335–56).

Greenhouse, Steven. 1998. Groups Reach Agreement for Curtailing Sweatshops. *New York Times,* November 11, A18.

Greenstone, J. David. 1977. *Labor in American Politics.* Chicago: University of Chicago Press.

Greer, Scott. 1998. Health Care as Labor Market Strategy: American Business and the Failure of Health Care Reform. Paper presented at the SASE annual conference, UN campus. Vienna, Austria, August 15–20.

Greider, William. 1987. *Secrets of the Temple: How the Federal Reserve Runs the Country.* New York: Simon & Schuster.

———. 1997. *One World, Ready or Not: The Manic Logic of Global Capitalism.* New York: Simon & Schuster.

Grossman, Richard L., and Frank T. Adams. 1996. Exercising Power over Corporations through State Charters. In Mander and Goldsmith (1996, 374–89).

Groves, Harold M. 1974. *Tax Philosophers: Two Hundred Years of Thought in Great Britain and the United States,.* ed. Donald J. Curran. Madison: University of Wisconsin Press.

Gustafsson, S. S., and F. P. Stafford. 1998. Equity-Efficiency Tradeoffs and Government Policy in the United States, the Netherlands, and Sweden. In Barnett and Boocock (1998, 211–44).

Gutmann, Amy. 1987. *Democratic Education.* Princeton, N.J.: Princeton University Press.

Hacker, Andrew. 1997. *Money: Who Has How Much and Why.* New York: Simon & Schuster.

———. 1999. Who's Sticking to the Union? *New York Review of Books,* February 18, 45–48.

Hacker, Jacob S. 1997. *The Road to Nowhere: The Genesis of President Clinton's Plan for Health Security.* Princeton, N.J.: Princeton University Press.

———. 1998. The Historical Logic of National Health Insurance: Structure and Sequence in the Development of British, Canadian, and U.S. Medical Policy. *Studies in American Political Development* 12 (spring): 57–130.

Hall, Peter A., ed. 1989. *The Political Power of Economic Ideas: Keynesianism across Nations.* Princeton, N.J.: Princeton University Press.

Hall, Richard, and Frank W. Wayman. 1990. Buying Time: Moneyed Interests and the Mobilization of Bias in Congressional Committees. *American Political Science Review* 84: 797–820.

Halstead, Ted, and Clifford Cobb. 1996. The Need for New Measurements of Progress. In Mander and Goldsmith (1996, 197–206).

Handlin, Oscar, and Mary Flug Handlin. 1969. *Commonwealth: A Study of the Role of Government in the American Economy: Massachusetts, 1774–1861.* Cambridge, Mass.: Harvard University Press.

Hansen, Susan B. 1983. *The Politics of Taxation: Revenue without Representation.* New York: Praeger.

Hansen, W. Lee, and Burton A. Weisbrod. 1969. *Benefits, Cost, and Finance of Public Higher Education.* Chicago: Markham.

Hanushek, Eric A. 1996. School Resources and Student Performance. In Burtless (1996, 43–73).

Harberger, Arnold C. 1962. The Incidence of the Corporation Income Tax. *Journal of Political Economy* 70 (June): 215–40.

———. 1983. The State of the Corporate Tax: Who Pays It? Should It Be Replaced? In Walker and Bloomfield (1983, 161–70).

Hargreaves, Deborah. 1999. Pensions Will Squeeze European Budgets. *Financial Times,* November 23, 3.

Harrington, Michael. 1962. *The Other America: Poverty in the United States.* New York: Macmillan.

Harris, Richard. 1966. *A Sacred Trust.* New York: New American Library.

Hassel, Bryan C. 1998a. The Case for Charter Schools. In Peterson and Hassel (1998, 33–51).

———. 1998b. Charter Schools: Politics and Practice in Four States. In Peterson and Hassel (1998, 249–71).

Hatano, Giyoo, and Kayoko Inagaki. 1987. A Theory of Motivation for Comprehension and Its Application to Mathematics Instruction. In *The Monitoring of School Mathematics: Background Papers,* vol. 2, ed. Thomas A. Romberg and Deborah M.

Stewart, chap. 13. Madison: Wisconsin Center for Education Research, University of Wisconsin.

Hattam, Victoria C. 1992. Institutions and Political Change: Working-Class Formation in England and the United States. In Steinmo, Thelen, and Longstreth (1992, 155–87).

Hausman, Jerry A. 1981a. Income and Payroll Tax Policy and Labor Supply. In Meyer (1981, 173–202).

———. 1981b. Labor Supply. In Aaron and Pechman (1981, 27–72).

Hayek, Friedrich A. von. 1994 [1944]. *The Road to Serfdom.* Chicago: University of Chicago Press.

Heard, Alexander. 1960. *The Costs of Democracy.* Chapel Hill: University of North Carolina Press.

Heckman, James, Anne Layne-Farrar, and Petra Todd. 1996. Does Measured School Quality Really Matter? An Examination of the Earnings-Quality Relationship. In Burtless (1996a, 192–289).

Hedges, Larry V., and Rob Greenwald. 1996. Have Times Changed? The Relation between School Resources and Student Performance. In Burtless (1996a, 74–92).

Heidenheimer, Arnold, Hugh Heclo, and Carolyn Adams. 1990. *Comparative Public Policy.* New York: St. Martin's.

Heinz, John, Edward Lauman, Robert Nelson, and Robert Salisbury. 1993. *The Hollow Core: Private Interests in National Policy Making.* Cambridge, Mass.: Harvard University Press.

Henneman, Todd. 1998. San Jose OKs "Living Wage" Plan. *San Francisco Chronicle,* November 18, 1, 24.

Herrnstein, Richard J., and Charles Murray. 1994. *The Bell Curve: Intelligence and Class Structure in American Life.* New York: Free Press.

Herzenberg, Stephen A., John A. Alic, and Howard Wial. 1998. *New Rules for a New Economy: Employment and Opportunity in Postindustrial America.* Ithaca, N.Y.: Cornell University Press.

Hess, Frederick M. 1999. *Spinning Wheels: The Politics of Urban School Reform.* Washington, D.C.: Brookings.

Hibbs, Douglas A., Jr. 1987. *The American Political Economy: Macroeconomics and Electoral Politics in the United States.* Cambridge, Mass.: Harvard University Press.

———. 1994. The Partisan Model of Macroeconomic Cycles: More Theory and Evidence for the United States. *Economics and Politics* 6(1): 1–23.

Hicks, Alexander M., and Duane H. Swank. 1992. Politics, Institutions, and Welfare Spending in Industrialized Democracies, 1960–82. *American Political Science Review* 86(3): 658–74.

Hightower, Jim. 1997. The Next Best Thing to Slaves. Reprinted in *Funny Times,* November 1998, 7.

Hill, Paul T., Lawrence C. Pierce, and James W. Guthrie. 1997. *Reinventing Public*

Education: How Contracting Can Transform America's Schools. Chicago: University of Chicago Press.

Himmelstein, David U., and Steffie Woolhandler. 1994. *The National Health Program Book: A Source Guide for Advocates.* Monroe, Me.: Common Courage.

Hobbes, Thomas. 1996 [1651]. *Leviathan.* Cambridge, England: Cambridge University Press.

Hoffman, Saul D., and Laurence S. Seidman. 1990. *The Earned Income Tax Credit.* Kalamazoo, Mich.: W. E. Upjohn Institute for Employment Research.

Hofstadter, Richard. 1963. *The Progressive Movement 1900–1915.* Englewood Cliffs, N.J.: Prentice-Hall.

Hollander, Dore. 1996. Nonmarital Childbearing in the United States: A Government Report. *Family Planning Perspectives* 28(1): 29–32, 41.

Holzer, Marc, and Kathe Callahan. 1998. *Government at Work: Best Practices and Model Programs.* Thousand Oaks, Calif.: Sage.

Horwitz, Morton J. 1977. *The Transformation of American Law, 1780–1860.* Cambridge, Mass.: Harvard University Press.

———. 1992. *The Transformation of American Law, 1870–1960: The Crisis of Legal Orthodoxy.* New York: Oxford University Press.

Howard, Christopher. 1997. *The Hidden Welfare State: Tax Expenditures and Social Policy in the United States.* Princeton, N.J.: Princeton University Press.

Hoxby, Caroline M. 1998. Analyzing School Choice Reforms That Use America's Traditional Forms of Parental Choice. In Peterson and Hassel (1998, 133–55).

Huber, Evelyne, Charles Ragin, and John D. Stephens. 1993. Social Democracy, Christian Democracy, Constitutional Structure and the Welfare State. *American Journal of Sociology* 99(3): 711–49.

Huber, Evelyne, and John D. Stephens. 1998. Internationalization and the Social Democratic Model. *Comparative Political Studies* 31(3): 353–97.

Imig, Douglas R. 1996. *Poverty and Power: The Political Representation of Poor Americans.* Lincoln: University of Nebraska Press.

Immergut, Ellen. 1992. The Rules of the Game: The Logic of Health Policy-Making in France, Switzerland and Sweden. In Steinmo, Thelen, and Longstreth (1992, 57–89).

Iversen, Torben, and Thomas R. Cusack. 1999. The Causes of Welfare State Expansion: Deindustrialization or Globalization? Unpublished paper. Cambridge, Mass.: Harvard University, Center for European Studies.

Jackson, Kenneth T. 1985. *Crabgrass Frontier: The Suburbanization of the United States.* New York: Oxford University Press.

Jacobs, Lawrence R. 1993. *The Health of Nations: Public Opinion and the Making of American and British Health Policy.* Ithaca, N.Y.: Cornell University Press.

———. 1995. The Politics of America's Supply State: Health Reform and Medical Technology. *Health Affairs* 14(2): 143–57.

References

Jacobs, Lawrence R., and Robert Y. Shapiro. 1998. Myths and Misunderstandings about Public Opinion toward Social Security. In Arnold, Graetz, and Munnell (1998, 355–88).

———. 2000. *Politicians Don't Pander: Political Manipulation and the Loss of Democratic Responsiveness.* Chicago: University of Chicago Press.

Jacobson, Gary C. 1978. The Effects of Campaign Spending in Congressional Elections. *American Political Science Review* 72:769–83.

Jacoby, Sanford M. 1993. Employers and the Welfare State: The Role of Marion B. Folsom. *Journal of American History* 80(2): 525–56.

James, Estelle, Gary Ferrier, James Smalhout, and Dimitri Vittas. 1999. Mutual Funds and Institutional Investments: What Is the Most Efficient Way to Set Up Individual Accounts in a Social Security System? NBER Working Paper no. W7049. Stanford, Calif: National Bureau of Economic Research.

Jencks, Christopher. 1992. *Rethinking Social Policy: Race, Poverty, and the Underclass.* Cambridge, Mass.: Harvard University Press.

———. 1994. *The Homeless.* Cambridge, Mass.: Harvard University Press.

———. 1996. Comment on School Spending. In Fuchs (1996, 91–105).

Jencks, Christopher, Susan Bartlett, Mary Corcoran, James Crouse, David Eaglesfield, Gregory Jackson, Kent McClelland, Peter Mueser, Michael Olneck, Joseph Schwartz, Sherry Ward, and Jill Williams. 1979. *Who Gets Ahead? The Determinants of Economic Success in America.* New York: Basic.

Jencks, Christopher, and Paul E. Peterson, eds. 1991. *The Urban Underclass.* Washington, D.C.: Brookings.

Jencks, Christopher, and Meredith Phillips, eds. *The Black-White Test Score Gap.* Washington, D.C.: Brookings.

Jencks, Christopher, Marshall Smith, Henry Acland, Mary Jo Bane, David Cohen, Herbert Gintis, Barbara Heyns, and Stephan Michelson. 1972. *Inequality: A Reassessment of the Effect of Family and Schooling in America.* New York: Harper & Row.

Johnson, Nicholas, and Iris J. Lav. 1997. *Are State Taxes Becoming More Regressive?* Washington, D.C.: Center on Budget and Policy Priorities.

Jorgenson, Dale W., and Ralph Landau, eds. 1993. *Tax Reform and the Cost of Capital: An International Comparison.* Washington, D.C.: Brookings.

Kaestle, Carl F. 1983. *Pillars of the Republic: Common Schools and American Society, 1780–1960.* New York: Hill and Wang.

Kasten, Richard, Frank Samartino, and Eric Toder. 1996. Trends in Federal Tax Progressivity, 1980–93. In Slemrod (1996, 9–50).

Katz, Michael B. 1987. *Reconstructing American Education.* Cambridge, Mass.: Harvard University Press.

———. 1990. *The Undeserving Poor: From the War on Poverty to the War on Welfare.* New York: Pantheon.

————, ed. 1993. *The "Underclass" Debate: Views from History.* Princeton, N.J.: Princeton University Press.

————. 1996. *In the Shadow of the Poorhouse: A Social History of Welfare in America.* Tenth anniversary ed., rev. & updated. New York: Basic.

Katzenstein, Peter J. 1984. *Corporatism and Change: Austria, Switzerland, and the Politics of Industry.* Ithaca, N.Y.: Cornell University Press.

————. 1985. *Small States in World Markets: Industrial Policy in Europe.* Ithaca, N.Y.: Cornell University Press.

Katznelson, Ira, and Aristide Zolberg, eds. 1986. *Working-Class Formation: Nineteenth-Century Patterns in Western Europe and the United States.* Princeton, N.J.: Princeton University Press.

Keene, Karlyn. 1983. What Do We Know about the Public's Attitude on Progressivity? *National Tax Journal* 56:371–76.

Keith, Timothy Z., and Ellis B. Page. 1985. Do Catholic High Schools Improve Minority Student Achievement? *Educational Researcher* 22:337–48. Reprinted in Kretovics and Nussel (1994, 239–50).

Keyssar, Alexander. 1986. *Out of Work: The First Century of Unemployment in Massachusetts.* New York: Cambridge University Press.

————. 2000. *The Right to Vote: The Contested History of Democracy in the United States.* New York: Basic. Forthcoming.

Kilborn, Peter T. 1998. Reality of the H.M.O. System Doesn't Live Up to the Dream. *New York Times.* October 5, 1, 16.

Kinder, Donald R., and Lynn M. Sanders. 1996. *Divided by Color: Racial Politics and Democratic Ideals.* Chicago: University of Chicago Press.

King, Ronald Frederick. 1993. *Money, Time and Politics: Investment Tax Subsidies and American Democracy.* New Haven, Conn.: Yale University Press.

Kingdon, John W. 1984. *Agendas, Alternatives, and Public Policies.* Boston: Little, Brown.

Kitschelt, Herbert. 1994. *The Transformation of European Social Democracy.* New York: Cambridge University Press.

Kitschelt, Herbert, Peter Lange, Gary Marks, and John D. Stephens, eds. 1999. *Continuity and Change in Contemporary Capitalism.* New York: Cambridge University Press.

Klausen, Yvette. 1999. The Declining Significance of Male Workers: Trade-Union Responses to Changing Labor Markets. In Kitschelt et al. (1999, 261–91).

Koegel, Paul, et al. 1996. The Causes of Homelessness. In *Homelessness in America,* ed. Jim Baumohl. Phoenix, Ariz.: Oryx Press.

Kohut, Andrew. 1998. *Deconstructing Distrust.* Washington, D.C.: Pew Research Center.

Korpi, Walter. 1983. *The Democratic Class Struggle.* London: Routledge & Kegan Paul.

Kotlikoff, Laurence J., and Jeffrey Sachs. 1999. It's High Time to Privatize. In *Controversies in American Public Policy,* ed. John Hird and Michael Reese, 211–16. New York: St. Martin's/Worth.

Kotz, Nick. 1971. *Let Them Eat Promises: The Politics of Hunger in America.* Garden City, N.Y.: Doubleday.

Kozol, Jonathan. 1991. *Savage Inequalities.* New York: HarperCollins.

Kretovics, Joseph, and Edward J. Nussel, eds. 1994. *Transforming Urban Education.* Boston: Allyn and Bacon.

Kushnick, Louis, and James Jennings. 1999. *A New Introduction to Poverty: The Role of Race, Power, and Politics.* New York: New York University Press.

Kuttner, Robert. 1996. *Everything for Sale: The Virtues and Limits of Markets.* New York: Knopf.

Ladd, Everett Carll, and Karlyn H. Bowman. 1998. *What's Wrong: A Survey of American Satisfaction and Complaint.* Washington, D.C.: AEI Press.

Lafer, Gordon. 1999. Captive Labor: America's Prisoners as Corporate Workforce. *American Prospect* 46 (September–October): 66–71.

LaLonde, Robert J., and Robert H. Topel. 1991. Labor Market Adjustments to Increased Immigration. In Abowd and Freeman (1991, 167–99).

Lambert, Peter J. 1993. *The Distribution and Redistribution of Income: A Mathematical Analysis.* 2nd ed. New York: Manchester University Press.

Lane, Robert Edwards. 1991. *The Market Experience.* New York: Cambridge University Press.

Leff, Mark H. 1983. Taxing the "Forgotten Man": The Politics of Social Security Finance in the New Deal. *Journal of American History* 70(2): 359–81.

———. 1984. *The Limits of Symbolic Reform: The New Deal and Taxation.* New York: Cambridge University Press.

Lerman, Robert I. 1996. Building Hope, Skills, and Careers: Creating a Youth Apprenticeship System. In Garfinkel, Hochschild, and McLanahan (1996, 136–72).

Leuchtenburg, William Edward. 1963. *Franklin D. Roosevelt and the New Deal, 1932–1940.* New York: Harper & Row.

Leung, Frederick. 1999. The Traditional Chinese Views of Mathematics and Education: Implications for Mathematics Education in the New Millennium. In *Rethinking the Mathematics Curriculum,* ed. Celia Hoyles, Candia Morgan, and Geoffrey Woodhouse, 240–47. London: Falmer.

Levine, Andrew. 1998. *Rethinking Liberal Equality: From a "Utopian" Point of View.* Ithaca, N.Y.: Cornell University Press.

Levitan, Sar A., Garth L. Mangum, and Stephen L. Mangum. 1998. *Programs in Aid of the Poor.* 7th ed. Baltimore: Johns Hopkins University Press.

Levy, Frank. 1998. *The New Dollars and Dreams: American Incomes and Economic Change.* New York: Russell Sage.

Lewis, Charles, Alejandro Benes, Meredith O'Brien, and the Center for Public Integrity. 1996. *The Buying of the President.* New York: Avon.

Lijphart, Arend. 1994. Democracies: Forms, Performance, and Constitutional Engineering. *European Journal of Political Research* 15:1–17.

Lindahl, Erik. 1958 [1919]. Just Taxation—A Positive Solution. In Musgrave and Peacock (1958, 168–76).

Lindblom, Charles E. 1977. *Politics and Markets: The World's Political-Economic Systems.* New York: Basic.

Link, Bruce, et al. 1995. Life-time and Five-Year Prevalence of Homelessness in the United States: New Evidence on an Old Debate. *American Journal of Orthopsychiatry* 65(3): 347–54.

Lipset, Seymour Martin. 1996. *American Exceptionalism: A Double-Edged Sword.* New York: W. W. Norton.

Lipset, Seymour Martin, and William Schneider. 1983. *The Confidence Gap: Business, Labor, and Government in the Public Mind.* New York: Free Press.

Locke, John. 1952 [1690]. *The Second Treatise of Government,* ed. Thomas P. Reardon. New York: Macmillan.

———. 1960 [1690]. *Two Treatises on Government,* ed. Peter Lasslett. New York: Mentor.

Locke, Richard, Thomas Kochan, and Michael Piore, eds. 1995. *Employment Relations in a Changing World Economy.* Cambridge, Mass.: MIT Press.

Lohmann, Susanne. 1998. An Information Rationale for the Power of Special Interests. *American Political Science Review* 92(4): 809–27.

Longworth, Richard C. 1998. *Global Squeeze: The Coming Crisis for First-World Nations.* Chicago: Contemporary Books.

Loprest, Pamela. 1999. Families Who Left Welfare: Who Are They and How Are They Doing? Discussion Paper no. 99-02. Washington, D.C.: Urban Institute.

Lubove, Roy. 1968. *The Struggle for Social Security 1900–1935.* Cambridge, Mass.: Harvard University Press.

MacDonald, Maurice. 1977. *Food, Stamps, and Income Maintenance.* New York: Academic Press.

Mackinson, Larry, ed. 1997. *The Big Picture: Where the Money Came From in the 1996 Elections.* Washington, D.C.: Center for Responsive Politics.

Maeroff, Gene I. 1988. Withered Hopes, Stillborn Dreams: The Dismal Panorama of Urban Schools. *Phi Delta Kappan* 69:632–38. Reprinted in Kretovics and Nussel (1994, 32–45).

Mander, Jerry, and Edward Goldsmith, eds. 1996. *The Case against the Global Economy and for a Turn toward the Local.* San Francisco: Sierra Club Books.

Mankiw, N. Gregory. 1998. *Principles of Economics.* Fort Worth, Tex.: Dryden.

Manski, Charles F. 1994. Systemic Educational Reform and Social Mobility: The School Choice Controversy. In Danziger, Sandefur, and Weinberg (1994, 308–29).

References

Marger, Martin. 1999. *Social Inequality*. Mountain View, Calif.: Mayfield.

Markusen, Ann, Peter Hall, Scott Campbell, and Sabina Deitrick. 1991. *The Rise of the Gunbelt*. New York: Oxford University Press.

Marmor, Theodore. 1973. *The Politics of Medicare*. Chicago: Aldine.

———. 1999. *The Politics of Medicare*. 2nd ed. New York: Aldine de Gruyter. Forthcoming.

Marmor, Theodore R., and Jerry L. Mashaw. 1997. The Case for Social Insurance. In Greenberg and Skocpol (1997, 78–108).

Marmor, Theodore R., Jerry L. Mashaw, and Philip L. Harvey. 1990. *America's Misunderstood Welfare State: Persistent Myths, Enduring Realities*. New York: Basic.

Martin, Cathie J. 1991. *Shifting the Burden: The Struggle over Growth and Corporate Taxation*. Chicago: University of Chicago Press.

———. 2000. *Stuck in Neutral: Business and the Politics of Human Capital Investment Policy*. Princeton, N.J.: Princeton University Press. Forthcoming.

Massey, Douglas S., and Nancy A. Denton. 1993. *American Apartheid: Segregation and the Making of the Underclass*. Cambridge, Mass.: Harvard University Press.

Massing, Michael. 1998. The Blue Revolution. *New York Review of Books,* November 19, 32–36.

Mauer, Mark. 1999. *Race to Incarcerate*. New York: New Press.

Mayer, Jane, and Jill Abramson. 1994. *Strange Justice: The Selling of Clarence Thomas*. Boston: Houghton Mifflin.

Mayer, Susan E. 1997. *What Money Can't Buy: Family Income and Children's Life Chances*. Cambridge, Mass.: Harvard University Press.

McCarty, Nolan M., Keith T. Poole, and Howard Rosenthal. 1997. *Income Redistribution and the Realignment of American Politics*. Washington, D.C.: AEI Press.

McChesney, Fred S. 1997. *Money for Nothing: Politicians, Rent Extraction, and Political Extortion*. Cambridge, Mass.: Harvard University Press.

McCloskey, Robert G. 1994. *The American Supreme Court,* revised by Sanford Levinson. Chicago: University of Chicago Press.

McClosky, Herbert, Paul J. Hoffmann, and Rosemary O'Hara. Issue Conflict and Consensus among Party Leaders and Followers. *American Political Science Review* 54(2): 406–27.

McConnell, Grant. 1966. *Private Power and American Democracy*. New York: Knopf.

McGerr, Michael. 1986. *The Decline of Popular Politics*. New York: Oxford University Press.

McKeown, Timothy J. 1999. The Global Economy, Post-Fordism, and Trade Policy in Advanced Capitalist States. In Kitschelt et al. (1999, 11–35).

Meier, Deborah. 1995. *The Power of Their Ideas: Lessons for America from a Small School in Harlem*. Boston: Beacon.

Mellon, Andrew W. 1924. *Taxation: The People's Business*. New York: Macmillan.

Metcalf, Gilbert E. 1996. The Lifetime Incidence of State and Local Taxes: Measuring Changes during the 1980s. In Slemrod (1996, 59–88).

Mettler, Suzanne. 1998. *Dividing Citizens: Gender and Federalism in New Deal Public Policy.* Ithaca, N.Y.: Cornell University Press.

Meyer, Laurence H., ed. 1981. *Supply-Side Effects of Economic Policy.* Boston: Kluwer-Nijhoff.

Mieskowski, Peter M. 1967. On the Theory of Tax Incidence. *Journal of Political Economy* 75 (June): 250–62.

———. 1972. The Property Tax: An Excise Tax or a Profits Tax? *Journal of Public Economics* 1 (April): 73–96.

Mill, John Stuart. 1923 [1848]. *Principles of Political Economy.* London: Longmans.

Miller, Arthur H. 1974. Political Issues and Trust in Government: 1964–1970. *American Political Science Review* 68(3): 951–72.

Miller, Preston J., ed. 1994. *The Rational Expectations Revolution: Readings from the Front Line.* Cambridge, Mass.: MIT Press.

Millman, Joel. 1997. *The Other Americans: How Immigrants Renew Our Country, Our Economy, and Our Values.* New York: Viking.

Mischel, Lawrence, Jared Bernstein, and John Schmitt. 1999. *The State of Working America, 1998–99.* Ithaca, N.Y.: Cornell University Press.

Model, Suzanne. 1993. The Ethnic Niche and the Structure of Opportunity: Immigrants and Minorities in New York City. In *The "Underclass" Debate: Views from History,* ed. Michael B. Katz. Princeton, N.J.: Princeton University Press.

Moffitt, Robert. 1992. Incentive Effects of the U.S. Welfare System: A Review. *Journal of Economic Literature* 30(1): 1–61.

Moon, Marilyn. 1996a. *Medicare Now and in the Future.* 2nd ed. Washington, D.C.: Urban Affairs Press.

———. 1996b. What Medicare Has Meant to Older Americans. *Health Care Financing Review* 18(2): 49–59.

———. 1999. Medicare Matters: The Value of Social Insurance. Washington, D.C.: Urban Institute. From the Urban Institute web site.

Mosteller, Frederick. 1995. The Tennessee Study of Class Size in the Early School Grades. *Future of Children* 5(2): 113–27.

Moynihan, Daniel P. 1973. *The Politics of a Guaranteed Income: The Nixon Administration and the Family Assistance Plan.* New York: Vintage.

Munnell, Alicia H., ed. 1987. *Lessons from the Income Maintenance Experiments.* Boston: Federal Reserve Bank of Boston.

Murray, Charles. 1984. *Losing Ground.* New York: Basic Books.

Murray, Shailagh. 1999. Drop in Food Stamp Rolls Is Mysterious and Worrisome. *Wall Street Journal,* August 2, A20.

Musgrave, Richard A. 1996. Progressive Taxation, Equity, and Tax Design. In Slemrod (1996, 341–56).

References

Musgrave, Richard A., K. Case, and H. Leonard. 1974. The Distribution of Fiscal Burdens and Benefits. *Public Finance Quarterly* 2:259–300.

Musgrave, Richard A., and Peggy B. Musgrave. 1980. *Public Finance in Theory and Practice*. 3rd ed. New York: McGraw-Hill.

Musgrave, Richard A., and Alan T. Peacock, eds. 1958. *Classics in the Theory of Public Finance*. New York: McGraw-Hill.

Myrdal, Alva. 1971. *Toward Equality*. Stockholm: Prisma.

National Coalition for the Homeless. 1999a. How Many People Experience Homelessness? Fact Sheet no. 2. From NCH web site, (visited 8/5/99).

———. 1999b. Who Is Homeless? Fact Sheet no. 3. From NCH web site, (visited 8/5/99).

Nelson, Richard. 1996. *The Sources of Economic Growth*. Cambridge, Mass.: Harvard University Press.

Nelson, Robert L., and William P. Bridges. 1999. *Legalizing Gender Inequality: Courts, Markets, and Unequal Pay for Women in America*. New York: Cambridge University Press.

Nielsen, Waldemar A. 1985. *The Golden Donors: A New Anatomy of the Great Foundations*. New York: Dutton.

Nissen, Bruce, ed. 1999. *Which Direction for Organized Labor? Essays on Organizing, Outreach, and Internal Transformations*. Detroit: Wayne State University Press.

North, Douglass Cecil. 1966. *The Economic Growth of the United States, 1790–1860*. New York: Norton.

Nozick, Robert. 1974. *Anarchy, State, and Utopia*. New York: Basic.

O'Connor, Julia S., and Greg M. Olsen, eds. 1998. *Power Resources Theory and the Welfare State: A Critical Approach*. Toronto: University of Toronto Press.

Oestreicher, Richard. 1988. Urban Working-Class Political Behavior and Theories of American Electoral Politics, 1870–1940. *Journal of American History* 74: 1257–86.

Okun, Arthur M. 1975. *Equality and Efficiency: The Big Tradeoff*. Washington, D.C.: Brookings.

Olson, Mancur, Jr. 1965. *The Logic of Collective Action: Public Goods and the Theory of Groups*. Cambridge, Mass.: Harvard University Press.

Orfield, Gary, et al. 1984. *Chicago Study of Access and Choice in Higher Education: A Report to the Illinois Senate Committee on Higher Education*.

Osborne, David, and Ted Gaebler. 1993. *Reinventing Government: How the Entrepreneurial Spirit Is Transforming the Public Sector*. New York: Penguin.

Page, Benjamin I. 1983. *Who Gets What from Government*. Berkeley: University of California Press.

———. 1997. Trouble for Workers and the Poor: Economic Globalization and the Reshaping of American Politics. Paper delivered at the annual meeting of the Midwest Political Science Association, Chicago, April 10–12.

———. 1999. Is Social Security Reform Ready for the American Public? Paper delivered at the annual meeting of the National Academy of Social Insurance, Washington, D.C., January 30–31.

Page, Benjamin I., and Robert Y. Shapiro. 1992. *The Rational Public: Fifty Years of Trends in Americans' Policy Preferences.* Chicago: University of Chicago Press.

Patel, Kant, and Mark E. Rushefsky. 1995. *Health Care Politics and Policy in America.* Armonk, N.Y.: M. E. Sharpe.

Patterson, James T. 1981. *America's Struggle against Poverty 1900–1980.* Cambridge, Mass.: Harvard University Press.

Patterson, Orlando. 1999. What to Do When Busing Becomes Irrelevant. *New York Times,* July 18, sec. 4, p. 17.

Patterson, Thomas E. 1993. *Out of Order.* New York: Knopf.

Pear, Robert. 1998a. As H.M.O.'s Drop Medicare, Many Are Left in Quandary. *New York Times,* September 19, 1, 10.

———. 1998b. Most States Meet Work Requirement of Welfare Law. *New York Times,* December 30, A1, A12.

Pechman, Joseph A. 1977. *Federal Tax Policy.* 3rd ed. Washington, D.C.: Brookings.

———. 1985. *Who Paid the Taxes, 1966–1985.* Washington, D.C.: Brookings.

———. 1986. Pechman's Tax Incidence Study: A Response. *American Economic Review* 76 (December): 1219–20.

———. 1987. *Federal Tax Policy.* 5th ed. Washington, D.C.: Brookings.

Pechman, Joseph A., and Benjamin A. Okner. 1974. *Who Bears the Tax Burden?* Washington, D.C.: Brookings.

Persson, Torsten, and Guido Tabellini. 1994. Is Inequality Harmful for Growth? *American Economic Review* 84(3): 600–21.

Peterson, Paul. 1981. *City Limits.* Chicago: University of Chicago Press.

———. 1998. School Choice: A Report Card. In Peterson and Hassel (1998, 3–32).

———. 1999. Top Ten Questions Asked about School Choice. In Ravitch (1999, 317–54).

Peterson, Paul E., and Bryan C. Hassel, eds. 1998. *Learning from School Choice.* Washington, D.C.: Brookings.

Peterson, Paul E., David E. Myers, William G. Howell, and Daniel P. Mayer. 1999. The Effects of School Choice in New York City. In *Earning and Learning: How Schools Matter,* ed. Susan E. Mayer and Paul E. Peterson, 317–54. Washington, D.C.: Brookings.

Peterson, Peter G. 1988. *On Borrowed Time: How the Growth in Entitlement Spending Threatens America's Future.* San Francisco: ICS Press.

Phelps, Edmund S., ed. 1973. *Economic Justice: Selected Readings.* Harmondsworth, England: Penguin.

Physician Task Force on Hunger in America. 1985. *Hunger in America: The Growing Epidemic.* Middletown, Conn.: Wesleyan University Press.

Pierson, Paul. 1994. *Dismantling the Welfare State?* New York: Cambridge University Press.

Pigou, A. C. 1920. *The Economics of Welfare*. London: Macmillan.

———. 1952 [1920, 1932]. *The Economics of Welfare*. 4th ed. London: Macmillan.

Piven, Frances Fox, and Richard A. Cloward. 1971. *Regulating the Poor: The Functions of Public Welfare*. New York: Vintage.

———. 1977. *Poor People's Movements: Why They Succeed, How They Fail*. New York: Pantheon.

———. 1989. *Why Americans Don't Vote*. New York: Pantheon.

Pollin, Robert. 1998. Living Wage, Live Action. *Nation,* November 23, 15–20.

Pontusson, Jonas, and Peter Swenson. 1996. Labor Markets, Production Strategies, and Wage-Bargaining Institutions: The Swedish Employer Offensive in Comparative Perspective. *Comparative Political Studies* 29(2): 223–50.

Poole, Keith T., and Howard Rosenthal. 1997. *Congress: A Political-Economic History of Roll Call Voting*. New York: Oxford University Press.

Poterba, James. 1989. Lifetime Incidence and the Distributive Burden of Excise Taxes. *American Economic Review* 79(2): 325–30.

———. 1996. Government Intervention in the Markets for Education and Health Care: How and Why? In Fuchs (1996, 277–304).

Protess, David, and Rob Warden. 1998. *A Promise of Justice*. New York: Hyperion.

Quadagno, Jill. 1988. *The Transformation of Old Age Security: Class and Politics in the American Welfare State*. Chicago: University of Chicago Press.

———. 1994. *The Color of Welfare*. New York: Oxford University Press.

Quinn, Dennis. 1997. The Correlates of Change in International Financial Regulation. *American Political Science Review* 91(3): 531–51.

Rauch, Basil, ed. 1957. *The Roosevelt Reader: Selected Speeches, Messages, Press Conferences, and Letters of Franklin D. Roosevelt*. New York: Rinehart.

Ravitch, Diane, ed. 1998. *Brookings Papers on Education Policy 1998*. Washington, D.C.: Brookings.

———, ed. 1999. *Brookings Papers on Education Policy 1999*. Washington, D.C.: Brookings.

Rawls, John. 1971. *A Theory of Justice*. Cambridge, Mass.: Harvard University Press.

Reich, Robert B. 1991. *The Work of Nations: Preparing Ourselves for 21st Century Capitalism*. New York: Random House.

———. 1997. *Locked in the Cabinet*. New York: Knopf.

Reischauer, Robert D., Stuart Butler, and Judith R. Lave, eds. 1998. *Medicare: Preparing for the Challenges of the 21st Century*. Washington, D.C.: National Academy of Social Insurance.

Revkin, Andrew C. 1999a. As Need for Food Grows, Donations Steadily Drop. *New York Times,* February 27, 1, 17.

————. 1999b. Plunge in Use of Food Stamps Causes Concern. *New York Times,* February 25, 1, 17.

————. 1999c. Welfare Policies Alter the Face of Food Lines. *New York Times,* February 26, 1, 16.

Reynolds, Morgan, and Eugene Smolensky. 1977. *Public Expenditures, Taxes, and the Distribution of Income: The United States, 1950, 1961, 1970.* New York: Academic Press.

Rich, Michael J. 1993. *Federal Policymaking and the Poor: National Goals, Local Choices, and Distributional Outcomes.* Princeton, N.J.: Princeton University Press.

Rifkin, Jeremy. 1995. *The End of Work: The Decline of the Global Labor Force and the Dawn of the Post-Market Era.* New York: Putnam.

Roberts, Michael L., Peggy A. Hite, and Cassie F. Bradley. 1994. Understanding Attitudes toward Progressive Taxation. *Public Opinion Quarterly* 58 (Summer): 165–90.

Robins, Philip K. 1985. A Comparison of the Labor Supply Findings from the Four Negative Income Tax Experiments. *Journal of Human Resources* 20(4): 567–82.

Roemer, John E. 1996. *Theories of Distributive Justice.* Cambridge, Mass.: Harvard University Press.

Rosenbaum, James E. 1995. Changing the Geography of Opportunity by Expanding Residential Choice: Lessons from the Gautreaux Program. *Housing Policy Debate* 6(1): 231–69.

Rosenberg, Gerald N. 1991. *The Hollow Hope: Can Courts Bring about Social Change?* Chicago: University of Chicago Press.

Rosenberg, Nathan. 1982. *Inside the Black Box: Technology and Economics.* New York: Cambridge University Press.

Rosenstone, Steven J., and John Mark Hansen. 1993. *Mobilization, Participation, and Democracy in America.* New York: Macmillan.

Rosenstone, Steven J., and Raymond E. Wolfinger. 1978. The Effect of Registration Laws on Voting Turnout. *American Political Science Review* 72(1): 22–45.

Rothman, Robert. 1999. *Inequality and Stratification.* Upper Saddle River, N.J.: Prentice-Hall.

Rousseau, Jean-Jacques. 1977 [1754]. A Discourse on the Origin of Inequality. In *The Social Contract and Discourses,* trans. G. D. H. Cole, rev. J. H. Brumfitt and John Hall, 27–114. New York: E.P. Dutton.

Rushefsky, Mark E., and Kant Patel. 1998. *Politics, Power and Policy Making: The Case of Health Care Reform in the 1990s.* Armonk, N.Y.: M. E. Sharpe.

Sabato, Larry J., and Glenn R. Simpson. 1996. *Dirty Little Secrets: The Persistence of Corruption in American Politics.* New York: Times Books.

Saloma, John S., III. 1984. *Ominous Politics: The New Conservative Labyrinth.* New York: Hill and Wang.

References

Samuelson, Paul A. 1954. The Pure Theory of Public Expenditure. *Review of Economics and Statistics* 36:387–89.

———. 1955. Diagrammatic Exposition of a Theory of Public Expenditure. *Review of Economics and Statistics* 37:350–56.

Sassen, Saskia. 1996. *Losing Control? Sovereignty in an Age of Globalization.* New York: Columbia University Press.

Sassoon, Donald. 1996. *One Hundred Years of Socialism: The West European Left in the Twentieth Century.* New York: New Press.

Schattschneider, E. E. 1935. *Politics, Pressures and the Tariff.* New York: Prentice-Hall.

———. 1960. *The Semisovereign People: A Realist's View of Democracy in America.* New York: Holt, Rinehart and Winston.

Schieber, Sylvester, and John B. Shoven. 1999. *The Real Deal: The History and Future of Social Security.* New Haven, Conn.: Yale University Press.

Schlozman, Kay Lehman, and John T. Tierney. 1986. *Organized Interests and American Democracy.* New York: Harper & Row.

Scholz, John Karl. 1993–94. Tax Policy and the Working Poor: The Earned Income Tax Credit. *Focus* (Institute for Research on Poverty, University of Wisconsin): 15(3): 1–12.

Schor, Juliet B. 1992. *The Overworked American: The Unexpected Decline of Leisure.* New York: Basic.

Schuldiner, Allan. 1999. *Influence Inc.: The Bottom Line on Washington Lobbying.* Washington, D.C.: Center for Responsive Politics.

Schultze, Charles L. 1971. *The Distribution of Farm Subsidies: Who Gets the Benefits?* Washington, D.C.: Brookings.

Schwarz, John E. 1988 [1983]. *America's Hidden Success: A Reassessment of Public Policy from Kennedy to Reagan.* Rev. ed. New York: Norton.

Seelye, Katharine Q. 1999. Recipients of Welfare Are Fewest since 1969. *New York Times,* April 11, A17.

Sen, Amartya, ed. 1970. *Growth Economics: Selected Readings.* Baltimore: Penguin.

———. 1997 [1973]. *On Economic Inequality.* Enlarged ed. Oxford, England: Clarendon Press.

Sennett, Richard, and Jonathan Cobb. 1972. *The Hidden Injuries of Class.* New York: Random House.

Shapiro, Carl, and Joseph Stiglitz. 1984. Equilibrium Unemployment as a Worker-Discipline Device. *American Economic Review* 74:433–44.

Shapiro, Isaac, and Robert Greenstein. 1997. *Trends in the Distribution of After-Tax Income: An Analysis of Congressional Budget Office Data.* Washington, D.C.: Center on Budget and Policy Priorities.

Shefter, Martin. 1986. Trade Unions and Political Machines: The Organization and

Disorganization of the American Working Class in the Late Nineteenth Century. In Katznelson and Zolberg (1986, 17–78).

Shuman, Michael H. 1998. Going Local: Devolution for Progressives. *Nation,* October 12, 11–15.

Sidgwick, Henry. 1907 [1893]. *The Method of Ethics.* 7th ed. London: Macmillan.

Simmons, James R. 1992. Economic Theory of Democracy Revisited and Revised. *New Political Science* 23 (Fall): 29–49.

Skidmore, Max. J. 1999. *Social Security and Its Enemies: The Case for America's Most Efficient Insurance Program.* Boulder, Colo.: Westview.

Skocpol, Theda. 1992. *Protecting Soldiers and Mothers: The Political Origins of Social Policy in the United States.* Cambridge, Mass.: Harvard University Press.

———. 1995. *Social Policy in the United States: Future Possibilities in Historical Perspective.* Princeton, N.J.: Princeton University Press.

———. 1997. *Boomerang: Health Care Reform and the Turn against Government.* New York: Norton.

Slaughter, Thomas P. 1986. *The Whiskey Rebellion: Frontier Epilogue to the American Revolution.* New York: Oxford University Press.

Slemrod, Joel. 1992. Do Taxes Matter? Lessons from the 1980s. *American Economic Review* 82:250–56.

———, ed. 1996. *Tax Progressivity and Income Inequality.* New York: Cambridge University Press.

———, ed. 1999. *Tax Policy in the Real World.* New York: Cambridge University Press.

Smeeding, Timothy. 1992. Why the U.S. Antipoverty System Doesn't Work Very Well. *Challenge* 35 (January/February): 30–35.

Smith, Adam. 1976 [written 1766–76]. *An Inquiry into the Nature and Causes of the Wealth of Nations.* Chicago: University of Chicago Press. Cannan ed., orig. pub. 1904.

Smith, Daniel A. 1999. Howard Jarvis, Populist Entrepreneur: Reevaluating the Causes of Proposition 13. *Social Science History* 23(2): 173–210.

Smith, James Allen. 1991. *The Idea Brokers: Think Tanks and the Rise of the New Policy Elite.* New York: Free Press.

Snow, David A., and Leon Anderson. 1993. *Down on Their Luck: A Study of Homeless Street People.* Berkeley: University of California Press.

Solon, Gary. 1999. Intergenerational Mobility in the Labor Market. In *Handbook of Labor Economics,* vol. 3, ed. Orley Ashenfelter and David Card. New York: Elsevier.

Solow, Robert M. 1998. Guess Who Pays for Workfare? *New York Review of Books,* November 5, 27–28, 36–37.

Solow, Robert M., Gertrude Himmelfarb, Anthony Lewis, Glenn C. Loury, and

John E. Roemer. 1998. *Work and Welfare,* ed. Amy Gutmann. Princeton, N.J.: Princeton University Press.

Sorauf, Frank J. 1988. *Money in American Elections.* Glenview, Ill.: Scott, Foresman.

Starr, Paul. 1982. *The Social Transformation of American Medicine.* New York: Basic.

Stedman, Lawrence C. 1998. An Assessment of the Contemporary Debate over U.S. Achievement. In Ravitch (1998, 53–121).

Stefancic, Jean, and Richard Delgado. 1996. *No Mercy: How Conservative Think Tanks and Foundations Changed America's Social Agenda.* Philadelphia: Temple University Press.

Steinberg, Laurence, B. Bradford Brown, and Sanford M. Dornbusch. 1996. *Beyond the Classroom: Why School Reform Has Failed and What Parents Need to Do.* New York: Simon & Schuster.

Steiner, Gilbert Y. 1971. *The State of Welfare.* Washington, D.C.: Brookings.

Steinmo, Sven. 1995. Why Is Government So Small in America? *Governance: An International Journal of Policy and Administration* 8(3): 303–34.

Steinmo, Sven, Kathleen Thelen, and Frank Longstreth, eds. 1992. *Structuring Politics: Historical Institutionalism in Comparative Analysis.* New York: Cambridge University Press.

Steinmo, Sven, and Jon Watts. 1995. It's the Institutions, Stupid! Why Comprehensive National Health Insurance Always Fails in America. *Journal of Health Politics, Policy and Law* 20(2): 329–89.

Stephens, John D. 1979. *The Transition from Capitalism to Socialism.* Urbana: University of Illinois Press.

Steuerle, C. Eugene. 1992. *The Tax Decade: How Taxes Came to Dominate the Public Agenda.* Washington, D.C.: Urban Institute.

———. 1997. Social Security in the Twenty-First Century: The Need for Change. In *Social Security and the 21st Century,* ed. Eric Kingson and James Schulz. New York: Oxford University Press.

Steuerle, C. Eugene, and Jon Bakia. 1994. *Retooling Social Security for the 21st Century.* Washington, D.C.: Urban Institute.

Stevenson, Harold W., and Shinying Lee. 1998. An Examination of American Student Achievement from an International Perspective. In Ravitch (1998, 7–52).

Stith, Kate, and Jose A. Cabranes. 1998. *Fear of Judging: Sentencing Guidelines in the Federal Courts.* Chicago: University of Chicago Press.

Stolper, Wolfgang F., and Paul A. Samuelson. 1941. Protection and Real Wages. *Review of Economic Studies* 9(1): 58–73.

Streeck, Wolfgang. 1992. *Social Institutions and Economic Performance: Studies of Industrial Relations in Advanced Capitalist Economies.* Newbury Park, Calif.: Sage.

Sundquist, James L. 1968. *Politics and Policy: The Eisenhower, Kennedy, and Johnson Years.* Washington, D.C.: Brookings.

Swank, Duane. 1992. Politics and the Structural Dependence of the State in Democratic Capitalist Nations. *American Political Science Review* 86(1): 38–54.

———. 1996. Funding the Welfare State, Part I: Global Capital and the Taxation of Business in Advanced Market Economies. Paper delivered at the annual meeting of the American Political Science Association, San Francisco, August 29–September 1.

Swenson, Peter. 1997. Arranged Alliance: Business Interests in the New Deal. *Politics and Society* 25(1): 66–116.

———. 2000. *Labor Markets and Welfare States: Employers in the Making of the American and Swedish Systems.* Forthcoming.

Tanzi, Vito. 1995. *Taxation in an Integrating World.* Washington, D.C.: Brookings.

Tawney, R. H. 1961 [1931]. *Equality.* New York: Capricorn.

Teixeira, Ruy. 1992. *The Disappearing American Voter.* Washington, D.C.: Brookings.

Thelen, Kathleen Ann. 1991. *Union of Parts: Labor Politics in Postwar Germany.* Ithaca, N.Y.: Cornell University Press.

Tobin, James. 1994. Poverty in Relation to Macroeconomic Trends, Cycles, and Policies. In Danziger, Sandefur, and Weinberg (1994, 147–67).

Townsend, Peter. 1993. *The International Analysis of Poverty.* New York: Harvester Wheatsheaf.

Trachtenberg, Alan. 1982. *The Incorporation of America: Culture and Society in the Gilded Age.* New York: Hill and Wang.

Trattner, Walter I. 1999. *From Poor Law to Welfare State: A History of Social Welfare in America.* 6th ed. New York: Free Press.

Triest, Robert K. 1996. The Efficiency Cost of Increased Progressivity. In Slemrod (1996, 137–69).

Trutko, John, Nancy Pindus, Burt S. Barnow, and Demetra Smith Nightingale. 1999. *Early Implementation of the Welfare-to-Work Grants Program.* Washington, D.C.: Urban Institute.

United Kingdom. 1942. *Social Insurance and Allied Services* (Beveridge Report, Cmd 6404). London: HMSO.

United Nations Development Programme. 1999. *Human Development Report 1999.* New York: Oxford University Press.

United Nations General Assembly. 1948. Universal Declaration of Human Rights. In *Basic Documents of the United Nations,* ed. Louis B. Sohn, 132–35. Brooklyn, N.Y.: Foundation Press, 1956.

U.S. Bureau of Justice Statistics. 1999. *Correctional Populations in the United States, 1996.* From BJS web site.

U.S. Bureau of the Census. 1975. *Historical Statistics of the United States, Colonial Times to 1970.* Washington, D.C.: U.S. Government Printing Office.

———. 1999a. Current Population Reports, Series P60-206, *Money Income in the United States: 1998.* Washington, D.C.: U.S. Government Printing Office.

————. 1999b. Current Population Reports, Series P60-207, *Poverty in the United States: 1998.* Washington, D.C.: U.S. Government Printing Office.

U.S. Conference of Mayors. 1998. *A Status Report on Homelessness in America's Cities: 1998.* Washington, D.C.: U.S. Conference of Mayors.

U.S. Congressional Budget Office. 1998. Social Security and Private Saving: A Review of the Empirical Evidence. CBO Memorandum. July. Washington, D.C.: Congressional Budget Office.

U.S. Department of Agriculture, Economic Research Service. 1998. *Structural and Financial Characteristics of U.S. Farms, 1995: 20th Annual Family Farm Report to the Congress.* Agriculture Information Bulletin no. 746.

U.S. Department of Commerce, Bureau of the Census. *Annual Survey of Governments: State Tax Collections.* Washington, D.C.: U.S. Government Printing Office.

U.S. Department of Education, National Center for Education Statistics. 1996. *Out-of-Field Teaching and Educational Equality.* Washington, D.C.: National Center for Education Statistics.

————. 1999. *Digest of Education Statistics 1998.* Washington, D.C.: U.S. Government Printing Office.

U.S. Department of Health and Human Services. 1996. *1996 Green Book Overview of Entitlement Programs.* Washington, D.C.: U.S. Government Printing Office. From DHHS web site (visited 8/9/99).

U.S. Federal Old-Age and Survivors Insurance and Disability Insurance Trust Fund, Board of Trustees. 1999. *1999 Annual Report of the Board of Trustees of the Federal Old-Age and Survivors Insurance and Disability Insurance Trust Funds.* Washington, D.C.

U.S. Health Care Financing Administration. 1996. *Health Care Financing Review: Statistical Supplement.* Baltimore: Health Care Financing Administration.

————. 1998. *Health Care Financing Review: Medicare and Medicaid Statistical Supplement.* Baltimore: Health Care Financing Administration.

U.S. Office of Management and Budget. 1998. *Budget of the United States Government, Fiscal Year 1999.* Washington, D.C.: U.S. Government Printing Office.

————. 1999. *Budget of the United States Government, Fiscal Year 2000.* Washington, D.C.: U.S. Government Printing Office.

U.S. Office of the President. 1999. *Economic Report of the President.* Washington, D.C.: U.S. Government Printing Office.

U.S. Social Security Advisory Board. 1998. *Social Security: Why Action Should Be Taken Soon.* Washington, D.C.: Social Security Advisory Board.

U.S. Social Security and Medicare Boards of Trustees. 1999. *Status of the Social Security and Medicare Programs: A Summary of the 1999 Annual Reports.* Washington, D.C.

van Zandt, David. 1993. The Lessons of the Lighthouse: "Government" or "Private" Provision of Goods. *Journal of Legal Studies* 22:47–72.

Verba, Sidney, Kay Lehman Schlozman, and Henry E. Brady. 1995. *Voice and Equality: Civic Volunteerism in American Politics.* Cambridge, Mass.: Harvard University Press.

Vickrey, W. 1945. Measuring Marginal Utility by Reaction to Risk. *Econometrica* 13:319–33.

Viteritti, Joseph P. 1998. School Choice and State Constitutional Law. In Peterson and Hassel (1998, 409–27).

von Mises, Ludwig. 1951 [1922]. *Socialism: An Economic and Sociological Analysis,* trans. J. Kahane. New Haven, Conn.: Yale University Press.

Walker, Charls E., and Mark A. Bloomfield, eds. 1983. *New Directions in Federal Tax Policy for the 1980s.* New York: Ballinger.

Wallerstein, Michael. 1999. Wage-Setting Institutions and Pay Inequality in Advanced Industrial Societies. *American Journal of Political Science* 43(3): 649–80.

Webber, Michael J., and G. William Domhoff. 1996. Myth and Reality in Business Support for Democrats and Republicans in the 1936 Presidential Election. *American Political Science Review* 90(4): 824–33.

Weir, Margaret. 1992. *Politics and Jobs: The Boundaries of Employment Policy in the United States.* Princeton, N.J.: Princeton University Press.

Weiss, Linda. 1998. *The Myth of the Powerless State.* Ithaca, N.Y.: Cornell University Press.

Weissert, Carol S., and William G. Weissert. 1996. *Governing Health: The Politics of Health Policy.* Baltimore: Johns Hopkins University Press.

West, Darrell M., and Burdett A. Loomis. 1998. *The Sound of Money: How Political Interests Get What They Want.* New York: W. W. Norton.

Western, Bruce. 1993. Postwar Unionization in Eighteen Advanced Capitalist Countries. *American Sociological Review* 58(2): 266–82.

———. 1997. *Between Class and Market: Postwar Unionization in the Capitalist Democracies.* Princeton, N.J.: Princeton University Press.

White, Richard. 1991. *"It's Your Misfortune and None of My Own": A History of the American West.* Norman: University of Oklahoma Press.

Wilensky, Harold, and Charles Lebeaux. 1965. *Industrial Society and Social Welfare.* New York: Free Press.

Wilgoren, Jodi. 1999. Quality Day Care, Early, Is Tied to Achievements as an Adult. *New York Times,* October 22, A16.

Wilson, William J. 1987. *The Truly Disadvantaged: The Inner City, the Underclass, and Public Policy.* Chicago: University of Chicago Press.

———. 1996. *When Work Disappears: The World of the Urban Poor.* New York: Random House.

Witte, John F. 1985. *The Politics and Development of the Federal Income Tax.* Madison: University of Wisconsin Press.

———. 1993. The Milwaukee Parental Choice Program. In *School Choice: Exam-*

ining the Evidence, ed. Edith Rasell and Richard Rothstein. Washington, D.C.: Economic Policy Institute.

———. 1999. *The Market Approach to Education: An Analysis of America's First Voucher Program.* Princeton, N.J.: Princeton University Press.

Wittman, Donald A. 1973. Parties as Utility Maximizers. *American Political Science Review* 67:490–98.

Wolf, Charles. 1993. *Markets or Governments.* Cambridge, Mass.: MIT Press.

Wolfe, Barbara. 1996. A Medicaid Primer. *Focus* (Institute for Research on Poverty, University of Wisconsin) Spring.

Wolff, Edward N. 1995. *Top Heavy: A Study of the Increasing Inequality of Wealth in America.* New York: Twentieth Century Fund.

———. 1998. Recent Trends in the Size Distribution of Household Wealth. *Journal of Economic Perspectives* 12(3): 131–50.

Wolin, Sheldon S. 1960. *Politics and Vision: Continuity and Innovation in Western Political Thought.* Boston: Little, Brown.

Wong, Kar-yiu. 1995. *International Trade in Goods and Factor Mobility.* Cambridge, Mass.: MIT Press.

Wood, George H. 1992. *Schools That Work: America's Most Innovative Public Education Programs.* New York: Penguin.

Woodward, Bob. 1994. *The Agenda: Inside the Clinton White House.* New York: Simon & Schuster.

Yeric, Jerry, and John Todd. 1996. *Public Opinion: The Visible Politics.* 3rd ed. Itasca, Ill.: E. E. Peacock.

Zinberg, Dorothy S. 1993. Putting People First: Education, Jobs, and Economic Competitiveness. In *Empowering Technology: Implementing a U.S. Strategy,* ed. Lewis M. Branscomb, 235–65. Cambridge, Mass.: MIT Press.

Zucchino, David. 1997. *Myth of the Welfare Queen.* New York: Simon & Schuster.

INDEX

A

Aaron, Henry, 87, 259

Abecedarian Project, 174, 175

abilities, and equal opportunity, 165–66, 167

ability-to-pay theory of taxes, 128–29

abortion, 170

accomplishments, government programs and, 290–93

accounting tricks, and corporate taxes, 134, 140

Acheson, Dean, 73

acrobats, in safety net image, 247–48

administrative costs: of Disability Insurance, 93; of Food Stamps, 256; of insurance companies and charities, 93, 256; of Medicaid, 271–72; of OASI, 93; of private retirement accounts, 91; of Social Security, 79

adverse selection problem, in insurance, 39, 57

AFDC. See Aid to Families with Dependent Children

AFDC mothers, stereotypes of, 276

affirmative action: and higher education, 196–97; in hiring, 233

AFL, 230

AFL–CIO: lobbying expenditures by, 242; revival of, 231

Africa, GDP per capita in, 13–14

African Americans: commodities distribution and, 252; higher education and, 196–97; homelessness and, 264–65; imprisonment of, 221; job discrimination and, 232–33; as military personnel, 212, 337n. 28; poverty and, 21; segregation of, 178, 182, 183; social class and parents of, 192, 334n. 78; unions and, 229–30

African-American workers, immigration and wages of, 240

agribusinesses, subsidy of, 251–52

agricultural subsidies, 250–52

agriculture, in early United States, 12. See also farms

Aid to Families with Dependent Children (AFDC): benefit levels of, 275; childbearing and, 275, 276–77; cycling in, 277; dependency and, 276, 277–78; effects of on work, 278–79; error rates in, 256; fraud in, 275; generations on, 277–78; history of, 274; independence effect of, 277; long-

Aid to Families with Dependent Children (AFDC) (*continued*)
term recipients of, 277; marriage and, 275, 276, 277; opposition to, 48; poverty gap and, 278; sequel to, 218–19; size of, 275; states' role in, 275; welfare-to-work and, 217–18; work incentives and, 275, 276, 278–79. *See also* Temporary Assistance for Needy Families; welfare reform
aircraft, 213
Alabama: Medicaid benefits in, 332n. 27; regressive taxes in, 152
Alan Guttmacher Institute (AGI), 331n. 17
Alaska, and prenatal care, 172
alcohol, taxes on, 145–46
alcohol abuse, and homelessness, 263, 264, 265
Alexander, Jeff, 342n. 1
Almost Home, 268
Altman, Robert, 73
American Association of Retired Persons (AARP), 114; lobbying expenditures by, 341n. 103
American Automobile Manufacturers Association, lobbying expenditures by, 242
American Federation of Labor (AFL), 230. *See also* AFL–CIO; labor unions
American Medical Association (AMA): lobbying expenditures by, 341n. 103; political role of, 112–13
American Petroleum Institute, 114
Amway, soft money from, 341n. 104
antipoverty politics, 283–85; interest groups and, 283–84, 285; political parties and, 283
antitrust policy, 38
apprenticeship programs, 190–91; price supports and, 251; soft money from, 341n. 104
Arizona: charter schools in, 189; food seekers in, 258
Arkansas, alternative schools in, 189
Asia: financial crisis, 238; GDP per capita in, 13–14; immigration from, 240; U.S. investment in, 238
assessment practices, and property tax, 150

asset-based redistribution, 315n. 33, 316n. 42
assets, liquidation of and estate taxes, 329n. 63
asthma, 270
Australia: corporate taxes in, 141; economic growth in, 64; health insurance in, 99; income inequality in, 30, 64; infant mortality in, 119; medical costs in, 99; poverty rate in, 24; public sector employment in, 338n. 47; rich-to-poor ratio in, 30; tax levels in, 133

B

Baker, Howard, 120
Ball, Robert, 87
Baltimore, living wage in, 226
bankruptcy, alleged: of Medicare, 102–3; of Social Security, 83–89
Barlett, Donald, 158
battered women, 265, 267
Becker, Gary, 52
behavior, controllability of, 59, 60–61, 122–24
Belgium: economic growth in, 64; income inequality in, 30, 64; public sector employment in, 220; tax levels in, 133; trade volume in, 234
Bell Atlantic: lobbying expenditures by, 242; PAC contributions to Republicans by, 244
"Bell Curve" and inherited intelligence, 192, 335n. 79
benefits theory of taxation, 127–28
beriberi, 250
Beveridge Report, 122
birth: equal opportunity and, 168–70; out of wedlock, 276
birth control, 169–70; government role in, 169–70; poor people and, 170; programs, effects of, 332n. 20
Blackfoot Indians, and commodities distribution, 252
Blank, Rebecca: on elderly and disabled, 275; on Food Stamps, 255; on jobs and wages, 53; on Medicaid, 271; on mobility pro-

grams, 209; on Social Security and poverty, 81; on stereotypes of poor, 21; on unemployment and poverty, 204; on work loss and AFDC, 278

Blinder, Alan, 204

Bluestone, Barry, 1

Boeing: lobbying by, 213; lobbying expenditures by, 242; PAC contributions of, 244

bond holders, and inflation, 206

Boskin, Michael, 321n. 35

Boston: living wage in, 226; low-income housing in, 268

Bowles, Samuel, 315n. 33, 316n. 42

Brady, Henry, 65

Braun, Denny, 29

Britain. *See* United Kingdom

Brown v. Board of Education, 181

Browning, Edgar, 131

Brunei, GDP per capita in, 13

Buckley v. Valeo, 306–7

budget (U.S. federal), size of, 77

budget balancing, 206–8

budget deficits: economic performance and, 41–42; measurement problems and, 42

bureaucratic influence, on schooling, 187

Burnham, Walter Dean, 66

Burtless, Gary, 131, 180

Bush, George H. W., 198, 257

business: antipoverty politics and, 283; conflict of with labor, 241–43; education politics and, 197, 198; opposition of to guaranteed work, 224; opposition of to minimum wage, 225; PAC contributions by, 69–70, 242–43, 244; political contributions by, 69–70, 284; political power of, 68–71, 242–43; privileged position of, 341n. 105; representation of by interest groups, 69–70; Republican Party and, 243–44; right turn by, 70, 73–74, 113; welfare state role of, 241. *See also* business firms

business costs, and egalitarian policies, 4–5

business cycle: controversy about, 206; government stabilization and, 41; inequality at peak of, 1–2; length of, 204; persistence of, 205; poverty and, 18, 203; welfare reform and, 281

business firms: influence of on public debate, 109; lobbying expenditures by, 242; right turn by, 70, 73–74, 113; role of in Democratic Party, 72–74; role of in Social Security Act, 110–11; soft money contributions by, 341n. 104. *See also* business; interest groups; *specific firm names*

Business Roundtable, lobbying expenditures by, 242

busing, for school desegregation, 182

C

California: education politics in, 198; progressive income taxes in, 152, 153; school finance equalization in, 179; school quality in, 198

campaign contributions: by business, 69–70, 242–43, 244, 284, 341n. 104; class bias in, 68; income level and, 306, 347n. 5; by labor, 69–70, 242–43, 244, 284, 341n. 104

campaign finance reform, 306–7

Canada: corporate taxes in, 141; doctors in, 112; health insurance in, 99–100; homelessness in, 262; incarceration rate in, 221; income inequality in, 30; medical costs in, 99–100; payroll tax rate in, 142; poverty rate in, 24; rich-to-poor ratio in, 30; tax levels in, 133; trade with, 236; U.S. investment in, 238

Canadian health care system: as model for United States, 105, 118–19, 272–73; popularity of, 109

capital: flight, 63; income from ownership of, 17–18; property tax and, 149, 150; return on, 16

capital gains: home sales and, 260; omission of from income data and, 27, 311n. 22; special tax treatment of, 135–36; taxes on, and economic growth, 209–10 capital mobility, 237–39; acceleration of, 237–38; constraints on egalitarian policies by, 63–64; corporate taxes and, 134, 140; government policies and, 238; poverty and inequality and, 238; protection of U.S. workers from, 238–39. *See also* globalization

capital punishment, and the innocent, 222

capitalism: and freedom, 36; and U.S. economic growth, 14

Card, David, 225

Carnegie report on schools, 185

Carville, James, 273

categorical imperative, 128

Catholic Charities USA, government help to, 257

Catholic schools. *See* schools, Catholic

Center for Budget and Policy Priorities, 70–71, 268

Center for Responsive Politics, 242, 284

Central Park East schools, 183–84, 333–34n. 57

Chamber of Commerce: lobbying expenditures by, 242; opposition of to social insurance, 324n. 103

charitable agencies, and homeless shelters, 266–67

charitable contributions: amount of, 257; to poor and nonpoor, 257

charitable giving, displacement of by public spending, 343n. 24

charities, private, 257–58; administrative costs of, 256; public funding of, 257; substitution of for government, 257, 343n. 24

charter schools, 189–90; arguments for, 190; poverty and inequality and, 190; religion and, 190

Chicago: living wage in, 226; low-income housing in, 268–69; rental voucher wait in, 262; segregation in, 178

child care, 174–76

Child Care and Development Fund, 176

child labor, regulation of abroad, 239

child nutrition, and schools, 173–74

child support, 171

childbearing: AFDC and, 275, 276–77; equal opportunity and, 168–70. *See also* birth control

children: equal opportunity and, 49–51, 165–76; participation of in AFDC, 275; political representation of, 283–84; poverty rate among, 21–22; recommendations on, 294–95; working-poor families and, 25

Children's Defense Fund, 281, 284

China: GDP per capita in, 13–14; imports from, 236; military spending by, 211–12; U.S. investment in, 237, 238; voluntary trade limits and, 235

Chinese schools, and student equality, 168

Chinese workers, competition with, 301

choice, in schooling, 185–90

Christian Coalition, lobbying expenditures by, 341n. 103

Chubb, John, 186–87

cigarette taxes, 145–46; lobbying against, 120

circus imagery, and safety nets, 247–48

Citicorp, and EBT, 343n. 23

Citizens Board of Inquiry, 250

Citizens for Tax Justice, 151, 158

Civil Rights Act: higher education and, 196; job discrimination and, 232; school desegregation and, 181–82

Civilian Conservation Corps, 54

Clark, Joseph, 249

class divisions, exacerbation of by inequality, 45

class size, educational effects of, 183, 184

Cleveland: public housing wait in, 261; school vouchers in, 334n. 68; segregation in, 178

clinics, community health, 172–73, 273

Clinton administration: business and, 74, 244; free trade priority of, 244; tax progressivity and, 157–58; teachers and, 184

Clinton health plan: business and, 114; demise of, 113–14

coal miners, disability spending for, 78 table 4.1

Coase, Ronald, 314n. 12

codetermination of wages, 229

Cold War: leftist union leaders and, 230; military spending and, 211–12

Coleman, James, 186

Coleman report: on educational opportunity, 180; on peer effects, 181

collective goods. *See* public goods

college, frequency of completing, 190. *See also* education, higher

commodities distribution, 252–53; history and effects of, 252; politics of, 252

Common Cause, 71

common schools, ideal of, 177–78

communitarian arguments, against income inequality, 44–46

community activity, class bias in, 68

community development, 209

Community Development Block Grants, 337n. 22

community health clinics, 172–73, 273

comparable worth laws, 233

compensatory education, 159–60, 179–80

compensatory efforts, for equal opportunity, 294–95

competition and schools. *See* school choice

competition, international. *See* globalization

competition, market, and invisible hand, 34

competitive advantages, of United States, 301

competitiveness of United States: egalitarian policies and, 4–5, 301–2. *See also* economic growth; globalization

Comprehensive Employment and Training Act (CETA): effects of, 54, 215–16, 219; politics of, 220

confidence in government, loss of, 2–3, 309nn. 2, 4

Congress of Industrial Organizations (CIO), 230, 231. *See also* AFL–CIO

congressional roll-call votes, and party affiliation, 108

Connecticut: AFDC benefits in, 275; housing and welfare reform in, 268

Consumer Price Index (CPI): adjustment of poverty line and, 23; real income growth and, 301n. 1

contraceptive services, effects of, 332n. 20

contributions, political: by business and labor, 69–70, 242–43, 244, 284, 341n. 104; class bias in, 68; income level and, 306, 347n. 5

control of events, and social insurance, 56. *See also* moral hazard

corporate charters, social obligations in, 8, 35

corporate income tax: capital mobility and, 140; constraint of globalization on, 133–34, 140–41; depreciation allowances in, 138; incidence of, 139–40; integration of with personal income tax, 141–42; nominal rates of, 139; progressivity of, 141–42; rates of in United States and advanced countries, 141; as source of federal revenue, 125–26, 126 fig. 5.1, 139

corporations: as creatures of government, 35; political power of, 68–71, 242–43. *See also* business; interest groups

correctional supervision, 338n. 49

cost-benefit analysis, measurement problems in, 40

crack cocaine users, harsh treatment of, 223, 338n. 50

"creaming," and school choice, 188

credentials effect. *See* screening hypothesis

creditors, and inflation, 206

crime: decline in, 222; drugs and, 223; nonviolent, 222–23; poverty and, 222–23

criminals, and prison, 222

D

Daly, Gerald, 269

Danziger, Sheldon, 27, 53, 224, 278

day care: employer-provided, 175–76; low-income children and, 176; middle class and, 175–76

Death Row, innocent inmates on, 222

debt, national, Social Security and payoff of, 85

debtors, and inflation, 206

declining marginal utility, of money, 43–44, 128, 129, 131

deduction, tax. *See* tax deduction

defense. *See* military

deinstitutionalization of mentally ill, 264

Democratic Leadership Council, 74

Democratic Party: and antipoverty policies, 283; and business investors, 72–74, 113, 244; and education policies, 198; and egalitarian policies, 71–72; and free trade, 235; and labor unions, 243–44; and low-income voter turnout, 66; and pro-worker policies, 243–44; and social insurance programs, 107–8; and the South, 73, 111; and tax policy, 155, 156, 157

democratic-statist tax regimes, 330n. 95

demograms, 47

Denmark: austerity in, 133; public sector employment in, 220; tax levels in, 133

Denton, Nancy, 182

dependency, AFDC and, 276, 277–78

depreciation allowances, 138

Depression, Great, unemployment in, 207, 336n. 14

Detroit, segregation in, 178

development of self, inequality and, 45, 46

Deverell, Bill, 342n. 1

Diamond, Peter, 91

Dillon, Douglas, 73

Disability Insurance (DI): administrative costs of, 93; benefit levels of, 92, 322n. 42; eligibility reviews for, 93; number of beneficiaries of, 92, 93; Reagan-era purge in, 92–93, 264; spending on, 78 table 4.1, 92

disability insurance, public, 92–96; federal spending on, 78 table 4.1, 92; government workers and, 94–95; social insurance logic of, 92; veterans and, 95

disasters, social insurance and, 56–57

discouraged workers, 203, 204

discrimination: in employment, 232–33; in higher education, 196–97. *See also* racism; segregation

disenfranchisement of workers, 66, 230

dislocated workers, 236; retraining of, 216–17

diversified quality production, 56

divorce rates, guaranteed incomes and, 47–48. *See also* marriage

doctors and AMA, 112

Domhoff, William, 73

double taxation, 140, 327n. 43

Dow Jones Industrial Average (DJIA), rise of since 1980, 29, 297, 346n. 3

draft, military, and inequality, 212

Drew, Elizabeth, 318n. 79

drug abuse: homelessness and, 263, 264, 265; medical treatment of, 223

drug crimes, prison and, 223

Dye, Thomas, 195

E

Earned Income Tax Credit (EITC): after-tax wages and, 55; Clinton administration and, 157; effect of on work, 228; graduated benefits of, 279; lump-sum payment of, 228; maximum level of, 227, 279; payroll taxes and, 143; refundable feature of, 227; size of, 227–28, 279; spending on, 228; work incentives and, 132–33, 227, 278–79

earnings, effect of family background on, 20, 51, 312n. 26

Eastern Europe, opening of to investment, 237

Eastern European immigrants, 230

Eastman Kodak, and New Deal, 111

economic competition, and social insurance policies, 114–16

economic fluctuations, effects of on wages, 18

economic growth: constraints on egalitarian policies and, 61–64; free enterprise system and, 14; government aid in, 14; government role in, 40–43; history of, 11–14; income equality and, 64, 209–10; poverty and, 208–9

Economic Policy Institute, 70

economic rights, 285; affordability of, 286; benefits of, 286 economic stability, government role in, 40–43

economics: language of, 33; ordinal basis of, 130

economists, and justice, 130, 326n. 12, 340n. 84

economy, management of, 203–10

Edgeworth, F. Y., 129

Edison Electric Institute, lobbying expenditures of, 242

education: compensatory, 159–60, 179–80; equal opportunity and, 50, 51, 159–60, 168; importance of, 52; improving, 199–200, 294–95; income inequality and, 160; market failure and, 161–65; positive externalities in, 163–64; poverty and inequality and, 51–52; public goods and, 52, 164; public provision of, 162–65; role of peers in, 179–80, 181; screening hypothesis in, 160, 192, 193–94; what works in, 180–81, 183–85. See also job training; schools

education, elementary and secondary, 176–90; market failures in, 164; what works in, 180–81, 183–85. See also schools

education, higher: discrimination in, 196–97; economic returns from, 192–93; effect of on earnings, 191–94; exacerbation of inequalities by, 191–92, 195–96; frequency of college graduation, 190; government research expenditures on, 195; government spending on, 194–96; market failures in, 163–64; non-economic benefits of, 194; states' role in, 192, 195; student aid for, 194–95; tax expenditures on, 195

education effects, methodological problems in studying, 180, 184, 192–93

education politics: globalization and, 199; interest groups in, 198, 199; low visibility and, 199; political parties in, 198; states and localities in, 198–99

education and training programs: recommendations on, 294–95; successes of, 291–92

educational establishment, 199

effective tax rates, defined, 135. See also taxes

efficiency, xi, 6; government role and, 32; school choice and, 185; tradeoff of with equity, 46, 56

efficiency gains, justice or welfare and, 340n. 84

effort, equal opportunity and, 166, 167–68

egalitarian policies: business costs and, 4–5; globalization and, 61–64; interest groups as obstacles to, 68–71; overcoming obstacles to, 74–75, 300–307; participation biases as obstacle to, 65–68; party investors and activists as obstacles to, 71–74; political obstacles to, 61–74; strength of in Europe, 63, 316–17n. 55; support for by income level, 65

Ehrenreich, Barbara, 24

El Paso (Tex.), indigent medical care and, 270

elderly: encouraging work by, 88; fraction of the poor, 22; medical needs of, 100; out-of-pocket medical costs of, 102; reliance of on Social Security, 79; Social Security and poverty among, 79–80, 81

elderly and disabled: focus of Medicaid on, 272; proportion of public assistance going to, 275

election holidays, U.S. lack of, 66

election of 1936, business money in, 73

election of 1980, business desertion of Democrats in, 113; business money in, 70, 73

election of 1994 (congressional), effect of turnout bias on, 67

elections, effect of money on, 70. See also campaign contributions; political participation; political parties; voter turnout

electronic benefit transfer (EBT), 256, 258, 343n. 26

Elementary and Secondary Education Act: school desegregation and, 181–82; Title I help to low-income areas, 179

emergency rooms, 270

employer retirement plans, tax expenditures on, 79

employer-provided day care, 175–76

employers, job training and, 162, 163

employment. *See* jobs; wages; work

employment, public sector, in United States and other countries, 220–21

employment, public service, 219–21; and military service, 212. *See also* jobs

Employment Service, 217

England, theories of government in, 33–34. *See also* United Kingdom

Enterprise Foundation, 269

enterprise zones, 209

entitlement, Social Security as, 82

environment: international agreements on, 237, 239; public service jobs and, 220

environmental degradation, and GDP, 14

Environmental Working Group, 71

Equal Employment Opportunity Commission (EEOC), 232

equal opportunity: abilities and, 165–66, 167; accidents of life and, 45–46; broad conception of, 50–51; childbirth and, 168–70; for children, 49–51, 155–76, 176–90, 294–95; education and, 50, 51, 159–60, 168; effort and, 166, 167–68; equal results and, 51, 167; estate taxes and, 147; family background and, 51; government action and, 45–46; higher education and, 191–92, 196–200; job discrimination and, 232–33; liberties and, 167; poverty and inequality and, 49–51; prenatal and infant care and, 172–73; school choice and, 188–89; starting line and, 50, 166–67; what to make equal, 50–51

equality, complete: arguments against, 44, 46; under simple utilitarian model, 44

equality, economic growth and, 64, 209–10

equality of sacrifice, 129

equilibrium, economic, quickness of approach to, 4

equity, tradeoff of with efficiency, 46, 56

error rates: in AFDC, 256; in Food Stamps, 256; in Medicaid, 256; in SSI, 256

estate and gift taxes: avoidance of, 148; progressivity of, 146–48; rates of, 147–48; as source of federal revenue, 126

estate taxes: equal opportunity and, 147; liquidation of assets and, 329n. 63

Ethiopia, GDP per capita in, 13, 26

Europe: GDP per capita in, 13; incarceration rate in, 221; maintenance of welfare states in, 63, 316–17n. 55; pressure on social insurance in, 115; pressure on unions in, 231; public sector employment in, 220; Social Democratic parties in, 66, 67; strength of labor unions in, 229; trade volume in, 234; trade with, 236; universal health insurance in, 99; voter turnout in, 65, 66; U.S. investment in, 238. *See also specific countries*

European countries: day care and, 176; gasoline taxes in, 145; global pressures on employment policies of, 244–45

European Union, 235

European welfare states, and global pressure, 133, 316–17n. 55

excise taxes: early U.S. history of, 155; regressivity of, 145–46; sin and, 145; as source of federal revenue, 126 fig. 5.1, 144–45

exclusion, tax. *See* tax exclusion

executive compensation, level of, 29

exports, from United States, 235–36

externalities: definition of, 37, 39; government action and, 37, 39; inefficiency of markets and, 37

F

factor price equalization, 340n. 96

failure: government, 39–40; market, 37–40 (*see also* insurance; public goods; social insurance)

Fair Labor Standards Act, minimum wage and, 225

fair treatment, collective help and, 46

family: background, effect of on occupation

and earnings, 20, 51, 192, 312n. 26; background, political participation and, 68; planning, 169–70; size, income statistics and, 27, 310n. 3; values, guaranteed incomes and, 48. *See also* birth control; income, family

Family Assistance Plan (FAP), 47, 283

Family Support Act: child support and, 171; work placement and, 217–18

farm income stabilization, 78 table 4.1, 250–52

farm insurance, 251

farm subsidies: beneficiaries of, 251–52; import quotas and, 250–51; price supports and, 250–52; spending on, 78 table 4.1, 250–51

farms: family, 251; number of, 251

fathers, fleeing child support, 171

feasibility, political, 246

Federal Agriculture Improvement and Reform Act (FAIR), 251

federal government revenue, sources of, 125–26, 126 fig. 5.1

Federal Housing Authority (FHA), mortgage programs of, 260

Federal Insurance Contribution Act (FICA), tax regressivity and, 83

Federal Reserve Board, monetary policy and, 42

federal taxes, 134–48

federalism: and educational experimentation, 199; and egalitarian policies, 317n. 57

Feldstein, Martin, 80

Ferguson, Thomas, 72, 73–4, 111, 244

fertility effect, of AFDC, 276–77

Field Foundation, 254

Finland: economic growth in, 64; income inequality in, 30; tax levels in, 133

fiscal policy, defined, 41, 205. *See also* economy; macroeconomic policy

floor, solid, imagery of, 249

Florida, regressive taxes in, 152

Folsom, Marion, 111

food: commodities distribution of, 252–53; costs of to poor people, 24; decline in donations of, 258; infant and prenatal, 172–73; need for, 249; right to, 258–59; schools and, 173–74. *See also* Food Stamps

food budget, poverty definition and, 22–23

food insecurity, 255

Food for Peace, 252

food programs, 172–74, 249–59

Food Stamps: administrative costs of, 256; comprehensiveness of, 253, 254; effects of, 254–55; error rates in, 256; fraud in, 256; history of, 254; improving, 258–59; means test for, 253; participation in, 254, 255; payment levels of, 227, 253; stigma and, 255–56, 258–59

Ford Motor Company, and health care, 114

Forrestal, James, 73

foundations, charitable, 148; right wing, 285

Four Freedoms, 285

Fourier, Charles, 45

fragmented government, and egalitarian policies, 327n. 24

France: corporate taxes in, 141; day care in, 175; income inequality in, 30; infant mortality in, 119; medical costs in, 99; poverty rate in, 24; prisoners in, 223; tax levels in, 133; unionization rate in, 110

fraud: AFDC and, 275; disability payments and, 92–93; Food Stamps and, 256; Medicaid and, 272

free enterprise, economic growth and, 14

free riding: insurance market failure and, 57; organization of interest groups and, 69; private retirement insurance and, 58

free speech, economic rights and, 285

freedom, 6; capitalism and, 36; effects of inequality on, 45, 46; importance of, 32; from want, 285

Freeman, Richard, 1, 229, 243

Friedman, Benjamin, 320n. 13

Friedman, Milton: on income redistribution, 43; on limited government, 36; on

Friedman, Milton (*continued*)
monetarism, 206; on negative income tax, 47; on school choice, 185
Full Employment Act, 224
Fullerton, Don, 141

G

Galbraith, James K., 18, 53, 208
Gale, William, 327n. 35
Galveston (Tex.), indigent medical care in, 270
Gans, Herbert, 284
Gap, sweatshops and, 239
Garfinkel, Irwin, 49
Gary (Ind.), segregation in, 178
gasoline taxes, 145–46; regressivity of, 146; in United States and other countries, 145
Gatreaux program, and racial integration, 183
GDP per capita, in United States, 286
GDP per household, in United States, 286
gender. *See* women
General Agreement on Tariffs and Trade (GATT), 235
General Electric, and New Deal, 111
General Motors: lobbying expenditures by, 242; poor and, 284
Genuine Progress Indicator (GPI), decline in, 14
Germany: active labor market policies in, 56, 302; corporate taxes in, 141; employer-provided training in, 331n. 7; health coverage history in, 99; imports from, 236; inequality and economic growth in, 64; medical costs in, 99; payroll tax rate in, 142; poverty rate in, 24; pressure on retirement in, 89, 321n. 35; prisoners in, 223; public sector employment in, 220; retiree growth in, 321n. 35; tax levels in, 133; trade volume in, 234; unemployment insurance in, 115; union role in, 229
Gibbs, David, 70
Giddens, Anthony, 51

gift taxes, 146–48. *See also* estate and gift taxes
gifts, tax-free making of, 148
Gingrich, Newt, 67
Gini coefficient: of disposable income inequality in OECD countries, 29–30; of family income inequality, 29; of income inequality "pregovernment" and "postgovernment," 31
Gintis, Herbert, 315n. 33, 316n. 42
global solutions, 5
globalization, economic, 3–5; capital mobility and, 237–39; coping with, 300–305; corporate income taxes and, 133–34, 140–41; education politics and, 199; egalitarian policies and, 61–64; employment policies and, 244–45; European welfare states and, 133, 316–17n. 55; government capacity and, 3–5, 61–64; immigration and, 239–41; income taxes and, 134; increased inequality and, 28; international economic policy and, 233–41; international policies to cope with, 304–5; overblown fears of, 301; policies that advance competitiveness in, 301–2; political effects of, 64; social insurance and, 114–16, 302–3; tax progressivity and, 303–4. *See also* capital mobility; immigration; trade
globalization, political, 5, 64
Golden Rule, 45
Goldman Sachs, and Clinton administration, 74, 244
Goldwater, Barry, 89
Goodman, Ellen, 233
Gordon formula, 322n. 38
Gottschalk, Peter, 27, 53, 224
government: capacity of, 3–5, 61–64; effectiveness of, xi, 2; failure of, 39–40; for the people, v, 43, 307–8; functions of, 33–46; loss of confidence in, 2–3, 309nn. 2, 4; successes of, 290–93
government employees: disability insurance for, 94–95; social insurance spending for, 77, 78 table 4.1

government employment, wage levels and, 54–55. *See also* public service employment

government procurement, wage levels and, 53–54

Great Britain. *See* United Kingdom

Great Depression, unemployment in, 207, 336n. 14

Greenspan, Alan, 208

Greenstone, J. David, 244

gross domestic product (GDP): international comparisons of per capita, 13–14; neglect of nonmonetary factors in, 14; per capita in United States, 12, 310n. 5; per household in United States, 12, 310n. 6

gross national product (GNP), rise of per capita in United States, 12

guaranteed income: advantages of, 47, 273, 282; costs of, 282; divorce rates and, 47–48; family values and, 48; intensive care and, 282–83; 1960s and 1970s proposals for, 47; poverty and inequality and, 47–48; recommendations on, 299; rejections of, 47; work incentives and, 47–48, 282

guaranteed work: arguments pro and con, 54–55; business opposition to, 224; poverty and, 224; public opinion on, 224

Gumperz, John, 342n. 1

gun control, health and, 119–20

guns, taxes on, 145

H

Habitat for Humanity, 269

Hacker, Andrew, 29

Hansen, Mark, 66

Harriman, Averell, 73

Harrington, Michael, 21

Harvey, Philip, 117

Hausman, Jerry, 131

Havel, Vaclav, 268

Hayek, Friedrich, 314n. 6

Head Start: effects of, 174–75; funding of, 175

health: effects of Medicaid on, 271; nonmedical influences on, 119–20

health care, 269–73; infant and prenatal, 172–73; universal, 272–73. *See also* medical care

health clinics, 172–73

health insurance: employer-provided, 77; lack of, 269–71, 323n. 63; public, 98–106

health maintenance organizations (HMOs): cost containment and, 104; problems with, 118

Heard, Alexander, 72

Hedges, Larry, 180

Herbert, Bob, 239

Heritage Foundation, 285

higher education. *See* education, higher

Hispanics: higher education and, 196–97; immigration and wages of, 240; military personnel and, 212; poverty and, 21; school segregation of, 182. *See also* Latinos

Hobbes, Thomas, 33, 44

Hochschild, Jennifer, 49

home, need for, 268

home health care, in Oregon, 106

home mortgage interest, tax deductibility of, 259–60

home ownership: imputed rent from, 136; tax breaks for, 259–60

home sales, tax exclusion of capital gains on, 260

homeless people: characteristics of, 263–66; number of, 262–63; stereotypes about, 263; turnover among, 263

Homeless Relief Act, 266

homeless shelters: charitable agencies and, 266–67; comprehensive services in, 267; funding of, 266; mixed record of, 267; shortage of, 263

homelessness: African Americans and, 264–65; children and, 265; defined, 343–44n. 42; drug and alcohol abuse and, 263, 264, 265; housing costs and, 266; immigrants and, 265; lack of spouse or partner and, 265–66; men and, 265; mental illness and, 263–64; old people and, 265; poverty and, 265–66; sexual abuse and, 265, 267;

homelessness (*continued*)
veterans and, 265; whites and, 265; women and, 265, 267

homemaking work, neglect of in GDP, 14

Hoover Institution, 285

hospital emergency rooms, 270

House of Representatives (U.S.), party polarization in, 243

housing: affordable, 268–69; middle-class subsidies for, 259–60; need for, 259, 262; self-help in, 269; transitional, 267. *See also* homelessness

housing assistance: poor families receiving, 261; spending on for low-income people, 262

housing costs: home, shelter, prison, and hospital compared, 268; homelessness and, 266

housing, public. *See* public housing

Houston (Tex.), rental voucher wait in, 262

Howard, Christopher, 157

Hughes Aircraft, lobbying by, 213

human capital: broad conception of, 51, 52; defined, 51, 159; market imperfections and, 163; poverty and, 51–52. *See also* education

human poverty, in United States and other advanced countries, 30

humanity, common, sense of, 45

hunger: in the 1990s, 255; in United States, 249–50, 255

Hunger in America, 250

hunger counties, 250

Hyde amendments, 170

I

Iceland, public sector employment in, 338n. 47

Illinois: proportional income taxes in, 152; regressive taxes in, 152

immigrants: homelessness and, 265; union weakness and, 230

immigration: costs and benefits of, 63, 240, 241; free, 239–40; geographic concentration of, 239, 240; illegal, 240; impact of on poverty and inequality, 239–41; service industries and, 239; upsurge in, 239–40. *See also* globalization

impartiality, tax progressivity and, 128

import quotas, agricultural, 250–51

imports: increase of, 235–36; job displacement and, 216–17; job retraining and, 236; wage drops and, 236. *See also* globalization

imputed rent: owner-occupied homes and, 136; tax exclusion of, 259, 260

incarceration rates, international comparisons of, 221

incentives: material, usefulness of, 17; nonmaterial, 55–56. *See also* saving, private; work

income: after-tax distribution of, 154–55; effect of family background on, 20, 51, 192, 312n. 26; wages as share of, 18

income, disposable: distribution of, 29–30; relative inequality in, 31

income, family: distribution of by quintiles, 27–28; Gini coefficient of inequality in, 29; inadequacy of monetary measures of, 14; increased inequality in, 28; median vs. mean, 14; methodological problems with trends in, 310n. 3; post-1973 decline and stagnation of, 13; postwar rise in, 12–13; share of received by top 5 percent, 27

income, guaranteed, 282–83. *See also* guaranteed income

income, household: distribution of by income quintile, 27–28; GDP per household and, 13; Gini coefficient of inequality in, 29–30; increased inequality in, 27–28; postgovernment distribution of, 31; pregovernment distribution of, 30–31; share of received by top 5 percent, 27

income inequality: causes of increase in, 28–29; communitarianism and, 44–46; economic growth and, 64, 209–10; education and, 160; effect of public goods spending on, 210–14; effect of social insurance on,

116–17; effect of Social Security on, 81–83; effect of taxes on, 153–55; extent and nature of, 25–31, 205; government reduction of, 31; imports and, 236; increase in, 1, 27–28; international comparisons of, 29–30; job and wage policies and, 245–46; military spending and, 212–13; postgovernment, 31; pregovernment, 30–31; religious arguments and, 45; self-interest arguments and, 44; social contract and, 45; social order and, 44, 45; unemployment and, 203–5; utilitarianism and, 43–44, 128–31

income level, political participation and, 65, 68

income maintenance, 273–83; work and, 273–74

income redistribution: as approach to poverty and inequality, 48–49; methods of, 49; privatization as barrier to, 90; role of taxes in, 128; social insurance and, 58–59. *See also* tax progressivity; *specific taxes*

income replacement ratio: Social Security, 82–83; Unemployment Insurance, 98

income tax, individual (federal): globalization and, 134; nominal rates of, 134, 137; progressivity of, 134–38; as source of federal revenue, 125, 126 fig. 5.1. *See also* corporate income tax

income tax, state, 152–53

increasing returns to scale: defined, 38; market failure and, 38–39

independence effect, of AFDC, 277

India: GDP per capita in, 13–14; U.S. plants in, 238

Indian. *See* Blackfoot Indians; Native Americans

Indian Law Resource Center, 70

Indiana: AFDC benefits in, 278; proportional income taxes in, 152

Indianapolis, school choice in, 188

individual retirement accounts: administrative costs of, 91; tax expenditures on, 79. *See also* Social Security privatization

industrialization, of United States, 12

inequality. *See* poverty and inequality

inequality, economic. *See* income inequality; wealth

inequality, political: interest group power and, 68–71; as obstacle to egalitarian policies, 64–74; overcoming, 74–75; 300–307; participation biases and, 65–68; party investors and activists and, 71–74. *See also* campaign contributions; lobbying; political participation; voter turnout

inequality express, 1–2

infant mortality: international comparisons of, 119; Medicaid and, 271; U.S. rate of, 325n. 119

infant nutrition and health care, 172–73

inflation: adjustment of poverty line for, 23; defined, 205; effects of, 206; effects of macroeconomic policy on, 40–43; effects of on rich and poor, 42–43; erosion of minimum wage and, 225–26; tradeoff of with unemployment, 41, 207–8; wage gains and, 224

information asymmetries: and insurance markets, 57; and market failure, 39

infrastructure, public service jobs and, 220

inheritance of wealth, equal opportunity and, 147

insurance: adverse selection problem in, 39; moral hazard problem in, 59, 60, 123–24

insurance, private: administrative costs of, 256; disability and, 92; failures in markets for, 57, 58; farming and, 251; medical care and, 99; retirement and, 58, 89–90; unfairness in, 58

insurance, public. *See* social insurance

insurance, social. *See* social insurance

insurance industry, attack on Clinton health plan by, 114

intelligence: and earnings, 20, 192, 311n. 17; genetic factors in inheritance of, 20, 192, 311n. 17

intelligence quotient (IQ), correlation of with income, 311n. 17

interest group power: difficulty of measuring, 68–69, 70; historical evidence of, 70; quantitative evidence of, 70; techniques of, 69, 70

interest groups: antipoverty policy and, 283–84; bias of toward producers, 69–70; education politics and, 198, 199; job politics and, 241–43; myth of balance among, 284; political power of, 68–71; progressive, 70–71; redistributive policies and, 69–70; social insurance politics and, 109–14; tax politics and, 156, 157

interest rates, effect of, 42, 206, 208

international agreements: coping with globalization, 5, 304–5; on environment and working conditions, 237, 239

international economic policy, 233–41

international trade policies, protection of U.S. workers and, 237

interpersonal comparisons: justice and, 130; of utility, 129, 130. See also economists

investment. See economic growth; education; human capital; saving, forced; saving, private; saving, public; saving rate

investment, public, and Social Security Trust Fund, 58

investment tax credit, 138

investor gains, 297

invisible hand, 34

invisible homeless, 263

Iowa, progressive income tax in, 152

Iraq, 211

Italian immigrants, 230

Italy: corporate taxes in, 141; public sector employment in, 220; tax levels in, 133

J

Jacobs, Lawrence, 102

jail. See prisons

Japan: corporate taxes in, 141; economic growth in, 64; educational success of, 184–85; imports from, 236; incarceration rate in, 221; infant mortality in, 119; medical costs in, 99; payroll tax rate in, 142; prisoners in, 223; public sector employment in, 338n. 47; tax levels in, 133; voluntary trade limits and, 235

Japanese schools, and student equality, 168

Jencks, Christopher, 263, 309n. 1

Jews, higher education and, 196

Job Bank, 217

Job Corps, effects of, 191

Job Opportunity and Basic Skills (JOBS), 217–18

job politics, 241–45; CETA and, 220; economic growth and, 244–45; global constraints and, 244–45; political parties and, 243–44

Job Service, 217

job training, externalities in, 162, 163

Job Training Partnership Act (JTPA), 214–15; effects of, 215

job training programs, 190–91, 214–19; for dislocated workers, 216–17; effects of, 215–16, 217; skimpiness of, 214, 215; welfare-to-work, 217–19

job transitions, and imports, 236, 238

job and wage programs, 201–46; poverty and inequality and, 53–56; recommendations on, 245–46, 296–97; successes of, 292. See also wages

jobs: creation of, 219–21, 223–24; discrimination in, 232–33; displacement from, 216–17; ex-welfare recipients and, 280–81; guaranteed, 223–24 (see also guaranteed work); imports and retraining for, 236, 237; placement in, 214–19; public goods spending and, 210–14; right to, 223–24. See also public service employment; wages

Johnson, Lyndon B., 107, 283

Johnson, William, 131

justice, interpersonal comparisons and, 130, 326n. 12, 340n. 84

K

Kant, Immanuel, 128

Kasten, Richard, 137

Katz, Lawrence, 1
Kennedy, Robert, 249
Keynes, John Maynard, 41–42, 207
Keynesianism, 207
Keyssar, Alexander, 66, 230, 342n. 1
Knights of Labor, 230
Korea, imports from, 236
Korean war, military spending and, 211
Kozol, Jonathan, 178
Krueger, Alan, 225
Kuttner, Robert, 16
kwashiorkor, 250

L

labor, conflict of with business, 241–43
labor costs, wages as, 241
labor market centralization, 229, 316–17n. 55, 339n. 75
labor market policy, active, 56, 302
labor markets, 15–20; advantages and disadvantages of, 201–2; and wage justice, 228–29. See also jobs; marginal product theory; wages
labor supply. See jobs; work
labor unions: antipoverty politics and, 283; antiunion attitudes and, 231; collective benefits of, 229; contributions to Democrats by, 69–70, 244; Democratic Party and, 243–44; encouraging, 228–32; European, 110, 229, 231; history of, 230–31; job politics and, 241–43; lobbying expenditures by, 242; monopoly power and, 228–29; New Deal and, 111; PAC contributions by, 69–70, 242–43, 244; political weakness of, 242; revival of, 231; soft money contributions by, 341n. 104; total political contributions by, 284; wages and, 228–29; workforce coverage by, 230
labor union weakness, 69–70, 110, 242; causes of, 229–31; government policy and, 231
laissez-faire doctrine, macroeconomic policy and, 41
Lamm, Don, 342n. 1
Landrum-Griffith Act, 231

Latin America: GDP per capita in, 13–14; immigration from, 240; U.S. investment in, 238
Latinos: higher education and, 196–97; job discrimination and, 233; residential segregation of, 178. See also Hispanics
law and order, as government function, 33, 34–5
lawsuits, job discrimination and, 232–33
legal arrangements, voter turnout and, 66–67
leisure, loss of and GDP, 14
Levitan, Sar, 171
Levy, Frank, 12, 27
liberalism, practical, 3
libertarianism, 36
liberties, equal opportunity and, 167
liberty, xi, 2, 6; school choice and, 185
life expectancy: rise of, 12; Social Security benefits and, 320n. 19
lifetime earnings, Social Security smoothing of, 82
lifetime income models, of tax incidence, 141, 146, 149–50, 151
lighthouse, as public good, 38
Lincoln, Abraham, v, 43, 307–8
Lindahl, Erik, 127–28
living wage, 226; protection of city employees by, 339n. 62
lobbying, tax deductibility of, 8
lobbying expenditures, by business and labor, 242, 341n. 103
Locke, John, 33–34, 127
Lockheed Martin, lobbying by, 213
Loprest, Pamela, 280
Los Angeles: immigration to, 239, 240; living wage in, 226; rental voucher wait in, 262
Louisiana, regressive taxes in, 152
Lovett, Robert, 73
Low Countries, payroll tax rates in, 142
low-income people, support for egalitarian policies by, 65
luck: disasters and, 60; wages and, 16–17, 19

Luxembourg, GDP per capita in, 13
luxury taxes, 145

M

macroeconomic policy, 40–43, 203–10; wage levels and, 53
Maeroff, Gene, 178
magnet schools, 189
majority rule, 7
make-work, 54–55, 219–20
Malaysia, capital controls in, 238
malnutrition: in America, 249–50; Food Stamps and, 254–55. *See also* food; nutrition
marasmus, 250
marginal product theory of wages: nature of, 15; validity of, 15–20. *See also* labor markets; wages
market economy, establishing foundations of, 34–37
market failure, 37–40; education and, 161–65; externalities and, 37; public goods and, 37–38. *See also* insurance
markets, labor. *See* labor markets; marginal product theory of wages; wages
markets, private, government entanglement in, 36
Marmor, Theodore, 57, 117
marriage: AFDC and, 275, 276, 277; among poor people, 21–22; childbirth and, 168–69; guaranteed incomes and, 47–48
married-couple families, as fraction of the poor, 22
Marshall, Alfred, 15
Martin, Cathie Jo, 325n. 113
Maryland, welfare reform and, 280
Mashaw, Jerry, 117
Massachusetts: alternative schools in, 189; school inequality in, 179; welfare reform and, 280
Massey, Douglas, 182
maximin criterion, 45
McCloy, John J., 73

McConnell, Grant, 70
McDermott, James, 119
McDonnell Douglas, lobbying by, 213
McGovern, George, 47
McKinney Act, 266
McLanahan, Sara, 49
means-tested expenditures, effects of on poverty gap, 325n. 114
media: cynicism about government and, 3; poverty stereotypes in, 21
median incomes, relative poverty and, 26
Medicaid: administrative costs of, 271–72; birth control and, 169, 170, 332n. 20; effects of on poor, 271; elderly and disabled and, 272; error rates in, 256; fraud and overpayments in, 272; limited coverage of, 271, 272; long-term care and, 105–6; nursing home coverage by, 272; pregnant women and children and, 172; proportion of poor covered by, 272; size and cost of, 271, 272; social insurance and, 106; spending on, 77, 78 table 4.1; state variations in benefits, 172, 332n. 27
medical care: effectiveness of prenatal, 50; federal spending on, 78 table 4.1; infant and prenatal, 172–73; policy improvement, 117–20, 297, 298–300; right to, 269, 272; social insurance logic and, 98–99; universal, 272–73. *See also* health; health care; health clinics; health insurance; health maintenance organizations (HMOs)
medical insurance: employer-provided, 77; lack of, 99, 269–71, 323n. 63; private, 99
medical insurance, public, 98–106; AMA role in, 112–13; universality of, 117–19, 272–73
medical treatment, drug abuse and, 223
Medicare: alleged bankruptcy of, 102–3; AMA campaign against, 112–13; co-payments in, 101; coverage of, 101–2; Democratic responsibility for, 107; financial pressure on, 102–3; increased coverage of elderly and, 100; number of bene-

ficiaries, 100; premiums for, 100; public opinion on, 108–9; redistributive effects of, 101; spending on, 77, 78 table 4.1, 100–101

Medicare costs: containment of, 103–5; Prospective Payment System (PPS) and, 104; rise in, 103

Medicare Hospital Insurance (HI), 100, 101

Medicare Supplemental Medical Insurance (SMI), 100, 101

medicine: preventive, 270; socialized, 273

Medigap insurance, 102, 105

Mellon, Andrew, 157

Memphis, rental voucher wait in, 262

Menchik, Paul, 329n. 62

mental hospitals, number of patients in, 264

mental illness: deinstitutionalization and, 264; homelessness and, 263–64

merit, wages and, 16–17

Mexico: illegal immigration from, 240; U.S. investment in, 237–38

Miami, immigration to, 239, 240

Michigan: proportional income taxes in, 152; regressive taxes in, 152; welfare reform and, 280

Midwest, commodities distribution and, 252

military draft, 212

military equipment, 213

military operations, 212–13

military personnel, 212

military policies, wage levels and, 54

military spending: as percentage of GDP, 211; poverty and inequality and, 212–13; as share of federal budget, 211

milk marketing orders, 250

Mill, John Stuart, 129

Milwaukee: living wage in, 226; school choice in, 187; segregation in, 178

minimum wage: erosion of by inflation, 25; levels of, 225–26

minimum wage laws: business opposition to, 225; economists and, 225; effects of, 225;

good wages and, 55; limited role of, 226–27; at state level, 226; unemployment and, 55, 225

Minnesota: alternative schools in, 189; charter schools in, 189

Mishel, Lawrence, 313n. 40

missiles, 213

Mississippi: AFDC benefits in, 275, 278; Medicaid benefits in, 172, 332n. 27; prenatal care and, 172

Missouri, school inequality in, 179

Mitchell, George, 120

mobility programs, 209

mobilization of voters, U.S. failure at, 66

Moe, Terry, 186–87

Moffitt, Robert, 278

monetarism, 206

monetary policy: defined, 205; nature of, 42. *See also* macroeconomic policy

money: declining marginal utility for, 43–44, 128, 129, 130–31; effect of on elections, 70; effect of on schools, 179–81

money, political, 8; class bias in giving, 68; givers of to political parties, 72–73; giving of by income level, 306, 347n. 5; reforms to control, 306–7. *See also* campaign contributions; interest groups; lobbying expenditures

money, tight, 42, 206, 208

money supply: government management of, 35–36; macroeconomic policy and, 206

monopoly: Adam Smith and, 36; natural, 38–39

Montana: commodities distribution and, 252; progressive income taxes in, 152

moral hazard: defined, 59; social insurance and, 59, 60, 123–24; unemployment insurance and, 121–22

mothers, never-married, among the poor, 21

mothers, single: frequency of among poor people, 22; as society-wide phenomenon, 22

Motor Voter law, 67
Musgrave, Richard, 30

N

Nation at Risk, A, 185
National Academy of Social Insurance (NASI), 316n. 49
National Association of Manufacturers (NAM), lobbyists from, 242
National Coalition for the Homeless, 262–63, 281, 284
National Educational Association (NEA), on high schools, 178
national emergencies, tax system and, 155–56
national health insurance, 118–19. *See also* medical insurance
National Labor Relations Act, 231; business role in, 73; origins of, 243
National Labor Relations Board (NLRB), 231
National Rifle Association (NRA), 120
national sovereignty, economic globalization as threat to, 62–64
Native Americans: casino gambling and soft money from, 341n. 104; higher education and, 196–97; military personnel and, 212; poverty rates among, 21. *See also* Blackfoot Indians
natural monopoly: defined, 38; government regulation and, 38–39; market failure and, 38–39
natural rate of unemployment, 41, 207
natural rights, 33, 285; to property, 127
necessities, basic: guaranteeing, 298–300; right to, 249, 285–87; successes in providing, 293
needs, basic, 247–87; poverty and inequality and, 59–61
negative income tax: Milton Friedman and, 43, 47; 1960s and 1970s proposals for, 47
Negative Income Tax experiments, labor supply and, 132, 133
neighborhood effects: defined, 37; and externalities, 39

Netherlands: infant mortality in, 119; poverty rate in, 24; public sector employment in, 220; tax levels in, 133; trade volume in, 234
New Deal: business role in, 72, 73, 244; practical liberalism and, 3; racial discrimination in, 111, 338n. 44; South role in, 111; tax policy in, 156
New Hampshire, state financing of schools in, 333n. 38
New Jersey: housing and welfare reform in, 268; progressive income taxes in, 152; welfare reform and, 280
New Mexico, state financing of schools in, 333n. 38
New Party, living wage and, 226
New York City: food charity cuts in, 258; immigration to, 239, 240; living wage in, 226; public homeless shelters in, 267; public housing wait in, 261; rental voucher wait in, 262; school choice in, 187, 288
New Zealand: gasoline taxes in, 145; infant mortality in, 119; public sector employment in, 338n. 47
Newark, rental voucher wait in, 262
Nike, sweatshops and, 239
ninety-ten ratio, in OECD countries, 30
Nixon, Richard: Food Stamps and, 254; Social Security amendments and, 107
Nixon administration: antipoverty policies and, 283; Family Assistance Plan and, 47
nominal tax rates, defined, 134
nonexcludible consumption: defined, 37; public goods and, 37–39
nongovernmental organizations (NGOs), international boycotts and, 239
nonrival consumption: defined, 37; public goods and, 37–39
North American Free Trade Agreement (NAFTA), 235; investment in Mexico and, 237–38; protection of workers and, 237
North Korea, 211
Northrop Grumman, lobbying by, 213
Norway: income inequality in, 30; public sec-

tor employment in, 220; tax levels in, 133

nursing homes, 105–6

nutrition: infant and prenatal, 172–73; schools and, 173–74. *See also* food; malnutrition

O

Oakland (Calif.), public housing wait in, 261

obstacles, political: to egalitarian policies, 61–74; overcoming, 74–75, 300–307

occupational status, family background and, 20, 51, 192, 312n. 26

Ohio, progressive income taxes in, 152

Okner, Benjamin, 137

Okun, Arthur, 46

old age pensions: globalization and, 115; social insurance for, 57–59. *See also* social insurance

Old Age and Survivors Insurance (OASI), 78–92; spending on, 77, 78 table 4.1. *See also* Social Security

Old Age, Survivors and Disability Insurance (OASDI): Social Security as rubric for, 77; spending on, 77. *See also* Social Security

old people, homelessness and, 265. *See also* elderly

Operation Dixie, 230, 231

opportunity, equal. *See* equal opportunity

order, social, income inequality and, 44, 45

ordinalist economic theory, 130; and justice, 326n. 12, 340n. 84

Organization of Economic Cooperation and Development (OECD) countries: income inequality in, 29–30; rich-to-poor ratios in, 30

organizing politically, 7

P

PAC contributions: by business, 69–70, 242–43, 244; by labor, 69–70, 242–43, 244

PACs, nonrepresentation of poor people by, 284

Page, Alexandra, 318n. 81

Page, Ben R., 322n. 39

Page, Eleanor, 334n. 75

Page, Mary R., xii

Page, Timothy, 335n. 91

parents, equal opportunity for children and, 50–51

participation, political. *See* political participation

participation bias, reforms to reduce, 305–7

parties, political. *See* political parties

partner, lack of and homelessness, 265–66

party affiliation, voting in Congress and, 108

party differences, between Republicans and Democrats, 71–74

party mobilization, voter turnout and, 66, 67

party polarization, House of Representatives and, 243

party systems, voter turnout and, 65–66

Patterson, Orlando, 182

payroll taxes: as contributions to social insurance, 144; income cap on, 87, 88, 120, 143–44; poverty line and, 227; rates compared internationally, 142; regressivity of, 142–44; as source of federal revenue, 126 fig. 5.1, 142

Pear, Robert, 324n. 82

Pechman, Joseph, 48, 131–32, 137

peers, role of in education, 179–80, 181

Pell Grants, 194

Pennsylvania: proportional income taxes in, 152; regressive taxes in, 152

people, government by and for, v, 43, 307–8

Perry Preschool Program (Ypsilanti, Mich.), 174, 175

Peterson, Paul, 153

Peterson, Peter G., 321n. 23

Philip Morris: lobbying expenditures by, 242; PAC contributions of to Republicans, 244; poor people and, 284; soft money from, 341n. 104

Phillips curve, 207

Pigou, Arthur, 37, 129

Pittsburgh, SRO housing in, 268
Planned Parenthood, 169
policies: designing, 6; enacting, 7
policy tools, choice among, 40
political action, 7
political contributions: by business and labor, 284; income level and, 306, 347n. 5
political feasibility, 246
political money, reforms to control, 306–7. *See also* campaign contributions; lobbying
political obstacles: to egalitarian policies, 61–74; overcoming, 74–75, 300–307
political organizations, class bias in membership of, 68
political participation: family background and, 68; income level and, 68, 306, 347n. 5; inequalities in, 65–68; reforms to reduce bias in, 305–7; beyond voter turnout, 67–68. *See also* voter turnout
political parties: antipoverty politics and, 283; free trade and, 235; job politics and, 243–44; money and activists in, 71–74; social insurance politics and, 107–8
political reform, 5, 7–8; recommendations for, 305–7
politics: of antipoverty policy, 283–85; of commodities distribution, 252; of education, 197–99; of employment policies, 241–45; of social insurance, 107–16; of tax policy, 155–58
pollution, market failure and, 37
poor people: African Americans among, 21; characteristics of, 21–22; elderly among, 22; homelessness and, 266; Latinos among, 21; members of married-couple families among, 22; never-married mothers among, 21; nonrepresentation of by PACs and contributors, 284; single men among, 22; single women living alone among, 22; stereotypes of, 21–22; urban ghetto residents among, 21; whites among, 21, 22; workers among, 21; youth among, 22
poverty: birth control and, 168–70; consequences of, 23; crime and, 222–23; depen-
dency and, 21; duration of, 21; economic growth and, 208–9; education and, 159; effect of inflation on, 206; effect of Social Security on, 79–80, 81; effect of welfare reform on, 280–81; effect of welfare-to-work programs on, 218; European standard of, 24; extent of in United States, 2, 20–23; guaranteed work and, 224; imprisonment as policy on, 221–23; invisibility of, 21; minimum wage and, 226; 1960s decline in, 21; 1970–80s rise in, 21; official definition of, 22–23; politics of, 283–85; preschooling and, 165; relative conception of, 25–26; single motherhood and, 22; among social groups, 21–22; unemployment and, 204, 205. *See also* income inequality
poverty and inequality: effect of public goods spending on, 210–14; government role in dealing with, 43–46; impact of immigration on, 239–41; jobs and good wages, military spending and, 212–13; jobs policies and, 245–46; public goods and, 40
poverty and inequality, approaches to: education and human capital, 51–52; equal opportunity, 49–51; guaranteed income, 47–48; jobs and good wages, 53–56; progressive taxes, 48–49; safety nets and basic needs, 59–61; social insurance, 56–59
poverty gap: effect of social insurance and means-tested expenditures on, 325n. 114; reduction of by AFDC, 278; reduction of by social insurance, 116
poverty line: adjustment of for inflation, 23; level of, 20
poverty politics, 283–85; interest groups and, 283–84; political parties and, 283
poverty rates: among African Americans, 21; among children, 21–22; among elderly, 21; among Hispanics, 21; among Native Americans, 21; among whites; international comparisons of with United States, 23–24
poverty spells, 21

Powell, Colin, 212

pregovernment income distribution: difficulty of knowing, 30; importance of, 30, 31

prenatal care, cost effectiveness of, 50

prenatal nutrition and health care, 172–73

preschooling: cost effectiveness of, 50; effects of, 174–75; government role in, 164–65; poverty and inequality and, 165. *See also* day care; equal opportunity, for children; Head Start

preventive medicine, 270

price supports, agricultural, 250–52

prison option, 221–23

prisoners, work and, 222

prisons: African Americans in, 221, 223; cost of, 221–22, 268; incarceration rates internationally, 221; population of, 221

privatization: of old age insurance, 58–59; and protection of the poor, 321–22n. 37; of Social Security, 89–92

producer's surplus, 16

production, jointness of, 16

profits, 16

progressive taxes: approach to poverty and inequality, 48–49; arguments concerning, 127–34; defined, 48, 125. *See also* tax progressivity; taxes

property, natural right to, 127

property rights, establishment of, as government function, 33–35, 36

property tax: assessment practices and, 150; incidence of, 149; payments, deductibility of, 259–60; progressivity of, 149–50; revolt, 150; as source of revenue, 126, 148–49

proportional taxes, defined, 125

Prospective Payment System (PPS), Medicare costs and, 104

protectionism, 237

psychiatric hospital bed, cost of, 268

public debate, business firms' influence on, 109

public goods: defined, 37; education and, 164; efficient provision of, 127–28; market failure and, 37–38; military, 211–13; nonex-cludibility and, 37–38; nonrival consumption and, 37–38; peaceful, 213–14; poverty and inequality and, 40; provision of as government function, 37–40; spending on, 210–14

public health, importance of, 119–20

Public Health Service Act, Title X and birth control, 169

public housing, 260–61, 262; demolition of blighted, 261; waiting in vain for, 261; working families and, 261

public interest groups, 70–71

public opinion: on guaranteed work, 224; on labor unions, 231; on Medicare, 108–9; mobilizing, 7; social insurance, 88, 108–9; on Social Security, 83, 88, 108; tax politics and, 156, 158

public sector employment, in United States and other countries, 220–21

public service employment, 219–21; efficiency of, 54–55; good wages and, 54–55; military and, 212–13; wage subsidies and, 220

public works, Adam Smith and, 36–37

Public Works Administration (PWA), 219, 220

Puritanism, American social policy and, 274

Q

Quadagno, Jill, 111

Quinn, Dennis, 134

R

race to the bottom, 4, 63; and corporate taxes, 141

racial discrimination: in employment, 232–33; in higher education, 196–97; in New Deal 111, 338n. 44. *See also* equal opportunity; segregation

racial segregation, in schools, 181–83. *See also* equal opportunity; segregation, residential

racism, wars against the poor and, 284

railroad workers, social insurance spending for, 77, 78 table 4.1

rational benevolence, 128

rational expectations, macroeconomic policy and, 207

Rawls, John, 45, 123, 128

Raytheon, lobbying by, 213

Reagan, Ronald: business and election of, 70, 73; on Food Stamps and gin, 256; on welfare queens, 275

Reagan administration: disability purge by, 92–93, 264; military buildup and, 211; tax policy of, 157

recession: defined, 206; of early 1990s, 204–5; macroeconomic policy and, 40–43

Reciprocal Trade Act, 235; business role in, 244

recommendations, 293–300; on children, 294–95; on education and training, 294–95; on guaranteeing necessities, 298–300; on jobs and wages, 296–97; on social insurance, 297–98

redistribution of income: as approach to poverty and inequality, 48–49, 46n. 31. See also income inequality; tax progressivity

reform, economic, 8

reform, political, 5, 7–8; recommendations for, 305–7

regressive taxes, defined, 125

Reich, Robert, 52

reinventing government, 6

Reischauer, Robert, 87

relative income, social functioning and, 26

relative poverty, 25–26; median incomes and, 26

religion: charter schools and, 190; school choice and, 187–88

religious ideas, inequality and, 45

religious missions, homeless shelters and, 266–67

religious worship, charitable contributions for, 257

rental assistance, 260, 261–62

rental subsidies, 261, 262

rental vouchers, 261–62; wait for, 262

Republican Party: business and, 72–74, 243–44; education policy and, 198; egalitarian policies and, 71–72; free trade and, 235; proworker policies and, 243–44. See also campaign contributions; interest groups; political parties

research, government spending on, 195

residential segregation: amelioration of, 346n. 2; school segregation and, 178, 182–83

retirement age: delaying for Social Security, 88; effect of Social Security on, 80–81

retirement insurance, private, 89–90, 91

retirement insurance, public, 78–92; and social insurance for, 57–59

Reuther, Walter, 230

revenue: federal government sources of, 125–26, 126 fig. 5.1; state and local government sources of, 126

Reynolds, Morgan, 30

Rhode Island, progressive income taxes in, 152

Ricardo, David, 234

rich-to-poor ratio, in United States and other OECD countries, 30

right to basic necessities, 249, 285–87; affordability of, 286; implementation of, 286–87

Right-to-Work laws, 231

right turn, by business, 70, 73–74, 113

right-wing foundations, 285

rights: economic, 285–86; to food, 258–59; to medical care, 272; natural, 33, 127, 285

risk aversion, tax progressivity and, 128

Rivera, Diego, 219

Robins, Philip, 278

Rogers, Diane, 141

Rogers, Joel, 73, 226

Roosevelt, Franklin D., 3, 107, 156, 285

Rosenstone, Steven, 66

Rousseau, Jean-Jacques, 45

Rubin, Robert, 73, 74, 244

Rubinow, I. M., 319n. 1

runaways, teenage, 265

Russia: military spending by, 211–12; opening of to investment, 237

S

safety net: as approach to poverty and inequality, 59–61; limited need for, 248–49; metaphor of, 59–60, 247–48

safety net programs: recommendations on, 298–300; successes of, 293

salaries. *See* executive compensation; wages

sales taxes: regressivity of, 145–46, 151–52; as source of state and local revenue, 126

San Antonio, school choice in, 188

San Francisco, low-income housing in, 268

San Jose, living wage in, 226

saving, forced, Social Security and, 82

saving, private: effect of retirement insurance on, 58; effects of taxes on, 131–34; government subsidy of, 89; Social Security and, 80–81; wage inequality and, 55–56

saving, public, and Social Security surpluses, 81

saving rate: national, 310n. 6; personal, 132

Scaife Foundation, 285

Scandinavia: infant mortality in, 119; payroll tax rates in, 142; public sector employment in, 220; retrenchment in, 317n. 55; union role in, 229

Scandinavian countries, trade volume in, 234

Schattschneider, E. E., 69, 70

Schegloff, Manny, 342n. 1

Schlozman, Kay, 65

Scholastic Aptitude Tests (SATs), trends in, 185

school bond issues, 198–99

school breakfasts, 173–74

school busing, 182

school choice: arguments for, 185; charter schools and, 189–90; effects of on inequality, 188–89; effects of on public schools, 188–89; multiple public districts and, 189; religious issue in, 187–88

school effects, methodological problems in studying, 180, 184, 193

school lunches, 173; effects of, 254–55

school organization, effects of, 187

school vouchers, 186, 187, 188, 189, 190

schooling, bureaucratic influence on, 187

schools, Catholic: educational effects of, 186; enrollment in, 162; minorities' gains in, 186, 287; religious freedom and, 187–88; tuition costs at, 164, 331n. 9

schools, charter, 189–90

schools, common, ideal of, 177–78

schools, elementary and secondary, 176–90; federal role in, 176–77; rise of public, 177; state and local role in, 176

schools, private: educational effects of, 186, 187; effects of on public schools, 187; enrollment in, 162; tuition costs at, 164

schools, public, 176–90; abolition of, 185–86; effects of money and resources in, 179–81; enrollment in, 162; historical rise of, 163, 177; inequality in, 177–78, 179, 180; meager resources for poor students in, 178; rationale for, 162–65; segregation and, 178, 181–83; what works in, 183–85. *See also* day care; education; equal opportunity; preschooling

Schultze, Charles, 252

Schwarz, John, on hidden success, 293

scope of conflict, 199

screening hypothesis: in education, 160, 192; in higher education, 193–94

Seattle, low-income housing in, 268

Second Harvest, 258

Segal, Dan, 342n. 1

segregation, racial, in schools, 181–83

segregation, residential: amelioration of, 346n. 2; school segregation and, 178, 182–83

self-development, inequality and, 45, 46

self-help, in housing, 269

self-interest, income inequality and, 44

Sen, Amartya, 26

Seniors Coalition, lobbying expenditures by, 341n. 103

separation of powers, and egalitarian policies, 317n. 57, 327n. 24

Serbia, 211

service industries, and immigration, 239

sexual abstinence, 169. *See also* birth control

sexual abuse, homelessness and, 265, 267

sexual profligacy, 22

shelter, need for, 259. *See also* housing

shelters, homeless. *See* homeless shelters

Sidgwick, Henry, 45, 128

Sierra Leone, GDP per capita in, 13–14

single-parent families, poverty and, 168–69

single-room occupancy hotels (SROs), destruction of, 266

sin taxes. *See* excise taxes

skill premium, 191–92; education efforts and, 52; increased inequality and, 28; international competition and, 238

Slemrod, Joel, 132

Smith, Adam, 34, 36–37, 234

Smolensky, Eugene, 30

social class, parental transmission of, 20, 51, 192, 312n. 26

social contract, inequality and, 45

social democracies, and globalization, 316–17n. 55. *See also* Europe

Social Democratic parties: absence of in United States, 110; and voter turnout, 66, 67

social functioning, relative income and, 26

social goods. *See* public goods

social insurance: as approach to poverty and inequality, 56–59; broad conception of, 122–24; controllability of behavior and, 122–24; effects of on poverty, 116; farmers and, 251; globalization and, 114–16; improving, 116–24, 297–98; income redistribution and, 58–59, 116–17; interest groups and, 109–14; Medicaid and, 106; moral hazard and, 59, 60, 123–24; nature of, 57; payroll taxes as contributions to, 144; political parties and, 107–8; politics of, 107–16; private saving and, 58; privatization of, 58–59; public opinion and, 88, 108–9; retirement and, 57–59, 89–90; spending on, 77, 78 table 4.1; SSI and, 95–96. *See also* insurance; Social Security

social insurance expenditures, effects of on poverty gap, 325n. 114

social insurance logic: broad conception of, 122–24; disability insurance and, 92; guarantee of basic necessities and, 249; medical care and, 98–99; retirement insurance and, 89–90

social insurance politics, 107–66; global constraints and, 114–16; interest groups and, 109–14; political parties and, 107–8; public opinion and, 88, 108–9

social insurance programs: accomplishments of, 290–91; and globalization, 302–3; Democratic Party and, 107–8; recommendations on, 297–98

social interaction, effects of extreme inequality on, 45

social mobility, 20; and family background effects, 20, 51, 192, 312n. 26

social movements, of poor people, 284, 285

Social Security: accomplishments of, 290; administrative costs of, 79, 93; demographic pressure on, 84; effect of on poverty, 79–80, 81; effects of on savings and work, 80–81; as entitlement, 82; globalization and, 115, 302–3; increased progressivity in, 83; measures to strengthen, 120–21; pay-as-you-go financing of, 86; privatization of, 89–92; public opinion on, 88, 108; redistributive effects of, 81–83; reliance of elderly on, 79

Social Security Act: business firms' role in, 73, 110–11; Democratic Party and, 107; social insurance programs and, 77

Social Security "bankruptcy": measures to avert, 84, 87–89; payoff of national debt and, 85; receding dates of, 85

Social Security benefits: income replacement ratios and, 82–83; levels of, 78–79; life expectancies and, 320n. 19; proposed cuts in, 84, 87–88; reduction of poverty by, 79–80, 81; taxation of, 83; unpopularity of cuts in, 88

Social Security privatization: administrative costs and, 91; free riders and, 91; investment returns in, 90, 91; political unraveling and, 91–92; protection of the poor and, 321–22n. 37; redistribution and, 90; transition problem in, 90–91

Social Security revenue: expected shortfalls in, 87; payroll tax cap and, 87, 88

Social Security surpluses, 84–85; expected end of, 86–87; public investment of, 58, 81; Reagan years and, 86

Social Security taxes. *See* payroll taxes

Social Security Trust Fund, as accounting device, 84–85, 86

socialized medicine, 273

soft money contributors, 242–43, 341n. 104

Solow, Robert, 219

Soros, George, 29

soup kitchens, 257, 258

South: commodities distribution and, 252; Democratic Party role of, 73; labor union weakness and, 230, 231; New Deal role of, 111

South Dakota, regressive taxes in, 152

Southeast Asia, imports from, 236

sovereignty, economic globalization as threat to, 62–64

spouse, lack of and homelessness, 265–66

stagflation, 113, 207

standard of living, rise of in United States, 12, 13

Standard Oil, New Deal and, 111

starting line, and equal opportunity, 50, 166–67

state and local taxes: most regressive states, 151–52; as sources of revenue, 126, 148–49

state income taxes: progressivity of, 152–53; as source of revenue, 152

Steel, James, 158

stereotypes: of AFDC mothers, 276; of homeless people, 263; of poor people, 21, 22

stigma, Food Stamps and, 255–56

stock market: long-run returns from, 322n. 38; rise in, 29, 297, 347n. 3

Streeck, Wolfgang, 56

student loans, 194–95

successes, government programs and, 290–93

Supplemental Security Income (SSI): benefit levels of, 96; coverage of, 96; error rates in, 256; number of recipients, 96; social insurance and, 95–96; spending on, 78 table 4.1

Swank, Duane, 134

sweatshops abroad, 239

Sweden: active labor market policies in, 302; austerity in, 133; centralized wage bargaining in, 339n. 75; corporate taxes in, 141; globalization and employment policies of, 244–45; income inequality in, 30; labor union density in, 229; poverty rate in, 24; public sector employment in, 220; tax levels in, 133

Swedish welfare state, role of business in, 241

Swenson, Peter, 111, 241, 319n. 86

Switzerland: inequality and economic growth in, 64; poverty in, 24; public sector employment in, 338n. 47; tax levels in, 133

Swope, Gerald, 111

sympathy, extended, 45

T

Taft-Hartley Act, 231

Tanzania, GDP per capita in, 26

tariffs: historical struggles over, 155; as source of federal revenue, 126, 144–45

Tawney, R. H., 44

tax credit: child and dependent care, 175; low-income housing, 262; refundability of, 227

tax deduction: high-income taxpayers and, 136; of home mortgage interest, 259–60; of property tax payments, 259–60

tax exclusion, 135–36; of capital gains on home sales, 260; of employer-provided day care, 175–76; of imputed rent, 259, 260 tax expenditures: on EITC, 228; on employer retirement plans, 79; on employer-provided health insurance, 77; on higher education, 195; on home ownership, 259–60; on IRAs and Keogh plans, 79; politics of, 156–57

tax incidence: lifetime income models of, 141, 146, 149–50, 151; property tax and, 149

tax levels, in United States and other countries, 133

tax loopholes, 156

tax philosophers, 48

tax politics: interest groups in, 156, 157; national emergencies and, 155–56; political parties and, 155, 156, 157; public role in, 156, 158

tax progressivity: arguments concerning, 127–34; corporate income tax and, 141–42; defined, 48, 125; estate and gift taxes and, 146–48; excise taxes and, 145–46; globalization and, 303–4; income tax and, 134–38; net extent of, 153–55; property tax and, 149–50; sales taxes and, 151–52; in U.S. history, 134, 156; utilitarian theory of, 128–29; worst states for, 151–52

tax proportionality, defined, 125

tax rates: effective, defined, 135; nominal, defined, 134

tax reform, 158

tax regimes, democratic-statist, 330n. 95

tax regressivity, defined, 125

tax shelters, 136

tax system, possibility of fairness in, 291

taxation: ability-to-pay theory of, 128–29; benefits theory of, 127–28; of capital gains, effect of on economic growth, 209; double, 140, 327n. 43; of Social Security benefits, 83

taxes: deductibility of lobbying expenses from, 8; effects of on savings and work, 131–34; federal, 134–48; net effect of on income inequality, 153–55; net effective rates of, 153–55; progressive, as approach to poverty and inequality, 48–49; state and local, 148–53; timing of economic activity and, 132. See also corporate income tax; excise taxes; income tax; payroll taxes; property taxes; sales taxes

teacher-pupil ratios, effects of, 183, 184

teacher quality, educational effects of, 180, 183, 184

Teagle, Walter, 111

teenage runaways, 265

Temporary Assistance for Needy Families (TANF), 279–81; provisions of, 279

Tennessee, regressive taxes in, 152

terrible ten states, tax regressivity and, 151–52

test scores, declines and rises in, 180, 185

Texas: education politics in, 198; indigent medical care in, 270; Medicaid benefits in, 332n. 27; regressive taxes in, 152

Thomas, Clarence, 232

Thompson, Tommy, 279

tight money, 42, 206, 208. See also macroeconomic policy; monetary policy

tobacco companies, lobbying by, 120

Tobin, James, 204

trade, free, 234–37; Clinton administration priority for, 244; costs and benefits of, 62–63; political parties and, 235. See also globalization

trade, international: as GDP share, 234; gains and losses from, 233–35; increased volume of, 234, 235–36; lowering of barriers to, 235; wage competition and, 233–34, 236–37. See also globalization

trade adjustment programs, 216–17

trade unions. See labor unions

tradeoff: between efficiency and equity, 46, 56; between unemployment and inflation, 41, 207–8

training. See education; job training; schools

trust in government, decline of, 2–3; 309nn. 2, 4

tuition costs, 164

U

underclass, 284

underemployment, 203, 204

unemployment: effects of macroeconomic policy on, 40–43; effects of on rich and poor, 42–43; imports and, 236; inequality and, 203–5; minimum wage laws and, 55; natural rate of, 41, 207; poverty rate and, 204, 205; tradeoff of with inflation, 41, 207–8

unemployment frequency, 204

unemployment insurance: availability of work and, 122; measures to improve, 121–22; moral hazard and, 121–22

Unemployment Insurance (UI): benefit levels of, 96, 98; coverage of, 96, 97–98; fraction of unemployed helped by, 96, 98; hassle and stigma in, 97; regressive financing of, 97; regulatory function of, 97; spending on, 78 table 4.1, 96; state variations in, 98; time limits of, 97

unemployment rate: defined, 203; level of, 203, 204–5; alternative measures of, 335–36n. 3

unionization rates: in France, 110; international comparison of, 110

unions. *See* labor unions

United Auto Workers (UAW), 230; lobbying expenditures by, 242

United Kingdom: corporate taxes in, 141; homelessness in, 262; income inequality in, 29–30; medical costs in, 99; payroll tax rate in, 142; poverty rate in, 24; prisoners in, 223; public sector employment in, 220; rich-to-poor ratio in, 30; socialized medicine in, 99, 273; tax levels in, 133

Universal Declaration of Human Rights: on jobs and wages, 223–24; on standard of living, 285–86

universal health care, 272–73. *See also* medical insurance

universal health insurance, Canadian model of, 105

universality, Food Stamps and, 258–59

universities: elite, and inequality, 195–96; exacerbation of inequality and, 191–92, 195–96; research in, 195; state, 192, 195. *See also* education, higher

University of California, affirmative action and, 197

Upward Bound, 197

urban empowerment zones, 209

Urban Institute, 280

urban renewal, loss of housing and, 266

users' fees, 326n. 5

utilitarian theory: of income inequality, 43–44; of tax progressivity, 128–29

utilitarianism, defined, 43

utility functions, for money, 43–44, 129–31

V

value-added taxes, regressivity of, 145–46

Vance, Cyrus, 73

veil of ignorance, 128

Verba, Sidney, 65, 68

Vermont, progressive income taxes in, 152

Veterans Administration (VA), home mortgage programs of, 260

veterans: disability compensation for, 95; homelessness and, 265; social insurance spending for, 77, 78 table 4.1

Vietnam war, military spending and, 211

Virginia, Medicaid benefits in, 332n. 27

vocational education, 190–91. *See also* job training

Volcker, Paul, 208

volunteer military, 212

volunteerism, 257–58

von Mises, Ludwig, 314n. 6

voter registration, personal requirement of, 66–67

voter turnout: causes of class bias in, 65–66; effect of on 1994 election, 67; effects of class bias in, 67; in Europe, 65, 66; income level and, 65, 68; legal arrangements and, 66–67; levels in presidential and

voter turnout (*continued*)
nonpresidential years, 346–47n. 4; party mobilization and, 66, 67; party systems and, 65–66; reforms to increase, 305–6; in United States, 65, 346–47n. 4
voting rights: disenfranchisement of workers and, 230; imprisonment of African Americans and, 221
vouchers: for day care, 176; rental, 261–62; for schooling, 186, 187, 188, 189, 190

W

wage, living, 226
wage bargaining, centralized, 229, 316–17n. 55, 339n. 75
wage competition, international: international agreements and, 237, 239; through trade, 233–34, 236–37
wage drops, U.S. imports and, 236
wage equalization: limits of, 55–56; work incentives and, 55–56
wage gains, inflation and, 224
wage justice, labor market and, 228–29
wage levels: effects of welfare reform on, 219; government employment and, 54–55; government procurement policies and, 53–54; macroeconomic policy and, 53; minimum wage laws and, 55
wage policies, improving, 245–46
wage subsidies, public service employment and, 220
wages: after-tax, and EITC, 55; as approach to poverty and inequality, 53–56; external influences on, 18–19; fairness of, 15–20, 43; family background and, 20, 51, 192, 312n. 26; labor unions and, 228–29; luck and, 16–17, 19; marginal product theory of, 15–20; naturalness of, 15; public goods spending and, 210–14; raising, 224–33, 296–97; right to, 223–24; as share of total income, 18; women's, 233; workers' characteristics and, 19–20. *See also* jobs
Wagner Act, 231
want, freedom from, 285

war against the poor, 284–85
Washington (state), regressive taxes in, 151–52
Washington, D.C.: low-income housing in, 268; public housing wait in, 261
waste, Food Stamps and, 256
wealth: income from ownership of, 17–18; increase of in stock market, 297; inheritance of, 18; unequal ownership of, 18
wealthy people: negative effects of inequality on, 45; number of, 29
weaponry, high-tech, 213
weapons spinoffs, 337n. 30
Webber, Michael, 73
welfare, 274–79. *See also* Aid to Families with Dependent Children
welfare queens, 275
welfare reform: and availability of good jobs, 281; and business cycle, 281; and continued poverty, 280–81; and drop in Food Stamp use, 255; and drop in welfare rolls, 280; effects of, 218–19; and TANF, 279–81; and wage competition, 219; and welfare-to-work programs, 218–19; and work by ex–welfare recipients, 280–81
welfare rolls, reduction of, 218–19, 280
welfare states, European, globalization and, 63, 133, 316–17n. 55
welfare-to-work programs, 217–19; child care and, 176; effects of, 218
Wellstone, Sen. Paul, 119
Whiskey Rebellion, 155
White, Annie, 249–50
white flight, 182
whites: frequency of among the poor, 21, 22; poverty rates among, 21
Wilson, William Julius, 53, 224
Wisconsin, welfare reform in, 279
Wolff, Edward, 18
women: higher education and, 196–97; homelessness and, 265, 267; job discrimination and, 232–33; job training and, 215, 217–19; labor-force participation of, 233; New Deal and, 111–12; public sector and

employment of, 220; Social Security benefits to, 79; wages of, 233

Women, Infants, and Children (WIC) program, 172; commodities distribution and, 253; effects of, 254–55

women's shelters, 265, 267

work: AFDC and, 48; effect of AFDC on, 278–79; effect of EITC on, 228; effect of taxes on, 131–34; elderly and, 88; ex-welfare recipients and, 280–81; frequency of among poor families, 21; importance of, 48; income maintenance and, 273–74; material incentives for, 17; preparing people for, 294–95; prisoners and, 222; right to, 223–24

worker protection, through international trade policies, 237

workers: disenfranchisement of, 230; dislocated, retraining of, 216–17; unfriendly U.S. policies toward, 243

Workers' Compensation: amount spent on, 94; benefit levels of, 94; coverage of, 94; state variations in, 94

Workforce Investment Act (WIA), 215–17

work, guaranteed. See guaranteed work

work incentives: AFDC and, 275, 276, 278–79; EITC and, 132–33, 227; guaranteed incomes and, 47–48; nonmaterial, 55–56; retirement insurance and, 58; Social Security and, 80–81; wage equalization and, 55–56

working conditions, 24; international agreements on, 237, 239

working families, public housing and, 261

working poor: characteristics of, 25; children of, 25; life of, 24–25; minimum wage and, 25

working-class Americans, disenfranchisement of, 66, 230

Works Progress Administration (WPA), 219, 220; good wages and, 54

World Trade Organization (WTO), 235; democratizing, 304; resistance of to worker protection, 237

Y

young people, as fraction of the poor, 22